A History of Religion in America

A History of Religion in America: From the End of the Civil War to the Twenty-First Century
provides comprehensive coverage of the history of religion in America from the end of the
American Civil War to religion in post-9/11 America. The volume explores major religious
groups in the United States and examines the following topics:

- The American Civil War
- Immigration's impact on American religion
- The rise of the Social Gospel
- The fundamentalist response
- Religion in Cold War America
- The 1960s counterculture and the backlash
- Religion in post-9/11 America

Chronologically arranged and integrating various religious developments into a coherent
historical narrative, this book also contains useful chapter summaries and review questions.
Designed for undergraduate religious studies and history students *A History of Religion in
America* provides a substantive and comprehensive introduction to the complexity of religion in American history.

Bryan F. Le Beau is retired from the University of Saint Mary, Leavenworth, KS, where he
served as Professor of History, Provost, and Vice President for Academic Affairs. He is the
author of several books on American cultural and religious history.

For student and instructor resources to accompany *A History of Religion in America*, visit the dedicated companion website at:

www.routledge.com/cw/lebeau

Perfect for use in the classroom or as an aid to independent study, the website includes:

- Recommended Further Reading
- Supplementary Chapter Information
- Audio Chapter Introductions

The companion website includes material which covers both volume one: *A History of America, from the First Settlements through the Civil War* and volume two: *A History of America, From the End of the Civil War to the Twenty-First Century.*

A History of Religion in America

From the End of the Civil War
to the Twenty-First Century

Bryan F. Le Beau

Routledge
Taylor & Francis Group

LONDON AND NEW YORK

First published 2018
by Routledge
2 Park Square, Milton Park, Abingdon, Oxon OX14 4RN

and by Routledge
711 Third Avenue, New York, NY 10017

Routledge is an imprint of the Taylor & Francis Group, an informa business

© 2018 Bryan F. Le Beau

British Library Cataloguing-in-Publication Data
A catalogue record for this book is available from the British Library

Library of Congress Cataloging-in-Publication Data
A catalog record for this book has been requested

ISBN: 978-1-138-71129-7 (hbk)
ISBN: 978-1-138-71133-4 (pbk)
ISBN: 978-1-315-16308-6 (ebk)
ISBN: 978-1-138-05991-7 (2 volume set, pbk)

Typeset in Times New Roman
by Apex CoVantage, LLC

Visit the companion website: www.routledge.com/cw/lebeau

Contents

Figures

Table

Acknowledgments

Books such as this may take only a few years to write, but they rely on a professional lifetime of research. And even then, the author is heavily dependent on the scholarship of others to fill in the gaps in the story that even a lifetime of research cannot fill. I am deeply grateful for all those who contributed – albeit unknowingly in most cases – to the story I have told. I hope that I have fairly represented their work.

As with all of my past publications, this book would not have been possible without the professional research assistance, willing and encouraging ear, and good counsel of my wife and outstanding reference librarian, Chris Le Beau. I owe so much of my career to her.

I want to acknowledge the very capable assistance of my editors at Routledge, Taylor and Francis Group. Their editorial assistance from the very start has been invaluable. And finally, I want to thank the several readers who took the time to review this book while it was still at the manuscript stage and to offer much wise advice. My book is far better for all of their insights.

Introduction

The principal themes of this history of religion in America are growth, diversity, adaptation, and accommodation, which are actually major themes in American history as a whole, religious or secular. These themes help to explain the unique persistence of religion in America, when it appears to be in decline throughout most of the Western world. This history focuses on religion in the context of American history. But it also addresses questions concerning that history, namely the challenges posed to religious bodies living outside the boundaries of traditional beliefs or even belief itself, as well as the resistance to new religions – at least new to the United States – which has waxed and waned but nevertheless persisted over the centuries. Studying such resistance helps us not only to better understand the history of religion in America but also our cultural underpinnings and our understanding of ourselves as a people.

Although each chapter is organized around a particular theme, this story of religion in America is told more or less chronologically. The themes provide the central points around which this history has been written. The chronological approach affords the opportunity to make connections between religious and secular history, thereby presenting a more coherent story. It also shows how secular events – immigration, urbanization, economic depression, and international affairs – influenced, and in many cases were influenced by, religious developments. The two have been inextricably linked and cannot be understood properly in isolation.

And finally, two things quickly occur to anyone who has tried to write such expansive histories. First, given the limits of space, it is impossible to include everything and still provide enough depth to provide a satisfactory level of understanding. As a result, this history is somewhat subjective, and readers will find that some religious groups and topics have been excluded. Second, the author must rely on the work of hundreds of scholars, past and present, who have devoted their professional lives to the study of various topics of religion in American history. I hope this single volume has done justice to their very fine scholarship, much of which has been cited in the endnotes and recommendations for further reading following each chapter.

In the way of a brief overview, Chapter 1 picks up the story of religion in American history from the end of the American Civil War, which was not only the crucial, even seminal, event in American secular history, but which also served to reshape and redirect American religious history. Both the nation and its churches were torn asunder, and although both would survive and even grow stronger, they would be significantly changed by the experience as well as by what followed. During the decades following the Civil War, the United States witnessed a dramatic increase in the number and variety of religious organizations in the United

States, as well as in denominational affiliation both in real numbers and in percentage of the overall population. That growth, however, was not without its challenges, posed largely by the arrival of immigrants of differing faiths, schisms among denominations already present in the United States, and the spawning of yet new faiths. All clung to their own theological identities, while at the same time insisting on their place under the ever-expanding "sacred canopy" of religion in America.

All of this led to a sense of loss of national unity and to an attempt to restore that unity by joining the disparate new religious practices and beliefs in a familiar, commonly accepted, domesticated "American" – preferably Protestant – civil religion. This movement took on issues related to, but not strictly, religious, namely temperance and Sabbath-day laws, and placed greater emphasis on public schools as a major force in Americanization. This thrust for national unity helped give rise to the Third Great Awakening, the religious revival that swept America at the end of the nineteenth century. Also taking center stage was the World's Parliament of Religions held in Chicago in 1893 – the same year in which the United States celebrated (a year late) the 400th anniversary of Columbus's arrival in the Americas. The Parliament showcased the great diversity of faiths in the world. But it also attempted to make the case that out of a diversity of faiths could be found a common core of beliefs, a universalism of faiths, a lesson yet to be fully embraced in the United States though the alternatives were becoming increasingly unrealistic in a nation already among the most diverse on earth.

Of major importance to the story of religion in America at the end of the nineteenth and start of the twentieth centuries was the Social Gospel, which was largely the product of the Industrial Revolution, immigration, and urbanization. As will be discussed in Chapter 2, the resulting social, cultural, and economic conflicts challenged not only how Americans viewed themselves but also how they viewed the purpose of religion, taking many churches beyond the salvation of souls. The Social Gospel Movement will be discussed in the context of the Populist and Progressive Movements, Social Darwinism, and Andrew Carnegie's Gospel of Wealth, the most popular rendering of the capitalist ethos of the time, in semi-religious terms. Also discussed is the role of women in reform, operating largely from a religious base in such areas as temperance, peace, and civil liberties, as well as suffrage. The chapter will conclude with a discussion of American missions abroad, which mirrored, if not served as an extension of, the Social Gospel Movement.

Chapter 3 expands on earlier, passing references to the specter of the higher criticism and science and what they forebode for revealed religion. It will address what has come to be known as "the golden age of agnosticism," wherein for the first time the idea of not believing in God, or some sort of deity, was no longer seen as a "a bizarre aberration," but rather as a plausible alternative to the still-dominant theism. Various developments converged to open the door to unbelief, including Enlightenment skepticism, Biblical criticism, Darwinian evolution, and scientific naturalism. Doubters may not have had sufficient proof to actually deny the existence of God, but they could stop one step short of unbelief to suggest that they simply did not have enough information to affirm their belief in God, thus, the appearance, at least formally, of agnosticism, a term coined by British scientist Thomas Huxley in 1869. In the mid-nineteenth century, American atheists and agnostics advanced their cause through organizations such as the Free Religious Association and the Ethical Culture Federation, but perhaps the greatest asset to American freethought in the nineteenth century was the "Great Agnostic" or "Pagan Prophet" Robert Ingersoll. Ingersoll's public lectures, especially "Why I Am an Agnostic," delivered during the 1870s and 1880s, were among the most talked about of their time, largely because of the credibility he established by his impeccable reputation. As will be explained, one of the most dramatic, contrasting developments at the end of the nineteenth century was the rise of Holiness, Pentecostalism, and Fundamentalism.

Although often in the shadow of histories that focus on manifestations of the Jazz Age – flappers, gangsters, speakeasies, and other popular aspects of the "roaring twenties" – religion in the 1920s was exciting in its own way. Its most visible figures were as aggressive, flamboyant, and controversial as secular stars. Chapter 4 will open with a discussion of the first two decades of the twentieth century, when the fundamentalists formalized their position, demanded assent, and would not compromise. This led to the showdown between fundamentalists and modernists in 1925 in Dayton, Tennessee in what has often been called "the trial of the century." Among the more prominent evangelicals to be highlighted will be William "Billy" Sunday, the professional baseball player turned preacher; "God's Flapper," Aimee Semple McPherson; and African American "jazzmen" preachers Daddy Grace and Father Divine. Finally, as will be discussed, the "roaring twenties," which posed one set of challenges to religion, were followed by the "Great Depression," which presented yet others.

And then came Pearl Harbor – and Chapter 5. Upon American entrance into World War II, churches performed two crucial functions. They offered consolation, solace, and peace of mind, to those shocked by the inhumanities they witnessed. Like many other institutions, they also rallied to support the cause through a wide variety of services at home and abroad. The 1930s were marked by various antiwar conferences and agreements, heartily supported by most American churches, but although a significant portion of the population continued to campaign to "Keep America Out of the War," resistance largely dissipated after December 7, 1941. Most churches (Mennonites and Quakers among notable exceptions) that had hoped to eliminate war, seeing it as evil, changed their position to explain that war was evil, but sometimes a necessary evil, propounding a "just war" position on entering the war. The "just war" position came up again, however, with the dropping of the atomic bomb on Hiroshima and Nagasaki, prompting some to argue that the only alternative to the total world disaster atomic bombs forecast was "repentance and regeneration," led by the nation's moral and religious forces.

As if on cue, the call for repentance and regeneration was answered by a number of revivalists, the most prominent of whom was Billy Graham, on whom Chapter 6 will dwell at some length. At the same time, the Cold War got its start and dominated the thinking – and fears – of most Americans in the second half of the 1940s and the 1950s. Anticommunism was not new to the United States. It began soon after the Russian Revolution of 1917 and fluctuated thereafter until the pitting of the two world powers, the US and the USSR, in the wake of World War II fueled the flames to new heights. Although not without reason to fear the Soviet Union, that fear in the United States led to considerable demagoguery and witch-hunts led early on by the House Un-American Activities Committee, and later by Joseph McCarthy and his Senate Investigating Committee. This chapter will recall the wide use of the phrase "atheistic Communism," and how that led to the shunning not only of those suspected of atheism, but also of liberal Christians, the net effect of which was to weaken the latter's moral leadership. Nevertheless, or perhaps as the result of the need to reaffirm their allegiance to Christian America and opposition to the godless, communist Soviet Union, mainstream religion in America prospered throughout the 1950s and rallied behind symbolic changes such as adopting "In God We Trust" as the national motto and including "under God" in the Pledge of Allegiance. The chapter will close by addressing the subject of religion in the courts, during which constitutional issues of free exercise and separation of church and state took center stage.

The 1960s and 1970s were a period of turmoil for all aspects of life in America, including religion. Some have referred to the decades as "revolutionary," pointing to the civil rights movement and battles over abortion, aid to parochial schools, the free exercise of religion and separation of church and state, the proliferation of new religious movements, and more. Chapter 6 opens with the election of 1960 and the victory of the nation's first Roman Catholic president, John F. Kennedy. That election, building on strong Roman Catholic anti-communism and furthered by the reforms inaugurated by Pope John XXIII and Vatican II, ushered in a new era of Catholic acceptance. That will be followed by a discussion of the civil rights movement, the Mexican migrant workers movement led by Catholic layman Cesar Chavez, the role of the churches in the anti-Vietnam War movement, and the feminist and environmental movements. *Roe v. Wade*, wherein the US Supreme Court tackled one of the most divisive issues of the time, abortion, will be discussed, as well as gay rights.

The dramatic expansion of religious diversity following changes in the immigration law of 1965 led not only to the proliferation of different religious groups, but also to the growing influence of religions no longer Christian or even Western. This posed a challenge to mainstream America. But so too did the proliferation of homegrown new religions or religious communities among countercultural spiritual seekers, mostly the young and disillusioned with traditional Western religions. What slowed this course and contributed to the disappearance of many of the new religious communities were the mass suicide in 1978 of over 900 followers of Jim Jones in Jonestown, Guyana, to which they had moved from California, and the siege and inferno of the Branch Davidian compound in Waco, Texas in 1993, which led to the deaths of 74 true believers.

The difficulties of the 1960s and 1970s were often blamed on liberal leadership in the nation's political, social, and cultural arenas and what many saw as an increasingly secular society. By the late 1970s, Chapter 7 shows, many Americans believed the time had come for more conservative leadership. Accordingly, the scene of American religion shifted, beginning with the election of the openly acknowledged born-again, Southern Baptist President Jimmy Carter, and peaking with the election of President Ronald Reagan in 1980. The leading force in this conservative Christian movement was the Moral Majority, led by Baptist minister Jerry Falwell. When it disbanded in 1989, it was replaced by the Christian Coalition, led by Pat Robertson, television preacher and presidential candidate. The issues remained the same, but the focus shifted to organizing a political electorate prepared to achieve its ends through the ballot box. Robertson's candidacy did not survive the Republican primaries, but the more mainstream, but religious, conservative, George H. W. Bush, Reagan's vice president, would assume the presidency if only for one term. He would be followed by the more liberal, "New Democrat" Bill Clinton, who faced considerable opposition by conservative Republicans in Congress. Chapter 7 will conclude with an analysis of the premillennialist dilemma faced by many evangelicals at the end of the twentieth century – those who anticipated that the arrival of the new millennium would coincide with the Second Coming – and the major issues embraced by the New Christian Right, namely abortion, the Equal Rights Amendment, the Promise Keepers, prayer in the schools, and creationism versus evolution.

This history of religion in America will end with a short Chapter 8 – perhaps better seen as an epilogue – looking at religion in post-9/11 America. It tends to raise more questions, than it answers, questions that will take time to answer, as the course of religion in America has often proved unpredictable. The first decade of the twenty-first century began on a troubling note and continued to face difficulties thereafter. Although by the slimmest of margins – some would say only with the intervention of the Supreme Court – the election of George W. Bush in 2000 appeared to reassert the dominance of the religious right in America. But that was followed by the devastating attacks of 9/11, a massive counterterrorism effort, two wars that lasted for the entire decade, and two major economic recessions. The Presidential Election of 2008, which resulted in the election of the first President of color, was seen by many as a vote for major change and a renewed sense of optimism, neither of which materialized or at least lasted, as witnessed in the Election of 2016. In brief, the immediate results of the events of 9/11 were a brief renewed sense of national unity, which had both positive and troubling aspects. But even that was followed by disunity and conflict.

The chapter opens with an analysis of the changing American religious landscape in the early years of the twenty-first century, arguing that the United States remains the most religious developed nation in the world, as well as the most religiously diverse, but that signs of potentially significant changes appear in the offing. The point will be made that the United States remains dominantly Christian but that mainline Protestant churches, the "founding churches" of the nation, are in decline. Possible reasons for this will be discussed, including the argument made for secularization, which has been anticipated for decades. But also included will be data pointing to the still small, but consistently increasing, number of agnostics and atheists and the more significant growth of those unaffiliated with, disaffected from, organized religion. The total of all three groups now approximates nearly one in five Americans. The chapter and book end with some discussion of the impact of Hispanic immigration and the state of Muslims in America in the twenty-first century, or more particularly in the wake of 9/11, on the one hand presenting a summary of anti-Muslim activity in the United States, but on the other hand pointing to the lessons of history, which suggest that this too may pass – in time.

Chapter 1

The challenges of immigration, growth, and diversity

The challenges of immigration

Roman Catholics

Dramatic challenges to ecclesiastical community occurred among Roman Catholics in the second half of the nineteenth century as the result of the massive immigration of Catholics from various previously underrepresented nations. Unlike earlier Catholic immigration, which was dominantly Irish, Catholic immigration at the close of the nineteenth and start of the twentieth centuries was composed of Italians, Poles, and other Europeans – with a fair number of Mexicans (see Figure 1.1). Confronted with a Catholic Church with a decidedly Irish character, led by a church hierarchy almost exclusively Irish, who were unfamiliar with, and often disdainful of, their customs, the new arrivals insisted on maintaining their ethnic and religious identity.

One notable case-in-point that set the tone for many immigrant communities across the country occurred in Scranton, Pennsylvania, among the city's Polish Catholics. Despite their rapidly growing numbers in the 1880s and 1890s, they found themselves governed by a less than culturally sensitive Irish bishop. When their protests turned to riots, mediators proposed that those among the Polish Catholics who were dissatisfied organize a parish of their own. They did just that and soon other ethnic groups followed their example until in short order nearly every community of any size with different immigrant Catholic populations sported Polish, Irish, French, Italian, and Hispanic Catholic parishes. The Polish, however, did not stop there. Whereas nearly all other ethnic Roman Catholic parishes remained loyal to the diocese and the larger church organization from which they originated, Polish Catholics moved toward greater ecclesiastical independence, in 1904 forming the Polish National Catholic Church in America.[1]

As referenced earlier, another group of Roman Catholics that came to the United States in the nineteenth century in large numbers – or perhaps more accurately put, found themselves in the United States – did not come from Europe, but rather from the Mexican territories in the American Southwest annexed as a result of Texas independence and the Mexican-American War of 1846–1848. At least on paper, their rights were to be guaranteed under the Treaty of Guadalupe Hidalgo. Of some 80,000 Mexicans residing in the new territories, over 90 percent elected to become US citizens and were to have "all the rights of citizens of the United States, according to the constitution." The property and civil rights of those who chose not to become citizens were to be protected, as well. The Mexican population throughout the Mexican Cession, however, was soon overwhelmed by Anglo Americans and most of their rights were swept aside. They found themselves treated as second-class citizens, and many lost their lands – up to 75 percent in New Mexico. Still Hispanic Americans retained their culture and held fast to their Roman Catholic religion.[2]

The modernist crisis and its impact on American Catholics

It is important to note that these challenges to ecclesiastical community among Roman Catholics occurred at the same time that, as a result of this massive immigration of new Catholic communities, Roman Catholicism became the largest single Christian denomination in the United States. The unofficial Protestant establishment remained by virtue of its overall numbers, inclusive of its many denominations, but the upstarts clearly posed a challenge to the Protestant Reformation diaspora that became the United States. Although hardly of one confession, based on a long history of religious warfare in Europe, Protestants were largely of one mind in identifying Roman Catholics as outsiders and as a threat to both the American Protestant presumption of homogeneity and commitment to religious freedom. As we have seen, the roots of this problem extend to the vary founding of the British colonies of North America. But the situation became particularly explosive, even violent, in the two decades leading up to the Civil War.

Protestant fears of the incongruity of Roman Catholics to American republicanism were enhanced by various pronouncements from the Vatican, which American Protestants assumed would dictate policy to American Catholics. In response to reform movements and revolutions, which date to the French Revolution and its attacks on the established Catholic Church, but that peaked in 1848 throughout Europe and that posed a threat to Catholic European establishments everywhere, the papacy issued a series of statements, which confirmed in the minds of many American Protestants of Rome's opposition to liberty of conscience and the separation of church and state. In 1832, Pope Gregory XVI set the tone for what was to follow in an encyclical that read in part: "From the polluted fountain of indifference flows that absurd and erroneous doctrine or rather raving, in favor and in defense of 'liberty of conscience.'" Although the Civil War would temporarily distract the nation from this particular concern, the controversy would reignite after the war and peak in the last decade of the nineteenth and first two decades of the twentieth century. In this later phase, however, it would be tied to what is known as the Modernist Crisis in the Roman Catholic Church.

The most controversial statement in the Modernist Crisis came in 1907 from Pope Pius X. In the encyclical, *Pascendi dominici gregis* (Feeding the Lord's Flock), Pope Pius labeled modernism as the "synthesis of all heresies" and its proponents as laying "the axe not to the branches and shoots, but to the very roots, that is, to the faith and its deepest fires . . . so that there is no part of Catholic truth from which they hold their hand, none that they do not strive to corrupt."[3] Central to the Pope's statement was his assumption that the ideas that called into question the Church's centuries-old teachings came not from its external enemies alone, but from those members of the Church's leadership whose roles might position them to pose an even greater threat to the Church. The result, as Darrell Jodock has described it, was a condemnation of modernism, "with such vehemence, and the measures prescribed to prevent its growth . . . so stringent [including the establishment of Councils of Vigilance in each diocese to detect and root out such heresies] that it virtually slammed the door on any historical study of the Bible, on theological creatively, and on church reform . . . for the next three decades."[4]

In sum, Pius X's immediate goal in pushing back against the modernist movement was to affirm papal authority and the teaching authority of the church (referred to as the *magisterium*), claiming that the church and its leadership alone had inherited authority in religious matters from the apostles. But, in doing so, he saw the modernist movement as having the potential not only to weaken ecclesiastical authority, but also to emancipate science in every field of investigation without fear of conflict with the church; to emancipate the state, which would cease to be answerable to religious authority; and to emancipate private conscience from being answerable to any higher law.[5]

Two points should be made here. First Pius X's encyclical did not occur in isolation or without precedent. In some respects, it can be seen as the most definitive statement on a situation that had been developing within the church for decades. The importance of Gregory XVI's encyclical of 1832 in launching the antimodernist movement has already been mentioned. His successor Pius IX, who served in office from 1846 to 1878, became "an icon of defiance" of modernism in the Church. His *Syllabus of Errors* (1864) offered a sweeping rejection of modernity, as did the First Vatican Council (1869–1870) with its endorsement of papal authority, even infallibility in certain matters, the nuances of which were largely missed by the general population.[6]

Modernist Catholics were excommunicated and books associated with the movement placed on the *Index of Forbidden Books*. There was Leo XIII's position taken in 1893 in *Providentisimus Deus* (On the Study of Holy Scripture), which rejected scientific biblical criticism when not pursued in a spirit of faith (to be enforced by the Pontifical Biblical

Figure 1.1 Ellis Island, Gateway to America

Source: Archive Pics/Alamy Stock Photo

Commission). But more important for our purposes was his *Testem benevolentiae* (Witness to Our Goodwill, 1899), in which he rejected by specific reference, "Americanism," which by then had come to symbolize in the eyes of the Vatican modernism itself. To be more specific, while proclaiming his affection for the American people and their bishops, Leo XIII rejected efforts to adapt the church's teachings to the modern world that America represented: "The Catholic faith is not a philosophical theory that human beings can elaborate, but a divine deposit that is to be faithfully guarded and infallibly declared." Similarly, Leo insisted that there is a difference between authority in the church and government, because of the divine nature of the church: "Whereas the state exists by the free will of those associated with it, the church is based upon its own infallible teachings. To be preserved from private error, members of the church must thus submit to that infallible authority."[7]

As Lester Kurtz has explained, in his denouncing Americanism as heresy, Leo XIII was not so much condemning what was occurring in the United States, where adherence to modernist thought was far less widespread than in Europe and Catholics remained loyal to the Vatican to a greater extent, but rather attempting to discourage European interpretations of how American Catholics felt about the conflict between democracy and monarchism:

> Those [Europeans] who regarded republicanism as inherently anti-Catholic accused some members of the American Catholic elite of seeking to undermine the church and its authority by supporting 'liberals, evolutionists, [and] Americanists' and by talking forever of liberty, of respect for the individual, of initiative, [and] of natural virtues.[8]

Other Protestant Christian divisions tied to growing ethnic diversity

Ethnic immigration divisions similar to those that occurred among Roman Catholics surfaced among Lutherans. Swedish, Danish, Norwegian, Finnish, and Icelandic Lutherans refused to affiliate with their German brethren when they arrived, resulting in twenty-four different Lutheran groups by the end of the nineteenth century. Other, and more pronounced, examples reflecting the divisive impact of immigration and ethnicity resulted in the creation of several branches of the Eastern Orthodox Church in America: Russian, Greek, Albanian, Armenian, Bulgarian, Romanian, Syrian, Serbian, Ukrainian, and others.[9]

And finally, there is the case of the Dutch, where immigration resulted in separation, not tied to ethnicity but to theology and ecclesiology, the late arriving Dutch differing in both areas from their predecessors. Dutch Reformed immigrants who arrived in the nineteenth century found that those who had migrated as much as two centuries earlier from the same tiny land and from the same church had lost enough of their Calvinist base and fidelity to the Heidelberg Confession that they felt the need to establish their own church. In 1857, they formed the Christian Reformed Church in North America.[10]

Jews

Similar challenges occurred among American Jews, who, as we have seen, had been in the United States since the seventeenth century. By the mid-nineteenth century, that earlier, largely Sephardic Jewish population (of Spanish and Portuguese ancestry) was greatly outnumbered by immigrants of German extraction, called Ashkenazi. This increasingly

successful and liberal Jewish population was in turn confronted by a number of more orthodox Jews from Eastern Europe – 2.5 million by 1920 – that threatened not only to overwhelm
them in numbers but in culture and theology. The most visible result of this confrontation
was the unique development in the United States of separate Reformed, Conservative, and
Orthodox branches of American Judaism.[11]

Jewish immigration from Eastern Europe, largely from Russia and Russian controlled
neighboring areas, was driven by the bloody pogroms of 1881, 1891, and 1905 and the search
for a better way of life in America. We are reminded that the words welcoming immigrants
to the United States through New York Harbor, inscribed on the Statue of Liberty ("Give me
your tired, your poor / Your huddled masses yearning to be free") were written by the Jewish
poet Emma Lazarus. But not even all Jews then living in the United States were always welcoming. German Jews, among whom Rabbi Isaac Mayer Wise – himself an immigrant from
Bohemia, who served as president of the Hebrew Union College in Cincinnati – was the
most prominent leader, were committed to a process of Americanization. Unlike their East
European brethren – technically Yiddish-speaking Ashkenazic Jews – German Jews found
in America a world in which they were not forced behind ghetto walls to live in isolation and
fear for their lives. German Jews were free to worship as they pleased, but also to become
more American, if they chose, which most did.[12]

Given their far different recent life-experiences, Eastern European Jews set different goals
upon arriving in America. Basically, what they wanted was to be left alone to practice their
religion without fear or intimidation, and their religion continued to cling to un-Reformed
ancient law, or Torah. As Gaustad and Schmidt summarized it:

> Every obstacle that could be thrown in the path of ritual purity and communal wor-
> ship had been thrown; every burden that could be thrust upon observant Jews had been
> pressed upon them, their families, their children. Now they had come to a land where
> they could worship without fear, and they wanted to do just that. They did not wish to
> hear of reform; they wished rather for the freedom to be observant.[13]

Positioned in between those who resisted change, Orthodox Jews, and those who welcomed change, Reform Jews, were Conservative Jews. The architect of Conservative
Judaism – or the Conservative Jewish Movement – was Solomon Schechter. Moldavian
born, Schechter arrived in America in 1902 to become president of the Jewish Theological
Seminary of America in New York City. He found nothing in American citizenship, which
was incompatible with Jews observing the dietary laws, sanctifying the Sabbath, fixing a
Mezuzah (an excerpt from the Hebrew Bible) on their door posts, refraining from unleav-
ened bread on Passover, or perpetuating any other law essential to the preservation of Judaism. "In this great, glorious and free country," Schechter concluded, "we Jews need not
sacrifice a single iota of our Torah; and, in the enjoyment of absolute equality with our fellow
citizens, we can live to carry out those ideas for which our ancestors so often had to die."[14]

Asians

Although we will return to this story in greater detail when we reach 1965 and passage of a
new immigration policy that lowered discriminatory policies toward Asians, note should be
made here of the first wave of immigration to the United States of Chinese and a few Japanese, bringing with them even more "foreign" religions.

Many Chinese, mostly young men, came to the West Coast to work the gold fields and mining camps. Others came as migrant agricultural workers and laborers on the transcontinental railroad. But many were also brought in as cheap labor and used as strike breakers throughout the country, thereby being seen as posing a threat to American labor. When the number of Chinese immigrants topped 300,000 by 1880, one-tenth of the population of California, Washington passed the Chinese Exclusion Act (1882), which suspended all immigration from China for ten years. The Act was renewed at that point and a decade later made indefinite. Similar sentiments arose in response to Japanese immigration, commonly referred to as the "Yellow Peril," that led to the Gentlemen's Agreement of 1907 and 1908 between the governments of Japan and the United States halting that migration as well.[15]

As to their religious traditions, the first Chinese immigrants usually remained faithful to traditional Chinese beliefs, which were Confucianism, ancestral worship, Buddhism or Daoism. The number of Chinese migrants who converted to Christianity remained low. They were mainly Protestants, who had already been converted in China where foreign Christian missionaries (who had first arrived en masse in the mid-nineteenth century) had strived to Christianize the nation with relatively minor success. Christian missionaries had also worked in the Chinese communities and settlements in America, but nevertheless their religious message found few who were receptive. It has been estimated that during the first wave until 1882, less than 20 percent of Chinese immigrants accepted Christian teachings.[16]

"Lived religion" in ethnic communities

It is commonly argued by historians of religion that the beliefs and rituals of any particular group cannot be fully understood without a clear understanding of the daily lives of its members. This has been explored in various accounts of Native Americans and African Americans, but much the same approach can be taken with many of those religious groups considered in this chapter. By way of example, it would be particularly appropriate to look at the beliefs and rituals of immigrant groups whose religion of choice might have been shared by other Americans, but whose practices differed for cultural, social, and even economic reasons, thereby setting them apart from others practicing the same faith.

This type of scholarship goes by various names: "popular religion," "lived religion," or "theology in the streets." Perhaps this is easier to understand when shown by contrasting the two ways in which religion can be studied. The first, and more traditional, approach is to study a religious group's religious beliefs, scriptures, symbols, and prayers. While not ignoring all of this at the macro level, the second explores local places of worship, rituals, and practices, both formal and informal, and the lives of the people who lived those religious practices in their daily lives. In this way, scholars of lived religion argue, we can better understand the totality of a people's deepest values and ethical convictions, as well as their perceptions of, and efforts to order, their reality. A classic study of this genre is Robert Orsi's examination of the people of Italian Harlem at the turn of the twentieth century and their annual religious celebration of the feast of the Madonna.[17]

Italian Harlem

Orsi studied the *festa* of the Madonna of Mount Carmel on East 115th Street in New York City, a festival that flourished among Italian immigrants and their American born children as long as the Italian neighborhood persisted, by-and-large through the end of World War II.

He examined the rituals involved in what was basically a twenty-four-hour-long celebration that began at midnight on July 16, but that in some form could go on for the better part of a week. The annual *festa* was not native to New York; it was celebrated in southern Italy, which prompted Orsi to explore the reasons why Italian immigrants chose to reproduce the ritual in their new home and why new arrivals, who took pride in their origins in different communities in southern Italy, could come together in this one communal ritual.

The highlight of the *festa* was the procession, which began in the afternoon after a solemn high mass. Thousands of Italians from every walk of life – rich and poor, prominent and not, part of organized groups such as women of the Altar Sodality and those entering with their families or even alone – gathered in front of the church and along the procession route, which included bands that played Italian and American music. Those in the procession followed a large statue of La Madonna del Carmine, brought to the United States from Italy specifically for that church. Mounted on a float, decorated with flowers and white ribbons, the procession began amidst fireworks and trailed incense and "haunting sounds of southern Italian religious chanting" through every street in the Italian quarter of East Harlem.[18]

At the rear of the procession walked the penitents. All walked barefoot; some crawled on hands and knees. Women carried heavy candles and wax body parts, which they would deliver to the church at the end of the procession. At that point, they and others entered the sanctuary, again barefoot, some on hands and knees, and a few dragging their tongues along the floor as they approached the altar. They presented their petitions, or expressed their gratitude, to the Madonna, as well as the body parts, as many had come to be healed or to give thanks for a loved one who had been healed. Upon its arrival from Italy the statue of La Madonna had been placed on the altar of the downstairs church, reflecting the status of the Italian immigrant Catholics. It was not until 1923 that the statue was moved to the main church on the first floor, signaling their arrival, at least in Italian Harlem, as well as leading to a moderation of the more extreme elements of the procession and supplications of the penitents.[19]

Orsi raises the following questions commonly posed by scholars of popular religion in reference to the Feast of the Madonna of 115th Street, the answers to which must be left to the reader of his book: "What did this devotion mean to the immigrants and their children in the new land? How could this devotion not only survive the sea change but take on a new and powerful life in New York City? What does the devotion reveal about the immigrants' values and hopes? What does it teach us about the nature of their religious faith?"[20] And to this, although it takes us beyond the years included in this chapter, readers might find interesting Elizabeth McAlister's essay, "The Madonna of 115th Street Revisited," which takes the story of the Madonna of Mount Carmel to the end of the twentieth century, during which time Haitians, with their mix of Afro-Haitian, Voodoo and Catholic spirituality, replaced Italians in the East Harlem neighborhood and adapted the historic *festa* to their own needs.[21]

Another example of "lived religion" can be found in Jack Kugelmass's *The Miracle of Interval Avenue: The Story of a Jewish Congregation in the South Bronx*. At the same time that Italian immigrants were following the construction of railroad lines into Harlem, Jews began moving further north in the Bronx. As noted earlier, this was the period of mass migration of East European Jews, who, after settling on the Lower East Side of Manhattan, sought the less congested lands of Brooklyn and the Bronx. By 1930, six years after this particular period of European mass migration to New York ended, 600,000 Jews lived in the Bronx or about half the borough's residents. And it was in the heart of the South Bronx, whose population remained stable for the next fifteen years, that the Jewish community of Interval grew up. Jack Kugelmass tells the story of Interval, whose synagogue at its peak served some 500 worshippers with weeknight study groups for adults and an afternoon religious school for children. Much like the Italian neighborhood of Mount Carmel, Interval succumbed to out-migration. The miracle to which Kugelmass refers in his title is that the community lasted as long as it did – past the Second World War – if with ever declining numbers that regularly called into question whether a sufficient number of adult Jewish males (ten) could be mustered to constitute the *Minyan* necessary for ritual purposes. Symbolic of the community's hopes, ambitions, and even expectations, he writes, was the one-story synagogue, or *Shul*, with the two-story façade intended to front a second story that was never built.[22]

The challenge of diversity

More native born religions added to the stew

In the years prior to the Civil War, new religions were born on American soil, which added to the nation's growing diversity of faiths: the Church of Jesus Christ of Latter-day Saints, or the Mormons, for example. Among others that appeared after the Civil War were Jehovah's Witnesses and Christian Science. The roots of Jehovah's Witnesses can be traced to 1872 and a small Bible study group led by Charles Taze Russell. With Russell's guidance, the group focused on those passages in the New Testament that spoke of Christ's Second Coming and concluded that the Second Coming was near. It would be preceded by a cosmic struggle between Satan and Jehovah, but they believed millions of believers would never die. By 1879, Jehovah's Witnesses had their own publication, *The Watchtower*, and their first national assembly in Chicago. And in 1909, they established their world headquarters in Brooklyn, New York.[23] Christian Science will be discussed later in this chapter, for reasons that will be made clear at that point.

Impact of freedom on African American religion

Prior to the Civil War the quarrel over slavery led to divisions within long established "white" churches, Baptists and Methodists, in particular, as well as the exit of African Americans from mainstream Protestant organizations to form their own churches: the African Methodist Episcopal Church, organized in 1816, and the African Methodist Episcopal Zion (AMEZ) Church, established in 1821. Both black churches appeared in the North, however, whereas in the South, black Methodists did not separate from the Methodist Episcopal Church, South, to create their own denomination until 1870.

A similar story surrounds the separation of black Baptists and the creation of independent black Baptist churches after the Civil War, which in turn helped mitigate the debilitating effects of segregation. In 1896, in the midst of the Jim Crow Era, black Baptist pastor E. K. Love of Savannah, Georgia, said: "It never was true anywhere, and perhaps never will be, that a Negro can enjoy every right in an institution controlled by white men that a white man can enjoy." Love's comment came the year after formation of the National Baptist Convention, in 1895, which made official what began in 1880 when black Baptists organized their own missionary organization. Three years later the NBC established its own publishing house and embarked upon a lobbying effort to improve the lot of African Americans. These black Baptists – some 2 million strong by 1900 – turned the tables on white missionaries by organizing a missionary effort to take their decidedly Christian gospel "back to Africa." As a spokesman for the

National Baptists put it in 1903: "A great work remains to be done for the race in this and other lands." The National Baptist Convention continued to expand in the twentieth century and became the largest predominantly African American denomination in the United States.[24]

Impact of expansion on Native Americans

As we have seen in Chapter 1, by the mid-nineteenth century, most Native American tribes were relocated west of the Mississippi, where, it was said, they would be beyond the ever-expanding white population. That all changed in the wake of the Civil War, when Americans flooded into the West – the population living in the region increasing from 7 to 17 million between 1870 and 1890. This influx of Americans forced the Plains Indians onto increasingly smaller, less desirable tracts of land, overwhelmed the Native American food supply, including the buffalo (whose numbers dropped to only a few hundred by 1880), and challenged the Plains Indians very way of life, which was deemed uncivilized by those moving west. In the process, Native American religion – still numbering approximately 200 separate religions – continued to be challenged and to respond as it had in centuries past.[25]

From the 1860s to the 1880s, the federal government tried to force the Plains Indians onto reservations, where they were to be protected from outsiders, provided with food and other essentials, and "civilized." Reservations only further degraded the Native Americans' way of life by making them wards of the state, a condition made official by the United States Supreme Court in 1884 and 1886. Indians responded in different ways, none of which were successful. In 1864, one group of Cheyenne and Arapaho, mostly older men, women, and children, complied with an order to relocate to Big Sandy Creek in Colorado Territory with a guarantee of safety, only to be massacred by federal troops. Others refused to be relocated, prompting military action, as was the case in 1877 when troops chased 800 Nez Perce Indians across the Northwest, killing many in the process before they surrendered. The most infamous of Indian battles, however, occurred in June 1876, when 2,500 Lakotas led by Chiefs Sitting Bull and Crazy Horse surrounded and annihilated their pursuers, 256 government troops led by Colonel George Custer near the Little Big Horn River in Montana.

These continuous armed conflicts, as well as an awakening among some to the tragedy unfolding before them through publications such as Helen Hunt Jackson's *A Century of Dishonor* (1881), persuaded some officials and reformers that more peaceful means of dealing with the Native Americans were needed. Most often this meant that they had to be "uplifted" through their adoption of the white man's ways and had to abandon their "savage" way of life. In 1887, Congress passed the Dawes Severalty Act, which reversed its reservation policy authorizing the dissolution of commonly owned Native American property and granting allotments to individuals. Those who accepted such allotments would be awarded citizenship, a legal status not afforded all Native Americans until 1924. The idea was that private property ownership, with the expectation that they would learn to farm the land, would create useful citizens and in time integrate those Indians who accepted their new way of life into the larger, white society. Put another way, the plan was to destroy their tribal relations and traditional way of life.

After the Civil War, as the Indian Wars were coming to an end, and as the reservation system was being put into place, the US government encouraged the education of Native American children. Christian missionary schools were located on, or near, reservations, but closely allied with this plan was the determination that they would be assimilated more quickly if their children were taken from their families and educated at a distance at white-run boarding schools. The first and best known of these boarding schools, as it provided a model for those to follow, was the Carlisle School in Pennsylvania, founded by Richard Henry Pratt in 1879. After the Civil War, Pratt led the 10th Cavalry Regiment, which became known as the Buffalo Soldiers, on the southern plains. The cavalry, that included Native American scouts as well as African American soldiers, captured and transported seventy-two Native American prisoners to Fort Marion in St. Augustine, Florida, where Pratt resolved to improve their lot by caring for their physical condition, as well as their education. He organized volunteers to teach them the white man's language and culture, which included Christianity. When the prisoners were released, in 1878, seventeen went to Hampton Institute, a historically black institution established after the Civil War for freedmen, and which became the model for the Carlisle Industrial School authorized the next year by an act of Congress.[26]

Like most Americans at the time, Pratt believed that Native Americans should be uprooted from their tribal past in order to be fully assimilated into white society, or to put it more bluntly: "Kill the Indian in him, and save the man." This meant erasing any trace of Native American customs, language, and religion from their children, including their Indian names, and leading them to replace these with the white man's names and ways, which included adopting the practice of private property, building homes, learning to farm the land and/or a trade, and embracing Christianity. To that end, at Carlisle and other boarding schools, in addition to English, mathematics, history, drawing and music, Indian boys were taught farming and carpentry, and girls learned sewing and cooking. All were taught Christianity and expected to attend church in town. Carlisle also developed an "outing" program, wherein, in order to accelerate their assimilation, the children were sent to spend time with white families, often living with them for an extended period of time.[27]

The first Carlisle students came from the Lakota tribe, at the recommendation of Spotted Tail and Red Cloud, but by the time the school closed in 1918, under pressure from the Bureau of Indian Affairs, nearly 12,000 children followed from 140 tribes, as many as 1,000 a year at one point. Moreover, by 1902 Carlisle provided the model for 26 Indian boarding schools the Bureau of Indian Affairs established across the country, in addition to more than 450 schools run by Catholic and Protestant missionary schools that operated on the same basic "civilizing" premise.[28]

The Carlisle School has a mixed legacy of educational ideals and results. Some of those who attended Carlisle or other Indian boarding schools were assimilated, but by most accounts, the full promise of these institutions was not realized. Most of the graduates returned to their families demoralized and confused as to their identity and place in the world. Hundreds of children died at Carlisle, most from infectious diseases, although some would argue that the new climate and separation anxiety added to their mortality. More than 175 were buried at the school, mostly those who died of tuberculosis, given its contagious nature; the bodies of most of the others were returned to their families. Corporal punishment – from a slap of a ruler on the hand to confinement and hard labor, with a few reports of children having their mouths washed with lye soap for speaking in their tribal languages – was accepted for such transgressions as speaking their native tongues or attempting to escape.[29]

The Ghost Dance

Plains Indians resisted the changes being forced upon them through religion, a recourse made difficult by the Indian Religious Crimes Code of 1883, which made many Indian religious ceremonies illegal. Many ceremonies were driven underground, while others remained visible but were often seen as threatening. The best known was the Ghost Dance.

The Ghost Dance, variously referred to as a revitalization movement but also a crisis cult, originated with the Northern Paiute prophet Wodziwob in 1870. But in 1889–1890, another Northern Paiute, Wovoka, also known as Jack Wilson (Wilson being the name of a family for whom he worked for a time), whose medicine man father may have been involved in the 1870 movement, transformed the dance into a religious ritual and was thereafter recognized as the messiah or prophet of the Ghost Dance.[30]

Wovoka, born sometime between 1856 and 1863, fell sick during a solar eclipse on January 1, 1889. When he recovered, he claimed to have visited the spirit world, where he encountered his dead ancestors, all living blissfully amidst great abundance, and received a message he was to disseminate among other Native Americans upon his return to earth. That message was that the world would soon be restored to a pure pre-white-man state of peace and abundance, which Native Americans, living and resurrected, would inherit. In order to ensure the arrival of this new promised-land, and prepare to inherit it, Wovoka taught that Native Americans should shun the ways of the whites and live in peace with one another, meditate, pray, sing, and engage in the Ghost Dance.[31]

The Ghost Dance involved several nights – by some reports three, by others five – in a circle (its actual Indian name was Nanigukwa, meaning "dance in a circle") until dancers reached a trance-like state in which they entered the spirit world and made contact with their ancestors. Dancers who achieved such visions, Wovoka taught, would themselves have a confirming vision of the day when the buffalo would return and white civilization would disappear, "when the entire Indian race, living and dead, will be reunited upon a regenerated earth, to live in aboriginal happiness, forever free from death, disease, and misery."[32]

Wovoka's visions offered both a hopeful message for revitalization and instructions on how to bring it about. Further, by some estimates, it also reflected the fusion of Christian and Native American religious elements. The Wilsons were devout United Presbyterians and by various reports shared their religious views, including the resurrection and its meaning for Christians, with the young Wovoka. Ethnologist James Moody interviewed Wovoka in 1896 and recorded the prophet's account of his vision: "When the sun died [a reference to the solar eclipse], I went up to heaven and saw God and all the people who had died a long time ago. God told me to come back and tell my people they must be good and love one another, and not fight, or steal or lie. He gave me this dance to give to my people." If those to whom he bore this message obeyed his instructions, Wovoka continued, "they would at last be reunited with their friends in this other world, where there would be no more death or sickness or old age."[33]

Although a common element in the various interpretations of Wovoka's vision was the disappearance of whites from the earth, most Ghost Dancers foreswore violence. To that point, historians have variously referred to the religion as "accommodative," "reformist," and "redemptive." But some, like the Lakota Sioux – devastated by the wars of the 1870s, suffering from confinement to a drought-stricken reservation and dying from disease and starvation because of inadequate food allotments – took a more militant, or apocalyptic, stance. They believed that resistance would speed the arrival of the promised new day, a perception made all the more threatening when the dancers donned sacred "ghost shirts" that they believed would repel the white man's bullets.[34]

As the Ghost Dance ritual spread across the West to the Sioux, Cheyenne, Comanche, Shoshone, Arapaho, and other tribes, government agents became alarmed that the emotional frenzy it created would lead to renewed armed uprisings and outlawed it. When Chief Sitting Bull embraced the Ghost Dance, attracting even larger numbers to the ritual, white leaders concluded that a major Indian uprising was imminent. Particularly alarming was the situation among the Lakota Sioux on the Pine Ridge Reservation in South Dakota, where the dance appeared to have reached a fevered pitch. In December 1890, the US 7th Cavalry (Custer's old regiment) attempted to disarm a group of Indians moving toward Pine Ridge. Encountering the band at Wounded Knee Creek, on December 29, fighting broke out resulting in the deaths of an estimated 150 Lakota men, women, and children. The Ghost Dance did not entirely disappear at that point. It continued to be practiced in parts of the country where it did not raise alarms. But following the Wounded Knee Massacre, armed Native American resistance faded away.[35]

Black Elk Speaks

Witness to the Lakota Ghost Dance and resulting killings was Black Elk, whose recollections were collected and published in 1932 by John G. Neihardt. Neihardt interviewed the Oglala Lakota tribal elder/holy man on the Pine Ridge Reservation in South Dakota, and decades later, the resulting book became a national best seller. It was one of the most influential books of the 1960s among those with a renewed interest in Native American religion, as well as those involved in the American Indian Movement.

In Neihardt's account, Black Elk looks back at his experiences as a young man, which included the Battle of the Little Bighorn, Wounded Knee, touring with Buffalo Bill's Wild West Show, and the Ghost Dance movement. But it also portrays Black Elk as an elderly holy man, reflecting on life in pre-reservation days, on boyhood memories, village and family life, and religious rituals. The mood is set on the very first page, when, Black Elk says:

> My friend, I am going to tell you the story of my life, as you wish; and if it were only the story of my life I think I would not tell it. . . . It is the story of a life that is holy and is good to tell . . . [and] now that I can see it all as from a lonely hilltop, I know it was the story of a mighty vision given to a man too weak to use it; of a holy tree that should have flourished in a people's heart with flowers and singing birds, and now is withered; and of a people's dream that died in bloody snow.[36]

Black Elk, the son of a Lakota warrior and medicine man, received the first of his many visions at age 9. Although muddled in several specifics in their various retellings over the decades and cast in imagery that has been subject to differing interpretations, Black Elk recalled that he had suddenly taken ill and was unresponsive for several days, during which time he was carried by two spirit men – Thunder Beings according to some accounts – up to the sky to meet Six Grandfathers in a lodge of flaming rainbows:

> And while I stood there I saw more than I can tell and understood more than I saw; for I was seeing in a sacred manner the shapes of all things in the spirit, and the shape of all shapes as they must live together like one being. And I saw the sacred hoop of my people was one of many hoops that made one circle, wide as daylight and as starlight, and in the center grew one mighty flowering tree to shelter all the children of one mother and one father. And I saw that it was holy.[37]

The grandfathers, seen by Native Americans as kind, loving, and the sources of great wisdom, explained that Black Elk's destiny was to be a holy man in a period of "great troubles" for his people, and as Black Elk grew up, he experienced the many crises his people faced in the closing years of the nineteenth century. In his later years, he reflected on those experiences, and although his words would be inspirational to many, as Tracy Neal Leavelle has commented, his closing words seem to be those of a man defeated: Although a person to whom "so great a vision was given" in his youth, "you see me now a pitiful old man who has done nothing, for the nation's hoop is broken and scattered. There is no center any longer, and the sacred tree is dead."[38]

Although ostensibly a biography of an important Native American, and by extension a commentary on the fate of the Sioux, at the close of the nineteenth century, *Black Elk Speaks* has been the subject of numerous interpretations. As Michael Steltenkamp, for one, has argued, Black Elk's accounts, as reported by John G. Neihardt, presents a romanticized view of pre-reservation days, that came to an end with Wounded Knee. By extension, Plains Indians became romanticized as well. As Steltenkamp summarized it:

> So evocative is Black Elk's characterization [in *Black Elk Speaks*], that it was been expropriated and utilized on behalf of diverse forms of special pleading. Environmental activists, Indian militants, anthropologists, historians, religionists, students of Americana and others have gleaned from Black Elk passages that bolster or refute whatever convention Native themes they choose because, it appears, his representation has become the conventional stereotype par excellence.[39]

From a religious perspective, which is our primary concern here, Black Elk's life was more complex, and interesting historically, than a reading of Neihardt's book might suggest. Following his years as holy man, in 1904, Black Elk became a Roman Catholic, a catechist, and a leader in the local Catholic church. Moreover, Black Elk was actively involved in establishing Catholicism beyond the Lakota of the Pine Ridge Reservation to the Arapahos, Winnebagos, Omahas, and others. When asked to explain the conversion, his daughter Lucy later explained that, while a medicine man, in a time of the tremendous reversals of fortune, he had experienced considerable inner turmoil and in time concluded that "the son of God had called him to lead a new life." In sum, Black Elk's conversion resulted in an integration of the two religious traditions.[40]

Neihardt did not include this part of his life, which in number of years exceeded that of Black Elk's pre-Catholic life. In fact, Joseph Epes Brown later reported that, while working on *The Sacred Pipe*, he had been in communication with Neihardt and that the poet admitted that his depiction of Black Elk was greatly embellished and was only based on Black Elk's recollections. Neihardt did this, some have speculated, because it would have compromised Black Elk's Indianness, as the poet turned biographer clearly wanted to show. Or, given that Black Elk welcomed the teaching of Jesuit missionaries and the conversion experience, it would have flown in the face of the dominant idea of "close-minded [missionary] zealots bent on destroying Native culture."[41]

Black Elk's daughter, Lucy, later insisted that her father realized this omission and provided Neihardt with additional material for the book, which never appeared. The addition, although never conclusively identified, may well have been the letter Black Elk wrote on January 26, 1934. Written from the Holy Rosary Mission on Pine Ridge Reservation and titled "Black Elk Speaks Again – A Last Word," Black Elk wrote:

> Listen, I speak some true words. A white man made a book and told what I had spoken of olden times, but the new times he left out. So I speak again, a last word. . . . In the last thirty years I am different from what the white man wrote about me. I am a Christian.

I was baptized thirty years ago. . . . I am now converted to the true Faith in God the Father, the Son and the Holy Ghost. . . . Thirty years ago I was a real Indian and knew a little about the Great Spirit. . . . I was a good Indian; but now I am better . . . St. Paul also turned better when he was converted. I now know that the prayer of the Catholic Church is better than the prayer of the Ghost-dance.[42]

Peyote ceremonialism

Lucy, Black Elk's daughter, commented that, when her father traveled the Plains espousing Catholicism, he commonly faced opposition from Native Americans who were embracing a new religious expression, at least new among them, namely peyote ceremonialism. Derived from a cactus native to the region, the Indians of Mexico and what would become the American Southwest used peyote both as a medicine and to commune with the spirit world before the arrival of Europeans. Peyote ceremonialism, however, commonly involving all-night ritualistic use of the hallucinogenic, inducing an intense spiritual experience, spread beyond the Southwest to other Native American groups at about the same time as the Ghost Dance.[43]

The principal promoter of the peyote religion, in its late nineteenth-century form, was the Comanche Quanah Parker, who claimed to have been healed by a medicine man who used the plant while in the Southwest. Parker brought the ritual home to Oklahoma and became a practitioner of what became known as the "Half Moon Ceremony," a reference to the curved shape of the earth-composed altar, which opened to the East and that served as the centerpiece of the ritual. The "cross fire" ceremony, which involved a horseshoe-shaped altar with a mound of dirt at one end, was added later. The ritual, which commonly began at sundown on Saturday and ended Sunday morning, included, in addition to consuming peyote, prayer, songs, water rituals, and contemplation. The ritual was believed to allow communion with the spirit world from which one could gain knowledge and power, as well as healing.

Peyotists, as they were often called, commonly believed in one god, who was responsible for giving humans the sacred peyote medicine. Among some tribes, that god was Mescalito, who was peyote personified. Among others, its ceremonial use included aspects of Christian beliefs, symbols, and even rituals including Jesus as spiritual guardian and intercessor. Christian influences can be seen in this and other aspects of the ritual, although it was always a mix of Christian and Native American elements. A more explicitly Christian version of this ritual can be found in the previously mentioned cross fire ceremony, wherein practitioners expressly sought Christ in their visions.[44]

Although getting ahead of ourselves a bit, government officials frowned on the use of peyote, even in a religious ceremony, and sought to suppress it. They failed, and in 1918, practitioners founded the Native American Church, which continued the use of peyote in a more formally organized church. In 1990, the United States Supreme Court, in *Employment Division, Department of Human Resources of Oregon v. Smith*, placed in jeopardy American Indian use of peyote in their religious ceremonies. In 1994 and 1996, Congress countered with amendments to the American Indian Religious Freedom Act of 1978 providing for its continue use when used for "bona fide traditional ceremonial purposes in connection with the practice of a traditional Indian religion."[45] But in its ruling in *City of Boerne v. Flores* in 1997, the Supreme Court declared those amendments unconstitutional.

Calls for unity amidst rapidly increasing diversity

In 1900, four-fifths of American church members belonged to the eight largest denominations. The smallest of the eight, the Episcopalians and Congregationalists, were the largest during the Colonial Period. By 1900, they numbered about 600,000 each, still much larger than those not among the top eight, but clearly a far cry, proportionately, from what they once were. The number of denominations was greatly expanded, but most remained comparatively small. Further, at American independence, church membership was estimated at 17 percent of the total population. By 1900, that number approached 50 percent, the growth among Roman Catholics leading the pack, followed by Methodists and Baptists. But also notable was the rise of the Disciples of Christ from an upstart faith to take its place among the top eight and, although not yet a contender, the Church of Jesus Christ of Latter-day Saints, which by 1890 numbered a quarter million.[46]

All of this, as well as the previously discussed wave of immigration, led to a sense of loss of national unity. And, as religious historian Edwin Gaustad has put it: "All this difference made Americanization the great cause of many native born whites: to take all that 'foreignness' in language, custom, dress, and religion and somehow to melt it all down into a familiar, domesticated English – speaking 'American' – preferably Protestant and Bible believing."[47]

Further, although as the nineteenth century drew to a close, one-third of Americans regularly went to church and nearly three-fifths of these to evangelical churches, the prevailing opinion, espoused most vociferously by the press, was of "a church in crisis and threatened with decline." To their observation, the mainstream Protestant churches had grown complacent in dealing both with the challenges of immigration and diversity and with the problems associated with both, including urbanization, industrialization, unionization, labor strikes, and outright acts of violence such as the Haymarket Square riot and bombing of 1886. As an editorial in the *Boston Journal* put it, church-goers too often were fed "religious services designed to tickle the ear without awakening the conscience or purifying the heart."[48] The warning did not fall on deaf ears. In fact, it led to a two-step response, the first of which became America's Third Great Awakening (the second will be addressed in the next chapter).

The Third Great Awakening

By the end of the nineteenth century, the perceived threats facing the nation and the need to respond to the evils they portended, became the cause of many, especially among the native born, leading to a reemphasis on the nation's mainstream Protestant foundation. And this helped spark yet another major revival, referred to as the Third Great Awakening, which swept the nation especially its northern urban areas.[49]

A most unlikely revivalist, Boston shoe clerk Dwight L. Moody, proved instrumental to the awakening. Moody was born on a farm in Northfield, Massachusetts, in 1837 into a family of nine children that struggled to make ends meet after their father died when Dwight was only four. Raised in the Unitarian church, Dwight moved to Boston when he turned 17 to work in his uncle's shoe store, whereupon his uncle required him to attend the Mount Vernon Congregational Church. Within a year, in April 1855, he was converted to evangelical Christianity. The following month, Moody applied for church membership but was rejected. As his Sunday School teacher, Edward Kimball, later commented on Moody's rejection: "I can truly say . . . that I have seen few persons whose minds were spiritually darker than was his when he came into my Sunday school class; and I think the committee of the Mount Vernon Church seldom met an applicant for membership more unlikely ever to become a Christian of clear and decided views of Gospel truth, still less to fill an extended sphere of public usefulness." Moody proved Kimball wrong. Almost exactly one year later, Moody was accepted into the church, soon after which, still only age 18, Moody moved to Chicago.[50]

Moody remained committed to making his fortune in business, but he could not resist the calling to preach the gospel. He joined the Plymouth Congregational Church where he spent his business after-hours providing Sunday school classes for young men from Chicago's notorious slum, Hell's Kitchen. But when he began to recruit some of those same boys to join him in his rented pew, causing concern among his fellow congregants, Moody took his Sabbath School classes to the Wells Street Mission School. In 1859, he took them to the North Market Hall, where he gave himself totally over to spreading the word of God among the city's poor youth.[51]

Moody's first Sunday school meetings were modest in their numbers. Armed with only a fifth grade education, his earliest observers commented how, amidst his considerable zeal, he could not pronounce many of the words in the various biblical passages he chose as his texts. Moody persisted, however, and within a year began to attract audiences averaging 650 with 60 volunteers from various churches serving as teachers. He became so well known that President Elect Abraham Lincoln attended and spoke at one of Moody's Sunday school meetings on November 25, 1860.[52]

Moody's work with the poor attracted the city's press corps, his success a hallmark of his revival activities. Some characterized his use of the press as that of "an ostentatious self-seeker," but Moody saw his collaboration with the press as mutually supportive activities. As Moody would later explain to his detractors: "It seems to me a good deal better to advertise and have a full house, than to preach to empty pews. . . . This is the age of advertisement and you have to take your chances."[53]

After the Civil War, Moody continued to enhance his reputation for his mission of mercy among the poor, especially young men who came in increasingly large numbers in search of work. Some six years after its founding, what began as a mission Sunday school at North Market Hall blossomed into the Illinois Street Church. When that building was destroyed in the Great Chicago Fire of 1871, it was replaced by a temporary structure, the North Side Tabernacle, which three years later was replaced by the more permanent Chicago Avenue Church (renamed The Moody Church after his death). At its opening, the Chicago Avenue Church proudly advertised that unlike many of the city's other churches, it would not rent pews. It "was built by the poor people, for the poor people, and belongs to the poor people." Moody also lent his efforts to the city's YMCA, which was organized in 1866 with the support of some of the city's wealthiest men of business – Cyrus McCormick and George Armour, to name just two – and with a mission similar to his, namely to evangelize and to provide wholesome activity for the city's rootless young men. Moody served as president of the YMCA from 1866 to 1870.[54]

In 1871, or early 1872, while walking the streets of New York, and Wall Street in particular, to raise money for the YMCA and his missionary efforts in Chicago, Moody had a new vision: "Preaching the Kingdom of God, not social work, would change the world." From that point on, he would devote his energies to the "evangelization of the world in this generation."[55]

Moody traveled to the United Kingdom where, in June 1873, he and gospel singer and hymn writer Ira D. Sankey, over the course of two years, led what the *Times* of London described as "the most remarkable [revival meetings] ever witnessed in England, Scotland, and even Catholic Ireland." Assisted and promoted by the Plymouth Brethren and the famous London Baptist preacher, Charles Spurgeon, Moody's popularity soared. His Greater London campaign, which began on March 9, 1875, included 285 meetings and 2,530,000 attendees. As the London *Morning Post* commented, educated listeners might have disdained Moody's massacre of the King's English, but the nightly crowds of 21,000 didn't seem to mind.[56]

The success Moody had in Britain and the coverage he received in the American press provided him with considerable momentum when he returned home in 1875. Moody began his American campaign in Brooklyn – commonly proclaimed "the wickedest city" in the nation – where even his biggest supporters feared his words would fall on deaf ears. But he attracted crowds that filled the "vast emptiness" of the Brooklyn Rink. As one report put it, when word got out about Moody's first, morning performance, fully 15,000 persons of all denominations, social classes, genders, and ages, massed at the Rink hours in advance. The crowd soon broke into "pushing, jostling, and scrambling" the likes of which had seldom been seen in the city. The police were called out to restore order but not before "women fainted, children screamed, hats were lost and shirts torn off." Just across the river, in New York City's Madison Avenue Hall, equally large crowds overwhelmed the facility's indoor seating of 5,000 and hundreds had to stand outside hoping to hear some of what Moody had to say and to the singing of hymns from the *Moody and Sankey Hymnbook*. A reporter covering the event found the calm and quiet of the attentive audience "remarkable." "Even the rough fellows who crowd the gallery passages make no sound," he wrote. President Ulysses Grant and some of the members of his cabinet attended a meeting on January 19, 1876.[57]

Moody's success continued unabated as he preached in Philadelphia and Boston in the East and out to the west coast to San Francisco, San Diego, and Vancouver, as well as several smaller cities along the way, spending five or six months in residence on occasion. And of course there was his triumphant return to the city of Chicago in October 1876, where one newspaper reported "the popular outpouring can't be compared to any event in Chicago history."[58]

Moody showed little regard for formal religion or denominationalism, but one of the distinguishing characteristics of Moody's revivals was his modern, masculine image. As one of his ministerial contemporaries, Lyman Abbott, put it: "As he stood on the platform [dressed in a black, three piece suit] he looked like a business man; he dressed like a business man; he took the meeting in hand as a business man would; he spoke in a business man's fashion; he had no holy tone." He appeared as "God's businessman," convincing those who observed him that he was ready "to convert and tame Chicago's restless working class." As Thekla Ellen Joiner concluded, Moody's sermons were intended to make the Gospel relevant to the men of Chicago and to win them over to the evangelical cause. This would in turn "tame the masses of uncontrolled, un-Christian men who threatened the city's social stability" and win back middle-class men, who had turned away from Christianity – Protestant Christianity to be more specific.[59]

Moody's sermons were simple and positive, and they discouraged any great emotional display. They stressed the need and opportunity for personal redemption, if only one took the initiative to be saved, and God's love: "Now, let me say, my friends, if you want the love of God in your hearts, all you have to do is to open the door and let it shine in. It will shine in as the sun shines in a dark room. Let him have full possession of your hearts." Moody understood men to be sinful. "We are wicked by nature," he preached:

> There is nothing good in us; the Bible teaches us that all the way through. But we are masters of our own fate. We cannot blame God or even Adam, for the solution to our problem has been given to us by God, and if we are lost it is because we spurn it. Though we are under the influence of the Devil, we can choose to believe the Gospel if we so wish. . . . And if we choose the gift of salvation, the blood of Jesus Christ redeems us. Christ paid the penalty; Christ died in our stead. And He did so because of His love for us.[60]

Moody came to embrace dispensationalism, which he had encountered among the Plymouth Brethren in Britain and which had a considerable following during the Gilded Age. Unlike the widespread postmillennialism of the previous century, dispensationalism was built on a premillennialist understanding that Christ would come before the millennium to establish it rather than after it was established on earth, something they believed was no longer possible. This led Moody to dismiss the social reform movements of contemporaries like Walter Rauschenbusch and what was known as the Social Gospel. The impact was immediate and profound: "I have felt like working three times as hard ever since I came to understand that my Lord was coming back soon. I look on this world as a wrecked vessel. God has given me a life-board and said to me, 'Moody, save all you can.'" As William Cooper has put it: "Revivalism now becomes a rescue mission, a spiritual raid in hostile territory, rooted in love and compassion geared solely to the salvation of sinners from a doomed, dying planet."[61]

But perhaps what most distinguished Moody's career as a revivalist was his concentration on methodology – how to choreograph, even construct, revivals that simply did not fail to attract the multitudes. As some have argued, Moody made revivals big business and provided a model for others to capitalize on in years to come. Moody transformed revivals into mass media campaigns involving enormous amounts of pre-event planning; careful preparation involving a veritable army of workers including local evangelical ministers, wealthy citizens, and lay people; ample financial support, all arranged in advance; and, especially, extensive publicity in the press. As Bruce Evensen has put it: "In Moody's world and since, the sacred and the profane have been mixed to serve mighty purposes and each other's interests. Moody needed the publicity, and the press needed a good story."[62]

In concluding this section, it should be noted that Moody did see the need for religious education, and he founded institutions he hoped would carry out that mission. In 1889, with considerable support from Emma Dryer, he was able to transform Chicago's Evangelization Society into a coeducational religious school, the Chicago Bible Institute, which was renamed the Moody Bible Institute in his honor, when he died. Support for the Institute came from some of the nation's wealthiest and most influential people, like Cyrus McCormick, John Wanamaker, and Henry Ward Beecher. Further, despite his success in Chicago, Moody chose to make his birthplace his permanent home, where he initiated other educational endeavors. He purchased a farm near Northfield, Massachusetts, where he founded the Northfield Bible Conference. The NBC hosted conferences attended by prominent Christian preachers and evangelists from America and England to lecture on various topics to hundreds of Christian visitors, at first focused on the doctrine of the Holy Spirit or how to commune with God, but in time being dominated by speakers on dispensational premillennialism. In 1879, he founded the Northfield Seminary for Young Women and, two years later, the Mount Hermon School for Boys. Both schools, dedicated to educating the poor and minorities of diverse religious backgrounds, later merged to form Northfield Mount Hermon School. Moody died in 1899.[63]

In the wake of Dwight L. Moody: evangelicalism versus reform

Moody's message avoided some of the burning social and political issues of the day, thereby being seen by some as out-of-date and unresponsive to the actual needs of the era. He was an evangelist, not a reformer. Fellow Congregationalist Josiah Strong saw things differently. He saw the need for social reform, as well as changing people's hearts. In *Our Country: Its Possible Future and Its Present Crisis*, published in 1895, Strong made the case for the adverse effects of American capitalism, including the exploitation of labor and the growing self-indulgence in money-making, as well as what he saw as the delusion that socialism could achieve a brotherhood of man without God. The present crisis, he explained, was not these issues per se, but rather the potential failure of Anglo-Saxon civilization, now centered in America, and pure Christian religion to counter the threat they posed. And the greatest threat to American Anglo-Saxon civilization and pure Christian religion was immigration and homegrown alien religious groups, such as the Mormons, and the non-Protestant diversity they represented. Strong and others blamed them for intemperance; political corruption; threats to free speech, free press, and free public education; and, in the case of the Mormons, a threat to the sanctity of marriage. These issues threatened not only the destiny of Christianity, but also of America, which by Strong's view of history, threatened the destiny of the world, as well. More on social reform in the next chapter.[64]

The World's Parliament of Religions

By the 1890s, the Third Great Awakening appeared to have peaked, especially as led by Dwight L. Moody, only to be reignited in response to Americans coming face-to-face with the great variety of religions in the world at the World's Columbian Exposition. Hosted by the city of Chicago in 1893, commemorating the 400th anniversary of Columbus's landfall in the New World (one year late), the World's Parliament of Religions certainly seemed appropriate, as it was Columbus's arrival in the New World that linked the world's continents and peoples, with the great variety of religions they represented. The Parliament, the idea for which came from Congregationalist John Henry Barrows, opened Americans' eyes to the great diversity of faiths in the world, many of which were already in the United States, if in small numbers. Moreover, it was organized around a theme, that amidst the dozens of religions represented at the Parliament a core of common truths could be discerned in which all people of all faiths could find comfort. Just how many of the estimated 27 million fairgoers found comfort in what they witnessed at the World's Parliament of Religions is unclear. What is clear is that many did not, which led to a brief, but highly energized, renewal of the Third Great Awakening.[65]

The Parliament was designed to be "a great university ready to attack the subject [religion] without prejudice and in the pure life of reason." It was intended to be ecumenical, but many – especially evangelicals, led by Moody in what would be his last grand revival – saw it as an opportunity to demonstrate the superiority of Christianity. Some saw it an opportunity to convert international visitors of other faiths, who would then return home to spread the word of Jesus.[66]

Although Chicago had become accustomed to periodic revivals over the past several years, taking full advantage of the large crowds attending the fair would call for a large sustained effort from the months of May through October. The Chicago Bible Institute became the campaign's unofficial headquarters, but other centers included Moody's Chicago Avenue Church and a newly erected Sunday School Building just outside the fairgrounds. By August, the revival was holding regular meetings in ten churches, seven halls, two theaters, and five tents. Moreover, the press made much of the World's Fair Revival and the numbers who were attracted to its meetings. No attendance records were kept, but by one estimate, the revival had its best day ever on September 23, sponsoring 64 different meetings held in 46 places with an estimated attendance of from 62,000 to 64,000 people. As reported in the *Chicago Herald* on June 19, 1893, although intended to reach the "heathen" or the masses, most of those who attended were "well dressed, sedate citizens, who joined in the prayers and swelled the chorus of the hymns." The Women's Christian Temperance Union's *Union Signal* reported that "the World's Fair Evangelization Campaign wrought more effectively for the Kingdom of God than all the combined forces of evil were able to accomplish against it."[67]

However, if we define a revival as a real or perceived quickening of faith of believers or the conviction and conversion of the fallen away or those who never believed, the real and long-term results are elusive and the subject of considerable and continuous reappraisal. As Jon Butler found, the Third Great Awakening was successful insofar as it promoted Protestant adherence. Between 1890 and 1916, he found, the percentage of Protestant church members in Chicago grew from 35 percent to 43 percent, an increase that was mirrored in other urban centers. But, once again, as is commonly believed among students of revivals, any lasting impact from revivals except in terms of temporary increased membership and sporadic social reforms is less clear.[68]

Women and religion in the late-nineteenth century

A final example of diversity and dissent for this chapter involves women in various Christian denominations. In the first half of the nineteenth century, the role of women in mainstream American Protestantism changed, that change reflecting changes in society, the economy, and culture that developed during the Early Republic. With the exception of the few women in more marginal religious organizations – Ann Lee among the Shakers, for example – women came to play a more active role in their various churches without ascending to positions of leadership, at least officially, or taking their place in the pulpits. They played an important role in a number of reform movements, including emancipation, only to find themselves left out when in the wake of emancipation, black men were afforded the vote but not women – black or white. Discouraged, but not defeated, American women's quest for full equality both in the nation's churches and society at large began anew after the Civil War.

Women continued to find the greatest success in their quest for leadership positions among new and still largely marginal churches, like Christian Science and holiness and pentecostal bodies, where women ministers were common. The holiness and pentecostal movements will be addressed in Chapter 3, but attention to Mary Baker Eddy and Christian Science would be in order at this point. As a young woman, Eddy suffered from multiple physical illnesses and nervous disorders, from which she found little relief from the common medical treatments of the day until she encountered fellow New Englander Phineas Quimby and his theories on the mental causes of physical disorders. Quimby's theories, which helped spark the New Thought movement, also led Eddy to develop a "science of health" that provided the basis for Christian Science and the substance of her book, *Science and Health with Key to the Scriptures*, first published in 1875. Four years later, she chartered the first Church of Christ, Scientist.[69]

Eddy based her ideas on the premise that physical matter was illusory or unreal and that only spirit was real. From that, she taught that ill health and false belief were closely related and that disease had no independent reality. Rather it was the product of mental error, and healing could not happen by medical treatment, but only by correcting that mental error by "right thinking." The proper activity of the mind, Eddy believed, could conquer "sin, sickness, and death." The name of her church was based on her belief that Jesus was the first "scientist" in that in his healing he demonstrated her understanding of the healing process. She pointed to passages in the New Testament, such as Matthew 9:2, in which Jesus healed a paralytic, the reading of which she believed led her to recovery from a life-threatening fall on the ice. Eddy insisted that the New Testament provided "all our recipes for healing," if properly understood. In 1883, she provided a guide to that understanding in her "Key to the Scriptures," which became central to her *Science and Health.*

Eddy insisted that Christian Science was Christian, but she caused considerable controversy with her insistence on the distinctive aspects of Christian Science and that only those with a specially revealed key to Scripture's interpretation, according to its "spiritual sense," could properly understand and provide authoritative Christian revelation. Claiming that she held that "key," she insisted that Christian Science was of divine origin and a dimension of the Second Coming of Jesus.

By the time of her death in 1910, the Church of Christ, Scientist was well established with more than 1,000 churches, and as many reading rooms, located in cities across the nation. To return to the focus of this section, however, Peter Williams, among others, has argued that Eddy's influence was greatest on Victorian women, who were "at the margins of the middle classes and unsure of their role in a rapidly urbanizing society." Donald Meyer has added that Christian Science and Eddy, by her example, provided a way by which such women could overcome their sense of powerlessness, exemplified by Eddy's use of the phrase "Our Father-Mother God, all harmonious" in her paraphrasing of the Lord's Prayer.[70]

Among more mainstream churches, the push for greater equality was more challenging, continually foiled by tradition and biblical injunction, at least as interpreted and enforced by male leaders. Typical for the time was the reasoning of Robert L. Dabney, a Presbyterian minister and theologian in Virginia. Writing in 1879, Dabney listed the many reasons why women should not be ordained. He argued that not all "progressive" innovations were biblical, women's ordination being one such example that also lacked any socially redeeming quality. Neither the Old nor New Testament made allowance for any office for women. Moreover, he added, women really were "weaker vessels," as was commonly believed, and thereby unfit for the responsibilities of ministerial office. And finally, the ascending of women to such high office threatened the foundation of Christian marriage itself. Thus, he proclaimed the idea of women's ordination "simply infidel" and insisted that Presbyterians have nothing to do with it.[71]

Elizabeth Cady Stanton begged to differ with Dabney. Stanton, outspoken on many women's rights issues, challenged those who relied on the Bible to buttress their arguments on gender inequality. "The Bible teaches that woman brought sin and death into the world," Stanton wrote in 1895, "that she precipitated the fall of the race, that she was arraigned before the judgment seat of Heaven, tried, condemned and sentenced." As a result: "Marriage was to be her bondage, childbearing her curse, and intellectual dependence her earthly fate." With that basic assumption in place, true equality for women could never be realized. She therefore called for a new critical understanding of the Bible or at least those parts that were being used to justify patriarchy. Stanton sought to provide that new critical understanding in *The Woman's Bible*, which she published in two volumes in 1895 and 1898. To those who criticized her revisions of what they deemed sacred and unalterable, she commented: "Come, come, my conservative friend, wipe the dew off your spectacles, and see that the world is moving."[72]

The world continued to move too slowly for Stanton and others, but women pioneers did carve out paths for women yet to come, and chief among them was Antoinette Brown Blackwell. Blackwell was admitted to Oberlin College, founded under the joint auspices of the Congregationalists and Presbyterians and among the earliest colleges to offer a college to educate both men and women. Neither the founding denominations nor the college, however, was prepared for what Blackwell chose to do upon completing her undergraduate degree, namely apply to continue her studies in the theology department, the path normally taken by those seeking ordination in the ministry. Blackwell persisted, however, and the college relented to the extent that it allowed her to pursue her theological studies, but it would not award her a degree, thereby presumably stopping her short of ordination. Nevertheless, Blackwell did succeed in being ordained a Congregationalist minister in 1853 – the first women ordained into the ministry by one of the major denominations – and for the rest of her life, she was a leading proponent of women's rights in general and women's ministry, in particular.[73]

An arena in which women gained significantly in their church leadership was in the Third Great Awakening. As detailed by Thekla Ellen Joiner, Dwight L. Moody and other evangelical ministers found women instrumental in his urban revivals, both in taking their message to the people, men and women included, and in Moody's case, symbolizing his two fold masculine-feminine message. More specifically, Moody balanced his masculine, business-like approach with the ideals of womanhood and domesticity, thereby appealing to men who had failed to live up to their domestic responsibilities and in the process lost that influence in their lives. The result was an "uncontrolled masculinity," which had led to public immorality, political corruption, and overall social decline. What Moody sought was nothing less than a modern Christian ideal, "a Christian manhood that, in many ways, was demanded by and depended upon female piety."[74]

While recognizing that the role of women in the churches dating to the early decades of the nineteenth century stood on the central Protestant values of piety, submission, domesticity, and sexual purity, by the end of the century, "evangelical men acquiesced to women's expanding influence in the home and church, [and] reform activism further tilted the moral balance in a feminine direction," elevating "the queen of middle-class domesticity, preserver of home and family, as society's ballast." Moody provided an example by encouraging evangelical women to take their "moralizing potential" to the streets. The result was that a burgeoning subculture of evangelical women took up their domestic assignment and formed associations that catapulted their moral influence into the public arena.[75]

An interesting case study of a woman evangelist whose career points to both the opportunities and the limits of women evangelicals is that of Emma Dryer. From 1864 to 1870, Dryer taught at the Illinois State Normal School during which time she gained the acquaintance of various YWCA missionaries and familiarized herself with Chicago's network of Protestant missions. In 1870, she resigned her teaching position to evangelize prostitutes and began to attend Moody's Illinois Street Church. Two years later Moody, whose Illinois Street Church had become the Chicago Avenue Church, hired Dryer to direct its Bible Work of Chicago, the purpose of which was to train people – especially women – to distribute Bibles and to lead prayer and Bible studies in city neighborhoods. Dryer herself worked in the Haymarket and Union Park neighborhoods, both poor and working class. After 1879, Dryer employed a more formal model she observed while in England, wherein she divided the city into districts and assigned a woman to live in each district, to organize prayer meetings in various homes, and to make house visits to read Scripture to women and children.[76]

Moody and Dryer shared the vision that Bible Work had both an educational and domestic purpose. As they saw it, the home had to be their prime target, as it was "the incubator of personal morality." But, as Thekla Ellen Joiner has argued, that role "conveyed authority and respectability to female workers. At a time when 'proper' society questioned the decency of any woman who ventured into urban space, missionaries like Dryer moved through city streets cloaked with the legitimacy of 'true womanhood' as they carried out their redemptive tasks."[77]

Similarly, Moody and Dryer were of like mind in their conservative yet utilitarian perspective on Bible Work. Both were influenced by premillennialism and wanted to save as many individuals as possible before the rapture, or Second Coming. And given the moral authority of womanhood and women's skills in urban work, both advocated women engaging in home and neighborhood work, as well as assuming more visible roles in more public forms of the ministry. Dryer, however, was the more socially conservative of the two and was intent on maintaining female respectability, refusing to allow Bible Workers to teach men or evangelize in areas dominated by men, such as saloons or prisons. Younger women, especially, needed protection and guidance, and their work should be limited to women and children. Nevertheless, Dryer's work soon attracted the attention and support of the city's elites, who funded many of the urban mission programs, the most prominent benefactor being Nettie McCormick, the widow of industrialist Cyrus McCormick.[78]

One telling difference between Moody and Dryer surfaced when Bible Work drew Dryer into association with other women's groups that were committed to addressing social issues – like the Woman's Christian Temperance Union, for example. Dryer early on allied with the WCTU, but as Moody became more exclusively focused on his revivals, Moody decided that temperance work only served as a distraction and threatened to break off his work with Dryer if she persisted in that area. She acquiesced, believing that her work with Moody was more important.[79]

Similarly, Dryer was influential in the formation of the Chicago Evangelization Society, which she originally envisioned becoming a woman's institution to educate young women for Christian work. She even proposed the idea to Moody, who at first was supportive despite his lack of interest in theological training, which he also saw as a distraction from the mission of saving souls. By 1886, Dryer's hope for her all female Institute was about to be realized when Moody abandoned the idea and decided it should be coeducational. His idea was to train "gapmen," men and women who could bridge the gap between the clergy and the laity and "lay their lives alongside of the laboring classes and the poor and bring the gospel to bear upon their lives." Moody set out to raise money for the institute only to run into opposition from Nettie McCormick, Dryer's benefactor, who viewed Moody's proposal as diminishing women's role in the newly formed institute and as a betrayal of Dryer's life goal. It took the intervention of Moody's wife, Emma, to reconcile the two sides and prevent their abandoning the project, the result of which was the incorporation of Dryer's Bible Work into the coeducational Chicago Evangelization Society. The Bible Work became the Ladies' Council of the Chicago Evangelization Society with Nettie McCormick as honorary president. Despite the successful merger, however, Dryer's strong desire for the Bible Work's success soon came into conflict with the Society's governing board, who accused her of refusing to work under Moody's leadership and interfering with her workers from doing the work Moody and the board expected of them. The board voted to separate the Bible Work from the Society, but Dryer refused to resign from her position on the Institute's Ladies' Council, which led the Board to dismiss her. Dryer spent the remaining years of her life dependent on the McCormick family for funds to support her smaller urban work. Her vision of a women's training school was subsumed by the department of "Ladies' Work" in the Moody Bible Institute.[80]

As Joiner has concluded, the Third Great Awakening "heightened woman's authority in the spiritual realm and empowered her in urban revival." But women did not participate as "totally free agents." Rather most, but certainly not all, "did not challenge the gendered dictates of evangelicalism; instead they accepted and promoted these dictates because they perceived such actions to be beneficial to their faith." A notable exception to the expectation of female deference is Frances Willard, another activist who became president of the Evanston College for Ladies (later merged with Northwestern University). Earlier in her career, Willard also allied herself with Moody and accompanied him on an eastern tour leading women's prayer meetings. When Willard shared a revival platform with a more liberal Universalist, however, Moody insisted that she desist. Willard refused and insisted on setting her own agenda. She broke with Moody and became an influential leader of the WCTU.[81]

Summary

The second half of the nineteenth century witnessed tremendous growth both in the number of religious organizations and in denominational membership. A large part of that increase resulted from schisms among already existing denominations as well as large-scale immigration, in the latter case consisting of people from south and eastern Europe, as well as Latin America and China, with differing religious beliefs and traditions. Understandably, immigrants experiencing a major disruption in their lives, severing ties with their native lands and not always being welcome in their chosen land, clung to their cultural, including religious, traditions, which provided them with personal and social cohesion. That combined with discord among existing denominations resulting in new sects, however, raised concerns among many Americans for national and religious unity. The response was to reaffirm mainstream Protestant dominance, as well as to incorporate the new arrivals into a common core of religious beliefs. The most visible manifestation of this concern was the Third Great Awakening. The most notable contrasting forecast of what was to come was the World's Parliament of Religions. By the 1920s, those who sought to limit immigration from suspect parts of the world carried the day with passage of exclusionary immigration laws, but longer term, they were unsuccessful in stemming the tide of religious diversity that continued to be the earmark of religion in America.

Review questions

1   The dramatic increase in immigration during the late nineteenth and early twentieth centuries impacted religion in America. Briefly describe that impact in general terms and then, by way of example, discuss why the arrival of Roman Catholic and Jewish immigrants posed a challenge to the already established Catholic and Jewish ecclesiastical communities.
2   What accounts for the proliferation of native born sects in this period?
3   How did historical developments in this period impact African American and Native American religion?
4   How did the role of women change in the churches?
5   How did Americans respond to the growing diversity in America?

Notes

1   Edwin S. Gaustad and Leigh E. Schmidt, *The Religious History of America*, rev. edn. (San Francisco, CA: HarperSanFrancisco, 2004), 211–2.
2   Jesse S. Reeves, "The Treaty of Guadalupe Hidalgo," *American Historical Review*, 10 (1905): 309–24. See also Richard Griswold del Castillo, *The Treaty of Guadalupe Hidalgo: A Legacy of Conflict* (Norman: University of Oklahoma Press, 1990).
3   An English translation of *Pascendi* and other papal encyclicals can be found in *The Papal Encyclicals*, ed. Claudia Carlen (Raleigh, NC: McGrath Publishing Company, 1981). *Pascendi* is in Volume III: 1903–1939, and those portions cites are on pages 72 and 89.
4   Darrell Jodock, "Introduction 1: The Modernist Crisis," in *Catholicism Contending with Modernity: Roman Catholic Modernism and Anti-Modernism in Historical Context*, ed. Darrell Jodock (New York: Cambridge University Press, 2010), 1, 7.
5   Arthus Vermeersch, "Modernism," in *The Catholic Encyclopedia* (New York: Robert Appleton Company, 1911), 10: 3. www.newadvent.org.cathen/10415a.htm; Lester R. Kurtz, *The Politics of Heresy: The Modernist Crisis in Roman Catholicism* (Berkeley: University of California Press, 1986), 33.
6   Papal infallibility was limited to the pope's pronouncements *ex cathedra* when, in discharging his duties as head of the church, defining a doctrine regarding faith or morals to be held by the church. The same Vatican Council pronounced that: "The Church of Christ is not a communion of equals in which all the faithful have the same rights." Rather some are given "the power from God . . . to sanctify, teach, and govern." Jodock, "Introduction 1," 18; Kurtz, *The Politics of Heresy*, 36.
7   Kurtz, *The Politics of Heresy*, 45–51; Jodock, "Introduction 1," 18. See also Paul Misner, "Catholic Anti-Modernism: The Ecclesial Setting," in *Catholicism Contending with Modernity: Roman Catholic Modernism and Anti-Modernism in Historical Context*, ed. Darrell Jodock (New York: Cambridge University Press, 2010), 56–87.
8   Kurtz, *The Politics of Heresy*, 44–5. See also Edward Elton Young Hales, *The Catholic Church in the Modern World* (New York: Doubleday, 1958); Marvin O'Connell, *Critics on Trial: An Introduction to the Catholic Modernist Crisis* (Washington, DC: Catholic University of America Press, 1994).
9   Gaustad and Schmidt, *The Religious History of America*, 216–17.
10   Gaustad and Schmidt, *The Religious History of America*, 217.
11   See Jonathan Sarna, *American Judaism* (New Haven, CT: Yale University Press, 2004).
12   Gaustad and Schmidt, *The Religious History of America*, 214. See Hasia R. Diner, *A Time for Gathering: The Second Migration, 1820–1880* (Baltimore, MD: Johns Hopkins University Press, 1992); James G. Heller, *Isaac M. Wise: His Life, Work, and Thought* (Cincinnati, OH: Union of American Hebrew Congregations, 1965).
13   Gaustad and Schmidt, *The Religious History of America*, 214. See Gerald Sorin, *A Time for Building: The Third Migration, 1880–1920* (Baltimore, MD: Johns Hopkins University Press, 1992).

14 Gaustad and Schmidt, *The Religious History of America*, 215. See Michael R. Cohen, *The Birth of Conservative Judaism: Solomon Schechter's Disciples and the Creation of an American Religious Movement* (New York: Columbia University Press, 2012).

15 Ruthanne Lun McCunn, *An Illustrated History of the Chinese in America* (San Francisco, CA: Design Enterprises, 1979). See Iris Chang, *The Chinese in America: A Narrative History* (New York: Penguin, 2004); Jean Pfaetzer, *Drive Out: The Forgotten War against Chinese Americans* (New York: Random House, 2007).

16 McCunn, *An Illustrated History of the Chinese in America*, 109–11.

17 Robert Orsi, *The Madonna of 115th Street: Faith and Community in Italian Harlem, 1880–1950* (New Haven, CT: Yale University Press, 1985); R. Stephen Warner, "Immigration and Religious Communities in the United States," in *Gatherings in Diaspora: Religious Communities and the New Immigration* eds. R. Stephen Warner and Judith G. Wittner (Philadelphia, PA: Temple University Press, 1998), 5.

18 Orsi, *The Madonna of 115th Street*, 6.

19 Orsi, *The Madonna of 115th Street*, 8, 10–1.

20 Orsi, *The Madonna of 115th Street*, 12–13.

21 Elizabeth McAlister, "The Madonna of 115th Street Revisited," in *Gatherings in Diaspora*, ed. R. Stephen Warner and Judith G. Wittner (Philadelphia, PA: Temple University Press, 1998), 123–60.

22 Jack Kugelmass, *The Miracle of Intervale Avenue: The Story of a Jewish Congregation in the South Bronx*, exp. edn. (New York: Columbia University Press, 1996).

23 See Marvin James Penton, *Apocalypse Denied: The Story of Jehovah's Witnesses* (Toronto: Toronto University Press, 1997).

24 Quoted in Gaustad and Schmidt, *The Religious History of America*, 218. The National Baptist Convention continued to expand in the twentieth century until it became the largest predominantly African American denomination in the United States. See The National Baptist Convention, USA, Inc., website: www.nationalbaptist.com/aboutus/history

25 Tracy Neal Leavelle, "American Indians," in *The Blackwell Companion to Religion in America*, ed. Philip Goff (Hoboken, NJ: Wiley-Blackwell, 2010), 405.

26 Stephanie Anderson, "On Sacred Ground: Commemorating Survival and Loss at the Carlisle Indian School," *Central PA Magazine* (May 2000). www.wordsasweapons.com/indianschool.htm

27 Jennifer Bess, "Casting a Spell: Acts of Cultural Continuity in Carlisle Indian Industrial School's the Red Man and Helper," *Wicazo Sa Review*, 26 (2011): 13–38. See Richard Henry Pratt, *The Indian Industrial School, Carlisle, Pennsylvania: Its Origins, Purposes, Progress, and the Difficulties Surmounted* (Carlisle, PA: Cumberland County Historical Society, 1979); Jacqueline Fear-Segal, "Nineteenth-Century Indian Education: Universalism versus Evolutionism," *Journal of American Studies*, 33 (1999): 329. See also Jacqueline Fear-Segal, *White Man's Club: Schools and the Struggle of Indian Acculturation* (Lincoln: University of Nebraska Press, 2007); "Carlisle Indian School," *The New Encyclopedia of the American West* (1998). http://credoreference.com/entry/americanwest/carlisle_indianschool

28 Anderson, "On Sacred Ground"; "Summary, in the White Man's Image" (2008). www.imdb.com/title/tt0371740/plotsummary?ref_=tt_stry_pl

29 See, for example: David Wallace Adams, *Education for Extinction: American Indians and the Boarding School Experience, 1875–1928* (Lawrence: University Press of Kansas, 1997); Anderson, "On Sacred Ground"; Mary Annette Pember, "A Painful Reminder" (November 28, 2007). www.diverseeducatoin.com/artman/publish/printer_10281.shtml

30 Michael Hittman, *Wovoka and the Ghost Dance*, exp. edn., ed. Don Lynch (Lincoln: University of Nebraska Press, 1997), ix, 3, 29, 47, 51; James Mooney, *The Ghost Dance Religion and the Sioux Outbreak of 1890* (Washington, DC: Smithsonian Institution – Bureau of American Ethnology Annual Report, 14 pt. 2, 1896), 791.

31 Hittman, *Wovoka and the Ghost Dance*, 27, 32, 64.

32 Hittman, *Wovoka and the Ghost Dance*, 63–4; Mooney, *The Ghost Dance Religion*, 777.

33 Jon Butler, Grant Wacker, and Randall Balmer, *Religion in American Life: A Short History*, 2nd edn. (New York: Oxford University Press, 2011), 289. Later in life, Wovoka also frequented a Baptist mission and temperance society in Nevada. Hittman, *Wovoka and the Ghost Dance*, 55, 57, 156; James Mooney, "The Indian Ghost Dance," *Proceedings and Collections of the Nebraska State Historical Society*, 16 (1911): 764, 772.

34 See, for example: Alice Kehoe, *The Ghost Dance: Ethnohistory and Revitalization* (New York: Holt, Rinehart and Winston, 1989); David F. Aberle, *The Peyote Religion of the Navaho* (Chicago: Aldine Publishing Co., 1966); Joseph Jorgensen, "Modern Movements," in *The Encyclopedia of Religion*, ed. Mircea Eliade (New York: MacMillan Publishing Company, 1987); Michael F. Steltenkamp, *Black Elk: Holy Man of the Oglala* (Norman: University of Oklahoma Press, 1993), 72. See also Mooney, *The Ghost Dance Religion*; Robert M. Utley, *The Last Days of the Sioux Nation* (New Haven, CT: Yale University Press, 1963); Gregory Smoak, *Ghost Dances and Identity: Prophetic Religion and American Indian Ethnogenesis in the Nineteenth Century* (Berkeley: University of California Press, 2006).
35 Steltenkamp estimates that over 200 died at Wounded Knee. Steltenkamp, *Black Elk*, 73.
36 John G. Neihardt, *Black Elk Speaks: Being the Life Story of a Holy Man of the Oglala Sioux* (Lincoln: University of Nebraska Press, 1961), x, 1; Navarre Scott Momaday, "To Save a Great Vision," in *A Sender of Words: Essays in Memory of John G. Neihardt*, ed. Vine Deloria, Jr. (Salt Lake City, UT: How Brothers, 1984), 31. Native American scholar N. Scott Momaday described *Black Elk Speaks* as "an extraordinary human document . . . the record of a profoundly spiritual journey, the pilgrimage of a people towards their historical fulfillment and culmination, towards the accomplishment of a worthy destiny." In 1953, based on his own interview of Black Elk, some sixteen years after Neihardt, Joseph Epes Brown recorded Black Elk's knowledge of Lakota's religious tradition in *The Sacred Pipe: Black Elk's Account of the Seven Rites of the Oglala Sioux*.
37 Raymond J. DeMallie, *The Sixth Grandfather: Black Elk's Teachings Given to John G. Neihardt* (Lincoln: University to Nebraska Press, 1984), 97.
38 DeMallie, *The Sixth Grandfather*, 25–30, 276; Leavelle, "American Indians," 398. The sensibility of "a man defeated" was made more pronounced and available to an even wider audience by Dee Brown in *Bury My Heart at Wounded Knee* (1970).
39 Steltenkamp, *Black Elk*, xiv–xv, 79.
40 Black Elk's first wife, who died in 1903, had become a Catholic, as had all three of their children. Steltenkamp, *Black Elk*, 36; Paul B. Steinmetz, *Pipe, Bible and Peyote among the Oglala Lakota* (1980; rpt. Knoxville: University of Tennessee Press, 1990), 62, 158–9; DeMallie, *The Sixth Grandfather*, 14, 59.
41 In 1972, Neihardt requested that the subtitle of his book be changed to "as told through the author" from the 1932 edition, "as told to the author." Steltenkamp, *Black Elk*, 19, 35, 87, 146. The dismissal of Black Elk's later years as a Catholic was perhaps best reflected in Vine Deloria's very popular *God Is Red*, which was published in 1973 in the midst of a Native American revitalization movement. Deloria largely dismissed Christianity's relevance, at least in any positive sense, for the Indian people. Vine Deloria, Jr., *God Is Red* (New York: Grosset and Dunlap, 1973), 201.
42 Transcribed in Steltenkamp, *Black Elk*, 84; DeMallie included much of this part of Black Elk's life in Raymond J. DeMallie, *The Sixth Grandfather*, 61.
43 Black Elk's daughter, Lucy, is quoted in Steltenkamp, *Black Elk*, 62. See Omer C. Steward, *Peyote Religion* (Norman: University of Oklahoma Press, 1993); Lee Marriott and Carol K. Rachlin, *Peyote* (New York: Thomas N. Crowell, 1971).
44 Marriott, *Peyote*, 1–5. See Stewart, *Peyote Religion*; William T. Hagan, *American Indians* (Chicago: University of Chicago Press, 1993).
45 American Indian *Religious Freedom Act, Portion Amended* (1996). www.cr.nps.gov/local-law/FHPL_IndianRelFreAct.pdf
46 Roger Finke and Rodney Stark, *The Churching of America, 1776–1990: Winners and Losers in Our Religious Economy* (New Brunswick, NJ: Rutgers University Press, 1992), 115–16.
47 Gaustad and Schmidt, *The Religious History of America*, 222.
48 Quoted in Bruce J. Evensen, *God's Man for the Gilded Age: D. L. Moody and the Rise of Modern Mass Evangelism* (New York: Oxford University Press, 2003), 183, 279–80.
49 Although most historians agree that this event qualified as the Third Great Awakening, William McLoughlin sees it as a continuation of a series of revival meetings held since the days of Charles G. Finney. William McLoughlin, *Revivals, Awakenings, and Reform* (Chicago: University of Chicago Press, 1978).
50 George Johnson, *What Will a Man Give in Exchange for His Soul?* (Bloomington, IN: Xlibris Corporation, 2011), 113–15. Kimball is quoted in Paul Moody, *The Shorter Life of D. L. Moody* (Whitefish, MT: Kessinger Publishing, 1997), 21.

51 Thekla Ellen Joiner, *Sin in the City: Chicago and Revivalism 1880–1920* (Columbia: University of Missouri Press, 2007).
52 Evensen, *God's Man for the Gilded Age*, 16.
53 Evensen, *God's Man for the Gilded Age*, 1, 25.
54 Joiner, *Sin in the City*, 38–40.
55 "Dwight L. Moody: Revivalist with a Common Touch," *Christian History*, August 8, 2008, 2. ChrisianHistory.net; William H. Cooper, *The Great Revivalists in American Religion, 1740–1944: The Careers and Theology of Jonathan Edwards, Charles Finney, Dwight Moody, Billy Sunday and Aimee Semple McPherson* (Jefferson, NC: McFarland and Co., 2010), 114.
56 Evensen, *God's Man for the Gilded Age*, 14, 40, 43.
57 Evensen, *God's Man for the Gilded Age*, 62, 67; Gaustad and Schmidt, *The Religious History of America*, 224.
58 Evensen, *God's Man for the Gilded Age*, 141. See Faith Bailey, *D. L. Moody* (Chicago: Moody Bible Institute, 1957, rpt. 1987).
59 Cooper, *The Great Revivalists in American Religion*, 112; Joiner, *Sin in the City*, 41–2, 88–9, 99; Stanley N. Gundry, *Love Them In: The Proclamation Theology of D. L. Moody* (Chicago: Moody Press, 1976); Evensen, *God's Man for The Gilded Age*, 22–3.
60 Gaustad and Schmidt, *The Religious History of America*, 224; Moody is quoted in: Cooper, *The Great Revivalists in American Religion*, 113, 118. See also Gundry, *Love Them In*.
61 Dwight L. Moody, "The Second Coming of Christ," in *The Best of D. L. Moody*, ed. William H. Smith (Chicago: Moody Press, 1971), 193; Cooper, *The Great Revivalists in American Religion*, 122.
62 Cooper, *The Great Revivalists in American Religion*, 123; Evensen, *God's Man for the Gilded Age*, 175, 177.
63 Johnson, *What Will a Man Give in Exchange for His Soul*, 113–15; Cooper, *The Great Revivalists in American Religion*, 116; Evensen, *God's Man for the Gilded Age*, 3, 6.
64 Cooper, *The Great Revivalists in American Religion*, 113. See Timothy P. Weber, *Living in the Shadow of the Second Coming: American Premillennialism* (Chicago: University of Chicago Press, 1987); Gaustad and Schmidt, *The Religious History of America*, 225–6.
65 Gaustad and Schmidt, *The Religious History of America*, 229–30.
66 Joiner, *Sin in the City*, 76, 83; Egal Feldman, "American Ecumenicism: Chicago's World's Parliament of Religions of 1893," *Journal of Church and State*, 9 (1967): 180–99.
67 Joiner, *Sin in the City*, 84–5, 106–7.
68 Jon Butler, "Protestant Success in the New American City, 1870–1920: The Anxious Secrets of Rev. Walter Laidlow," in *New Directions in American Religious History*, ed. Harry S. Stout and Darryl G. Hart (New York: Oxford University Press, 1997), 313; Cooper, *The Great Revivalists in American Religion*, 7.
69 For more on the relationship between New Thought, Phineas Quimby and Mary Baker Eddy, see Beryl Satter, *Each Mind a Kingdom: American Women, Sexual Purity, and the New Thought Movement, 1875–1920* (Berkeley: University of California Press, 1999).
70 The overview of Eddy and Christian Science was summarized from various sources, including Gaustad and Schmidt, *The Religious History of America*, 228–9; Peter Williams, *America's Religions: From Their Origins to the Twenty-First Century*, 3rd edn. (Urbana: University of Illinois Press, 2008), 337–9. On Eddy's influence on women of the time, see Donald Meyer, *The Positive Thinkers: Popular Religion from Mary Baker Eddy to Oral Roberts* (New York: Pantheon Books, 1980), ch. 2; Gail Thain Parker, "Mary Baker Eddy and Sentimental Womanhood," *New England Quarterly*, 43 (March 1970): 3–18; Satter, *Each Mind a Kingdom*, chs. 1 & 2.
71 Gaustad and Southwest, *The Religious History of America*, 221.
72 See Mary D. Pellauer, *Toward a Tradition of Feminist Theology: The Religious Social Thought of Elizabeth Cady Stanton, Susan B. Anthony, and Anna Howard Shaw* (Sandy, UT: Carlson Publishing, 1991).
73 Gaustad and Schmidt, *The Religious History of America*, 220–1. See Elizabeth Cazden, *Antoinette Brown Blackwell: A Biography* (Old Westbury, NY: Feminist Press, 1983).
74 Joiner, *Sin in the City*, 10, 89; Kathryn Teresa Long, *The Revival of 1857–1858: Interpreting an American Religious Awakening* (New York: Oxford University Press, 1998), 91.

75 Joiner, *Sin in the City*, 10, 43–4, 90; Colleen McDannell, *The Christian Home in Victorian America, 1840–1900* (Bloomington, IN: Indiana University Press, 1986), 42–5; Ann Taves, "Feminization Revisited: Protestantism and Gender at the Turn of the Century," in *Women and Twentieth-Century Protestantism*, ed. Margaret Lamberts Bendroth and Virginia Liesen Brereton (Urbana: University of Illinois Press, 2002), 317.
76 Joiner, *Sin in the City*, 45, 48.
77 Joiner, *Sin in the City*, 50–1. See Elizabeth Wilson, *The Sphinx in the City: Urban Life, the Control of Disorder, and Women* (Berkeley: University of California Press, 1991), 65.
78 Dryer did not always adhere to her own rules, at times taking her mission into city jails. Joiner, *Sin in the City*, 48, 50–1. See Weber, *Living in the Shadow of the Second Coming*.
79 Joiner, *Sin in the City*, 55, 57; Barbara Leslie Epstein, *The Politics of Domesticity: Women, Evangelism, Temperance in Nineteenth-Century America* (Middletown, CT: Wesleyan University Press, 1981), 115–46.
80 Joiner, *Sin in the City*, 57; Ruth Bordin, *Frances Willard: A Biography* (Chapel Hill: University of North Carolina Press, 1986), 89; Nancy Hardesty, *Women Called to Witness: Evangelical Feminism* (Knoxville, TN: University of Tennessee Press, 1999), 20–5; Epstein, *The Politics of Domesticity*, 115–46.
81 Joiner, *Sin in the City*, 57; Bordin, *Frances Willard*, 89.

Recommended for further reading

Adams, David Wallace. *Education for Extinction: American Indians and the Boarding School Experience, 1875–1928*. Lawrence: University Press of Kanas, 1997.
Cooper, William H. *The Great Revivalists in American Religion, 1740–1944: The Careers and Theology of Jonathan Edwards, Charles Finney, Dwight Moody, Billy Sunday and Aimee Semple McPherson*. Jefferson, NC: McFarland & Co, 2010.
Epstein, Barbara Leslie. *The Politics of Domesticity: Women, Evangelism, and Temperance in Nineteenth-Century America*. Middletown, CT: Wesleyan University Press, 1981.
Evensen, Bruce J. *God's Man for the Gilded Age: D. L. Moody and the Rise of Modern Mass Evangelism*. New York: Oxford University Press, 2003.
Joiner, Thekla Ellen. *Sin in the City: Chicago and Revivalism 1880–1920*. Columbia: University of Missouri Press, 2007.
Kehoe, Alice B. *The Ghost Dance: Ethnohistory and Revitalization*. New York: Holt Rinehart and Winston, 1989.
McAvoy, Thomas T. *The Americanist Heresy in Roman Catholicism: 1895–1900*. Notre Dame, IN: University of Notre Dame Press, 1963.
Neihardt, John G. *Black Elk Speaks: Being the Life Story of a Holy Man of the Oglala Sioux*. Lincoln: University of Nebraska Press, 1932.
Orsi, Robert Anthony. *The Madonna of 115th Street: Faith and Community in Italian Harlem, 1880–1950*. New Haven, CT: Yale University Press, 1985.
Steltenkamp, Michael F. *Black Elk: Holy Man of the Oglala*. Norman: University of Oklahoma Press, 1993.

Chapter 2

Industrialization, urbanization, and the Social Gospel, here and abroad

Billy Sunday and the fate of the Third Great Awakening

Some have argued that the Third Great Awakening died with Billy Sunday with a brief resurgence under Aimee Semple McPherson.[1] The position taken here is that, although Sunday and McPherson built on what Moody began, what resulted was so different both in intent and result that it is to do an injustice to what Moody built to include Sunday and McPherson in the same story. While Sunday was mentored by a disciple of Dwight L. Moody from whom he learned his proven techniques for organizing and staging a revival to attract the masses, Sunday's revivals became unabashedly dramatic performances where the audiences laughed at, cried over, and were entertained by the histrionics of a master showman in revivals almost entirely devoid of any Christian, or even spiritual, message. As William Cooper has written: Under Sunday, "the supernatural aspects of revivalism disappear, the methodology is exalted," money becomes more important than theology, and "the minister himself becomes corrupted by the very system he uses."[2]

Sunday (see Figure 2.1) was born in 1862 just outside Ames, Iowa, into a broken and impoverished family. He left home at the age of 15 and found success as a baseball player, landing a spot on various National League teams, including the Chicago White Stockings. The turning point in his life, however, came when he encountered a street-preaching team from Chicago's Pacific Garden Mission and accepted Christ as his savior. Sunday swore off alcohol, joined the Jefferson Park Presbyterian Church, and in 1891 became assistant secretary of the religious department of the Chicago YMCA. He became an evangelist and was prepared for that role by J. Wilbur Chapman, who had inherited Moody's mantle.[3]

Chapman gave up the revival circuit in 1895 and passed the mantle to Billy Sunday. Sunday began his preaching career on the "kerosene circuit" of small, rural agricultural towns in the Midwest, where he found his voice in his plain and simple message delivered in an entertaining manner. As the preacher who never graduated from high school often told those gathered to hear him, "I am a rube. . . . I am a graduate of the University of Poverty," and "I know no more about theology than a jackrabbit does about ping pong or an elephant about crocheting." As one small town newspaper headline in 1904 described his visit: "Evangelist Does Great Vaudeville Stunts in Tabernacle Pulpit," stunts that commonly involved doing flips on stage, challenging anyone in the crowd who sided with the forces of evil to fight him, shadow boxing with the devil, and his hallmark ballplayer-slide across home plate.[4]

As 1908 drew to a close, Sunday's star rose into the firmament and opportunities for crusades opened up in major towns and cities across the United States. The number of advance people and volunteers for each revival climbed into the thousands, while attendance grew into the tens of thousands at revivals that sometimes lasted several weeks. In 1917, Sunday's ten-week revival in New York City counted over 1.5 million attendees and over 98,000 self-proclaimed converts.[5]

Figure 2.1 Evangelist Billy Sunday

Source: Alpha Historica/Alamy Stock Photo

Between 1908 and 1920, Sunday earned over a million dollars. The rich and famous, like John D. Rockefeller, could be counted among his friends and supporters, and President Woodrow Wilson, among other prominent officials, publicly acknowledged Sunday's highly patriotic messages as a major force behind the World War I effort. Sunday and his wife indulged in new homes, new cars, tailored clothing, fur coats, jewelry, and other finery, none of which they made any attempt to hide but rather proclaimed them the will of God, Sunday's reward for spreading the gospel among his people and saving souls. But in 1920, the tide began to turn as the press began to expose the excesses of Sunday's lifestyle and his obsession with money. As reported in the press, whereas Dwight L. Moody never asked for money, Sunday did so in every sermon. The press also made public the dissolute lives of three of Sunday's five children, in one case ending in suicide. For more than a decade following his fall from grace, Sunday returned to the small towns where he got his start and to the much more modest income he left behind. He died in 1935.[6]

Reviews of Billy Sunday's revivals over the past several decades have been mixed. Some have credited him with giving expression to the fears of, and offering hope to, the American middle class as they transitioned from a largely rural, agrarian world to an urban, industrial, and demographically diverse environment. Others have discredited him as "a hypocrite shaking down dimwitted people for a pocketful of money." While a few have pointed to Sunday as developing the modern style of revivalism that promoted a new style of leadership built around the celebrity, traveling revivalist.[7] But to pronounce the death of revivalism in America upon Sunday's death was premature.

The Social Gospel in America

In 1921, Shailer Mathews, one of its prominent adherents, defined the Social Gospel as "the application of the teaching of Jesus and the total message of the Christian salvation to society, the economic life, and social institutions . . . as well as to individuals."[8] By then the Social Gospel movement, which grew up alongside the Third Great Awakening, had flourished for two decades and more. Walter Rauschenbusch, the intellectual leader of the movement, attributed its advent to publication of *Our Country* (1885) by Josiah Strong, which rallied those who saw the limitations of the awakening in dealing with the pressing matters of the day, or as some historians have put it, those that came to believe that "most Christians spent too much time trying to save the soul and not enough saving the body."[9]

White and Hopkins have written that, by "interacting with the changing realities and problems of an increasingly industrialized and urbanized nation," proponents of the Social Gospel viewed themselves as engaged in "a crusade for justice and righteousness in all areas of the common life." But it is also the case, that many Protestants feared the increasingly militant and foreign-born urban working class and what appeared to them to be escalating class warfare. Some sensed that their beliefs were being drowned out by the ever more diverse voices, cultures, and religions of the new arrivals and took up the cause of social justice for the poor in part as an attempt to expand the appeal of the Protestant church in cities where the Catholic Church and Judaism were popular among their large immigrant population. As a result, although it had Roman Catholic and Jewish participants, the Social Gospel was largely a Protestant movement.[10]

As Susan Curtis has described it, the Social Gospel "bolstered the age-old demand for individual regeneration with a powerful social message. It was a gospel that did not let the saved languish in smug self-satisfaction while the ills of society kept others from salvation." Social gospelers redefined the meaning of God, from the angry God of Jonathan Edwards to a more indulgent, even kind, God. But in exchange, God required men to be concerned with this life – its poverty, depravity, and injustice – as well as the afterlife, and to take responsibility for their brothers' and sisters' redemption, as well as their own. Some have argued that the Social Gospel was "a peculiarly American phenomenon in its interpretation of the Christian message and Church as having a role to play in the public sphere." A few have insisted that the Social Gospel was never an organized movement but, rather, that it attracted those who wished to apply social Christian ethics to the pressing social needs of the day, as portrayed daily by muckraking journalists and photographers like Jacob Riis.[11]

To this end, in 1908, on the heels of publication of Walter Rauschenbusch's Social Gospel classic, *Christianity and the Social Crisis* (1907), the Federal Council of Churches (FCC), newly formed from mainline Protestant churches, adopted the "Social Creed of the Churches," which called for measures to address the dehumanizing conditions of the industrial workplace, including the rights of workers to organize and bargain collectively, the elimination of child labor, and a shorter work week. The creed opened with the statement that it deemed it "the duty of all Christian people to concern themselves with certain practical industrial problems" and then proceeded to focus more specifically on "the right of workers to some protection against the hardships often resulting from the swift crises of industrial change"; "the protection of the worker from dangerous machinery, occupational disease, injuries and mortality"; "the abolition of child labor"; "such regulation of the conditions of toil for women as shall safeguard the physical and moral health of the community"; "the suppression of the 'sweating system'"; "the gradual and reasonable reduction of the hours of labor to the lowest practicable point, and for that degree of leisure for all which is a condition of the highest human life"; "a living wage as a minimum in every industry, and for the highest wage that each industry can afford"; and "the abatement of poverty." The creed concluded:

> To the toilers of America and to those who by organized effort are seeking to lift the crushing burdens of the poor, and to reduce the hardships and uphold the dignity of labor, this Council sends the greeting of human brotherhood and the pledge of sympathy and of help in a cause which belongs to all who follow Christ.

The creed was not binding on the member organizations, but it was adopted by many of its members over the next few years and commonly referenced by the rest.[12]

The goals of the FCC were perhaps most succinctly stated by one of its leading member churches, the Presbyterians: "The great ends of the church are the proclamation of the gospel for the salvation of humankind; the shelter, nurture, and spiritual fellowship of the children of God; the maintenance of divine worship; the preservation of truth; the promotion of social righteousness; and the exhibition of the Kingdom of Heaven to the world."[13] To implement those measures, the FCC established a string of churches, often called *institutional churches*, which were open seven days a week to provide meals, medical services, clothes, childcare and social activities. In 1911, they were joined in their efforts by the Men and Religion Forward Movement, wherein all of the major Protestant denominations joined forces to recruit men for the cause of Christian reform. It challenged men to devote their lives to making the Kingdom of God on earth a reality. The effectiveness of the Men and Religion Forward Movement was attested to by Walter Rauschenbusch: "The movement has probably done more than any other single agency to lodge the Social Gospel in the common mind of the church. It has made social Christianity orthodox."[14]

As will be further explained, proponents of the Social Gospel were mostly postmillennialists, in that they believed that humanity, especially Americans, could rid the nation of its various social evils, establish a kingdom of God on earth, and prepare the way for Christ's Second Coming. They developed their optimistic vision as a result of a theological liberalism that emerged out of their attempt to reconcile their Christian faith with evolution and the higher criticism. Also influential in the intellectual credibility it lent to the movement was the emergence of the new, and largely sympathetic, social science profession involving economics, political science, and sociology. All of these seemed to offer the possibility of building a new world that would ameliorate the dislocations of the new industrial age – as opposed to those who saw evolution as the basis for Social Darwinism or the weeding out of the unfit as a necessary step toward a new social order. And they were allied with leaders of the Progressive Movement, some referring to the Social Gospel as the religious expression of progressivism in that their theological and political liberalism complemented one another. But they never entirely merged operations as Social Gospel leaders commonly held more conservative positions on social issues and insisted on the role of Christianity as an ameliorating, even essential force.[15]

Walter Rauschenbusch, Washington Gladden, and Shailer Mathews

Walter Rauschenbusch, a Baptist minister serving Hell's Kitchen in New York, and the most articulate spokesman for the Social Gospel, criticized the excesses of capitalism and promoted a form of Christian Socialism. In response to unfettered capitalism, he favored a form of cooperative economics but believed that Christianity was central to the reform movement. He was among the most prolific writers of the movement, in 1892 joining forces with several other advocates of the Social Gospel in the Brotherhood of the Kingdom, which was dedicated to defining and disseminating the theology of the Social Gospel. As noted earlier, Rauschenbusch's *Christianity and the Social Crisis* came at a critical time in the Social Gospel Movement. In this call-to-arms, he found the roots of the movement in the first apostolate of Christianity, which grew out of Jesus's deep feeling for the social misery of the peasantry of Galilee, that followed him about with their poverty and their diseases, "like shepherdless sheep that have been scattered and harried by beasts of prey." Jesus had compassion for them and bade his disciples to care for them, to harvest the destitute, and to proclaim the kingdom of God.[16]

Rauschenbusch explained that the same situation was being repeated again in his time but on a vaster scale. "If Jesus stood today amid our modern life," he wrote, "with that outlook on the condition of all humanity, which observation and travel and the press would spread before him, and with the same heart of divine humanity beating in him, he would create a new apostolate to meet the new needs in a new harvest-time of history." The result would be "the great emancipation from barbarism and from the paralysis of injustice, and the beginning of a progress in the intellectual, social, and moral life of mankind to which all past history has no parallel." To those who would think his charge futile, Rauschenbusch observed: "Today, as Jesus looks out upon humanity, his spirit must leap to see the soul responsive to his call. . . . The harvest field is no longer deserted." "With all our faults and our slothfulness," he concluded, "we modern men in many ways are more on a level with the real mind of Jesus than any generation that has gone before. If that first apostolate was able to move mountains by the power of faith, such an apostolate as Christ could now summon might change the face of the earth." Rauschenbusch did not harbor any utopian delusion. "We shall never have a perfect social life," he offered, yet "we must seek it with faith. . . . The kingdom of God is always coming."[17]

In 1917, Rauschenbusch published *A Theology for the Social Gospel*, in which he announced: "We have a Social Gospel. We need a systematic theology large enough to match it and vital enough to back it." In creating that systematic theology, he reasoned, the Social

Gospel would become "a permanent addition to our spiritual outlook" and "constitute a stage in the development of the Christian religion." The individualistic gospel that had preceded the Social Gospel Movement had made clear the sinfulness of the individual, but it had not pointed to institutional sinfulness: "It has not evoked faith in the will and power of God to redeem the permanent institutions of human society from their inherited guilt of oppression and extortion." That had come to pass under the Social Gospel.[18]

Not to be outdone, Washington Gladden, though not a theologian by academic training, but rather a Congregational minister, led political crusades on behalf of workers and reform and authored nearly forty books and hundreds of articles challenging wealthy Christians to search their consciences, all of which earned him the title "father of the Social Gospel." Gladden was won over to the ministry by the then famous evangelist, Jedediah Burchard. Passing through a series of pastorates in New York and industrial towns in Massachusetts, Gladden came face-to-face with the struggle between labor and capital, including strikes, use of strike breakers, and confrontations with owners, which helped focus this as a fundamental concern in the Social Gospel he came to embrace. It also became the subject of a series of lectures in which he called for the application of Christian law to industrial society. The lectures were gathered in *Working People and Their Employers* (1876), which became "one of the first mileposts set by American Social Christianity." In 1882, Gladden began his ministry in Columbus, Ohio, where he remained for the rest of his professional life and became one of the most influential ministers in America.[19]

Central to Gladden's Social Gospel was his belief that salvation was both personal and social. In *Ruling Ideas of the Present Age*, published in 1895, he insisted that "the relations of men to one another in society are not contractual, but vital and organic . . . that no man reaches perfection or happiness apart from his fellow men." Gladden believed that the nation, led by an evangelical Protestant Christian church and its Social Gospel, was being purified by "finer conceptions of justice" and that salvation, realized with establishment of the kingdom of God on earth, was drawing near. Consistent with the heightened missionary atmosphere of the late nineteenth century, he saw the church as an instrument, a means toward the building of that kingdom, first to be realized in America but later throughout the world.[20]

His optimism notwithstanding, Gladden struggled with the industrial strife he witnessed and the widening breach between labor and owners. In 1886, labor strikes broke out across the country, including a particularly fierce confrontation in Cleveland, where Gladden was invited to address a mass meeting of laborers and employers. Workingmen outnumbered employers, but both were present and the atmosphere was tense. Gladden nevertheless succeeded in delivering a message marked by fairness and understanding, especially of labor, at one point declaring that, if "war is the order of the day, we must grant to labor belligerent rights." Gladden's address was published in *The Century Magazine* in May 1886, which was fortuitous given the bloody Chicago Haymarket riots of that month, and it became a chapter in one of his best-known books, *Applied Christianity: Moral Aspects of Social Questions* (1886). Gladden felt compelled, "as a Christian teacher, as the moral counselor and guide" of the men under his care, he wrote, "to . . . get at the rights" of the labor question. In doing so, he put forth his conviction that the teachings of Jesus contained the fundamental principles for the right ordering of society and that, when they were applied to the industrial situation, its deeper problems would be solved. That this position resonated with the people of Columbus can be attested to by Gladden's election to the city council in 1900 as an Independent, without actively campaigning for the position.[21]

Gladden responded to critics who charged him and by implication other Social Gospelers with being socialists with *Christianity and Socialism*. In brief, Gladden made clear that, although he believed that cooperation must replace competition in the realm of industry and that certain essential public service industries – like railroads and telegraphs – should come under governmental control and ownership, he was not a socialist. He believed that it was necessary to have private property firmly safeguarded and private enterprise strongly encouraged by the state.[22]

Gladden explained that it had only been in the last few years that people had begun to question the system as it exists and to seek answers in the words of Jesus. He made reference to communism and socialism, which were commonly cited alternatives. But neither had succeeded in meeting the needs of society, because neither was based on brotherhood, an understanding that "our deepest relation in human society is not to things, but to persons." He pointed out that twenty-five years earlier socialists had railed against religion intending "to root out the faith of God" and insisting that no one was worthy the title socialist unless s/he was an atheist. But that that was changing and that "men of broader wisdom" had come to realize that they had no quarrel with religion.[23]

Gladden thought it unwise to denounce socialism wholesale. Rather, he believed that there were "wholesome sentiments and reasonable aims" to be found in "true socialism." What was true socialism? "It is manifest . . . in the habit of regarding our work, whatever it may be, as a social function. The true socialist is one who never forgets that he is a member of society, and who always considers well the effect of what he is doing, not merely upon his own private fortunes, but also upon the common weal." The true socialist realizes his social duty and that making the best of oneself individually is not a separate thing from the duty of filling one's place in society. The two are one, and the latter is accomplished when the former is done."[24]

Also among the leading spokesmen for the Social Gospel Movement, was Shailer Mathews. As professor of theology and Dean of the University of Chicago's Divinity School, editor of two major journals, and the author of dozens of books and articles, Shailer, by Rauschenbusch's assessment, was the first to attempt a biblical basis for the Social Gospel. Though not ordained, he was active in the Baptist Church, and from 1912 to 1916, he served as president of the Federal Council of Churches, in which capacity he expanded the FCC's capacity for social service.[25]

Mathews argued that

> the message of the New Testament is expressed within the context, world-view, and language forms of an ancient culture. The task of interpreting that message for today's culture involves identifying and distinguishing both the substance of the message and its culturally determined thought-forms, finding functionally equivalent thought-forms in today's world-view, and re-expressing the message in a way comprehensible to current society and the religious problems that face it.

In doing so, Mathews identified Jesus as a source of Christian ethics. But he, like most Social Gospelers, understood that Jesus did not provide direct answers to the social dilemmas facing America at the turn of the twentieth century. To find those answers, to reclaim the relevance of Jesus to the modern world, it was necessary to draw "a distinction between Jesus' concrete, occasional, and often individually directed moral teachings on the one hand, and on the other hand the fundamental principles, or general moral attitudes, or the ideals that were either stated or were implicit in the concrete teachings." By way of example, Mathews pointed to Jesus' imperative of love, even sacrificial, of neighbor, and the value and dignity of every person.[26]

African Americans and the Social Gospel

The "Social Creed" largely ignored African Americans, although a number of Protestant leaders took up their cause in response to race riots at the turn of the century, the Niagara Declaration of 1905, lynchings, and Ku Klux Klan activity in the 1920s. They often supported the reform efforts of figures such as Ida B. Wells, Mary Church Terrell, and Mary McLeod Bethune, but they commonly refused African American membership in their reform organizations. As a result, until recently, the "black Social Gospel" has been often ignored, incorrectly so.[27]

A notable exception was Washington Gladden, who became an advocate for the rights of African Americans during Reconstruction. He supported the educational activities of the American Missionary Association (AMA), to which he was elected president at the start of the twentieth century, and he helped to form the National Association for the Advancement of Colored People (NAACP). Shortly after assuming the presidency of the AMA, Gladden championed the work of Booker T. Washington. In 1903, however, while attending Atlanta University's conference, "The Study of the Negro Problem," which he was invited to address, Gladden came into contact with, and became an advocate for, W.E.B. Du Bois and the ideas expressed in his newly published book, *The Souls of Black Folk* (1903). Without denying the importance of Washington's plan for industrial education as a means of economic advancement, Gladden was persuaded that Du Bois's championing of African Americans' higher education and his position that the Negro's economic plight was directly related to his political status was correct.[28]

The closing decades of the nineteenth century were marked by disenfranchisement and Jim Crow laws, which led to what has been described as the nadir of the African American experience, and not surprisingly, their response was somewhat unique. In the early decades of the twentieth century, Du Bois defined the problem African Americans faced. He criticized those like Washington, who he believed sought accommodation, as futile and helped launch the Pan-African Movement, the Niagara Movement, and the National Association for the Advancement of Colored People (NAACP), helping to radicalize the black Social Gospel. Largely excluded from the mainstream of the Social Gospel, many other African Americans hoped for a future golden day fulfilled in the millennial reign of God on earth. But that did not mean that they would not seek to prepare the way for the golden day.[29]

The concept of millennialism has been discussed earlier with its focus on a golden age yet to come, which for African Americans was tied to their Old Testament-based belief in their expected future entering the Promised Land. Like most white Americans, African Americans were largely postmillennialists, but there were important exceptions – namely those who felt the millennium could only be realized through Christ's intervention. However, as Fulop also pointed out, unlike most white premillennialists who sought personal rather than collective salvation in preparation for the Second Coming, African American premillennialists tended to stay engaged in the world, actively opposing the social and racial situation of African Americans and preparing for the millennium. Again, much like most whites, many African Americans believed that the millennium would be realized in the United States and even that the United States was the redeemer nation. And finally, unlike most white postmillennialists who sought to prepare the way for Christ's Second Coming both through the church and civil institutions, African Americans, largely denied access to those civil institutions, remained convinced that the church was the means by which the world would be purified and prepared for Christ's return. Many black ministers were optimistic about the transforming powers of Christianity on race relations because of their belief in the "fatherhood of God and the brotherhood of man."[30]

Among the most notable reform-minded African Americans was Lucius Holsey, bishop of the Colored Methodist Episcopal Church. He dedicated himself to the pursuit of a millennium without wars, corrupting institutions, drunkenness, and "slavery in every form." Another activist, AME Bishop R. H. Cain offered this vision of racial harmony and equality:

> Happy for the great country, happy for the negro and the nation when the great principles upon which our government is founded, when the genius of liberty as understood by the fathers, shall permeate this whole land . . . ; then there will be no discussion as to what of the negro problem. . . . There will be one homogeneous nation governed by intellectual, moral worth and controlled by Christian influences. There will be no East, no West, no North, no South, no Black, no White, no Saxon, no Negro, but a great, happy and peaceful nation.[31]

African American Christians found strength in Christian millennialism, because of its divinely inspired criticism against the present social order – criticism against the unjust and unequal treatment of African Americans as well as criticism against white Christianity, which did little if anything about it. But African Americans, especially in the urban north, nevertheless thought it necessary to take matters into their own hands, often through the AME and AMEZ churches. In 1906, AME minister Reverdy C. Ranson called upon black churches to take action. He made it clear that there should be no race problem in a Christian state erected on the "superstructure of 'the Fatherhood of God,' and its corollary, 'the Brotherhood of man.'" Its "crowning object," he wrote, was that at which Christ aimed, namely "to break down the middle wall of partition between man and man." America, he argued, had the right to call itself a Christian nation, as it was "the first nation that was born with the Bible in its hands." But the "Negro Question" had been with the nation from the time of its founding, and if the nation did not seriously address the problem, "American Christianity will un-christ itself."[32]

Ranson explained that those who brought Africans to America "had no thought of him as a human being" or of "admitting him even into the outer courts of opportunity for progress, much less according him the rights of a man." He was a slave, tied to the soil, with no opportunity to enjoy the fruits of his labor until "God's hour came." "God spoke from heaven," men's eyes were opened, the Civil War ensued, and out of the devastation of war, the slaves were set free. At the time of their freedom, Ranson continued, there were those who thought the freedman would be permitted to "tread the pathway of industrial opportunity," but that was not to be the case, as he was relegated "to the fringes of the industrial world." That he would be able to enter the doors of the banking, manufacturing, mercantile, and business offices open to all others became "a presumption amounting to impertinence." He referenced the work of Booker T. Washington and his Tuskegee Institute and the work he was doing to turn out young African Americans with "ability, coupled with high character," but which "counted for very little when they sought to enter the doors of industrial opportunity." The African American "should become a more skilled, and a more intelligent worker," he agreed, "but he should be permitted to work not only as a servant, but as a man, with all the opportunities open to him that are open to others no better qualified than he." That this was not happening, that the nation was not acting "in the spirit of Christ toward the black toilers of this land," was "the great and menacing danger" that surrounded the African American and the nation.[33]

Roman Catholics and the Social Gospel

As noted earlier, the Social Gospel was largely a Protestant movement, but Roman Catholics and Jews played a part as well. Most commonly, Roman Catholic leaders actively engaged in temperance, which they considered the biggest challenge facing Catholic immigrants, especially young single men. To some, it was one of the most destructive plagues to have befallen mankind, only exacerbated by saloons, which were a prime target of reformers. In 1884, the bishops of the Third Plenary Council of Baltimore urged pastors to do all in their power to persuade Catholic saloon keepers to desist in their sale of alcohol, while some went so far as to threaten the offenders with denial of Christian burial. But Catholic temperance placed primary emphasis on individual perfection, rather than on social reform, thereby setting it somewhat apart from the Social Gospel Movement.[34]

Perhaps the most radical Roman Catholic reformer of this period was Edward McGlynn, pastor of New York City's St. Stephen's Church. He was an early proponent of the ideas of Henry George expressed in his *Progress and Poverty* (1879) and George's insistence on the interrelated problems of labor and socialism. Of George's book, McGlynn wrote that he had never found "so clear an exposition of the cause of the trouble, involuntary poverty, and its remedy, as I found in that monumental work . . . and I did, as best I could, what I could to justify the teachings of that great work based upon the essence of all religion – the Fatherhood of God and the Brotherhood Man." Forbidden to speak on the controversial ideas espoused by Henry George, especially the single tax, McGlynn defied his superiors, insisting that the single tax was compatible with "the highest Christian truth and the best Christian justice": "Any man or set of men, who shall by law or in any other way deny, impair, diminish or restrain the equal rights of every human being, to the possession of the general bounties of nature . . . is guilty of blasphemy against the goodness of the universal Father." McGlynn was excommunicated for his defiance, although the church later reversed its decision.[35]

Others continued to be associated with socialism but somehow avoided any punitive action against them, the most prominent of whom was John Ryan. In 1906, fresh out of graduate studies at the Catholic University of America, Ryan published *A Living Wage: Its Ethical and Economic Aspects*, which, as one critic has put it, became the *Uncle Tom's Cabin* of the movement for minimum wage laws.[36]

Ryan acknowledged that, although "the great majority of fair-minded persons" believed that labor did not get its full share of the wealth it helped to create, there was little agreement as to what exactly that measure should be. Generally speaking, he wrote that those wages "should be sufficiently high to enable the laborer to live in a manner consistent with the dignity of a human being." This he called the "ethical minimum." More specifically, Ryan argued that the average family of that day could not live decently on less than $600 a year, and pointed out that at least 60 percent of adult male wage earners received less than this sum. Ryan suggested that "only those persons in control of the goods and opportunities of living" were in a position to do anything about this inequity, and they were morally responsible to do so. Further, the employer could not escape this duty "by taking refuge behind the terms of a so-called free contract": "The fact is that the underpaid laborer does not willingly sell his labor for less than the equivalent of a decent livelihood, any more than the wayfarer willingly gives up his purse to the highwayman." That, he insisted, was the result of the "superior economic force" of the employer.[37]

Ryan cast his net of responsibility even further. He wrote that others were complicit in this immoral situation, including the landowner, the loan-capitalist, the wealthy, the consumer, and even the state, which was morally compelled to force employers to pay a living wage whenever and wherever it can with the appropriate legislation. But he also insisted that a reconciliation would not be reached without religion, that is "without the aid of religious agencies and a larger infusion of the religious spirit into the minds and hearts of men." That would not be easy, he added, as people may be religious "in the ordinary meaning of the term," and still be so "thoroughly dominated by the ethical code of unlimited competition that they are blind to the many forms of moral wrong which that code sanctions. . . . In other words, they conform to the standard of business ethics, instead of to the standard of Christian ethics." That required a change of heart, which was the responsibility of the clergy.[38]

Ryan's *Living Wage* helped spark an increased flow of Catholic social justice literature. His later book, *Distributive Justice: The Right and Wrong of Our Present Distribution of Wealth* (1916), presented a framework for a plan for social justice. After World War I, the American bishops established the National Catholic Welfare Council, and Ryan was put in charge of its Washington office's social action department. He became an advisor to President Franklin D. Roosevelt and was nicknamed "Right Reverend New Dealer."[39]

Among the more moderate Roman Catholic social reformers was Bishop John Spalding of Peoria, Illinois. Spalding concerned himself with the city's degrading effect on the family, which he considered central to human relationships and moral development. He achieved national prominence for helping President Theodore Roosevelt and financier J. P. Morgan end the Great Coal Strike of 1902 as a member of the Arbitration Commission that awarded the miners a retroactive 10 percent wage increase and reduced daily work hours from 10 to 9. And there were Catholic benevolent societies like the Society of Saint Vincent De Paul, the Knights of Columbus, and the National Conference of Catholic Charities, which, much like their Protestant and Jewish counterparts, did much good.[40]

But then, as noted in Chapter 1, American Catholic reformers had to contend with the Modernist Controversy within the Roman Catholic Church, which called into question efforts at social reform. One such contender was James Cardinal Gibbons, Archbishop of Baltimore. When the Knights of Labor, two-thirds of whose American members were Roman Catholic, was condemned as a secret society in the Canadian Province of Quebec in 1884, Gibbons wrote to the Vatican opposing any such action in the United States, making the case for its existence and even for the Church's support. In his 1887 communiqué, he wrote of "the great chain of the social problems of our day, and especially of our country." "There exists among us," he explained, "as in the other countries of the world, grave and threatening social evils, public injustices, which call for strong resistance and legal remedy," among them "monopolies on the part of both individuals and of corporations," characterized by "avarice, oppression, and corruption." These, he argued, lay at the root cause of the problems and block any attempts to address them. He wrote of "the heartless avarice which, through greed of gain, pitilessly grinds not only the men, but particularly the women and children in various employments, mak[ing] it clear to all who love humanity and justice that it is not only the right of the laboring classes to protect themselves, but the duty of the whole people to aid them in finding a remedy." To this end, he concluded, the Knights of Labor played an important role, as "almost the only means to invite public attention, to give force to the most legitimate resistance, to add weight to the most just demands."[41]

Four years later, in 1891, Pope Leo XIII provided the foundation of labor policy for American Catholics in his encyclical, *Rerum Novarum*. In that document, the Pope recognized "the spirit of revolutionary change" that was sweeping much of the world, the elements of which were "unmistakable in the vast expansion of industrial pursuits . . . in the changed relations between masters and workmen; in the enormous fortunes of some few individuals, and the utter poverty of the masses," all of which filled "every mind with painful apprehension." He insisted that no solution to these problems could be found without the assistance of religion and of the Roman Catholic Church, in particular, and that the church must not neglect the duty to fulfill that obligation, noting especially the "working population themselves for whom We plead."[42]

As to labor, two years later, the Reverend James Leary explained to those gathered at the World's Parliament of Religions – speaking on what some would come to hail as the Magna Carta of Catholic social policy – "the wage-earner has rights which he cannot surrender, and which no man can take from him, for he is an intelligent, responsible being, owing homage to God and duties to human society. His recompense, then, for his daily toil cannot be measured by a heartless standard of supply and demand, or a cruel code of inhuman economics, for man is not a money-making machine, but a citizen of earth and an heir to the Kingdom of Heaven." In Pope Leo's words, employers must recognize that "their work-people are not their slaves; that they must respect in every way, his dignity as a man and as a Christian." But at the same time, workers must carry out "honestly and well all equitable agreements freely made" without resorting to violence or disorder." In that regard, the Church's assistance must "never be wanting," and it must be willing to intervene "by every means in their power . . . for the good of the people." Given the church's change of position on issues such as labor, trade unionism, and the right of the state to regulate private property in the public interest, at least liberal Protestants were willing to defend the Catholic Church against lingering anti-Catholic sentiment and activities. Catholic social activism, liberal Protestants believed, was evidence of the church's compatibility with American social liberalism.[43]

Jews and the Social Gospel

Much like the American Catholic Church, American Judaism did not produce a Social Gospel Movement comparable to that of American Protestantism, but it had a number of rabbis and laymen who contributed significantly to social reform, most notably among Reform Jews. That Reform Judaism was seriously concerned with ethical and social issues was made clear in its Pittsburgh Platform of 1885, which has been called "the embodiment of Reform ideology." It read, in part:

> In full accordance with the spirit of Mosaic legislation which strives to regulate the relation between rich and poor, we deem it our duty to participate in the great task of modern times, to solve on the basis of justice and righteousness the problems presented by the contrasts and evils of the present organization of society.[44]

Many liberal American Jews embraced the Social Gospel with its emphasis on the ethical and moral aspects of theology. They did not quarrel with the idea that the problems of the day were social problems, that, as the Protestant Social Gospeler Rauschenbusch wrote, "sin is lodged in social customs and institutions and is absorbed by the individual from his social group," that "the evils of one generation are caused by the wrongs of the generation that preceded, and will in turn condition the sufferings and temptations of those who come after." Even some Conservative Jews supported the aspirations of the Social Gospel, most notably Solomon Schechter, President of the Jewish Theological Seminary of America. He may have disagreed with his liberal colleagues over certain theological points, but he agreed with the idea of God's immanence and that for man "to work towards establishing the visible Kingdom of God in the present world" was "the highest goal religion can strive to reach."[45]

Rabbi Henry Berkowitz of Philadelphia explained the biblical basis for Reform Judaism's concern with social reform at the World's Parliament of Religions. In "The Voice of the Mother of Religions on the Social Question," Berkowitz declared that

> from the first Judaism proclaimed the dignity and duty of labor by postulating God, the Creator, at work, and setting forth the divine example unto all men for imitation, in the command, "Six days shalt thou labor and do all thy work." Industry is thus hallowed by religion, and religion in turn is made to receive the homage of industry in the fulfillment of the ordinance of Sabbath rest.

As such, he explained, Judaism had always opposed "the iniquity of self-seeking." "Love thyself" is axiomatic, but such self-love as an exclusive motive is entirely false, as per the biblical precept: "Thou shalt love thy neighbor as thyself." "In the reciprocal relation between the responsibility of the individual for society and of society for the individual lies one of Judaism's prime characteristics."[46]

The leading figure for social reform among American Jews, however, was Rabbi Stephen Wise, who studied the works of the Protestant Social Gospelers, especially Washington Gladden. For thirty years, Wise served as rabbi of the Free Synagogue of New York City. After the catastrophic Triangle Shirtwaist Factory Fire of 1911, in which 146 people died – most of them young women workers – he delivered one of his most impassioned speeches at a mass meeting at the city's Metropolitan Opera House. Wise opened by noting that the day ought to be a fast day for the citizens of New York, a day of guilt and humiliation, "a day of availing contriteness and redeeming penitence." The responsibility for the fire, he insisted, was not God's, but rather the inaction of man, "the greed of man," brought about "by lawlessness and inhumanity." It was neither a natural nor inevitable tragedy, but rather something that could have been prevented. It was not the result of the failure to enforce the law, but rather the wrong kind of laws. "Before insisting upon inspection and enforcement, let us lift up the industrial standards so as to make conditions worth inspecting . . . to afford security to the workers." Instead of merely seeking to blame, and shirking responsibility, he called on state, city, and business leaders to cooperate in planning ahead to redress justice and seek the remedy of prevention.[47]

Wise made clear that property should not be taken away without due process of law, but neither should life. "Alas, for another one of a multitude of proofs that we regard property as sacred, and are ready to suffer violations for the right," we treat life as if it "were not sacred but violable, and violable with impunity." This, he insisted, must be corrected if anything positive were to come from the fire and loss of life. Workers needed to be protected from "the incidents of the industrial regime." Women workers needed to be safeguarded in every way – economically, physically, morally, and spiritually – from "under-pay and undernourishment and insanitary housing, which seem to be the inevitable accomplishments of things as they are today." To this end, Wise did not spare the obligations of religion. He concluded:

> If the church and the synagogue were forces of righteousness in the world instead of being the faces of respectability and convention, this thing need not have been. If it be the shame and humiliation of the whole community, it is doubly the humiliation of the synagogue and of the church which have suffered it to come to pass.[48]

His strong sentiments notwithstanding, later that year, Wise was invited to speak at the annual banquet of the Chamber of Commerce of New York, "for the first and last time," he noted in his autobiography. Facing an audience that included the likes of Andrew Carnegie, James J. Hill, and J. P. Morgan, Wise drove home his views on labor and capital. He argued that the trade side of business should be moralized and the processes of creating and production, distribution, and consumption ethicized. No business order if not just can long endure, he explained, "if it be bound up with the evil of unemployment on the one hand and over-employment on the other, the evil of a man's under-wage and a child's toil, and all those social maladjustments incidental to our order which we lump together under the name of poverty." Charity could not bear that burden, alone, he insisted. Rather the situation demands "the daily meat and substance of justice" of a democracy, where "all the resources of nature by all the faculties of man" are used for the good of all.[49]

Wise argued that the conscience of the nation is not vital unless the nation protects its women and children in industry to the same extent that it protects its industries; unless it helps the masses of individuals who are suffering and perishing without the opportunity of real life to the same extent that it conserves the opportunity for initiative on the part of the individual. "The aim of democracy is not to be the production of efficient, machine-like men in industry. The first business of democracy is to be the industry of turning out completely effective, because completely free and self-determining, citizens."[50]

Much as was the case with Roman Catholics, the Social Gospel narrowed the theological gap between Jews and Christians. It became possible for Jews and Christians to talk about matters which for centuries had been held to be sacred and mutually exclusive. Liberal Jews and liberal Christians exchanged pulpits; they held interfaith worship services, a *Book of Common Worship* was compiled, and a handful of interfaith churches appeared. In 1918, the Central Conference of American Rabbis, composed of Reformed rabbis, committed to much the same goals as those expressed by the Federal Council of Churches. During the 1920s, the Central Conference of American Rabbis, the National Catholic Welfare Conference, and the Federal Council of Churches joined in challenging the twelve-hour-day and seven-day-week in the steel industry. But by then the ecumenical air was dissipating in the face of an increasingly vocal Zionist movement. The movement provoked the reappearance of anti-Semitism, encouraged in part by industrialist Henry Ford's fictional *The Protocols of the Elders of Zion*, which focused on the idea of supposed Jewish world domination. Both anti-Semitism and anti-Catholicism became the hallmarks of the revived Ku Klux Klan.[51]

Women and the Social Gospel

In earlier chapters, we looked at how women gradually played an increasingly more public and important role in America's religious institutions. Their progress was slow, however, and as late as the mid-nineteenth century, women seldom ascended to positions of leadership or took their place in the pulpit. In Chapter 1 we saw how women – Emma Dryer, for example – proved instrumental in Dwight L. Moody's urban revivals. And, we spoke of the ordination of Antoinette Brown Blackwell, who became the first woman ordained into the ministry by a major denomination. We now turn to a few of the women who continued to stride forward as part of the Social Gospel movement.

One of the less well-known, but important, case studies is that of Caroline Bartlett Crane. Born in Hudson, Wisconsin, in 1858, while still in her teens, Caroline Bartlett heard a stirring sermon by a Unitarian minister, which inspired her to set her sights on becoming a minister. After graduating from Carthage College in 1879, she held a variety of jobs, including teacher, principal, and newspaper reporter, before being accepted as a candidate for the ministry at the Iowa State Unitarian Conference. Her first church was the All Soul's Unitarian Church in Sioux Falls, Dakota Territory, where she remained for three years. In 1889, Bartlett became pastor of the First Unitarian Church of Kalamazoo, Michigan, in 1894 renamed the "People's Church."

In 1896, Bartlett married Augustus Warren Crane and two years later, under pressure from members of her congregation, who questioned whether it was appropriate for a married woman to continue in her ministry rather than devote her full energies to her husband and home, she resigned. But instead of returning to the confines of her home, she opted instead to pursue the life of a civic reformer. Among Crane's many concerns were the unsanitary conditions of slaughterhouses and the need for stringent inspection laws. When Upton Sinclair's *The Jungle* (1906) caused an uproar over conditions in Packingtown, dozens of cities invited Crane to carry out detailed inspections of their food processing plants. Under her leadership, Michigan laws were changed giving cities the power to regulate meatpacking. She organized Women's Civic Improvement Leagues to promote public health projects, and she served as a consultant in various public sanitation matters to more than sixty cities nationwide. By the end of the decade, *Collier's*, *Good Housekeeping*, and other magazines featured the "public housecleaner" as one of the nation's leading progressives. Also referred to as the "girl preacher," Crane impressed American progressives with her moral commitment to social redemption, embodying the blend of "true woman" and "new woman" that twentieth-century, middle-class Protestant women sought to become.[52]

Yet another woman who sought a new world through the Social Gospel was Elizabeth Stuart Phelps. In her novels, Phelps sought to create a gospel of social salvation that featured a benevolent God and that grew out of "the complicated patterns and unresolved tensions" she saw in the Victorian family. As such, what she created was a response to the Protestant religion in which she was raised, and against which she struggled, that "obscured the private anguish within the middle class American families that produced it."[53]

Elizabeth Stuart was born in 1844 in Boston. She lost her mother at age 8, which resulted in a close, but emotionally mixed, relationship with her father, Austin Phelps, professor of theology at Andover Theological Seminary, with whom she remained close even after she left home. Austin Phelps had only modest success as a Congregational minister in Boston. When he began to suffer from a number of debilitating illnesses, he moved to Andover Theological Seminary, which was run by his father-in-law. But as his health grew worse, he was forced into retirement at age 55. Left with three children, Austin Phelps' expectation was that his first born, Elizabeth, would conform to a socially acceptable mode of womanly behavior, something she adamantly refused despite the best efforts of her two stepmothers. Instead, at age 10, suggesting that she might follow in her mother's footsteps, she began to write stories for religious weeklies in time finding her way into *Harper's Magazine* and her first novel.[54]

Elizabeth Phelps rejected her father's conservative orthodoxy and embraced the liberal Social Gospel theology that became the mainstay of her many books, stories, and poems, chronicling her own quest for faith. In her first book, *Gates Ajar*, for example, Phelps challenged the evangelical position on sin and eternal retribution. "Instead of an afterlife of torment for the unrepentant, she pictured universal salvation from a deity who as 'a living presence, dear and real,' presided over a heaven that reproduced blissful middle-class family life." Phelps' critics – including her father – denounced her as a heretic and accused her of cheapening salvation rather than accepting God's justice, wisdom, and authority. "Heresy was her crime, and atrocity was her name," she wrote in *Chapters from a Life* (1896). She had "outraged the church" and "blasphemed its sanctities."[55]

Phelps took her most direct aim at the Social Gospel in *Friends: A Duet* (1881), *The Story of Jesus Christ* (1897), and *A Singular Life* (1894). Therein, she focused on life rather than on an afterlife and God and friends as sources of salvation. In *Friends*, for example, Charles wins the hand of Reliance and finds inner peace only after he begins to participate in reform activities to help the poor of his community. In *The Story of Jesus Christ*, as the title suggests, Phelps finds justification for her Social Gospel in the teachings of Jesus Christ, thereby lending it substance and offering her interpretation of Christ's story for modern Protestants.[56]

By most estimates, however, *A Singular Life* was Phelps' most important statement of her Social Gospel, and its chief protagonist, Emanuel Bayard, her principal Social Gospel figure. In the thinly veiled Christ story, replete with holy names and places, Bayard is portrayed as more than a mere minister. Shunned by members of his Congregational church for refusing to accept the doctrine of eternal damnation for the repentant, Bayard establishes another church among the fishermen of his seaside Massachusetts town. Following the example of many Social Gospel ministers of the day in their institutional churches, Bayard organizes social clubs and reading rooms, sets up lectures, and builds a gymnasium and bowling alley. He challenges those who insist that individuals alone have responsibility for their personal habits and salvation, only to reap the wrath of his fellow townspeople, some of whom are bent on taking his life. On the day he dedicates his chapel called Christ Love, one of them stones him to death, whereupon his fishermen disciples gather at his deathbed and vow to continue his work.[57]

There is no question that Jane Addams is among the best known of those engaged in social work during the era of the Social Gospel. Her famous Hull House, founded with Ellen Gates Starr in 1889, became the prototype of the settlement house movement in America, and in the process, Addams became the model settlement house leader. The main objective of the settlement house movement was to establish settlement houses in poor urban neighborhoods in which middle-class women would live and share knowledge and culture with their poor neighbors as well as alleviate the poverty of their neighbors and provide services such as daycare, education, and healthcare. Through Hull House, Addams fought for social justice, for women's rights, civil liberties, child labor laws, and even international peace. For our purposes, however, although the settlement house movement, including Hull House, sought to Christianize neighbors in the Protestant way of thinking, it is important to note that Addams rarely mentioned religion, or the Social Gospel, as part of her settlement mission, which has led some to conclude that her approach was essentially one of secular humanism.[58]

Among those women of the settlement house movement whose religious commitment was never questioned was Mary Eliza McDowell. She was a laywoman who accepted the Protestant Social Gospel, and her career as a settlement worker in the Chicago stockyards "provides an example of how the Social Gospel and progressive political culture became intertwined in the early years of the twentieth century." The "Angel of the Stockyards," as she came to be known, was born in Cincinnati, Ohio, in 1854 and raised in Chicago. She became active in Methodist social service work, as she later explained, from the moment a Methodist working man performed the laying on of hands on her, a ceremony that welcomed new members into the church. She took pride in knowing that a "carpenter who built boats on the Ohio River" rather than a "bishop of the apostolic succession" had blessed her. In that Methodist chapel, whose membership was made up largely of workers and which was evangelical in its orientation, her religion "became real" and involved her in everyday life rather than theological doctrines.[59]

Soon after moving to Chicago, McDowell and her father became engaged in a number of social service and religious activities. In 1871, for example, when the Great Chicago Fire left thousands homeless, they helped with the evacuation of the homeless, transporting them and their belongings to a hastily erected tent camp near their home. She helped organize the relief effort when assistance arrived from nearby states and was recognized for her efforts by an invitation to the White House to meet with President Rutherford B. Hayes and others seeking additional ways to assist in the disaster. In 1887, after meeting Frances Willard, she worked in the Women's Christian Temperance Union's kindergarten movement, and briefly taught in New York. McDowell became a Hull House resident in 1890, where she started a kindergarten and a woman's club. Inspired by the 1894 Pullman strike, she became interested in labor issues, and when University of Chicago faculty and graduate students established the University of Chicago Settlement near the city's stockyards, as a laboratory of social service, they chose McDowell to be the settlement house's director.[60]

It was at the University of Chicago Settlement that McDowell put her ideas on the Social Gospel into practice. "Settlement work," she wrote, "is one of the many expressions of the social conscience that is slowly but surely feeling its way into action." It also helped revitalize her religion, leading her to reject the destructive individualism she witnessed all around her. "Thirty odd years of living near to those in the struggle for existence," she wrote in an autobiographical article, "have . . . brought to my religious life a meaning that grows in value." The Social Gospel, she explained, was "a real religious faith," based on "both loving God with all your heart and your neighbor as if he were yourself." It also gave her life meaning, when she could no longer find fulfillment in, and rejected, the true womanhood model of the previous several decades.[61]

Under McDowell's leadership, the Chicago Settlement provided a wide range of services to the mostly immigrant families working in the stockyards. She began with a kindergarten but in 1896 rented four flats and an adjacent shop, which accommodated clubs, classrooms, lectures, and concerts. Not long after, McDowell purchased another four lots located on Gross Avenue, later renamed McDowell Avenue, and expanded her operations even further. She became involved in issues of sanitation, helping to get open garbage pits replaced by better disposal methods. She supported the packing-house workers in their 1904 strike, working to avoid violence and preserve union recognition, and later sought to expose and improve stockyard conditions. As she became increasingly more involved in social reform, she realized that to accomplish her goals faster she had to have political power. Therefore, in 1914, she became the Progressive Party's candidate for county commissioner. She was defeated, but in 1923, Mayor William E. Dever appointed her public welfare commissioner. McDowell was a founder of the Women's Trade Union League, wherein she worked for protective labor legislation for women and children. She was active in the women's suffrage movement, and after Chicago's 1919 race riots, she focused her activism on working to improve race relations. She established the first interracial committee for women and was actively involved in several interracial organizations, including the National Association for the Advancement of Colored People and the Chicago Urban League.[62]

The Social Gospel as literature

The Social Gospel was effectively promoted in popular literature as well as theological and social scientific books and essays. The work of Elizabeth Stuart Phelps has already been noted. But the best example of this was Charles Sheldon's novel *In His Steps* (1897). A Congregationalist minister located in Topeka, Kansas, Sheldon was committed to the Social Gospel and Christian Socialism, and his novels were among the best-selling books of the period. In brief, Sheldon's novels depicted the dilemma that Americans would face if they were confronted with an ethical decision, wherein they asked themselves, "What would Jesus do?"

The story opens with the unexpected appearance of a bedraggled stranger at a service presided over by the Reverend Maxwell, "satisfied with the conditions of his pastorate" for his equally self-satisfied congregation of the First Church of Raymond. The stranger announces that he is not an "ordinary tramp" – "though I don't know of any teaching of Jesus that makes one kind of tramp a tramp less worth saving than another." He was not drunk or crazy but rather harmless, and he had been wondering if he might say a word to those gathered. While the minister and his congregation sat in silence, the stranger explained that he had lost his job about ten months earlier, replaced by a machine, that his wife had died four months earlier, and that his daughter was staying with another family until he could find a job. He then proceeded to the heart of his message: What did Jesus mean when he said, "Follow me?" – that it was necessary for a disciple of Jesus to follow his steps, which were obedience, faith, love, and imitation when in all his wandering, few had bothered to offer him any support or even sympathy? "Somehow I get puzzled when I see so many Christians living in luxury and singing, 'Jesus, I my cross have taken, all to leave and follow thee,'" when his wife had died in a tenement in New York City "gasping for air" and his daughter suffered from starvation. "What I don't understand," he continued, is: "Is what you mean by following in his steps?" "What would Jesus do?" At last, the minister responded, stating that it was clear that people must be

> free of fanaticism on one hand and too much caution on the other. If Jesus's example is the example for the world, it certainly must be feasible to follow it. But we need to remember this great fact. After we ask the Spirit to tell us what Jesus would do and have received an answer to it, we are to act regardless of the results to ourselves.[63]

The impact of World War I on the Social Gospel

By stepping outside the churches to engage the political, social, and economic forces of their day, the Social Gospel transformed American Protestantism. Nevertheless, from the devastation of the World War I, the Social Gospel came under attack from proponents of a neo-orthodoxy that criticized the optimistic formulations of a theology that they believed did not deal seriously enough with either the transcendence of God or the reality of sin and evil. Although the Social Gospel Movement was not entirely a liberal movement, some Social Gospelers themselves grew disillusioned, doubting whether their goals of social reform were at all realistic. It is the case that most Social Gospelers did not favor the United States' entry into the war, as they saw it as destroying their hopes for God's kingdom on earth. The Federal Council of Churches renamed its Committee on War the Committee on Peace and International Relations, and the most outspoken in this group earned the disapproval, if not outright condemnation, of those who supported the war effort, labeling them un-American. Opposition to the war did not prevail, however, and in time, many of those who had opposed American entry into the war came to embrace it as providing Americans the opportunity to extend the Social Gospel to the world.[64]

The war did provide the mainstream Protestant Social Gospel a largely unchallenged level of legitimacy in the United States. But that triumph carried with it the seeds of destruction for the Social Gospel Movement, as reform became the mainstay of the nation's secular organizations rather than its churches. Perhaps anticipating such a fate, Shailer Mathews, as early as 1907, insisted that the mission of the church to society was specifically religious and spiritual, and he criticized liberal theology insofar as it tended to reduce Christianity and the church to an ethical or moral plane. As Roger Haight has explained, Mathews insisted that "the basic function of the Church is religious; and in that it is distinct from all other social institutions. The Church should never compromise its religious essence or be confused with other institutions. It is not meant to replace other social institutions with their specific goals." The church was not the government, not the school system, not primarily an agency for relief work. It "should not identify itself with any program or political or social reform, not by extension with any political party."[65] If the Social Gospel became less visible in the 1920s, however, it did not disappear. Further, by then it had taken on an important international dimension.

Religious missionary activity at the close of the nineteenth and opening of the twentieth centuries

It would be appropriate to conclude this chapter with a brief discussion of American missions abroad, which in large part served as an extension of the Social Gospel Movement. At the turn of the twentieth century, the United States became a global power, and so too did its churches. Americans were well aware of the economic difficulties and social problems they faced but were also confident that the twentieth century would be the "Christian century": "Evangelicals were certain that the universe was friendly both to the progress of Christianity and to the moral and spiritual advances in civilization for which the churches stood." And they believed that they were in the very vanguard of true progress, that Christianity was "the highest and purest form of religion in the world," and that it contained "the highest and purest conception of man and society."[66]

Tying all of this directly to missions, Sidney L. Gulick, missionary of the American Board of Commissioners for Foreign Missions, declared in 1897: "Christianity is the religion of the dominant nations of the earth. Nor is it rash to prophesy that in due time it will be the only religion in the world." And to those who might object to this aggressive stance, some dubbed imperialism, the Reverend Lyman Abbott provided this answer:

> It is said that we have no right to go to a land occupied by a barbaric people and interfere with their life. It is said that if they prefer barbarism, they have a right to remain barbarians. I deny the right of a barbaric people to retain possession of any quarter of the globe ... barbarism has no rights which civilization is bound to respect.[67]

Some have argued that America becoming a global power was the next logical step for a nation that, for the better part of the nineteenth century, pursued its "manifest destiny" across the North American continent. Others have argued that it was consistent with an outward looking ideology, whose roots could be traced to the planting of a "city on a hill" and the Puritans' sense of divine mission and "errand into the wilderness." By the end of the nineteenth century American missionaries had sailed to nearly every corner of the globe. First intended to teach native peoples about the Bible, missionary projects soon were extended to include social services, including schools and hospitals. In Africa, almost all leaders of the earliest independent states were educated in schools founded by European and American missionaries, including African Americans. By 1890, there were 100 missionary physicians in China, providing healthcare for 350,000 patients each year.[68]

As noted earlier, Walter Rauschenbusch credited publication of *Our Country* by Josiah Strong in 1885 as the advent of the Social Gospel Movement. It also served as a clarion call for Protestant American missions abroad. Strong wrote that as a "race" of people, the Teutonic people were representative of two great, closely related ideas, by which they deeply impressed themselves on the human family: civil liberty and spiritual Christianity. It was "the fire of liberty" that allowed the Teutonic people to rise up against the Pope and Protestantism to spread so rapidly. But European Teutonic Protestantism, he argued, had "degenerated into mere formalism," the result of which was that its state churches were "filled with members who generally know nothing of a personal spiritual experience." Spiritual Christianity was then to be found among Anglo-Saxons and their converts "for this is the great missionary race": "It is chiefly to the English and American peoples that we must look for the evangelization of the world."[69]

Predicting that, by the close of the twentieth century, Anglo-Saxons would outnumber all other civilized races in the world, Strong asked: "Does it not look as if God were not only preparing in our Anglo-Saxon civilization the die with which to stamp the peoples of the earth, but as if he were also massing behind that die the mighty power with which to press it?" He was confident not only that the Anglo-Saxon race would "eventually give its civilization to mankind," but also that North America would be "the great home of the Anglo-Saxon, the principal of his power, the center of his life and influence." America, he argued, with its "purest Christianity," would exercise controlling influence over the civilized world, and that would be "but the consummation of a movement as old as civilizations," the result of which would be what men had looked forward to for centuries." He left open the question as to whether "the feebler and more abject races" were going to be "regenerated and raised up" – whether that would be part of "God's plan to people the world with better and finer material."[70]

Eight years later, in 1903, in *The March of the Flag*, United States Senator Albert J. Beveridge reflected the unity of the secular and religious missionary message:

> It is a mighty people that He planted on this soil, a people sprung from the most masterful blood of history . . . a people imperial by virtue of their power, by right of their institutions, by authority of their heaven-directed purposes. . . . It is a glorious history our God has bestowed upon His chosen people . . . a history heroic with faith in our mission and our future . . . a history divinely logical.

Beveridge insisted that God had endowed Americans with "gifts beyond our deserts, and marked us as the people of His peculiar favor." As God's chosen people, he reasoned:

We cannot fly from our world duties; it is ours to execute the purposes of a fate that has driven us to be greater than our small intensions. We cannot retreat from any soil where Providence has unfurled our banner; it is ours to save the soil of liberty and civilization. For liberty and civilization and God's promises fulfilled, the flag must henceforth be the symbol and the sign of all mankind.[71]

Some would argue that America's first step on the world stage came with the Monroe Doctrine, a half-century earlier. And that it was less involved outside the Western Hemisphere than European powers in terms of actual conquest. But it did have a worldwide presence commercially, and in 1898, the United States annexed the Hawaiian Islands, extending its destiny half-way across the Pacific. The annexation is commonly explained in commercial terms, but it had its religious roots and underpinnings as well, as New England Congregational missionaries operated in Hawaii since the third decade of the nineteenth century. In that same year, the nation took its most intentional step toward a more international presence with its entrance into the Spanish-American War.

The reasons given for American action against Spain focused on a humanitarian effort to rescue Cuba from the abuses of Spanish control. But that it involved the annexation of the Philippines, keeping the islands out of the hands of European powers moving into the area, was a bonus in the minds of many, making it what Secretary of State John Hall called a "splendid little war." President William McKinley was only one of the more prominent leaders to add a religious flavoring to the Americans military venture by explaining that although at one point opposed to the war, with annexation he had come to see that it was the nation's duty "to educate the Filipinos, and uplift and civilize and Christianize them, and by God's grace, do the very best we could by them, as our fellow men for whom Christ also died." As two California newspapers (*California Christian Advocate* and *Pacific Advocate*) put it at the outbreak of the war: "The war is the Kingdom of God coming!" and "The cross will follow the flag. . . . The clock of the ages is striking."[72]

Not everyone agreed with the war, and US expansion through annexation of the Philippines, especially in the face of armed Filipino opposition. That included some of the most prominent evangelicals. With the coming of the war, William Jennings Bryan, the evangelical populist and three-time presidential candidate, made public his opposition to the war, if it would lead to annexation, on the grounds that annexation betrayed the Christian principles on which the nation was founded. Others opposed annexation of the Roman Catholic Philippines because they believed it would lead to an influx of "non-Christian, non-white immigrants" – read Catholics – to what they continued to see as a "Christian," meaning Protestant, nation. Still others argued that no matter how well intentioned, American civilization could not be exported to a non-Anglo-Saxon, "benighted" people. But these constituted minority views, which failed to influence the course of events. By 1900, there were over fifty mission boards in the United States and eight closely allied agencies in Canada sending missionaries abroad. There were nearly fifty auxiliary societies, and the total North American missionary staff overseas was about 5,000. By 1915, that number was estimated at 10,000, and by 1930 the movement involved tens of thousands of Americans abroad and millions at home.[73]

Protestant women made up a sizable portion of this new crop of American missionaries, including single women and those who accompanied their husbands to missionary outposts around the world and the many more who supported their efforts at home. By the end of the nineteenth century, the major Protestant denominations organized their own foreign missionary societies with women steadily increasing their membership until by 1890 women composed 60 percent of the American mission force. By 1914, more than 3 million American women supported the movement through direct participation abroad as doctors, nurses, and teachers; accompanying and assisting their ordained spouses; or by providing support at home, raising money and consciousness of missionary efforts around the world.[74]

Compared to men, women's approach was intimate and personal rather than directive. They associated their Christian mission with their domestic responsibility to instill moral character ("to renovate degraded man") and to breed refinement (to "clothe all climes with beauty"). Most American missionaries made clear their preference for influence rather than empire in China, but women were particularly adamant on this point. They were also insistent on limiting Western commercial efforts in China, especially those that encouraged the use of alcohol and tobacco as they had opium before then. Women in China were often seen as economic liabilities, less valued at birth and more likely to be abandoned, sold, or brutalized by their husbands in times of economic hardship. Women missionaries opposed this practice as well, employing "a female kind of authority" or "moral crusade . . . as guardians and founts of civilization." Women missionaries were seldom allowed to preach or work directly with men, so they focused on women and children, commonly offering their services as educators and healthcare workers, and in this regard, they made significant gains with this segment of the population.[75]

By the end of World War I, there was widespread unity among Protestants, and if to a somewhat lesser extent, among Catholics, that their commitment to social justice needed to extend beyond the United States to other nations around the globe. As the Federal Council of Churches put it, the war would "bring the Christian bodies in America into united service for Christ and the world." Although present all across the globe, in the Middle East, Latin America, Asia, and Africa by the end of World War I, by the 1920s, Protestant missionary efforts in China took center stage. The number of American missionaries more than doubled between 1890 and 1905 and doubled again by 1919 to 3300. In 1922, volunteer offerings for China topped $750,000 to support over a thousand missionary led elementary and secondary schools and more than 40 teacher-training institutes, to which would be added numerous colleges, seminaries, medical schools, and orphanages. By 1923, the American Bible Society sent nearly 20,000 Bibles to China along with more than 2 million related publications. Missionary enthusiasm grew out of a renewed interest in the development of a "New China" out of the ashes of the Boxer uprising of 1900, replacing military force with religious and cultural suasion.[76]

The Catholic Foreign Missionary Society of America was founded in 1911. The Maryknoll fathers (and nuns) focused their efforts on the Roman Catholic countries of Central and South America, and their efforts led to various missionary efforts, that, after World War I, the National Catholic Welfare Conference sought to coordinate and help promote. Like their Protestant counterparts, Catholic missionaries did not confine their efforts to spreading the teaching of the church. They too built and operated schools, hospitals, and orphanages and recruited native clergy that would more firmly plant their efforts in a more indigenous church.[77]

American religious missions in the wake of World War I

In 1919, Robert Speer, a Presbyterian but speaking for most Christians in his *New Opportunity of the Church* acknowledged that the West had done much harm to the non-West through "commercial exploitation, the liquor traffic, the slave trade . . . [and] the opium traffic." Missionary efforts, however, he contended, had and would continue to counter such destructive efforts: "It has joined with the wholesome moral sentiment existing among the people in a death struggle against the great iniquities that Western civilization [has] spread over the world." Nevertheless, as noted earlier, American missionary efforts abroad were not always welcome and often incurred sharp, even violent, resistance. In many cases, opposition arose to what William Hutchison has described as missionaries' "supercilious and often demeaning attitude toward religions that the recipient peoples considered integral to their own cultures." For others, it was the missionaries' mere foreignness that threatened local customs, cultures, and religions, many of which had long, rich traditions of their own. Such resistance grew particularly strong in China in the 1930s, but it was made more severe when Japan invaded in 1937, the result of which was the removal of nearly all foreign missions in that country.[78]

The Great Depression in the United States depleted the resources necessary for missionary efforts abroad, but the effort was even more seriously undermined by questions raised in some quarters as to the cultural imperialism such missionary efforts appeared to pose and from the growing tension between American liberal and conservative religious leaders and groups. Those who spoke to the former criticism, argued that nationalism was the dominant motive for American missionary efforts, or that American missionaries were mere "operatives to their American identity . . . that they were little more than spokespersons for national and social values." As seen earlier, nationalism was indeed integral to the movement, but Protestant missionaries were for the most part religiously sincere and earnestly sought to follow God's will as they understood it. They were "rooted both in a Christian, a-nationalistic zeal for expansion and active evangelization," William Hutchison has written, "and equally in a fervent belief, less obviously Christian but just as religious, that Americans were under special obligation to save and renovate the world." Or, as Robert Handy has put it,

> Greatly impressed by the achievements of Western, especially American, civilization, they attributed its remarkable progress primarily to the working of Christianity within it. Though they strove as Christians to keep the priority on spiritual religion and to be aware of the difference between faith and culture, it was not difficult in the spirit of those times, to lose the distinction and to see Christian civilization as a main outcome of faith, if not its chief outcome.[79]

The last objection, rising out of the gulf that arose between liberal and conservative Protestants, called into question, as it did within the Social Gospel Movement, whether such missionary efforts had, or even should have, as their primary mission evangelization or the many social services they provided. If the latter, why involve the churches? In considering this question, a report was commissioned and published in 1932 by the multidenominational Commission of Appraisal, titled *Re-Thinking Missions: A Layman's Inquiry after One Hundred Years*. It concluded that, although missionaries' initial purpose was to save souls, they had been of necessity drawn into caring for the minds and bodies, as well as the social life of those souls they engaged. These educational, medical, and social interests grew until in volume and variety, they then outranked the missionaries' original purpose. But by then, for reasons just noted, missionary efforts that had flourish for nearly a half-century or more, had begun to dissipate, although they never disappeared.[80]

Summary

Chapter 2 addressed concerns on the part of native born as to the influx of immigrants from parts of the world previously underrepresented in the United States with their differing cultural and religious traditions. It also considered another side of that issue, namely the influx of mostly poor, unskilled immigrants into the nation's cities, where they were joined by people from rural areas of the country, all of whom sought new economic opportunities. Many were successful in their quest, but others found their new industrialized, urban environments dens of poverty and exploitation. Most churches saw no alternative but to respond by providing a wide range of social services – better housing, healthcare, help in finding jobs – to meet the physical as well as the spiritual needs of the people. Among the churches, this took the form of what became known as the Social Gospel, which coincided with the secular progressive movement. The same commitment also led to an increased number of missionaries, largely Christian, who traveled throughout the world seeking to convert those they encountered to Christianity, but in the process building hospitals and schools and providing other services that benefited the local population. Their efforts raised questions as to whether the efforts of the missionaries were intended as well to pave the way for US business expansion abroad – even imperialism – and during the Great Depression, whether the time and money spent improving conditions abroad might be better used at home.

Review questions

1   How did the challenges of late-nineteenth and early-twentieth-century urban life give rise to the Social Gospel?
2   Explain the Social Gospel's underlying philosophy and how that philosophy was implemented by various religious organizations.
3   How did the Social Gospel impact the religious life of African Americans and women?
4   How did World War I impact the Social Gospel movement?
5   How were religious missions abroad a natural outgrowth of the Social Gospel movement at home?

Notes

1   See, for example: William H. Cooper, Jr., *The Great Revivalists in American Religion, 1740–1944: The Careers and Theology of Jonathan Edwards, Charles Finney, Dwight Moody, Billy Sunday, and Aimee Semple McPherson* (Jefferson, NC: McFarland & Company, Inc., 2010), 128.
2   Cooper, *The Great Revivalists*, 128.
3   Cooper, *The Great Revivalists*, 132; William G. McLoughlin, *Modern Revivalism* (New York: The Ronald Press Co., 1959), 420; William G. McLoughlin, *Billy Sunday Was His Real Name* (Chicago: University of Chicago Press, 1955), 1–34.
4   Cooper, *The Great Revivalists*, 132–3, 139–41; Lyle W. Dorsett, *Billy Sunday and the Redemption of Urban America* (Grand Rapids: W. B. Eerdmans, 1991), 88; McLoughlin, *Billy Sunday*, 35–72.
5   McLoughlin, *Billy Sunday*, xvii, xxvii.
6   Cooper, *The Great Revivalists*, 134–6, 138; Roger A. Bruns, *Preacher: Billy Sunday and Big-Time American Evangelism* (New York: W. W. Norton, 1992), 277; Dorsett, *Billy Sunday*, 132.
7   McLoughlin, *Billy Sunday*, vii, ix, 295; Cooper, *The Great Revivalists*, 130; Mark Noll, *The Scandal of the Evangelical Mind* (Grand Rapids: W. B. Eerdmans, 1995), 61–8.
8   Shailer Mathews. "Social Gospel," in *A Dictionary of Religion and Ethics*, ed. Shailer Mathews and Gerald Birney Smith (New York: The MacMillan Company, 1921), 416; also quoted in Ronald

C. White, Jr. and Charles Howard Hopkins, *The Social Gospel: Religion and Reform in Changing America* (Philadelphia: Temple University Press, 1976), xi.

9   Walter Rauschenbusch, *A Theology for the Social Gospel* (New York: The MacMillan Company, 1917), 2; Jon Butler, Grant Wacker, and Randall Balmer, *Religion in American Life: A Short History*, 2nd edn. (New York: Oxford University Press, 2011), 297.

10 White and Hopkins, *The Social Gospel*, xii; Susan Curtis, *A Consuming Faith: The Social Gospel and Modern American Culture* (Columbia: University of Missouri Press, 1991), 7–8.

11 Curtis, *A Consuming Faith*, 1–6; Roger Haight, "The Mission of the Church in the Theology of the Social Gospel," *Theological Studies*, 49 (1988): 477.

12 Curtis, *A Consuming Faith*, 3–4; White and Hopkins, *The Social Gospel*, xvi–xvii.

13 Jack B. Rogers and Robert E. Blade, "The Great Ends of the Church: Two Perspectives," *Journal of Presbyterian History*, 76 (1998): 181–6.

14 Walter Rauschenbusch, *Christianizing the Social Order* (New York: The MacMillan Company, 1912), 14, 19–20; Curtis, *A Consuming Faith*, 3–4.

15 Curtis, *A Consuming Faith*, 2. For more on this see Ronald C. White, Jr., *Liberty and Justice for All: Racial Reform and the Social Gospel, 1887–1925* (Louisville, KY: Westminster John Knox Press, 1990); Sydney Ahlstrom, *A Religious History of the American People* (New Haven, CT: Yale University Press, 1974).

16 Walter Rauschenbusch, *Christianity and the Social Crisis* (New York: The MacMillan Company, 1907), 414.

17 Rauschenbusch, *Christianity and the Social Crisis*, 415–17, 420–1.

18 Rauschenbusch, *A Theology for the Social Gospel*, 1–2, 5, 132.

19 Charles Howard Hopkins, *The Rise of the Social Gospel in American Protestantism* (New Haven, CT: Yale University Press, 1940), 27; Robert F. Handy, ed., *The Social Gospel in America, 1870–1920: Gladden Ely and Rauschenbusch* (New York: Oxford University Press, 1966), 19–24, 32, 38.

20 Handy, *The Social Gospel in America*, 27; Washington Gladden, *The Church and Modern Life* (New York: Houghton Mifflin, 1908), 85. See also Washington Gladden, *The Church and the Kingdom* (New York: Fleming H. Revell Company, 1894), an excerpt of which appears in Handy, *The Social Gospel in America*, 102–18; Washington Gladden, *The Nation and the Kingdom* (Boston: The American Board of Commissioners for Foreign Missions, 1909), excerpted in Handy, *The Social Gospel in America*, 135–53.

21 Washington Gladden, *Applied Christianity: Moral Aspects of Social Questions* (Boston: Houghton Mifflin, 1886), 125, 169, excerpted in Handy, *The Social Gospel in America*, 49–71.

22 Washington Gladden, *Christianity and Socialism* (New York: Eaton and Mains, 1905), 123–7.

23 Gladden, *Christianity and Socialism*, 47–9, 102–3, 136–7.

24 Gladden, *Christianity and Socialism*, 139–40, 148, 152–3.

25 Curtis, *A Consuming Faith*, 49; Shailer Mathews, *New Faith for Old: An Autobiography* (New York: The MacMillan Company, 1936).

26 Haight, "The Mission of the Church in the Theology of the Social Gospel," 482; Haight directly references Mathew's *The Social Teaching of Jesus* (1897). See also Shailer Mathews, *The Message of Jesus to Our Modern Life* (Chicago: University of Chicago Press, 1915), 26, 90; Shailer Mathews, *The Individual and the Social Gospel* (New York: Missionary Education Movement, 1914).

27 Ralph E. Luker, *The Social Gospel in Black and White: American Racial Reform, 1885–1912* (Macon, GA: Mercer University Press, 1988); White, *Liberty and Justice for All*. For a corrective to the absence of focus on the black Social Gospel, see Gary Dorrien, *The New Abolition: W. E. B. Du Bois and the Black Social Gospel* (New Haven, CT: Yale University Press, 2015).

28 White and Hopkins, *The Social Gospel*, 103–7.

29 Dorrien, *The New Abolition*, 15–16. For more on Du Bois, see David Levering Lewis, *W. E. B. Du Bois: A Biography: 1868–1963* (New York: Holt, 2009).

30 Timothy E. Fulop, "The Future Golden Day of the Race: Millennialism and Black Americans in the Nadir, 1877–1901," excerpted in Robert R. Mathisen, *Critical Issues in American Religious History: A Reader*, 2nd rev. edn. (Waco, TX: Baylor University Press, 2006), 495; see also Timothy E. Fulop and Albert J Raboteau, eds., *African-American Religion* (New York: Routledge/Taylor and Francis Group, 1997).

31 Fulop, "The Future Golden Day of the Race," 488–9; See also Fulop and Raboteau, *African-American Religion.*

32 Reverdy C. Ranson, *The Spirit of Freedom and Justice* (Nashville, TN: AMEC Sunday School Union/Legacy Publishing, 1926), 128–32.

33 Ranson, *The Spirit of Freedom and Justice,* 128–32.

34 See Jay P. Dolan, *Catholic Revivalism: The American Experience, 1830–1900* (Notre Dame, IN: University of Notre Dame Press, 1978).

35 White and Hopkins, *The Social Gospel,* 214–15.

36 Aaron I. Abell. *American Catholicism and Social Action: A Search for Social Justice, 1865–1950* (Notre Dame: University of Notre Dame Press, 1973), 88, 147–8; Richard T. Ely, "Introduction," in *A Living Wage: Its Ethical and Economic Aspects,* ed. John A. Ryan (New York: The MacMillan Company, 1906), xi–xiii.

37 Ryan, *A Living Wage,* vii–viii, 324–31.

38 Ryan, *A Living Wage,* 324–31.

39 Francis L. Broderick, *Right Reverend New Dealer: John A. Ryan* (New York: The Macmillan Company, 1963). See also Aaron I. Abell, *American Catholic Thought on Social Questions* (Indianapolis, IN; Bobbs-Merrill, 1968), 229–51.

40 Doris Kearns Goodwin, *The Bully Pulpit: Theodore Roosevelt, William Howard Taft, and the Golden Age of Journalism* (New York: Simon and Schuster, 2013), 318.

41 Gibbons letter is included in Henry J. Browne, *The Catholic Church and the Knights of Labor* (Washington, DC: The Catholic University of America Press, 1949), 365–78.

42 Leo XIII, "Rerum Novarum," in *The Church and Labor,* ed. John A. Ryan and Joseph Husslein (New York: The MacMillan Company, 1920), 57–9, 74–5, 77–8, 93–4.

43 White and Hopkins, *The Social Gospel,* 21–9; Leo XIII, "Rerum Novarum," 77–8, 93–4; White and Hopkins, *The Social Gospel,* 226–8.

44 Excerpted in White and Hopkins, *The Social Gospel,* 230.

45 Egal Feldman, "The Social Gospel and the Jews," *American Jewish Historical Quarterly,* 58 (1969): 308–16; see also White and Hopkins, *The Social Gospel,* 238–9.

46 White and Hopkins, *The Social Gospel,* 230–1.

47 White and Hopkins, *The Social Gospel,* 232; Carol H. Voss, *Rabbi and Minister: The Friendship of Stephen S. Wise and John Haynes Holmes* (Cleveland: World Press, 1964), 38–9; Stephen Wise, *Challenging Years: The Autobiography of Stephen Wise* (New York: Putnam's Sons Publishers, 1949), 62–4.

48 Wise, *Challenging Years,* 62–4.

49 Wise, *Challenging Years,* 60–1.

50 Wise, *Challenging Years,* 60–1.

51 Feldman, "The Social Gospel and the Jews," 308–16; Nathan R. Glazer, *American Judaism,* 2nd edn. (Chicago: University of Chicago Press, 1972), 141.

52 Curtis, *A Consuming Faith,* 59, 61. See also Caroline Bartlett Crane, *Everyman's House* (Garden City, NY: Doubleday, Page and Company, 1925), 128–9; Richard O'Ryan, *A Just Verdict: The Life of Caroline Bartlett* Crane (Kalamazoo: Western Michigan University, 1994).

53 Curtis, *A Consuming Faith,* 89.

54 Curtis, *A Consuming Faith,* 89–92; Elizabeth Stuart Phelps, *Chapters from a Life* (Boston: Houghton Mifflin, 1896), ch. 3.

55 Curtis, *A Consuming Faith,* 94–6; Elizabeth Stuart Phelps, *The Gates Ajar* (Boston: Fields & Osgood, 1868), 184; Phelps, *Chapters,* 110–30; Mary Angela Bennett, *Elizabeth Stuart Phelps* (Philadelphia: University of Pennsylvania Press, 1939), 1.

56 Elizabeth Stuart Phelps, *Friends: A Duet* (Boston: Houghton Mifflin, 1991); Elizabeth Stuart Phelps, *The Story of Jesus Christ* (Boston: Houghton Mifflin, 1897); Curtis, *A Consuming Faith,* 97.

57 Elizabeth Stuart Phelps, *A Singular Life* (Boston: Houghton Mifflin, 1894); Curtis, *A Consuming Faith,* 98. On Phelps literary work see Carole Farley Kessler, *Elizabeth Stuart Phelps* (Boston: Twayne Publishers, 1982).

58 Louise C. Wade, "The Heritage from Chicago's Early Settlement Housed," *Journal of the Illinois State Historical Society,* 60 (1967): 414; Howard Husock, "Bringing Back the Settlement House," *Public Welfare,* 51 (1993): 16–25; Louise K. Joslin, *Citizen: Jane Addams and the Struggle for Democracy* (Chicago: University of Chicago Press, 2005), 173–4, 181; Louise W. Knight, *Jane*

Addams: A Writer's Life (Champaign: University of Illinois Press, 2004), 170. See also Victoria Bissell Brown, *The Education of Jane Addams* (Philadelphia: University of Pennsylvania Press, 2003); Allen F. Davis, *American Heroine: The Life and Legend of Jane Addams* (New York: Oxford University Press, 1973); Jane Addams, *Twenty Years at Hull House* (New York: The MacMillan Company, 1910).

59 Curtis, *A Consuming Faith*, 157–8. For biographical information see Howard Wilson, *Mary McDowell, Neighbor* (Chicago: University of Chicago Press, 1928); Louise Carroll Wade, "Mary McDowell," in *Notable American Women: A Biographical Dictionary*, Paperback edition of volumes 1–3 (Cambridge, MA: Belknap/Harvard University Press, 1971), 2: 462–4.

60 Wilson, *Mary McDowell*, 9, 15–17, 21.

61 Curtis, *A Consuming Faith*, 161–2, 164–5; Wilson, *Mary McDowell*, 45–6, 216.

62 Wilson, *Mary McDowell*, 9, 15–7; Wade, "Mary McDowell," 462.

63 Summarized from Charles M. Sheldon, *In His Steps* (Chicago: John C. Winton Co., 1897).

64 Carl Degler, *Out of Our Past: The Forces That Shared Modern America* (New York: Harper & Row, 1950), 347; Curtis, *A Consuming Faith*, 10.

65 Curtis, *A Consuming Faith*, 194; Shailer Mathews, *The Church and the Changing Order* (New York: The MacMillan Company, 1907), 242; Haight, "The Mission of the Church in the Theology of the Social Gospel," 488–9. See also White and Hopkins, *The Social Gospel*; Handy, *The Social Gospel in America*.

66 Gaustad and Schmidt, *The Religious History of America*, 255; Robert T. Handy, ed., *A Christian America: Protestant Hopes and Historical Realities*, 2nd edn. (New York: Oxford University Press, 1984), excerpt in Mathisen, *Critical Issues in American Religious History*, 516–18.

67 Handy, *A Christian America*, in Mathisen, excerpt *Critical Issues in American Religious History*, 519, 521.

68 Mary Beth Norton, David M. Katzman, David W. Blight, Howard P. Chudacoff, Fredrik Logevall, Beth Bailey, Thomas G. Paterson, and William M. Tuttle, Jr., *A People and a Nation: A History of the United States*, 7th edn. (Boston: Houghton Mifflin, 2005), 2: 544.

69 Josiah Strong, *Our Country*, rev. edn. (New York: Baker and Taylor, 1892), 200–18; see also excerpt in Mathisen, *Critical Issues in American Religious History*, 505–6.

70 Strong, *Our Country*, 200–18; see also excerpt in Mathisen, *Critical Issues in American Religious History*, 507–8. For similar but later statements on Social Gospelers' support for foreign missions, see Walter Rauschenbusch, "Conceptions of Missions" (1892) included in Handy, *The Social Gospel in America*, excerpt in Mathisen, *Critical Issues in American Religious History*, 268–73; Washington Gladden, "The Nation and the Kingdom: Annual Sermon before the American Board of Commissioners for Foreign Missions" (1909) included in Handy, *The Social Gospel in America*, excerpt in Mathisen, *Critical Issues in American Religious History*, 135–53.

71 Albert J. Beveridge, "The March of the Flag" (1903) included in Mathisen, *Critical Issues in American Religious History*, 512–13, 515.

72 Susan K. Harris, *God's Arbiters: Americans and the Philippines, 1898–1902* (New York: Oxford University Press, 2011), 14; Mathisen, *Critical Issues in American Religious History*, 499. For more on how American missionaries urged annexation of the Philippines on religious grounds see Stuart Creighton Miller, *"Benevolent Assimilation": The American Conquest of the Philippines, 1899–1903* (New Haven, CT: Yale University Press, 1982).

73 Harris, *God's Arbiters*, 13, 16, 24, 27; Gaustad and Schmidt, *The Religious History of America*, 258; Handy, *The Social Gospel in America*, excerpt in Mathisen, *Critical Issues in American Religious History*, 522–3; William R. Hutchison, *Errand to the World: American Protestant Thought and Foreign Missions* (Chicago: University of Chicago Press, 1987), excerpt in Mathisen, *Critical Issues in American Religious History*, 526. See also Ian Tyrrell, *Reforming the World: The Creation of America's Moral Empire* (Princeton: Princeton University Press, 2010).

74 Jane Hunter, *The Gospel of Gentility: American Women Missionaries in Turn-of-the-Century China* (New Haven, CT: Yale University Press, 1984), excerpt in Mathisen, *Critical Issues in American Religious History*, 536; Gaustad and Schmidt, *The Religious History of America*, 266.

75 Hunter, *The Gospel of Gentility*, excerpt in Mathisen, *Critical Issues in American Religious History*, 537–42.

76 Gaustad and Schmidt, *The Religious History of America*, 260, 263, 267; Handy, *The Social Gospel in America*, excerpt in Mathisen, *Critical Issues in American Religious History*, 525; Hunter, *The Gospel of Gentility*, excerpt in Mathisen, *Critical Issues in American Religious History*, 537–42.

77 Gaustad and Schmidt, *The Religious History of America*, 268.
78 Gaustad and Schmidt, *The Religious History of America*, 267; Hutchison, *Errand to the World*, excerpt in Mathisen, *Critical Issues in American Religious History*, 527.
79 Hutchison, *Errand to the World*, excerpt in Mathisen, *Critical Issues in American Religious History*, 529, 533–4; Handy, *The Social Gospel in America*, excerpt in Mathisen, *Critical Issues in American Religious History*, 524.
80 William Ernest Hocking, *Re-Thinking Missions: A Layman's Inquiry after One Hundred Years by the Commission of Appraisal* (New York: Harper & Brothers, 1932).

Recommended for further reading

Bruns, Roger A. *Preacher: Billy Sunday and Big-Time American Evangelism*. New York: W. W. Norton, 1992.

Curtis, Susan. *A Consuming Faith: The Social Gospel and Modern American Culture*. Columbia: University of Missouri Press, 1991 (paperback edition 2001).

Dorrien, Gary. *The New Abolition: W. E. B. Du Bois and the Black Social Gospel*. New Haven, CT: Yale University Press, 2015.

Fairbank, John K. ed. *The Missionary Enterprise in China and America*. Cambridge: Harvard University Press, 1963.

Handy, Robert F. ed. *The Social Gospel in America, 1870–1920: Gladden, Ely and Rauschenbusch*. New York: Oxford University Press, 1966.

Hunter, Jane. *The Gospel of Gentility: American Women Missionaries in Turn-of-the-Century China*. New Haven, CT: Yale University Press, 1984.

Hutchison, William R. *Errand to the World: American Protestant Thought and Foreign Missions*. Chicago: University of Chicago Press, 1987.

Luker, Ralph E. *The Social Gospel in Black and White American Racial Reform, 1885–1912*. Macon, GA: Mercer University Press, 1998.

McLoughlin, William G. *Billy Sunday Was His Real Name*. Chicago: University of Chicago Press, 1955.

White, Ronald C. Jr. and C. Howard Hopkins. *The Social Gospel: Religion and Reform in Changing America*. Philadelphia: Temple University Press, 1976.

Chapter 3

Science versus religion

Action and reaction

The higher criticism

It could be said that the kind of textual analysis associated with the higher criticism dates to the third century, and the Christian scholar Origen. Origen argued that the Bible contained many unhistorical and literally false statements and that those seeking to understand the Bible should seek symbolic rather than literal truths. Our focus, however, is on the higher criticism that flourished throughout Europe and the United States at about the same time Darwin appeared on the scene, helping to erode public confidence in bedrock Christian beliefs concerning the authorship and divinely inspired teachings of the Bible. Further, the higher criticism provided the means by which churchmen, while continuing to rely on an argument from design could pull back from a strict biblical literalism seeking an interpretation of Scripture that reconciled recent science and the biblical story of creation.[1]

Higher criticism, or historical criticism, began with attempts to establish the original text of the Bible, free from mistranslations, but evolved into an investigation of the origins of the texts. The primary goal of the higher criticism was to ascertain a text's primitive or original meaning in its historical context. It sought to reconstruct the historical situation of the author and recipients of the text, which was accomplished by reconstructing the true nature of the events that the text describes. More specifically, the phrase higher criticism was applied to a type of biblical study that emerged in German universities in the eighteenth century, when biblical interpretation became a field of academic study relatively free of ecclesiastical control. These studies made it increasingly clear that the Bible, rather than being a single creation of divine origin, was a compilation of a variety of writings by various authors over a period of hundreds of years, thereby explaining the apparent confusion and errors contained therein. The higher criticism became an important force by the 1830s, when it migrated to the English-speaking world.[2]

The most influential of the higher critics was David Friedrich Strauss and his *Das Leben Jesu* (Life of Jesus) (1837). Simply put, Strauss operated from the principle that "before the critical historian could attempt to reconstruct the past, he must understand the presuppositions and conceptual modes of the era he wished to interpret." Applying the historical method to the New Testament, Strauss argued that nineteenth-century scholars did not share the same conceptual understandings as the authors of the Gospels. From that, he challenged not only the supernatural, or divinely revealed, interpretations of the Bible but also the historical accuracy of events related therein. Christianity, like all religions, Strauss concluded, originated in myth, or in "beliefs arising from the experiences and hopes of a community." In Christianity's case, the early Christian community was influenced by the Old Testament, the Jewish messiah, and Greek philosophy. The popular myths had been applied to Jesus, not by the Apostles, but by Jewish believers and had later become a part of the Gospel tradition.[3]

To a large extent, American theologians limited their work on the higher criticism to translating, interpreting, synthesizing, and popularizing the work of European scholars. Nevertheless, their work did make informed debate in the United States possible. The American response began soon after publication of Strauss's *Life of Jesus*, the reviews of which were so numerous that George Ellis, one of those reviewers, found it necessary to explain to his readers that the ideas contained in Strauss's book originated in Germany, not in the United States. Three academic centers responded most directly to the higher criticism – Harvard, Andover Seminary, and Princeton – and each responded differently. Harvard became the center of biblical criticism, beginning with Joseph Buckminster and Andrews Norton, who responded positively and welcomed it as a means by which to promote a critical knowledge of the Bible. At Andover Seminary, which became the center of conservative biblical studies, Moses Stuart and Edward Robinson addressed the higher criticism more cautiously. They taught it to their students, but they continued to insist on the inspiration of the Bible and its place as the final authority in all matters of religious faith and practice. While at Princeton Theological Seminary, Charles Hodge, recently returned from studies in Germany, mounted a countermovement to higher criticism through his journal, *The Biblical Repertory and Princeton Review.* In his influential *Systematic Theology*, Hodge stated that "the Scriptures of the Old and New Testaments are the Word of God, written under the inspiration of the Holy Spirit, and therefore infallible, and of divine authority in all things pertaining to faith and practice, and consequently free from all error, whether of doctrines, fact, or precept." This certainty, he added, was "not confined to moral and religious truths" but included as well "statements of facts, whether scientific, historical, or geographical."[4]

Liberal Protestants tended to fall in line with Norton, who believed that the ultimate goal of the biblical interpreter was to recover the true conceptions in the Bible and apply them to contemporary religion. Washington Gladden, whom we discussed in the previous chapter as an advocate of the Social Gospel, was among that group. In 1891, he published *Who Wrote the Bible: A Book for the People*, which is among the best known of American works on the higher criticism. Gladden wrote: "Many facts about the Bible are now known by intelligent ministers of which their congregations do not hear. An anxious and not unnatural feeling has prevailed that the faith of the people in the Bible would be shaken if the facts were known. The belief that the truth is the safest in the world, and that the things which cannot be shaken will remain after it is all told, has led to the preparation of this volume."[5]

More conservative Christians continued to respond to the higher critics with suspicion, even antagonism. Dwight L. Moody, for example, insisted that what was needed was "men who believe in the Bible from the crown of their heads to the soles of their feet; who believe in the whole of it, the things they understand, and the things they do not understand." But perhaps the most knowledgeable and articulate critic of higher criticism was Andover's Moses Stuart. Well aware that German scholars were in the vanguard of biblical studies, Stuart read widely among the German higher critics. Finding them, by his estimation, to be learned skeptics and labeling them "neologists," a term of disapprobation, Stuart feared that if not countered the day would come when their views would be accepted in America.[6]

The person who, among the early commentators on the higher criticism ended up sounding the loudest alarm among the movement's critics was Theodore Parker, an American Transcendentalist. Parker's first foray into the field came in 1840, with his review of Strauss's *Life of Jesus* in the *Christian Examiner.* Although at that point Parker mostly limited his comments to a review of the book's contents, where he did venture criticism, it was in reference to what he believed were Strauss's "fake principles, extreme conclusions, and extravagances." He argued that Strauss had concluded that the Gospels were not genuine without dealing adequately with the mass of external evidence to the contrary.[7]

Parker's assessment of the higher criticism took a more radical direction in his 1841 sermon, "The Transient and Permanent in Christianity," a title he took from a similarly titled essay by Strauss. While acknowledging the permanent elements of Christianity, Parker took aim at the transient, which included widely held views of the Bible, that he considered idolatrous. "Modern criticism," Parker explained with clear reference to the higher criticism,

> is fast breaking to pieces this idol which men have made out of the scriptures. It has shown that here are the most different works thrown together; that their authors, wise as they sometimes were, pious as we feel often their spirit to have been, had only that inspiration which is common to other men equally pious and wise; that they were by no means infallible, but were mistaken in facts or in reasoning – uttered predictions which time has not fulfilled; men who in some measure partook of the darkness and limited notions of their age, and were not always above its mistakes or its corruptions.

Parker went on to predict that the higher criticism would someday make impossible any adherence to the Bible as an infallible standard of truth, which he noted would be a step forward.[8]

The Civil War, the death of most of those who took seriously the higher criticism prior to the war, and the migration of biblical studies to seminaries rather than universities, where they would receive less rigorous academic attention, brought a lull in activity surrounding the higher criticism in the United States. The ideas central to the higher criticism, however, did not disappear. Indeed, by the end of the century, although divergent responses to higher criticism continued, for most serious biblical scholars there was no returning to earlier methods of biblical criticism. And by the 1920s, advocates of the higher criticism gained the ascendency, if primarily in liberal Protestant seminaries.[9]

Among those most active in the debate concerning the higher criticism after the Civil War were Philip Schaff of the Union Theological Seminary. Schaff's twenty-five volume collection, *A Commentary on the Holy Scriptures* (1865–1880), was the most detailed and in-depth explication of the work of leading German scholars of the higher criticism. In 1871, James Freeman Clark published *Ten Great Religions*, a comparative study that employed much of the methodology and findings of the higher critics. And in 1891 Orello Cone, of the theological school at St. Lawrence University, published *Gospel-Criticism and Historical Christianity*, a highly regarded study on the subject. The importance of this literature, as well as publication in the 1880s of a revised version of the King James Bible, which reflected some of the new scholarship, was that it limited, or at least called into question, the extent to which supernaturalism or divine revelation played in religion or man's understanding of God.[10]

Resulting heresy trials occurred throughout the closing decades of the century. Among Presbyterians alone, between 1883 and 1900, five theologians were brought to trial for heresy for favoring the results of the higher criticism, the best known of which was that of Charles A. Briggs. Briggs studied in Berlin, where he encountered the German critics firsthand. In 1874, he became professor of Hebrew at Union Theological Seminary in New York, leading the seminary to become an important center of Old Testament study in the United States. In 1880, he and Archibald Hodge became coeditors of a new theological journal, the *Presbyterian Review*, which Briggs determined to become a forum for discussion of the higher criticism. The result was a series of articles running from 1881 to 1883 that presented different points of view on the origin and inspiration of Scripture. To this, Briggs added his own book in 1883, *Biblical Study: Its Principles, Methods, and History, Together with a Catalogue of Books of Reference.* In 1890, Briggs was appointed to a new professorship of Biblical theology at Union Theological Seminary. On the occasion of his induction, however, he gave an inaugural address on the higher criticism endorsing the conclusions of a century's work in higher criticism, which resulted in the veto of his appointment by the New York Presbytery and in a trial for heresy. The trial resulted in an acquittal, but the decision was overturned by the Presbyterian General Assembly in 1893. Briggs was suspended from the ministry, but he found a new home in the Episcopal Church. More broadly, however, the war over higher criticism was subsumed by that over Darwinian evolution, which was not nearly as confined to academic or theological circles, but rather engaged the masses.[11]

Darwinian evolution

If higher criticism ignited a fire that threatened to consume revealed religion, or at least belief in a literal understanding of the Bible, Darwinian evolution added fuel to the fire. Charles Darwin, in *On the Origin of Species by Means of Natural Selection* (1859) (see Figure 3.1) and *The Descent of Man* (1870), called into question the argument from design and the special divine creation of man in what would come to be known as Darwinian evolution. Historian Richard Hofstadter has argued that "in some respects the United States during the last three decades of the nineteenth and at the beginning of the twentieth century was the Darwinian country." He pointed to American scientists, who for the most part were quick not only to accept the principle of natural selection but also to make important contributions to evolutionary science, as well as bring Darwin's theories on evolution into the academy – to Harvard, Yale, and the newly established Johns Hopkins.[12]

Hofstadter also pointed to "the enlightened American reading public, which became fascinated with evolutionary speculation . . . [and] gave a handsome reception to philosophies and political theories built in part upon Darwinism or associated with it." He pointed to a ten-year period, beginning in 1860, during which reaction to Darwin went from hostility to skepticism to approval to outright praise in the pages of the leading magazines and newspapers of the day. Edward Youmans saw the need for a popular magazine focused on scientific news and founded *Popular Science Monthly*, in whose pages Darwinism was amply discussed. Youmans, with publisher D. Appleton, organized the International Science Series, a set of books by outstanding science figures of the time including Darwin and those who supported Darwinian evolution in one form or another.[13]

The chief proponents of science and opponents of an orthodox religious view of creation in the United States were John William Draper and Andrew Dixon White. In 1871, John William Draper, English born visiting professor of medicine at New York University, published *The History of Conflict between Religion and Science*, which went through fifty printings and was translated into ten languages. In what bordered on the polemic, Draper reported on a history of conflict between science and religion in an attempt to "liberate us from the tyranny of religion." In 1896, Cornell University President Andrew Dixon White bolstered Draper's work with *A History of the Warfare of Science and Theology in Christendom*. White argued that religion and science were implacably opposed and that whenever science had been used in the interest of religion the result had been "the direst evils both to religion and science."

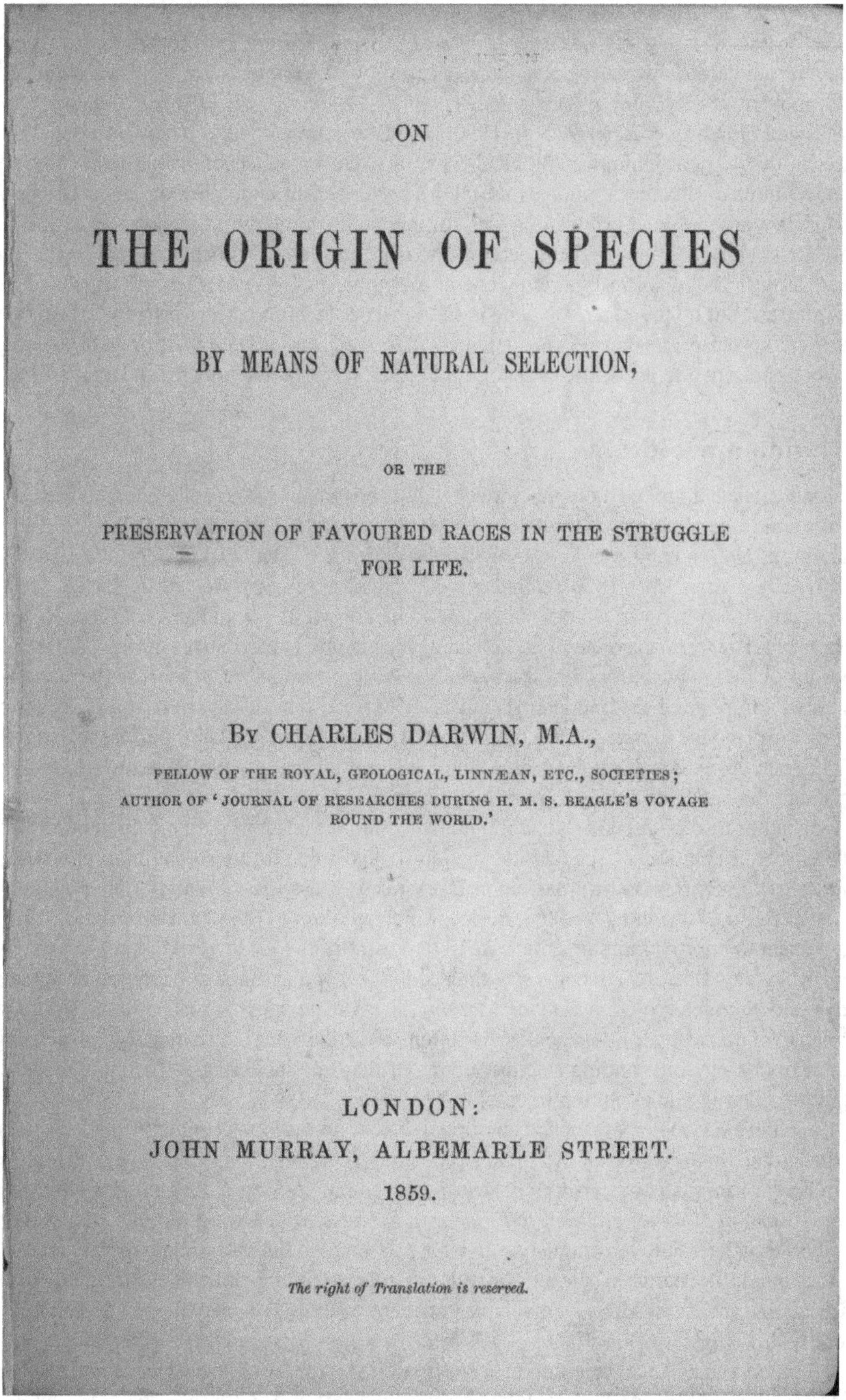

ON

THE ORIGIN OF SPECIES

BY MEANS OF NATURAL SELECTION,

OR THE

PRESERVATION OF FAVOURED RACES IN THE STRUGGLE FOR LIFE.

BY CHARLES DARWIN, M.A.,

FELLOW OF THE ROYAL, GEOLOGICAL, LINNÆAN, ETC., SOCIETIES;
AUTHOR OF 'JOURNAL OF RESEARCHES DURING H. M. S. BEAGLE'S VOYAGE ROUND THE WORLD.'

LONDON:
JOHN MURRAY, ALBEMARLE STREET.
1859.

The right of Translation is reserved.

Figure 3.1 The Origin of Species by Charles Darwin

And where scientific investigation had been left "untrammeled . . . no matter how dangerous to religion some of its stages may have seemed, for the time, it has invariably resulted in the highest good of religion and of science."[14]

The debate over evolution was drawn even before Darwin published *The Origin of Species*. John Herschel, Erasmus Darwin (Charles's grandfather), Jean Baptiste Lamarck, Georges Cuvier, and Charles Lyell paved the way for Darwin. The geological record with its fossil specimens pointing to a wide variety of species, was increasingly clear, forcing intellectuals of the day to consider the possibility that a reading of Genesis and its stories of creation ought not to be literal. Some began to imagine that the "age of rocks" may well be far older than the commonly ascribed 6,000 years, and that some form of evolution and diversification of species was possible, if only the means for such a process could be found. There were those who agreed with Lamarck that evolution followed the inheritance of acquired characteristics. Others preferred a more teleological evolutionary line of development established by God or divine creation. What Darwin and Alfred Russel Wallace (who conceived of the theory nearly simultaneously) added to the conversation were the means by which evolution occurred: random mutation and natural selection. Not only did this call into question the belief in fixed species, but it also threatened the widely held belief that man was the special creation of God. "If Darwinism was true," they would argue, "the wall between the animal kingdom and the human realm broke down altogether. . . . If man evolved through natural selection, if survival and adaptation, variation and struggle governed the course of development, it was hard to believe that an all-wise and all-beneficent Creator had presided over a single act of creation." Instead, the very idea "seemed to make life a mere variant of matter without mystery or spiritual meaning."[15]

Nearly forty years after its publication, elaborating on his thesis of the warfare between science and religion, Andrew Dickson White wrote that *The Origin of Species* "had come into the theological world like a plough into an ant hill. Everywhere those thus rudely awakened from their old comfort and repose had swarmed forth angry and confused."[16] Princeton theologian Charles Hodge summarized the position taken by those who opposed Darwinian evolution. He acknowledged that in order to account for the existence of matter and life, Darwin admitted of a creator, but Darwin said nothing of the nature of the creator and of the creator's relation to the world. Instead, he provided a theory as to the diversity of life on earth that was based on heredity, variation, overproduction, and natural selection. And therein lay the rub for Hodge. Natural selection, he reasoned, is selection made by natural laws "working without intention and design," or more specifically, without any "selection originally intended by a power higher than nature; or which is carried out by such power." Natural selection, Hodge argued, denied that it was a process originally designed or guided by intelligence, such as the activity that foresees an end and consciously selects and controls the means of its accomplishment.

> The conclusion of the whole matter is, that the denial of design in nature is virtually the denial of God. Mr. Darwin's theory is virtually atheistical; his theory, not he himself. He believes in a Creator. But when that Creator, millions on millions of ages ago, did something – called matter and a living germ into existence – and then abandoned the universe to itself to be controlled by chance and necessity, without any purpose on his part as to the result, or any intervention or guidance, then He is virtually consigned, as far as we are concerned to nonexistence. . . . We have then arrived at the answer to our question, What is Darwinism? It is Atheism.[17]

Other religious leaders, however, continued to embrace evolution as a revelation that would result in religious teachings being placed on a "firmer and broader foundation." The collapse of uncompromising opposition to evolution was foreshadowed as early as 1871, when James McCosh, the President of Princeton University, who had previously opposed Darwinian evolution, acknowledged his acceptance of the theory including natural selection, which he cautiously admitted was at least "a portion of the truth." In his *Christianity and Positivism* (1871), McCosh wrote that although

> Darwinism cannot be regarded as settled, I am inclined to think that the theory contains a large body of important truths which we see illustrated in every department of organic nature. . . . It does not contain the whole truth, and . . . it overlooks more than it perceives," he insisted, but "this principle [natural selection] is exhibited in nature working to the advancement of plants and animals from age to age."[18]

In *Evolution and Religion* (1886), the Reverend Henry Ward Beecher argued that "at first sight" the doctrine of evolution "seems to destroy the theory of intelligent design in creation, and in its earlier states left those who investigated it very doubtful whether there was anything in creation but matter, or whether there was a knowable God. So sprang up the agnostic school, which includes in it some of the noblest spirits of our day." Beecher argued, however, that the theory of evolution was restoring "the question of design in creation . . . in a larger and grander way, which only places the fact upon a wider space, and makes the outcome more wonderful." He found no conflict between "special creation, and the adaptation in consequence of it." The "old view" was that God created the earth and everything on the earth as it exists. "When the idea of the lily dawned on him, he smiled and said: 'I will make it'; and he made it to be just as beautiful as it is."[19]

Evolution, Beecher continued, "teaches that God created through the mediation of natural laws" – laws that God created – that led his creation through a process of slow growth, and not an instantaneous process. Over an immeasurable period of time, plants and animals alike were affected by their surrounding circumstances and either adapted to their environment and survived or did not adapt and perished. God designed "this mighty machine," Beecher insisted, "created matter, gave it its laws, and impressed upon it that tendency which has brought forth the almost infinite results on the globe and wrought them into a perfect system." In sum, Beecher wrote, what the doctrine of evolution accomplished, including the theory of natural selection, was "the deciphering of God's thought as revealed in the structure of the world." As such, it "lifted [divine design] to a higher place and made it more sublime than it ever was contemplated to be under the old reasoning."[20]

Lay scientists were similarly divided. Some, like Louis Agassiz, among the outstanding American naturalists, refused to accept Darwinism or any other form of evolution and continually posed scientific arguments against it. Agassiz charged Darwin with posing "a crude and insolent challenge to the eternal verities," which was, as well, "objectionable as science and abominable for its religious blasphemies." Others scientists believed that Darwin's theory was substantially correct and even that it undermined belief in God, or at least any certainty to his existence, or if God existed, God's direct role in creation. The British scientist Thomas Huxley – who coined the term *agnostic* in 1869 – was among the most outspoken of this group on both sides of the Atlantic. Huxley was notorious for his defense of Darwin, earning him the title "Darwin's bulldog." But his defense of Darwin was not unequivocal, especially as it pertained to the idea of natural selection as the means by which evolution occurred, which he was slow to accept. Thus, he identified himself as an agnostic, which was based on "a pretty strong conviction that the problem of God's existence was insoluble."[21]

Harvard's Asa Gray, one of the leading botanists of his day, and with whom Darwin corresponded before publication of his *The Origin of Species*, was among the earliest of the leading scientists in the United States to provide a reasoned defense of the position of reconciliation. He allowed that the alternative to belief in God was unacceptable, but he also insisted, in an attempt to counter any such sentiments, that Darwin was explicitly theistic and that natural selection did not challenge the argument from design. To those who insisted that the origin of species "be left in the realm of the supernatural," he replied that in doing so, they would arbitrarily limit the field of science without enlarging that of religion. Gray made clear what to him were the most cogent scientific objections to natural selection, but he also praised the theory for its studied scientific contribution to our understanding of the origin of species. He attacked Agassiz's theory of species as "theistic to excess" and praised Darwin's as an antidote. Natural selection, he continued, was not antagonistic to the theory of design in nature; rather, it could be considered one of the possible theories of the workings of God's plan.[22]

By the 1880s, religion was being forced to share its traditional authority with science, and American thought had been greatly secularized. Evolution had made its way into the churches themselves, and there remained few major figures in Protestant theology who still disputed it. For most, however, their faith remained unshaken, preferring to take the position that there was just not enough evidence to cause them to abandon their belief in some form of divinely guided creation. Once again, Thomas Huxley is a good example. On the one hand, Huxley would compare theologians to "strangled snakes" beside the cradle of Hercules, "crushed if not annihilated." On the other hand, he would allow that it was conceivable that evolution would yet prove that nature operated according to a divinely inspired purpose, which would be ascertained through science thereby providing a better basis upon which to rebuild religious belief for the future.[23]

"The golden age of agnosticism in America"

As historian James Turner has argued, by the second half of the nineteenth century due in large part to the challenges of science and the higher criticism, "agnosticism emerged as a self-sustaining phenomenon. Disbelief in God was, for the first time, plausible enough to grow beyond a rare eccentricity to stake out a sizable permanent niche in American culture." Addressed for the first time, at least publicly and perhaps mostly in intellectual circles, were the two key questions that would be central to consideration of doubt or unbelief, thereafter, not only whether belief in God was possible, in light of recent scientific advances, but also whether it was necessary.[24]

In the mid-nineteenth century, American skeptics, not just agnostics, organized and advanced their cause through periodicals such as the *Investigator* and the *Index* and organizations such as the Free Religious Association and the Ethical Culture Federation. The Free Religious Association (FRA) was formed by Octavius Brooks Frothingham, David Atwood Wasson, and William J. Potter to be a "spiritual anti-slavery society" to "emancipate religion from the dogmatic traditions it had been previously bound to." Although largely comprised of Unitarians, and although its membership consisted of theists and non-theists alike, the FRA was opposed to organized religion and to any supernaturalism in an attempt to affirm the supremacy of individual conscience and individual reason. Its members substituted "a divine faith in human nature for a faith in Christ." And although many rejected the divinity of Christ, most did not reject Jesus's example. Similarly, they did not shun the Bible but rather opposed its use as the revealed word of God. The FRA carried a message of the perfectibility of humanity, democratic faith in the worth of each individual, the importance of natural rights, and the affirmation of the efficacy of reason. The first public assembly was held in 1867 with an audience of Quakers, liberal Jews, radical Unitarians, Universalists, agnostics, spiritualists, and scientific theists. The first person to join the association at the original meeting was Ralph Waldo Emerson.[25]

Whereas the FRA was largely Unitarian, Ethical Culture was founded by Felix Adler, a German Jewish immigrant educated at the University of Heidelberg and a member of the FRA. It was at Heidelberg that Adler developed his vision for an ethical movement. When he returned from Germany in 1873, he shared his vision in a sermon with his father's congregation, the Reform Jewish Temple Emanuel in New York City, where he was expected to succeed his father as rabbi. Adler titled his sermon, "The Judaism of the Future": "The question for us to answer now," Adler told the congregation,

> is not . . . this reform or that reform . . . [but] is religion about to perish. . . . Religion not confined to church or synagogue alone shall go forth into the market place . . . laying its greatest stress not on the believing but in the acting out. A religion such as Judaism ever claimed to be, not of the creed but of the deed. . . . We discard the narrow spirit of exclusion and loudly proclaim that Judaism was not given to the Jews alone but that its destiny is to embrace in one great moral state the whole family of men.[26]

The congregation did not embrace Adler's vision, and he was never offered the position.

Adler took up a professorship at Cornell University from 1873 to 1875, but as the only Jew on the faculty, as well as a nascent ethical culturalist, he was challenged in certain circles as being an atheist and a threat to the Christian faith of the students. Although defended by Cornell's president Andrew Dixon White, he was not reappointed. Adler returned to New York, where in 1876 he gave a follow up sermon on "the plan of a new organization," wherein he concluded: "Diversity in the creed, unanimity in the deed. . . . This is the common ground where we may all grasp hands . . . united in mankind's common cause." It is to this sermon that the Ethical Culture movement points as its starting point.[27]

The New York Society for Ethical Culture was founded in 1877, but by 1886, similar societies had sprouted up in Philadelphia, Chicago, and St. Louis. In 1878, Adler was elected president of the Free Religious Association, but he found the group of prominent but often fiercely independent figures impossible to organize and rally behind his call for activism and resigned to focus on the Ethical Culture movement. In 1890, he founded the *International Journal of Ethics*, and in 1902, he assumed the position of professor of political and social ethics at Columbia University. He remained on the faculty at Columbia until his death, but among his other involvements were his appointment in 1908 as Theodore Roosevelt Professor at the University of Berlin. He also was active in the International Ethical Union, through which he developed the International Moral Education Congress, which began in 1908.[28]

Perhaps the best-known proponent of freethought in nineteenth-century America was the Great Agnostic, the Pagan Prophet, or the infidel personified, Robert Green Ingersoll. (see Figure 3.2) Ingersoll has also been referred to as the John the Baptist of American agnosticism and as the person without whom "the golden age of American freethought is as difficult to imagine as abolitionism without Garrison or the first wave of feminism without Stanton."[29]

Figure 3.2 Robert Green Ingersoll, The Great Agnostic

Source: Niday Picture Library/Alamy Stock Photo

Ironically, Ingersoll the skeptic was born in 1833 in Dresden, New York, to "an impassioned man of God, a revivalist whose converts were legion," but whose ardent abolitionism caused the family to move constantly from New York to Ohio, Illinois, Wisconsin, and elsewhere. It was at his father's knee and in his study that Robert was educated, except for a couple of brief stints in grammar schools and a religious academy at various stops on his minister father's itinerancy. When that phase of his education ended and he took odd jobs to support his family, he and his brother read the law and prepared for admission to the bar, whereupon in 1858 they set up business in Peoria, Illinois. The national financial collapse of 1857 notwithstanding the Ingersoll brothers did well and soon became involved in politics.[30]

After serving in the Union army during the Civil War, Robert Ingersoll returned to Peoria where he was honored for his service in the war, commonly referred to as Colonel Ingersoll, and resumed his legal career and involvement in politics, gradually moving away from the Democratic Party to support pro-Union and war Republicans running for office. In 1867, Illinois Governor Richard Oglesby appointed Ingersoll Illinois State Attorney General, and in the following year, he ran for governor of Illinois. He lost and never ran again for office, but he continued to gain national recognition for his oratory in support of the likes of Ulysses Grant and James G. Blaine in their campaigns for the presidency.[31]

Ingersoll was active outside of the political arena as well. He joined the National Liberal League (NLL), which was dedicated to the separation of church and state, the abolition of Sunday laws, civil recognition of religious holy days, and prayer and Bible reading in public schools. He also promoted universal education, women's suffrage, and repeal of the Comstock (censorship) laws. In 1877, Ingersoll was elected vice president of the NLL and in 1884 president of the American Secular Union (ASU), which was formed after the demise of the NLL. The ASU was more focused on the separation of church and state, including taxation of church property, elimination of chaplains in the military, and the banning of religious teaching in the public schools.[32]

Ingersoll became widely known as a "controversial, iconoclastic gadfly," but his reputation rested mostly on his spell-binding oratory on positions that most considered antireligious or anticlerical. It was a challenging time for skeptics, in that it was a period of labor unrest and fear of anarchism, often attributed to what many believed were atheistic immigrants, who did not share in America's supposed divine mission. Most biographers agree that Ingersoll's public agnosticism ultimately prevented his successfully running for, or being appointed to, political offices. But it is also the case that his public audiences were as large as any of the celebrated preachers of the day, and seldom antagonistic.[33]

Ingersoll delivered his first public speech in which he challenged religion in Peoria on May 14, 1866. In "Progress," he argued that throughout history the church had attempted to enslave the mind of man. As long as Ingersoll referenced the history of the Catholic Church in Europe, his audience found little with which to quarrel, but when he addressed his own, post-Reformation times, his criticism became more encompassing and raised some concern. But to that point, given his prominence in the community, his speech elicited little alarm. Moreover, although critical of organized religion, his was not an entirely negative or pessimistic message, as he believed in the progress of civilization. The church had slowed progress and almost succeeded in stopping it altogether, but ultimately it had failed. Human beings would eventually outgrow their primitive fantasies. "Every new religion has a little less superstition than the old," he argued, "so that the religion of science is but a question of time."[34]

On July 4, 1869, Ingersoll delivered an address in Sulphur Spring, Illinois. The event fell on a Sunday, which prompted some local religious leaders to denounce any open celebration on the Lord's Day. Ingersoll picked up on that criticism and made as the subject of his speech the struggle of early Americans for religious liberty. Still being a bit cautious, Ingersoll allowed that "every man on earth, under the Creator, has every right any other man can have" to worship as he pleases. Further, he offered that "our God is one of infinite mercy and tenderness," that "there are grand men in the church," and that the churches were "growing stronger every day." But he continued by offering signs of the wit, at time caustic, that won over those crowds that turned out to hear him. In reference to those who opposed Sunday activity of that kind, he recalled his childhood with his ministerial father: "I was educated on a different plan. I was not allowed to chew gum on Sunday. . . . If I was caught chewing gum, it was only another evidence of the total depravity of the human heart." His adult views, he continued, were decidedly more liberal.

> Come. Wear your hair as you please. I say, liberty to all. If I want to go to church, I'll go. If I want to hear a Calvinist preach, I will go – but I don't think I'll go this year. Let everybody do what he wants to do. It won't be long until the joss house [an old name for Chinese traditional temples] will be built by the side of the churches.[35]

From that point on, Ingersoll followed a busy schedule of public addresses. The following September Ingersoll was asked to speak on the centennial anniversary of the birth of the German naturalist, Alexander Friedrich Heinrich von Humboldt. Ingersoll used this occasion to speak about how Humboldt's scientific discoveries had demonstrated "the sublimest of truths – 'The Universe is Governed by Law!'" Further, the fact that "the universe is governed by law" was not proof of God's existence, as some liberal ministers had concluded, but "the death-knell of superstition." One of Humboldt's greatest accomplishments, Ingersoll continued, was "to do away with that splendid delusion called special providence." "All religions are inconsistent with mental freedom," he charged, its story of creation itself being founded on the ignorance and credulity that religion fosters." He delivered the same speech two weeks later in Cincinnati, at which time the Cincinnati *Times* reported that "Robinson's Opera House was crowded: "The renowned lecturer Col. R. G. Ingersoll . . . was escorted to the stage by a number of prominent citizens and introduced to the audience by the Mayor." In his introduction, the Mayor described Ingersoll as: "A brilliant, genial gentleman; a man of brains, a man greatly respected and admitted by all who know him, and greatly detested by many of those who do not agree with him in opinion." The newspaper reported that Ingersoll's remarks were frequently interrupted by "applause and cheers." As his biographer, Orvin Larson, has written, with his Humboldt speech, "the die was cast. . . . He was done temporizing. 'Humboldt' crystallized his convictions. . . . The infidel overcame the office seeker."[36]

Ingersoll gave pubic speeches on Thomas Paine, "the gods," and "heretics and Heresies," among other topics. But he delivered "Why Am I an Agnostic?" repeatedly during the 1870s and 1880s and published it in 1896. It is considered the clearest expression of Ingersoll's philosophy. His thesis was that organized religion, as represented by its leading theologians, had failed to provide a reasonable explanation of natural phenomena, thereby opening the door to agnosticism as a valid response. In commenting on the question of divine design of the universe, Ingersoll argued that the theist:

> sees with perfect clearness that matter could not create itself, and therefore he imagines a creator of matter. He is perfectly satisfied that there is design in the world, and that, consequently, there must have been a designer. It does not occur to him as necessary to account for the existence of an infinite personality. He is perfectly certain that there can be no design without a designer, and he is equally certain that there can be a designer who was not designed. . . . He takes it for granted that matter was created and that its creator was not.

As to the supposed divine inspiration of the Bible, Ingersoll asked how we could determine that the writers of the Bible were inspired but that Darwin and other secular writers – whose work he admitted he preferred – were not.[37]

That Ingersoll had reached the peak of his popularity by the early 1880s is suggested by his speech to some 6,000 people in Brooklyn, New York, on October 30, 1880. To begin, it should be noted that, in that year, Ingersoll was touring with one of his most provocative attacks not only on religion generally, but also on several of the nations' most influential denominations. In "What Must We Do to be Saved?" he concentrated on the New Testament and attacked not only Catholicism, a common and easy target at the time, but also Episcopalianism, Methodism, and Presbyterian. That he did not include the Baptists and others, he explained, was merely a matter of time and priority, although he made clear they were not above blame either. In brief, reflecting his study of the higher criticism, Ingersoll allowed that Matthew, Mark, and Luke presented a fundamentally decent, humane, and reasonable God. Where they did not, he ventured, was likely the result of later "interpolations." Where Christianity began to go astray, he charged, was with John, which was written much later and "by the church." In particular, Ingersoll attacked John's insistence that salvation depends on belief in Jesus Christ and following his teachings, as John reported them:

> Read Matthew, Mark, and Luke, and then read John, and you will agree with me that the first three gospels teach that if we are kind and forgiving to our fellows, God will be kind and forgiving to us. In John we are told that the only way to get to heaven is to believe something that we know is not so.[38]

Ingersoll was introduced for his speech in Brooklyn, New York, by perhaps the most famous minister in America, Henry Ward Beecher. "I am not accustomed to preside at meetings like this," Beecher began,

> only the exigency of the times could induce me to do it. . . . I stand not as a minister, but as a man among men, pleading the cause of fellowship and equal rights. . . . The gentleman who will speak tonight is in no conventicle or church. . . . and I take the liberty of saying that I respect him as the man that for a full score and more of years has worked . . . for the cause of human rights. I consider it an honor to extend to him, as I do now, the warm, earnest, right hand of fellowship.

According to press reports, Beecher's introduction was greeted with "tumultuous cheering and applause." Following Ingersoll's remarks, a reporter for the *New York Herald* questioned Beecher as to his opinion of the famous infidel. Beecher responded that he had never seen Ingersoll before that night, but that he regarded him "as one of the greatest men of this age. I am an ordained clergyman and believe in revealed religion. I am, therefore, bound to regard all persons who do not believe in revealed religion as in error." But, he continued, "I admire Ingersoll because he is not afraid to speak what he honestly thinks."[39]

To cite one last example of Ingersoll's criticism of Christianity, that would be his most popular and controversial public pronouncement on topics of broader interest, namely his "A Christmas Sermon," which appeared in the New York *Evening Telegram* on December 19, 1891. In the article, Ingersoll recalled that Christmas grew out of a pagan celebration of the winter solstice, and that its Christian overlay as the date upon which Christ was born was fabricated. Nevertheless, he added, he believed in Christmas, because it was set aside for joy and merriment. Christianity was good when it did that – when it promoted love and kindness. But, he continued, Christmas also symbolized the result of the triumph of Christianity over pagan belief, which not only failed to bring "tidings of great joy" but rather "filled the future with fear and flame, and made God the keeper of an eternal penitentiary, destined to be the home of nearly all the sons of men." Leaders of the religious community were outraged and called for a boycott of the newspaper. The newspaper welcomed the controversy. It explained that it had invited Ingersoll to submit the piece because, given the writer's prominence, it was newsworthy, and it invited submissions in response, which it published. Letters poured in on both sides of the issue, either praising Ingersoll and freedom of the press, or denouncing the article as blasphemous and having been sent into Christian homes to "greet the eyes of innocent children and pure women." The controversy led to the formation of the Society of Human Progress by Ingersoll and other freethinkers to further the freedom of speech and press.[40]

To conclude, we might ask: Did Ingersoll, with all his popularity, believe he was making a difference, that changes of substance would result from his oratory. As Martin Mary has pointed out, Ingersoll was of two minds on that subject. On the one hand, he predicted that infidelity would triumph, that "ten times as many infidels [exist] today as there were ten years ago." Christianity was dying of a "softening of the brain and ossification of the heart." On the other hand, he was well aware of the virulent nature of public sentiment in opposition to that which was branded infidelity. Reflecting on history and examples such as Thomas Paine, but also pointing to examples of his own day, Ingersoll acknowledged that there was no tolerance of freethought in America. The result, he speculated, was a reluctance on the part of freethinkers to acknowledge their unbelief and face public odium of being branded enemies of religion. The result, he admitted, was an uphill battle for freethought.[41]

Social Darwinism

Social Darwinism was an offshoot of evolution or the application of Charles Darwin's theory on social thinking. It made its appearance in the nineteenth century but was most dramatically expressed during the 1930s and 1940s. The name is used in reference to various social theories, which grew out of different interpretations and applications of the Darwinian concepts of natural selection, struggle for existence, and survival of the fittest. The degree to which those theories actually followed from Darwin's theory is subject to considerable debate. Darwin himself distanced himself from any applications of his idea of natural selection wherein humans should in any way advance the survival of the fittest or remain passive in the face of it. While acknowledging the survival of the fittest in nature, he insisted that in reference to the less fit among humans, "we could not check our sympathy, even at the urging of hard reason, without deterioration in the noblest part of our nature." He argued that it was highly probable that

> any animal whatever endowed with well-marked social instincts, the parental and filial affections being here included, would inevitably acquire a moral sense or conscience, as soon as its intellectual powers had become as well, or nearly as well, developed as in man. For firstly, the social instincts lead an animal to take pleasure in the society of its fellows, to feel a certain amount of sympathy with them, and to perform various services for them.[42]

The principal spokesmen for Social Darwinism in the nineteenth century were Herbert Spencer in England and William Graham Sumner, John Fiske, and Edward Youmans in the United States. Hebert Spencer made the most ambitious attempt to systematize the implications of evolution in fields other than biology, and he was particularly influential among liberal American Christian clergymen. In a letter to Herbert Spencer in 1886, for example, Henry Ward Beecher wrote: "The peculiar condition of American society has made your writings far more fruitful and quickening here than in Europe." By way of explanation, historian Richard Hofstadter wrote that Spencer's philosophy was well suited to the American scene at the end of the nineteenth century.

> It was a reassuring theory of progress based upon biology and physics. It was large enough to be all things to all men. . . . It offered a comprehensive world-view, uniting under one generalization everything in nature from protozoa to politics. Satisfying the desire of "advanced thinkers" for a world-system to replace the shattered Mosaic cosmogony, while at the same time assuring his reading public that whatever science might learn about the world the true sphere of religion – "worship of the Unknowable" – was by its very nature inviolable.[43]

Spencer was born into a lower-middle-class, non-conformist English family, from which he drew his disdain for state power. He was trained as a civil engineer, from which he developed an intense interest in science at a time when new scientific developments were widespread. And in his early years, he was on the staff of the *Economist*, a free-trade magazine that harbored some philosophically anarchist ideas. All of these various fields of knowledge and interest fed his Social Darwinism, his major work, *Synthetic Philosophy*, having been described as "an amalgam of the non-conformism of his family and the scientific learning so prominent in his intellectual environment." Among the dominant influences on the thinking that went into his Social Darwinism were Lyell's *Principles of Geology*, Lamarck's theory of evolutionary development, Malthus's population and resources prognosis, and Charles Darwin.[44]

In his first work, *Social Statics: The Conditions Essential to Human Happiness Specified*, published in 1851, Spencer attempted to strengthen *laissez-faire* with the imperatives of biology. He called for a return to natural rights and the right of every man to do as he pleased, subject only to the condition that he not infringe on the equal rights of others. The role of the state was to ensure that such freedom was not curbed. Spencer made clear even at this early date in the evolution of his thought, he believed that human adaption to the conditions of life, if allowed to happen, over the course of time human perfection was inevitable:

> The ultimate development of the ideal man is logically certain – as certain as any conclusion in which we place the most implicit faith. . . . Progress, therefore, is not an accident, but a necessity. Instead of civilization being artificial, it is a part of nature; all of a piece with the development of the embryo or the unfolding of a flower.[45]

Although not commonly recalled, Spencer did take some contradictory positions, including speaking out against the injustice of private land ownership and the rights of women and children. He was also a pacifist and an internationalist. Moreover, over time, his ardent opposition to state aid to the poor and unfit dissipated a bit, but it never entirely disappeared. State aid to the poor, he insisted, only impeded the natural growth of society. "The whole effort of nature is to get rid of such [the unfit], to clear the world of them, and make room for better." And he insisted that as nature was as insistent upon the fitness of mental character as upon physical character, "radical defects are as much causes of death in the one case as in the other." "If they are sufficiently complete [physically and mentally] to live, they do live, and it is well they should live. If they are not sufficiently complete to live they die, and it is best they should die." Accused of brutality in his application of biological concepts to social principles, Spencer insisted that he was not opposed to voluntary private charity to the unfit, since it had an elevating effect on the character of the donors and hastened the development of altruism, which he also believed would happen through the social evolutionary process. What he opposed was compulsory poor laws and other state measures that would interfere in the "natural order of things." Spencer further developed these ideas in his major works, *Progress: Its Law and Cause* (1857), *First Principles* (1860), and *Synthetic Philosophy* (1864).[46]

By the 1880s, Social Darwinism attracted considerable attention in the United States. As previously noted, Social Darwinism arrived in the United States at an opportune moment, when a politically conservative mood prevailed, resisting any "hasty and ill-considered reforms" or challenges to the status quo. Conservatives seized on Spenser's ideas that struggle for existence and survival of the fittest, when applied to humans and society suggested that nature would provide that the best competitors in a competitive situation would win, and that this process would lead to continuing improvement. Such reasoning provided a positive message for those participating in an increasingly challenging urban, industrialized world of disparate income and wealth. It implied that, while the hardships for the masses were inherent to nature's way, the free and unfettered process of Darwinian evolution meant progress.[47]

Proponents of Spencer's Social Darwinism in America included industrialists James J. Hill and John D. Rockefeller, but the most prominent of his disciples was Andrew Carnegie. In his autobiography, Carnegie explained how troubled he had been over the collapse of Christian theology, until he read Darwin and Spencer:

> I remember that light came as in a flood and all was clear. Not only had I got rid of theology and the supernatural, but I had found the truth of evolution. 'All is well since all grows better,' became my motto, my true source of comfort. Man was not created with an instinct for his own degradation, but from the lower he had risen to the higher forms. Now is there any conceivable end to his march to perfection.

In an article in the *North American Review*, Carnegie emphasized the biological foundations of the law of competition. "However much we may recoil from the seeming harshness of this law," he wrote, "It is here; we cannot evade it; no substitutes for it have been found; and while the law may sometimes be hard for the individual, it is best for the race, because it insures the survival of the fittest."[48]

As previously noted, among those most attracted to the idea of Social Darwinism and that sought to counter its critics in the United States were John Fiske, Edward Youmans, and William Graham Sumner. Each approached Social Darwinism through Hebert Spencer. Fiske, for example, a popular lecturer by the 1870s, focused on the philosophical and religious strains of Spencerianism. Born into a New England orthodox Congregational family, Fiske's personal journey took him from his conservative roots through the most liberal Christianity of his day, radical Unitarianism, but religion remained his primary concern. His first major work on Spencer's work was his *Outlines of Cosmic Philosophy* (1874), wherein he sought to calm any concerns about Spencer's religious ideas, and by implication about his own. The result was a philosophy that was Spencerian but also distinctly theistic, or as some put it, "cosmic theism." Fiske believed that human knowledge was limited and that there were certain "inconceivable notions" that underlie our experience of phenomena that we had to accept. That included our knowledge of the nature of existence itself, which for most remained the province of religion. Moreover, unlike Spencer, who became an agnostic and repudiated conventional religion, Fiske remained a theist and refrained from any attacks on existing churches.[49]

Edward Youmans did not make many significant intellectual contributions to Spencerian, or more broadly speaking, Social Darwinian thought in America. Rather, he focused on the applications of the latest scientific research and social thought. His greatest success, however, came with the appearance of *Popular Science Monthly*. Youmans started the magazine in 1872 out of frustration over the reluctance of journals such as *Atlantic Monthly, Harper's*, and the *Nation* to publish Spencer's work, or for that matter, anything proving controversial in the new science. Youmans included a stream of articles by and about Herbert Spencer, making it the source of more information on Spencer than any other publication. In those articles, Youmans not only included Spencer's words but also made clear his support for Spencer's social thought. As Youmans wrote in his Preface to *First Principles* by Herbert Spencer in 1865: "[If] we are not mistaken, it is [in America] that Mr. Spencer is to find his largest and fittest audience . . . [His writings] betray a profound sympathy with the best spirit of our institutions, and that noble aspiration for the welfare and improvement of society which can hardly fail to commend them to the more liberal and enlightened portions of the American public."[50]

By most accounts William Graham Sumner was "the most vigorous and influential" American defender of Social Darwinism during the closing decades of the nineteenth century, perhaps best introduced by the following words: "Let it be understood that we cannot go outside of this alternative: liberty, inequality, survival of the fittest; not-liberty, equality, survival of the unfittest. The latter carries society downwards and favors all its worst members."[51]

Born in Paterson, New Jersey, in 1840 to a family headed by an English laborer immigrant, Sumner entered Yale in 1859 to study theology. Following further studies at Geneva, Göttingen, and Oxford, where he was attracted to new developments in science and to the higher criticism, Sumner became a tutor at Yale where he stayed for the entirety of his remaining life except for brief stints as editor of a religious newspaper and rector of the Episcopal Church in Morristown, New Jersey. In 1872, he became Yale Professor of Political Science and Social Science, and during the remainder of that decade into the early 1890s, Sumner became widely known for his holy war against reformism, protectionism, socialism, and government intervention not only from his teaching post but even more effectively through publications such as *What Social Classes Owe to Each Other* (1883), "The Forgotten Man" (1883), and "The Absurd Efforts to Make the World Over" (1894).[52]

The financial crash of 1873 appears to have been a critical moment for Sumner, as he attributed the crash to the failure to apply science and the laws of nature to government management of the economy, pointing to untrained and incompetent legislators who arbitrarily passed legislation detrimental to the economy.[53] In 1879, he made clear his adoption of Spencer's application of the lessons of the animal world and Darwin's concept of survival of the fittest to society. In a lecture given in that year, Sumner took on those who would provide artificial means to care for the weak or the unfit. Such individuals, he said:

seem to be terrified that distress and misery still remain on earth and promise to remain as long as the vices of human nature remain. Many of them are frightened at liberty, especially under the form of competition. . . . They think it bears harshly on the weak. They do not perceive that here 'the strong' and 'the weak' are terms which admit of no definition unless they are made equivalent to the industrious and the idle, the frugal and the extravagant. They do not perceive, furthermore, that if we do not like the survival of the fittest, we have only one possible alternative, and that is the survival of the unfittest. The former is the law of civilization; the latter is the law of anti-civilization.[54]

Elsewhere, in his essays published in the *Nation* during the 1880s he was even more direct, even acerbic. "Poverty belongs to the struggle for existence," he insisted, "and we are all born into that struggle." And in that struggle there were but two alternatives, "The law of the survival for existence was not made by man. We can only, by interfering with it, produce the survival of the unfittest" – whom he on at least one occasion identified as "idiots, insane persons, cripples, etc." He admitted that society had to support such people, but if society attempted to support them equally, the "capital" it had accumulated over time would be reduced and its usefulness in improving society similarly lessened. He referred to Upton Sinclair and his fellow socialists as "puny meddlers, social quacks, who would try to break into the age-old process of societal growth at an arbitrary point and remake it in accordance with petty desires." So what hope did he hold out? "Let every man be sober, industrious, prudent, and wise, and bring up his children to be so likewise, and poverty will be abolished in a few generations."[55]

Sumner realized that his perspective on social evolution contradicted the traditional American ideology of equality and natural rights, as expressed in founding documents such as the Declaration of Independence and expounded upon repeatedly thereafter. But, he argued, from the perspective of evolutionary science, neither equality nor natural rights exist: "There can be no rights against nature except to get out of her whatever we can, which is only the fact of the struggle for existence stated over again." What were assumed to be natural rights, he countered, were simply "rules of the game of social competition which are current now and here" and that would cease to exist or even be necessary in time as society progressed to higher stages of existence.[56]

Further, Sumner elaborated, the idea of democracy, which most Americans held sacred, was transient, as it was based on the illusions of equality and natural rights. "Democracy itself, the pet superstition of the age," he wrote, "is only a phase of the all-compelling movement. If you have abundance of land and few men to share it, the men will all be equal." Sumner had to quarrel with democracy in this instance, where it provided for advancement based on merit it was "socially progressive and profitable." Where it was believed to be based on equality of acquisition, when in time abundance of land and an increased number of men occurred – reflecting Malthus in this case – he found democracy unintelligible and impractical. "Industry may be republican; it can never be democratic so long as men differ in productive power and in industrial virtue."[57]

At least for a time, the ideas of competition, natural selection and survival of the fittest not only provided cover for the nation's millionaires, and they were hailed as representing the best path and means – based on the leading science of the day – to the improvement, even perfection, of society itself. Beginning in the 1890s, however, exacerbated by the labor violence, agrarian protest, and rising urban poverty, the middle class began to repudiate "the wolfish struggle for existence," as one contributor to the *Arena* put it. In the face of an even more extreme position prompted by neo-Darwinists from abroad, they began "to shrink from the principle [Social Darwinism] had glorified, turned in flight from the hideous image of rampant competitive brutality, and repudiated the once heroic entrepreneur as a despoiler of the nation's wealth and morals and a monopolist of its opportunities." The result was greater acceptance of the Social Gospel, and the rise of the holiness, pentecostal, and fundamentalist movements, which turned away from and in some cases against what science, the higher criticism, and liberal Christianity had wrought.[58]

The holiness and pentecostal response

Any reconciliation among scientific and religious leaders at the close of the nineteenth century was not necessarily reflected among the rank and file of American Christians, most of whom remained true to their traditional, even literal, reading of Genesis and the idea of special, or divine, creation. Nevertheless, the increased visibility of Darwinism, the higher criticism, and skepticism sparked a reaction on the part of many Christians. There was the Spiritualist movement. It began in the late 1840s in Hydesville, New York, with a series of mysterious rappings that some interpreted as communications from the deceased and within a couple of decades attracted widespread attention. Many dismissed – and continue to dismiss – the phenomenon as just a bunch of misguided or fraudulent mediums who claimed to be able to communicate with the spirits of the dead on behalf of those who had lost love ones – including Abraham and Mary Todd Lincoln. Some historians, however, without necessarily approving of the practice, have found Spiritualism to be yet another reform movement dominated by women mediums, who also became advocates of women's rights. Ann Braude, for one, has argued that Spiritualism was attractive to women activists, who felt oppressed by the gender roles of traditional churches, and found that many spiritualists advocated woman's rights, reflective of a movement in which women were equal to men within Spiritualist practice. As Braude put it: "At a time when no churches ordained women and many forbade them to speak aloud in church, Spiritualist women had equal authority, equal opportunities, and equal numbers in religious leadership."[59]

A decidedly different, far larger, and more widespread response to skepticism and liberal Christianity became manifest in the rise of the holiness movement and pentecostalism, and soon thereafter, fundamentalism. The most direct origins of the holiness movement can be found in the second half of the nineteenth century within Methodism and its doctrine of holiness. Prior to the Civil War, American Methodism, born of the Second Great Awakening, through repeated rural camp meetings and urban revivals brought hosts of lower-class people into the fold. By the end of the war, many of this core constituency attained middle-class status and both their culture and taste became more middle class in the process and their religious ceremonies more restrained, even formal. This led to dissension in the ranks, among those who felt that the new more "respectable" religion was antithetical to the spiritual experience and emotional worship to which they had grown accustomed. In 1866, Methodists marked their centennial year with conventions as well as prayer gatherings and camp meetings that centered on the denomination's roots in holiness. The next year, in 1867, arguably as a direct outgrowth of the work of Phoebe Palmer in cultivating holiness ideas among Methodists in New York City, holiness seekers participated in a camp meeting in Vineland, New Jersey, which led to the formation of the National Camp Meeting Association for the Promotion of Holiness. Other holiness camp meetings and interdenominational gatherings soon followed, generating much press coverage and excitement. By 1886, holiness meetings were being held in every major city.[60]

The success of the holiness revival precipitated a growing separation of the holiness faction from the larger body of Methodist Church members. Nevertheless, holiness believers remained in the Methodist church until the 1880s, when denominational authorities felt compelled to rein them in. This pattern was repeated in other denominations in which holiness groups sprung up, such as the Baptists. What bothered denominational leaders most was holiness believers' apparent disregard for the authority, organization, and "established usage of the church." In 1881, the bishops of the Methodist Church, North rejected a lay appeal for a national holiness convention under church sponsorship, stating that is was their "solemn conviction that the whole subject of personal holiness . . . can be best maintained and enforced in connection with the established usages of the church." The bishops of the Methodist Church, South refrained from any official action until 1894, when in their annual address they denounced holiness believers' alleged claim to "a monopoly of the experience, practice, and advocacy of holiness" and their tendency to "separate themselves from the body of ministers and disciples." By then, however, holiness believers had already begun to leave the church, whether voluntarily or having been expelled, and began to establish their own churches. One of the earliest, the Church of God, began in 1880, followed by the Christian and Missionary Alliance in 1887, the Fire Baptized Holiness Church in 1895, and the Pilgrim Holiness Church in 1897. The largest denomination to emerge from the holiness movement was the Church of the Nazarene, which brought together several smaller groups in 1914.[61]

Basing his teachings on Matthew 5:48: "be perfect, as your heavenly Father is perfect," John Wesley, the eighteenth-century founder of Methodism, stressed the necessity for believers to seek "Christian perfection." That is to say, they were not only to seek justification, or conversion and the assurance of salvation by witness of the Holy Spirit, but also to achieve entire sanctification. They were not only to have the Holy Spirit descend upon them and be freed from sin and guilt but also through the grace of the Holy Spirit to achieve holiness, or perfection. If Scripture commanded one to be perfect, Wesley reasoned, a state of perfection must be possible. Wesley defined sin as "a voluntary transgression of a known law of God," or a voluntary act of the will to violate God's law. Wesley did not abandon the idea that people, even when entirely sanctified or in a state of Christian perfection, could not avoid sinful acts, where such acts were unintentional or committed out of ignorance of God's law. Further, he insisted that perfection, which involved a regeneration of the heart, was possible only through a lifelong gathering of God's grace, which enabled a person to be victorious in his or her struggle for perfection or sanctification. Nevertheless, this definition of sin conflicted sharply with Reformed and Puritan doctrine, which insisted that, given their naturally sinful and corrupt state, any form of Christian perfection was unobtainable. The two opposed views were synthesized during the evangelical revivals of the first half of the nineteenth century in America, most notably at the hands of Charles Finney.[62]

Finney and his associates in the revivals, especially Asa Mahan, developed what became known as the Oberlin Theology (named for the college at which it was developed). In brief, as detailed in Mahan's *The Baptism of the Holy Spirit* (1870), Finney emphasized the role of the will: Nothing is either sinful or righteous unless it be a free act of will. Finney insisted that the regenerate person is not expected to perform acts beyond his capacity. He must have the ability to choose the good in every instance of responsible choice. To choose correctly, however, "a special work of the Holy Spirit beyond mere regeneration, must completely overwhelm his will." Given this special work, defined so as to affirm both human free agency and complete dependency on God's gracious power, entire sanctification is attainable in this life. Finney preferred the phrase entire sanctification over perfection, even Christian perfection, so as to avoid concerns among those – especially schooled in the Reformed or Puritan tradition – who would have nothing to do with any pretense of perfection in any form.[63]

Concerns with social issues were an integral part of the holiness program. Some spoke in terms of the "worthy" versus the "unworthy" poor, thereby suggesting that only those worthy of God's grace deserved aid. But in their missionary efforts, especially in urban areas, holiness missionaries cast their net widely in an attempt to rescue men and women from drunkenness or prostitution. Similarly, there were those who argued that their church was not a benevolent institution but an institution dedicated to "winning lost souls to Christ and [thereby] being instrumental in redeeming the world." Nevertheless, even before the rise of the Social Gospel, most agreed that taking care of the immediate needs of the poor was an important first step in their redemption. During the 1880s and 1890s, they founded rescue missions, homes for fallen women, relief programs among immigrants, and other programs to ease the burden of the poor and engaged in organized social and political action to pass legislation concerned with women's and children's labor, better treatment of immigrants and blacks, and other social issues. Preaching the Gospel was their central aim, but social and evangelical work went hand in hand. "Uplifting the sinner, as well as saving his soul, was high among their priorities."[64]

All of this changed by the 1920s, as evangelical interest in social concerns – including holiness believers – disappeared in what has been called "The Great Reversal." Specifically as to how this was manifested in the fundamentalist movement during the 1920s will be addressed in the next chapter. As to holiness believers, as has been noted, although always of secondary importance social concerns, even political action, were common from 1865 until about 1900 when they began to diminish. The period has been better characterized as a period of transition from a Calvinist tradition, which had held sway in America from its founding, that saw political action as a means to advance the "kingdom of God," or the "New Israel," to a more pietistic view of political action as no more than a means to restrain evil. Gradually lost over time was Charles Finney's observation that the purpose of government was to promote holiness and that Christians are bound to exert their influence to secure legislation that is in accordance with the law of God. Finney did not believe that such political activity would divert from saving souls. Rather that it would promote "public and private order and happiness, [which] is one of the indispensable means of doing good and saving souls."[65]

This transition corresponded to the change from a dominantly postmillennial to premillennial world-view, the rise of dispensationalism (discussed in the next chapter), and the spread of the holiness movement. But in the case of the holiness movement, he insisted, it was not absolute. Most of those in the holiness movement continued to believe that governments were ordained by God to restrain evil. Therefore, politics was a means to do good. What was lost was the Calvinist-Puritan "view of the identity of the people of God with the advance of a religious-political kingdom." But even then, it was not lost completely, as holiness believers and other evangelicals continued to support Sabbath legislation and prohibition. Finally, to bring us back to where we opened this chapter, the crucial factor in the "Great Reversal" was the rise of the Social Gospel after 1900. By then, mainstream Protestant Christianity was becoming identified with liberalism and was viewed with great suspicion by many conservative evangelicals. The issue of evangelism versus social service became widely and hotly debated, and evangelicals grew increasingly critical of the goals of the Social Gospel, which they believed favored the latter at the expense of the former.[66]

The immediate origins of the pentecostal movement can be found in the holiness movement. In 1885, two black Baptist ministers, Charles H. Mason and Charles P. Jones, accepted holiness and began to preach it in Mississippi. Expelled by the local Baptist association for their new and unacceptable doctrines, they relocated to Memphis, Tennessee, where they organized the Church of God in Christ. At about the same time, some holiness believers began to adopt yet another experience beyond sanctification, baptism of the Spirit, which would result in their speaking in tongues, much as the disciples of Jesus did on the feast of Pentecost as recorded in the Acts of the Apostles. They also embraced prophesy, the ability to predict or reveal the meaning of events; healing, by prayer and/or touch; interpretation, the ability to translate and explain the meaning of what is spoken in otherwise unknown tongues; and judgment of sprits, the ability to determine if a prophesy or other spiritual gift is authentically from God. When this belief and practice was added to those that characterized holiness – Biblical literalism, personal ecstatic experience, strict moral values, congregational independence, and sanctification through a "second blessing" or second descent of the Holy Spirit – the movement split in two, some continuing in the holiness fold, others following the path of pentecostalism.[67]

The scriptural basis for pentecostalism came from the words of Paul in the New Testament, Acts 2:1–4, wherein he spoke of the descent of the Holy Spirit on Christ's disciples as tongues of fire on the Day of Pentecost. Believers sought to receive the baptism of the Holy Spirit themselves manifested in speaking in tongues, prayer, prophecy, and healing, whereby they would be prepared for Jesus's Second Coming, which many believed was imminent. Once again, the origins of this movement are difficult to determine definitively. But one definitive marker is a revival that took place in Topeka, Kansas, at the turn of the twentieth century. It was led by Charles Parham, an ordained Methodist minister whose background in faith healing and belief in baptism of the Holy Spirit, a sign of which was the ability to speak in tongues, or glossolalia, forced him out of that church.[68]

Parham started the College of Bethel on October 15, 1900, with a student body that consisted mainly of ministers or religious workers who had been associated with Methodist, Baptist, Quaker, and independent holiness churches and missions. What united them was their holiness persuasion and shared desire with Parham for a new experience of the Spirit. According to Holiness lore, the doctrine that speaking in tongues is the evidence of baptism in the Holy Spirit was miraculously revealed on January 1, 1901, when "fire fell" and one of Bethel Bible College's students, who along with her fellow students had been engaged in independent study and prayer, suddenly spoke in tongues. Although not present at the time, Parham set the stage for the revelation. Before leaving for a trip to Kansas City, he told his students to study the subject of baptism separately and in solitude. Further, he directed them to read carefully the second chapter of the book of Acts, saying, "The gifts are in the Holy Spirit and with the baptism of the Holy Spirit the gifts, as well as the graces, should be manifested. Now, students, while I am gone, see if there is not some evidence given of the baptism so there may be no doubt of the subject." Days later, returning from his trip, Parham called the students together and asked for their findings. He learned that the students had been engaged in prayer and worship, including a New Year's Eve "watch-night" service. The next evening they also held a worship service, and it was that evening that one of the students asked to be prayed for to receive the fullness of the Holy Spirit. Immediately after being prayed for, she began to speak in tongues. "To my astonishment," Parham reported, "they all had the same story, that while . . . different things occurred when the Pentecostal blessing fell . . . the indisputable proof on each occasion was, that they spoke with other tongues."[69]

Word spread quickly about the "strange sect" whose members claimed to speak strange languages. The press referred to Bethel as the "Parham School of Tongues" or to the school's prayer tower as "the tower of Babel." And although clearly meant in jest in most cases, Parham welcomed the publicity and set out to build on it with an "Apostolic Band" of seven workers. His tour often brought front-page coverage and in the process attracted those who at first might have been just curious, but in more than a few cases, adherents. In the spring of 1905, Parham traveled to the Houston-Galveston area, where he met up with several adherents of the Apostolic Faith Movement, a precursor of the still nascent pentecostal movement. The mission was successful, in large part due to Parham's well-publicized healing of the wife of a Houston attorney, who had been seriously injured in a streetcar accident, and by December, he was able to open a Bible school to "firmly establish this great growing work in Texas."[70]

A second and more influential moment occurred in 1906 in what came to be known as the Azusa Street (Los Angeles) revival. Influential in that event was William J. Seymour, one of Parham's students, an African American. Born a slave, Seymour was raised a Baptist but came to embrace the holiness movement, which he continued until he met Parham, at which point he embraced Parham's teachings on speaking in tongues and moved closer to pentecostalism. It seems that while in Houston, Seymour visited an African American mission and heard someone speak in tongues. That person was Lucy Farrow, an African American, who was associated with Parham and that frequently attended black missions. Impressed by what he witnessed, Seymour asked to be admitted to Parham's school and at risk of setting off white backlash, Parham accepted him.[71]

That was in 1905. In 1906, Seymour began preaching in a private home in Los Angeles until the number of those in attendance forced him to relocate to a vacant building on Azusa Street. He was preceded in his efforts by Neeley Terry, an African American from Los Angeles whom Seymour met while in Houston. On her return to Los Angeles, Neely persuaded her congregation to hire Seymour as an associate pastor, a post he accepted. Within days the revival was on, far exceeding what Parham had begun and accomplished in Houston. In many respects, Los Angeles was fertile ground for Seymour. At the time of his arrival, it was the fastest growing city in the United States. It had a substantial minority immigrant population of African Americans, Mexicans, southern and eastern Europeans, Chinese, and Japanese, most of whom were being shunned by the native white population. Moreover, the city was still reeling from the San Francisco earthquake, which Frank Bartleman, referenced later, interpreted as "the voice of God to the people on the Pacific Coast," which was "used mightily in conviction for the gracious after the revival."[72]

When Seymour arrived in Los Angeles a revival was already in progress, in which the expectations of pentecostal gifts and signs figured prominently led by F. B. Meyer and Frank Bartleman, both holiness preachers. Assisted by Lucy Farrow, already known for her speaking in tongues, recently arrived from Houston, Seymour overcame some initial and short-term resistance and attracted more than a thousand people to the 312 Azusa Street address, a rundown former African Methodist Episcopal (AME) Church, formerly occupied by a stable, warehouse and rooming house, in the center of the urban ghetto. The revival continued day and night for three years, during which time Seymour helped refine pentecostal doctrine, sermons almost always emphasizing Act 2: 4 or Mark 16:17–18.[73]

The emotionalism of the radical evangelical meetings of those who would become pentecostals was the movement's most striking characteristic. In the late 1890s, one observer reported that "people screamed until you could hear them for three miles on a clear night, and until the blood vessels stood out like whip cords." Another reported that their prayer meetings sounded like the "female ward of an insane asylum." But meetings were also characterized by singing, testifying, praying, speaking in tongues, the casting out of demons, and faith healings, all of which worked to further refine and institutionalize the Pentecostal doctrines of total sanctification, faith healing, baptism of the Holy Spirit, and the imminent Second Coming of Jesus. Bartleman offered the following description of what he witnessed at the Azusa Street Mission:

> No subjects or sermons were announced ahead of time, and no special speakers for such an hour. No one knew what might be coming, what God would do. All was spontaneous, ordered of the Spirit. We wanted to hear from God, through whoever he might speak. . . . We had no prearranged programme to be jammed through on time. Our time was the Lord's. We had real testimonies, from fresh heart-experience. . . . A dozen might be on their feet at one time, trembling under the power of God. . . . All obeyed God, in keenness and humility. . . . The Lord was liable to burst through any one. We prayed for this continually. Someone would finally get up anointed for the message. . . . It might be a child, a woman, or a man. It might be from the back seat, or from the front. It made no difference. We rejoiced that God was working.[74]

In large part as the result of the Azusa Street revival, its coverage in the press and the fanning out of participants to various parts of the country bearing witness as to what occurred in Los Angeles, pentecostalism spread rapidly. New pentecostal groups appeared informally in already established churches, but over time, as they became more committed to exclusively pentecostal doctrines, they organized more formally and in most cases adopted the name itself. By way of example, the Church of God in Christ, founded in 1897 as a holiness church moved into the pentecostal sphere as a result of the Azusa Street revival. It soon became the nation's largest black pentecostal denomination. The Assemblies of God followed a similar path, taking in several smaller pentecostal churches, until they formed the General Council of the Assemblies of God in 1914. And in the following year, a merger of holiness and pentecostal churches formed the Pentecostal Holiness Church. Soon, pentecostal churches could be found throughout the United States and abroad.[75]

By some reports, more than twenty different nationalities, including African Americans, Chinese, Indians, Mexicans, several European groups of immigrants, and Jews, participated in the Azusa Street revival. "No instrument that God can use is rejected," it was insisted, and for a while, the racial and ethnic minorities of Los Angeles found themselves welcome at Azusa where "some would discover there the sense of dignity and community denied them in the larger urban culture." And that was the case with many holiness and pentecostal churches, wherein whites and blacks worshipped in the same churches. Indeed, the African American Charles H. Mason ordained many white pentecostal ministers. By 1920, however, in nearly every case, the races separated into segregated churches. By 1914, after co-founder William J. Seymour ran afoul of white pentecostal segregationists, even the Azusa Street church had become a black congregation with an occasional white visitor. This was true in the South, but it also followed black migrants to the North.[76]

Between 1915 and 1930, the Great Migration brought large numbers of African Americans from the rural South to the urban North, and with them came their religious affiliations, including not only Baptists, still their largest gathering, but also pentecostal and holiness churches. Before the Great Migration, with some exceptions, African American churches developed independently in North and South, separated by regional economic, social, and political differences. African American Christians confronted racism in both sections of the country, but the expression of that racism and their ability to cope with it varied, as did expectations of the church's mission. Allan Spear wrote of the results of the Great Migration to Chicago:

> Of all aspects of community life, religious activities were most profoundly influenced by the migration. Before the war, the large, middle-class Baptist and Methodist churches had dominated Negro religious life. . . . Although they had not completely discarded the emotionalism of the traditional Negro religion, these churches had moved toward a more decorous order of workshop and a program of broad social concern. The migration brought to the city thousands of Negroes accustomed to the informal, demonstrative, preacher-oriented church of the rural south.[77]

Cities such as Chicago, New York, Philadelphia, and Detroit had their entire religious landscape significantly changed, not only by the increased presence of these denominations but also by the propensity for each of these groups to gather in small, often storefront, churches with memberships numbering only in the dozens, thereby offering the migrants a more closely knit sense of community in their strange new land. These storefront churches were often independent from mainline denominations; led by preachers with little, if any, formal theological training; marked by a preponderance of women among its members; and characterized by pentecostal ritual and holiness doctrine. In 1919, twenty holiness congregations were active in the city of Chicago. By 1928, there were fifty-six, and they contained 19 percent of all of the city's African American church members. As historian Bettye Collier-Thomas has found, holiness and pentecostal churches "empowered the oppressed and dispossessed." They insisted on the strict behavior of their members, including plain dress and shunning worldly activities such as dancing, consumption of alcohol, tobacco, and drugs, makeup, immoral sexual behavior, cursing, and even attending the concerts, movies, and the theater. At the same time, they encouraged honesty, thrift, hard work, and discipline.[78]

To conclude this section, although allied in their turning inward and to the Holy Spirit in search of a more personal alternative to liberal Christianity, holiness and pentecostalism were different, at least at the start. Holiness believers, for example, did not believe in speaking in tongues or emphasize ecstatic experiences, but placed greater emphasis on sanctification. Where they were alike was in their emphasis on conversion, or justification, and holding sacred Scripture, whereby "the Word continued to speak out against the world." Like many other religious groups before and after, they were restorationists, disillusioned with what they believed Christianity had become and sought to restore scriptural purity to Christianity. Over time, finding common ground was facilitated by changes made by each group to deemphasize doctrinal points that served to separate the two. For example, although some would argue that it had never been otherwise, pentecostals began to make clear that the much publicized speaking in tongues was not "the message of their movement, but rather a means by which the message was confirmed," the message being: "Jesus is coming soon." Also deemphasized, in the face of considerable negative press and abuse by supposed practitioners, was the miracle of healing closely tied to the casting out of demons, through the laying on of hands, prayer, or other means. And finally, although never completely abandoned, pentecostal insistence on the imminent Second Coming was unsustainable and deemphasized.

Changes such as these, while not impairing either group's message, paved the way for these movements to overcome their differences. Lines separating them became increasingly blurred, and believers from both traditions found their way into the same churches.[79]

Summary

This chapter has focused on the impact of developments in the fields of biblical criticism, namely the higher criticism, and Darwinian evolution. The first involved historical textual analyses of the Old and New Testaments, which challenged centuries-old, literal interpretations of both. The second challenged the hitherto accepted understanding of creation based on a literal reading of the Bible, by providing an alternative model based on modern science. The most troubling aspect of the latter for many was Darwin's theory of the origin of species and descent of man through a process of natural selection rather than the direct result of divine creation. One result was what some referred to as "the golden age of agnosticism." Most, however, sought to reconcile these new ideas through a more figurative reading of Scripture and a less direct role on the part of God in creation, thereby protecting the still-dominant commitment to revealed religion. Still others feared that seeds of doubt had been planted that left unchecked would lead to widespread unbelief, which left no room for compromise, giving rise, at least in part, to the holiness, pentecostal, and fundamentalist movements.

Review questions

1   What was the higher criticism and how did it impact revealed religion?
2   What was Darwinian evolution and how did it impact revealed religion?
3   Who was the most prominent agnostic in nineteenth-century America and why was he so successful? What were his major criticisms of established religions?
4   What was Social Darwinism? In what ways was it an offshoot of Darwinian evolution? In what ways was it different?
5   How did liberal and conservative religious leaders' responses to the higher criticism and Darwinian evolution differ?

Notes

1   Jerry Wayne Brown, *The Rise of Biblical Criticism in America, 1800–1870: The New England Scholars* (Middletown, CT: Wesleyan University Press, 1969), 3–4; Karen Armstrong, *The Case for God* (New York: Alfred A. Knopf, 2009), 244.
2   Merle Curti, *The Growth of American Thought*, 2nd edn. (New York: Harper & Brothers Publishers, 1951), 540–1, 582; Richard N. Soulen and R. Kendall Soulen, *Handbook of Biblical Criticism*, 3rd rev. edn. (Louisville, KY: Westminster John Knox Press, 2001), 78–9; Brown, *The Rise of Biblical Criticism in America*, 7.
3   Brown, *The Rise of Biblical Criticism in America*, 143, 146; Franklin L. Baumer, *Religion and the Rise of Scepticism* (New York: Harcourt, Brace and Company, 1960), 160; Armstrong, *The Case for God*, 248; Ira V. Brown, "The Higher Criticism Comes to America, 1880–1900," *Journal of the Presbyterian Historical Society*, 1 (1960): 193–212.
4   Brown, *The Rise of Biblical Criticism in America*, 8, 140; Charles Hodge, *Systematic Theology*, 3 vols. (New York: Charles Scribner and Company, 1873), 1: 152.
5   Brown, *The Rise of Biblical Criticism in America*, 79; Washington Gladden, *Who Wrote the Bible: A Book for the People* (Boston: Houghton Mifflin, 1891), 5.

6 Quote from Brown, "The Higher Criticism Comes to America," 207–8; Brown, *The Rise of Biblical Criticism in America*, 95–6.

7 Theodore Parker, "D. F. Strauss's *Das Leben Jesu*," *Christian Examiner*, 28 (1840): 307–9; Brown, *The Rise of Biblical Criticism in America*, 150–1.

8 Theodore Parker, "The Transient and Permanent in Christianity," in *Theodore Parker: An Anthology*, ed. Henry Steele Commager (Boston: Beacon Press, 1960), 47, 52, 58; Brown, *The Rise of Biblical Criticism in America*, 153–70, quote taken from 161.

9 Brown, *The Rise of Biblical Criticism in America*, 180–1; Brown, "The Higher Criticism Comes to America," 205.

10 Curti, *The Growth of American Thought*, 541–2; William N. Clarke, *Sixty Years with the Bible* (Charles Scribner's Sons, 1909), 97–8, 210–1, 120–1.

11 Brown, "The Higher Criticism Comes to America," 198–9, 204; Curti, *The Growth of American Thought*, 542.

12 Richard Hofstadter. *Social Darwinism in American Thought*, rev. edn. (New York: George Braziller, Inc., 1959), 21.

13 Hofstadter, *Social Darwinism in American Thought*, 4–5, 22–3.

14 John William Draper, *The History of Conflict between Religion and Science*, rpt. edn. (New York: Appleton, 1928); Armstrong, *The Case for God*, 252–4; Andrew Dixon White, *A History of the Warfare of Science and Theology in Christendom* (New York: Appleton, 1896); White, *A History of the Warfare of Science and Theology in Christendom* (excerpt), Robert R. Mathisen, ed., *Critical Issues in American Religious History*, 2nd edn. (Waco, TX: Baylor University Press, 2006), 399; Curti, *The Growth of American Thought*, 551.

15 Curti, *The Growth of American Thought*, 548. For more extensive coverage of scientific developments that led up to Darwin, see Peter J. Bowler, *Evolution: The History of an Idea*, 25th anniversary edn. (Berkeley: University of California Press, 2009), chs. 1–5.

16 White, *A History of the Warfare of Science and Theology in Christendom* (excerpt), 399.

17 White, *A History of the Warfare of Science and Theology in Christendom*, 400; Peter J. Bowler, "Evolution," in *Science and Religion: A Historical Introduction*, ed. Gary B. Ferngren (Baltimore, MD: The Johns Hopkins University Press), 223; Hofstadter, *Social Darwinism in American Thought*, 25–6; Charles Hodge, *What Is Darwinism?* (excerpt), Mathisen, *Critical Issues in American Religious Thought*, 376–81.

18 James McCosh, *Christianity and Positivism* (New York: Robert Carter & Brothers, 1871), 42, 63–4; Hofstadter, *Social Darwinism in American Thought*, 27; Henry Ward Beecher, "Progress of Thought in the Church," *North American Review*, 309 (1882): 99–100, 106–7.

19 James Moore, "Charles Darwin," in *Science and Religion: A Historical Introduction*, ed. Gary B. Ferngren (Baltimore, MD: The Johns Hopkins University Press, 2002), 213–14; Henry Ward Beecher, *Evolution and Religion* (excerpt), Mathisen, *Critical Issues in American Religious Thought*, 387; Curti, *The Growth of American Thought*, 550.

20 James Moore, "Charles Darwin," 213–14; Henry Ward Beecher, *Evolution and Religion* (excerpt), Mathisen, *Critical Issues in American Religious Thought*, 387; Curti, *The Growth of American Thought*, 550; Hofstadter, *Social Darwinism in American Thought*, 29–30.

21 Curti, *The Growth of American Thought*, 549; Louis Agassiz, "Evolution and Permanence of Type," *Atlantic Monthly*, 33 (1874), 92–101; Hofstadter, *Social Darwinism in American Thought*, 18; Christopher Lane, "When Doubt Became Mainstream," *The Chronicle (of Higher Education) Review* (March 25, 2011), B10–2, 15, an essay adopted from Christopher Lane, *The Age of Doubt: Tracing the Roots of Our Religious Uncertainty* (New Haven, CT: Yale University Press, 2011); Bernard Lightman, *The Origins of Agnosticism: Victorian Unbelief and the Limits of Knowledge* (Baltimore, MD: The Johns Hopkins University Press, 1987), 11, 13, 28. Gnosticism dates to the third century and to the Christian sect, which was expelled from the Church for claiming to possess superior knowledge of God from personal, divine revelation.

22 Hofstadter, *Social Darwinism in American Thought*, 13, 18, 28; Peter J. Bowler, *Monkey Trials and Gorilla Sermons: Evolution and Christianity from Darwin to Intelligent Design* (Cambridge, MA: Harvard University Press, 2007), 112–13; Curti, *The Growth of American Thought*, 530; Paul A. Carter, "The Ape in the Tree of Knowledge," in *Critical Issues in American Religious Thought*, ed. Robert R. Mathisen (Waco, TX: Baylor University Press, 2006), 408.

23 Carter, "The Ape in the Tree of Knowledge," 409. For more of the reception of Darwin's theory among scientists, see Bowler, *Evolution*, ch. 6; Hofstadter, *Social Darwinism in American Thought*, 29; William Albert Dembski, "The Design Argument," in *Science and Religion: A Historical Introduction*, ed. Gary B. Ferngren (Baltimore, MD: The Johns Hopkins University Press), 330, 339; Matthew Day, "Reading the Fossils of Faith: Thomas Henry Huxley and the Evolutionary Subtext of the Synoptic Problem," *Church History*, 74 (2005): 534, 548.

24 Martin E. Marty, *The Infidel: Freethought and American Religion* (Cleveland, OH: Meridian Books, 1961), 137–40, 142; James Turner, *Without God, Without Creed: The Origins of Unbelief in America* (Baltimore, MD: The Johns Hopkins University Press, 1985), 171; Lane, "When Doubt Became Mainstream," B10.

25 Sidney Warren, *American Freethought, 1860–1914* (New York: Gordian Press, 1966), 105. See also Stow Persons, *Free Religion: An American Faith* (Boston: Beacon Press, 1963).

26 Howard B. Radest, *Felix Adler: An Ethical Culture* (New York: Peter Lang, 1998), 10.

27 Radest, *Felix Adler*, 11.

28 Persons, *Free Religion*, 96; Radest, *Felix Adler*, 9–10, 117, 132; Turner, *Without God, Without Creed*, 205; Howard B. Radest, *Toward Common Ground* (New York: Frederick Ungar, 1969), 17–19, 29; Robert S. Guttchen, *Felix Adler* (New York: Twayne Publishers, 1974), 17–26; Felix Adler, *An Ethical Philosophy of Life* (New York: D. Appleton-Century Company, 1918); Felix Adler, *Creed and Deed* (New York ; G. P. Putman's Sons, 1877); Felix Adler, *The Reconstruction of the Spiritual Ideal* (New York: D. Appleton and Company, 1924).

29 Turner, *Without God, Without Creed*, 174; Marty, *The Infidel*, 140, 153; Susan Jacoby, *Freethinkers: A History of American Secularism* (New York: Metropolitan Books, 2004), 25, 157–64; Clarence Henley Cramer, *Royal Bob: The Life of Robert S. Ingersoll* (Indianapolis, IN: The Bobbs-Merrill Company, 1952), 18, 124–5.

30 Orvin Larson, *American Infidel, Robert G. Ingersoll: A Biography* (New York: The Citadel Press, 1962), 12, 19–35, 42–8; Cramer, *Royal Bob*, 20–1, 26, 34, 37, 40.

31 Cramer, *Royal Bob*, 39–46, 47–54, 67, 69, 75–95; Larson, *American Infidel*, 53–68, 90–4.

32 Peter M. Rinaldo, *Atheists, Agnostics, and Deists in America: A Brief History* (Briarcliff Manor, NY: DorPeter Press, 2000), ch. 6; Larson, *American Infidel*, 145; Cramer, *Royal Bob*, 175–7.

33 Roger E. Greeley, ed., *The Best of Robert Ingersoll, Immortal Infidel: Selections from His Writings and Speeches* (Buffalo, NY: Prometheus Books, 1983), xi.

34 Larson, *American Infidel*, 79–80; Turner, *Without God, Without Creed*, 174.

35 Larson, *American Infidel*, 99–100.

36 Turner, *Without God, Without Creed*, 181; Larson, *American Infidel*, 100–1; Cramer, *Royal Bob*, 99–100, 132.

37 Robert Green Ingersoll, "Why Am I an Agnostic? Part II" *The North American Review* (March 1890): 336–7; Warren, *American Freethought*, 86–7.

38 Larson, *American Infidel*, 158–9, 161–2; Robert Green Ingersoll, "What Must We Do to Be Saved?," in *The Works of Robert G. Ingersoll*, ed. C. P. Farrell (New York: The Dresden Publishing Co., 1900), 441–6.

39 Larson, *American Infidel*, 155–7; Cramer, *Royal Bob*, 192.

40 Cramer, *Royal Bob*, 165–6; Warren, *American Freethought*, 84; For a complete text of "A Christmas Sermon" go to: http://freethought.mbdojo.com/ingersollxms.html

41 Larson, *American Infidel*, 129, 173, 235–42; Marty, *The Infidel*, 148–50.

42 See Hofstadter, *Social Darwinism in American Thought*; Mike Hawkins, *Social Darwinism in European and American Thought, 1860–1945: Nature as Model and Nature as Threat* (Cambridge, England: Cambridge University Press, 1997) provide good starting points for a study of Social Darwinism in America. Curti, *The Growth of American Thought*, 576; Bowler, *Monkey Trials and Gorilla Sermons*, 35–8; Bowler, *Evolution*, 298–305. See Charles Darwin, *The Descent of Man and Selection in Relation to Sex*, 2nd edn. (London: John Murray, 1882), chap. 4.

43 Herbert Spencer, "The Instability of the Homogeneous," in *First Principles*, 4th American edn. (New York: D. Appleton & Company, 1900), 99–104. See also Hofstadter, *Social Darwinism in America*, 5, 31, 33; Bowler, *Monkey Trials and Gorilla Sermons*, 117–18.

44 Hofstadter, *Social Darwinism in America*, 35; Robert C. Bannister, *Social Darwinism: Science and Myth in Anglo-American Social Thought* (Philadelphia: Temple University Press, 1979), 7.

45 Herbert Spencer, *Social Statics: The Conditions Essential to Human Happiness Specified, and the First of Them Developed* (London: John Chapman, 1851), 79–80; Hofstadter, *Social Darwinism in America*, 40.

46 Spencer, *Social Statics*, 414–15, 325–44; Hofstadter, *Social Darwinism in America*, 37, 39, 41; Herbert Spencer, "A Theory of Population, Deduced from the General Law of Animal Fertility," *Westminster Review*, 57 (1852): 468–501, especially 499–500; See also Herbert Spencer, "The Development Hypothesis," in *Essays: Scientific, Political, and Speculative*, 3 vols. (New York: D. Appleton & Company, 1907), I, 107; Bowler, *Monkey Trials and Gorilla Sermons*, 114–15; Spencer, "The Instability of the Homogeneous," 530.

47 Hofstadter, *Social Darwinism in America*, 5–7; Hawkins, *Social Darwinism in European and American Thought*, 106.

48 Andrew Carnegie, *Autobiography of Andrew Carnegie* (Boston: Houghton Mifflin Co., 1920), 327; Andrew Carnegie, "Wealth," *North American Review*, 148 (1889): 655–7. For a discussion of how Social Darwinism differed from the rags-to-riches/Horatio Alger mythology, see Irwin G. Wyllie, *The Self-Made Man* (Piscataway, NJ: Rutgers University Press, 1954), 635; Bannister, *Social Darwinism*, 6–8; Raymond J. Wilson, ed., *Darwinism and the American Intellectual* (Homewood, IL: Dorsey Press, 1967), 93.

49 Milton Berman, *John Fiske: The Evolution of a Popularizer* (Cambridge, MA: Harvard University Press, 1961), 100; Hawkins, *Social Darwinism in European and American Thought*, 106–14; Bannister, *Social Darwinism*, 57. See also John Fiske, "The Progress from Brute to Man," *North American Review*, 117 (1873): 280–2.

50 Hofstadter, *Social Darwinism in America*, 5–7, 14; Bannister, *Social Darwinism*, 57, 69–71; John Fiske, *Edward Livingston Youmans: A Sketch of His Life* (New York: D. Appleton & Company, 1894), 68, 95.

51 Hofstadter, *Social Darwinism in America*, 51; Bannister, *Social Darwinism*, 98.

52 Bannister, *Social Darwinism*, 100.

53 Bannister, *Social Darwinism*, 103.

54 William Graham Sumner, *Essays of William Graham Sumner*, ed. Albert G. Keller and Maurice R. Davie, 2 vols. (New Haven, CT: Yale University Press, 1934), 2: 56.

55 William Graham Sumner, *War and Other Essays*, ed. Albert G. Keller (New Haven, CT: Yale University Press, 1911), 167–92; William Graham Sumner, "The Survival of the Fittest," *Index*, 4 (1884), 567; see also Bannister, *Social Darwinism*, 98, 105–6; Hofstadter, *Social Darwinism in America*, 61; Paraphrasing and quotes from William Graham Sumner, "Reply to a Socialist," in *The Challenge of Facts and Other Essays*, ed. William Graham Sumner (New Haven, CT: Yale University Press, 1914), 57–8, 219; Sumner, *Essays of William Graham Sumner*, I: 109.

56 William Graham Sumner, *What Social Classes Owe to Each Other* (New York: Harper & Bros., 1883), 135; William Graham Sumner, *Folkways* (Boston: Ginn & Co., 1906), 48; Sumner, *Essays of William Graham Sumner*, I: 358–62; Hofstadter, *Social Darwinism in America*, 59.

57 William Graham Sumner, *Earth-Hunger and Other Essays* (New Haven, CT: Yale University Press, 1913), 283–317; Sumner, *Essays of William Graham Sumner*, I: 104, 185; II: 165. Hofstadter has argued that Sumner found support for his view of democracy among the Founding Fathers. He argued that they feared democracy and through provisions in the US Constitution and the federal structure it created sought to limit it, but that because of "inherited dogmas" concerning the founding as a democratic nation, a tension existed from the start between "the democratic temper of the people and their constitutional framework." Hofstadter, *Social Darwinism in America*, 60.

58 Hofstadter, *Social Darwinism in America*, 201–4; Bannister, *Social Darwinism*, 11, 137–42.

59 Ann Braude, *Radical Spirits: Spiritualism and Women's Rights in Nineteenth Century America* (Boston: Beacon Press, 1989), 2–3 and passim.

60 Robert M. Anderson, *Vision of the Disinherited: The Making of American Pentecostalism* (New York: Oxford University Press, 1979), 29, 31; Grant Wacker, *Heaven Below: Early Pentecostalism and American Culture* (Cambridge, MA: Harvard University Press, 2001), 17; George M. Marsden, *Fundamentalism and American Culture: The Shaping of Twentieth-Century Evangelicalism, 1870–1925*, 2nd edn. (New York: Oxford University Press, 2006), 74; Timothy L. Smith, "The Holiness Crusade," in *The History of American Methodism*, ed. Emery S. Bucke, 3 vols. (Nashville, TN: Abingdon Press, 1964), 2: 608–27; Albert J. Raboteau, *Canaan Land: A Religious History of African Americans* (New York: Oxford University Press, 2001), 95.

61 Anderson, *Vision of the Disinherited*, 30–3; Catherine L. Albanese, *America: Religions and Religion*, 4th edn. (Belmont, CA: Thomson Wadsworth, 2007), 123; Edwin S. Gaustad and Leigh E. Schmidt. *The Religious History of America*, rev. edn. (San Francisco: HarperSanFrancisco, 2002), 282; Smith, "The Holiness Crusade," 608–27.

62 Marsden, *Fundamentalism and American Culture*, 73–4; Wacker, *Heaven Below*, 2.

63 Marsden, *Fundamentalism and American Culture*, 74–5; Wacker, *Heaven Below*, 2; Anderson, *Vision of the Disinherited*, 28–9; Albanese, *America: Religions and Religion*, 123; Gaustad and Schmidt, *The Religious History of America*, 281–2; Raboteau, *Canaan Land*, 95. For more on the historical development of sanctification in America, see John Leland Peters, *Christian Perfectionism and American Methodism* (Nashville, TN: Abingdon Press, 1956); Timothy L. Smith, *Revivalism and Social Reform* (New York: Harper & Row, 1965).

64 Marsden, *Fundamentalism and American Culture*, 81, 84–5; Smith, *Revivalism and Social Reform*, 148–77.

65 Marsden, *Fundamentalism and American Culture*, 86–92.

66 Marsden, *Fundamentalism and American Culture*, 86–91.

67 Anderson, *Vision of the Disinherited*, 28; Raboteau, *Canaan Land*, 95; on the early history of the Pentecostal movement, including its Holiness roots, see Joseph E. Campbell, *The Pentecostal Holiness Church, 1898–1948* (Franklin Springs, GA: The Publishing House of the Pentecostal Holiness Church, 1951). The Pentecostal belief in faith healing was derived in part from the New Thought movement, which was also foundational to Christian Science, as discussed earlier.

68 Anderson, *Vision of the Disinherited*, 43, 47–61; Albanese, *America*, 123; Gaustad and Schmidt, *The Religious History of America*, 282; Wacker, *Heaven Below*, 5; Bettye Collier-Thomas, *Jesus, Jobs, and Justice: African American Women and Religion* (New York: Alfred A. Knopf, 2010), 73.

69 Anderson, *Vision of the Disinherited*, 52–3, 55.

70 Anderson, *Vision of the Disinherited*, 57–61, 252–3, note 1.

71 Anderson, *Vision of the Disinherited*, 60; Wacker, *Heaven Below*, 6.

72 Anderson, *Vision of the Disinherited*, 60–1, 63, 67.

73 Anderson, *Vision of the Disinherited*, 63–5.

74 Wacker, *Heaven Below*, 1; Anderson, *Vision of the Disinherited*, 68–70. Bartleman suggested that the success of the Azusa Street revival was the result of its spontaneity and that success led to a dramatic increase in the mission's membership, which in turn required organization. The mission became the Apostolic Faith Gospel Mission, and a committee of twelve elders was appointed to handle finances and other administrative duties. Bartleman's response was to declare that Azusa had begun "to fail the Lord," and he left to found another church nearby for which he refused to set up any governance or even to name it. Anderson, *Vision of the Disinherited*, 70.

75 Anderson, *Vision of the Disinherited*, 74–5; Wacker, *Heaven Below*, 6; Raboteau, *Canaan Land*, 96; Albanese, *America*, 144–5; Cheryl J. Sanders, *Saints in Exile: The Holiness-Pentecostal Experience in African American Religion and Culture* (New York: Oxford University Press, 1996), 31.

76 Anderson, *Vision of the Disinherited*, 64–9; Albanese, *America*, 124; Gaustad and Schmidt, *The Religious History of America*, 282; Sanders, *Saints in Exile*, 29–31; Raboteau, *Canaan Land*, 97. For examples of Holiness and Pentecostal churches that originated or became segregated, see Sanders, *Saints in Exile*, 17–21; for more on early Pentecostal racism leading to segregated churches, see Ian MacRoberts, *The Black Roots and White Racism of Early Pentecostalism in the USA* (London: Macmillan Press, 1988).

77 Milton C. Sernett, *Bound for the Promised Land: African American Religion and the Great Migration* (Durham, NC: Duke University Press, 1997), 4; Allan Spear, *Black Chicago: The Making of a Negro Ghetto, 1890–1920* (Chicago: The University of Chicago Press, 1967), 174–5.

78 Collier-Thomas, *Jesus, Jobs, and Justice*, xxix, xxv, 25–6, 73–4, 84; Sernett, *Bound for the Promised Land*, 161, 188; Raboteau, *Canaan Land*, 96–7; Sanders, *Saints in Exile*, 17, 32–3. See also Bettye Collier-Thomas, *Daughters of Thunder: Black Women Preachers and Their Sermons, 1850–1979* (San Francisco, CA: Jossey-Bass Publishers, 1997); Anthea Butler, *Women in the Church of God in Christ: Making a Sanctified World* (Chapel Hill: University of North Carolina Press, 2007).

79 Edith L. Blumhofer, *Restoring the Faith: The Assemblies of God, Pentecostalism, and American Culture* (Champagne: University of Illinois Press, 1983), 1–5; Anderson, *Vision of the Disinherited*, 91–7; Albanese, *America*, 124 and 242; Gaustad and Schmidt, *The Religious History of America*, 284; Collier-Thomas, *Jesus, Jobs, and Justice*, 73.

Recommended for further reading

Anderson, Robert M. *Vision of the Disinherited: The Making of American Pentecostalism*. New York: Oxford University Press, 1979.

Bannister, Robert C. *Social Darwinism: Science and Myth in Anglo-American Social Thought*. Philadelphia: Temple University Press, 1979.

Blumhofer, Edith L. *Restoring the Faith: The Assemblies of God, Pentecostalism, and American Culture*. Champagne: University of Illinois Press, 1993.

Bowler, Peter J. *Evolution: The History of an Idea*, 25th Anniversary edn. Berkeley: University of California Press, 2009.

Hawkins, Mike. *Social Darwinism in European and American Thought, 1860–1945: Nature as Model and Nature as Threat*. Cambridge, England: Cambridge University Press, 1997.

Hofstadter, Richard. *Social Darwinism in American Thought*, rev. edn. New York: George Braziller, Inc., 1959.

Larson, Orvin. *American Infidel, Robert G. Ingersoll: A Biography*. New York: The Citadel Press, 1962.

Marsden, George M. *Fundamentalism and American Culture: The Shaping of Twentieth-Century Evangelicalism, 1870–1925*, 2 edn. New York: Oxford University Press, 2006.

Persons, Stow. *Free Religion: An American Faith*. Boston: Beacon Press, 1963.

Turner, James. *Without God, Without Creed: The Origins of Unbelief in America*. Baltimore: The Johns Hopkins University Press, 1985.

Chapter 4

Religion in America between the World Wars

Fundamentalism

As discussed in Chapter 3, liberal Christianity and its reaction to the higher criticism and Darwinian evolution met with an equally strong reaction from conservative Christians. We discussed the modernist and antimodernist movement in the Roman Catholic Church and its equivalent among Conservative and Orthodox Jews. But at the end of the chapter, we discussed in greater detail the Christian holiness and pentecostal movements. We now turn to the fundamentalist movement, which is often grouped with the holiness and pentecostal movements under the label evangelical. All three insisted on some sort of spiritual rebirth as a criterion for entering the kingdom of heaven and opposed the direction liberal Christians took at the close of the nineteenth and early twentieth centuries. Yet members of each subgroup often rejected being associated with the others. What set the fundamentalists apart from the others was the group's foundation on a series of pamphlets entitled *The Fundamentals*.[1]

The idea for publication of *The Fundamentals*, subtitled *A Testimony to the Truth*, is commonly credited to a Southern California millionaire oilman Lyman Stewart, who believed that someone had to challenge the inroads being made on Christianity by modernism in general, including modern science, but especially biblical criticism. Lyman was moved in that direction upon attending a revival sermon by A. C. Dixon in August 1909 in Los Angeles, California. Dixon was an evangelist well known for his militant and polemical attacks upon forces of unbelief. Upon listening to Dixon, Stewart concluded that something had to be done to convey the true message of the Bible to the people. "The spiritual welfare of the present generation requires it," Lyman wrote to his brother Milton on October 26, 1909. It would involve "the best and most loyal Bible teachers in the world" – a mix of laymen and ministers, all of whom were millenarian fundamentalists and largely dispensationalists, who would prepare "masterpieces" that would "count for both time and eternity." Stewart pledged an initial $300,000 to the project, which became a series of inexpensive paperback books, distributed free of charge "to every pastor, missionary, theological professor, theological student, YMCA and YWCA secretary, college professor, Sunday School superintendent, and religious editor in the English speaking world," totaling some 3 million volumes in all.[2]

His brother and business partner, Milton, joined Stewart in the project, and A. C. Dixon, then pastor of the Moody Church in Chicago, became the series' first editor. Despite what may be described as its mass-marketing effort, the public response was not what they hoped for. The publishers received many individual positive responses, but neither theological journals nor popular religious periodicals seemed to take much notice. Nevertheless, publication of *The Fundamentals* proved important for two reasons. First, although as shown in the last chapter that the roots of fundamentalism can be traced back at least to the mid-nineteenth century, it has been effectively argued that modern fundamentalism – especially as an organized movement – got its start with publication of *The Fundamentals*, which began in 1910 and included twelve volumes by 1915. *The Fundamentals* did more than give fundamentalists their name, however. They identified articles of belief, defined differences between themselves and others, and gave fundamentalists a common identity. When in 1920 the term "fundamentalist" was coined, it called to mind the articles of belief articulated in those volumes.[3]

Historians such as Norman Furniss and Stewart Cole have described fundamentalism as being based on a set of beliefs commonly referred to as its "five points": the Bible's infallibility; Christ's divinity, or virgin birth; Christ's atonement; Christ's resurrection; and his Second Coming, all of which, as explained later, originated as a declaration of the Presbyterian General Assembly in 1910. Michael Lienesch, however, has made a strong case for its also being an identity movement, at least in its formative stages, arguing that its early proponents – prior to its becoming a full-fledged political movement in the 1920s – "were less concerned with creating creeds than with constructing community, and less interested in developing a doctrine or ideology, than in establishing a sense of identity for themselves." Whichever is the case, and both are likely, *The Fundamentals* made clear what the fundamentalists stood for and even how their views changed over the five years during which the publications appeared.[4]

Stewart's plan was to avoid including essays that would perpetuate the differences that had occurred among conservatives over the past few decades. Selecting Dixon as editor was a step in the right direction, as he was widely regarded and respected among religious leaders across the spectrum of denominations. Dixon recruited a diverse, if conservative, editorial board of clergy and lay leaders. The board then selected an equally diverse group of sixty-four authors, mostly non-denominational and associated with independent Bible conferences, revival ministries, and missionary organizations. The inerrancy of the Bible dominated *The Fundamentals*, beginning with the essays in the first volumes, which provided commentaries on the Bible, and commonly assumed the Bible to be inspired, inerrant, clear, and unchanging in meaning over time, thereby leading inexorably to only one interpretation. The primary concern at that point was identifying which texts could be considered definitive, meaning free of later changes.[5]

Another common set of entries included personal testimonials by some of the leading revivalists of the day, including Reuben Torrey, Arthur Pierson, and James Gray, all of whom have been accurately described as protégés of Dwight L. Moody. These testimonials emphasized soul-saving, personal experience, and individual prayer. Written in a sermon format, they were seasoned with healthy doses of sentimentality, telling stories "of lost and troubled souls, rescued by the loving hand of the Holy Spirit." The soul-saving was not only from personal sin, however, but also from "the alienation of mass [modern and secular] society and the loneliness and anxiety it created.[6]

Underscoring these and other messages was a premillennialist assumption, or the expectation of an imminent Second Coming and dispensationalism, which was increasingly popular among conservative evangelicals, providing them with an alternative to the previously dominant postmillennialism. This nineteenth century iteration of an idea that stretches back in various forms to antiquity, can be attributed to the work of the nineteenth-century British preacher and writer, John Nelson Darby. But it had precedents in America as well.[7]

There were the Disciples of Christ, whose leader, Alexander Campbell, in his appropriately titled monthly journal, the *Millennial Harbinger*, commonly made use of the apocalyptic symbolism of Daniel and Revelation and the writings of prominent millenarians of the day. There were the Mormons in the first decades of their existence, whose anticipation of the millennium was reflected in their chosen name, "the Latter-Day Saints." Their journal was titled, the *Millennial Star*, and their millenarianism was so intense that Joseph Smith soon felt obliged to restrain his followers. There were the Shakers, as they were commonly known, or the Millennial Church of the United Society of Believers in Christ's Second Appearance. They believed that the Second Coming, or advent, had already occurred with the incarnation of God in Mother Ann Lee, the female complement to the Christ of the first advent.[8]

And there was William Miller, a self-educated farmer from Low Hampton, New York, who became the most famous millenarian in American history. Miller formulated a view of the end times, which by 1834 began to attract sufficient interest to cause him to abandon farming and devote himself to his advent message, largely throughout upstate New York and New England. With the help of the Reverend Joshua Himes, whom Miller attracted to his cause in 1839, and the use of periodical literature, their own hymnal, *The Millennial Harp*, and camp meetings, Miller attracted some 50,000 adherents.[9]

Miller's message more closely reflected, and was more emphatic in its insistence on, what would become central to American premillennialism thereafter. It was grounded on a literal reading of the prophecies of the Bible, which he believed would inevitably come to pass. In brief, Christ would return, the wicked would be judged, and the world would be cleansed by fire sometime between March 21, 1843 and March 21, 1844, a year held in common by many premillenarians in the United States and Britain. Although there were other reasons, those who arrived at that date did so largely because they believed that the prophecy of the 2,300 days referenced in Daniel 8 would be fulfilled then. Miller finally fixed on October 22, 1844, as the day of the second advent, but when that day and subsequent follow up attempts to correctly set the date passed and nothing happened, the result became known as "the Great Disappointment." Most of his followers abandoned him, but some joined other similarly thinking groups, including what became the Seventh-Day Adventists and the Russellites, named after their founder Charles Taze Russell, later to be known as the Jehovah's Witnesses. Premillennialism lived on but few thereafter, no matter how strong their conviction that Christ's Second Coming was imminent, would dare proclaim an actual date for his reappearance. As Sandeen put it: "It took a long time for Americans to forget William Miller," at least until John Nelson Darby.[10]

John Nelson Darby's theology, known ever since as dispensationalism, was critical to the development of fundamentalism, late nineteenth-century American millenarianism, and the *Scofield Reference Bible*, which became the Bible of fundamentalism. In brief, Darby determined that the history of the church had passed through a series of dispensations, or distinct ages, that included the current age, marked by apostasy, and which would be followed by Christ's Second Coming. Postmillennialists believed that Christ would return at the end of a thousand years of peace, which they believed was promised in apocalyptic Scripture and that they were confident would happen as the world continued to move in that direction. Darby's reading of Scripture arrived at a different conclusion, one that was also based on his reading of the current age as anything but promising of the perfect millennium, and in that, he had many who agreed. What separated Darby from some other premillennialists, and was distinctive of dispensationalism, was his teaching that the Second Coming would be preceded by a period of tribulation, a redemptive moment called the rapture, in which believers would be transported to heaven and spared the embattled period on earth that was to follow. In fact, Darby taught that there would be two second advents, or perhaps better put, two stages in the second advent. The first would be known only to those who, after waiting faithfully, would secretly become part of the rapture and disappear from the earth. The Second Coming, at which point Christ would defeat Satan and inaugurate a thousand years of peace and righteousness (the millennium) would happen only after the rapture, would be no secret, and would resemble the description in Matthew 24:27: "For as the lightning comes from the east and shines as far as the west, so will be the coming of the Son of man." Unlike Miller, Darby refused to set a date for the second advent or to attempt to correlate current earthly events with those predicted in Revelations.[11]

Darby believed that the true church could not be aligned with any existing denomination, suggesting even that to become a member of the "true church" one must leave one's denomination and exist only as a spiritual fellowship. The true church would be consummated at the Second Coming of Christ when its members, both living and dead, would be gathered to live with Christ in heaven. Darby visited the United States seven times between 1862 and 1877, and although at least at first he found the churches too worldly, even "inordinately wicked," he attracted many adherents from various denominations, especially among Baptists and Old School Presbyterians. For many, Darby's teachings seemed consistent with, and helped explain, the world around them marred by war, greed, and immorality. The prospect that Christ would soon come back to save the world, which seemed beyond saving in any other way, was their "Blessed Hope." Cyrus Scofield provided Scriptural substance to Darby's scheme in his *Scofield Reference Bible* published in 1909, the year before *The Fundamentals*, and that became the standard Biblical fundamentalist text. Darby's influence in America became increasingly more obvious in the final volumes of *The Fundamentals*, published on the eve and first stages of World War I, which was viewed by many with great foreboding. As Arno C. Gaebelein wrote in the eleventh volume, "the last days of the world are at hand and the time of the end is here."[12]

The Fundamentals were successful at the start because in the first volumes much of what was included appealed to some moderates, as well as conservatives. But as later volumes appeared, their message became less accommodating to non-conservatives. The targets of the later essays were predictable, namely the higher criticism, Darwinism, and those liberal Christians who sought accommodation with both. Their criticism was not very different from that which we have already discussed, namely that the assertions of both were based on faulty scholarship, that they were merely hypotheses, and that in time they would be discounted. Further, proponents of higher criticism and Darwinism, including accommodating theologians, were painted as elitists, dismissive of the common man and common sense, and often associated with colleges and universities. Where the essayist drew the line, for the most part, was in what they argued was science's prejudice against the supernatural and the miraculous, or as Reuben Torrey put it, science's "*a priori* hypothesis that certain things are impossible," which limited man's ability to know God.[13]

The Fundamentals found enemies in an increasingly secular contemporary culture. It was the result, they argued, of the state, under the guise of the US Constitution, assuring the separation of church and state by striking down any laws or activities that legislatures or courts saw as imposing on non-believers or even non-Christians. If left unchecked, the result would be a nation with no soul or moral framework and therefore likely to fail. In one essay, Presbyterian layman Robert Speer described contemporary culture as godless and without any moral foundation, as "a vain and empty thing," without any moral rudder, licentious, even lawless, and capable of plunging into anarchy if enough people were "mastered by the mob."[14]

Others stepped up their concern with what they saw as the incompatible natures of their fundamental faith with socialism and science. In the final essay of the collection, however, it might be said that Princeton theologian Charles Erdman offered the final and definitive statement in the matter, at least for the moment, that socialism and Christianity were antithetical and ultimately irreconcilable. "Christian socialism," he concluded, "is neither Christian nor socialism." In reference to science, as *The Fundamentals* drew to a close, essayists began to move away from their earlier insistence that there could be no conflict between science and religion, in that they operated in entirely different spheres, by insisting that science was not honoring that separation, but instead pretending to intrude on the world of religion. As Alexander White Pitzer wrote, science had "passed out of its proper sphere when it invade[d] the domain of the Invisible and the Infinite." He argued that science has crossed "the boundary of the known," or that which is known by observation and reason into that which can only be known through revelation, even denying that God "has revealed himself or can reveal Himself in his Word, His Son, His Spirit."[15]

The Fundamentals failed in their primary purpose to check the spread of modernism. But they did contribute significantly to the fundamentalist movement, which began years before they were published. "Fundamentals" were written among nearly all of the American Protestant denominations, but most notably among the two major denominations – the Presbyterians and Northern Baptists – and most dramatically the Disciples of Christ. The fundamentals came under attack and were rejected by the majority of the Presbyterian General Assembly, but that led in the 1930s to the separation of some of its members from the Presbyterian Church in the U.S.A. to form smaller, more conservative denominations.[16]

Northern Baptists, already separated from their southern brethren from before the Civil War, further divided when, in the 1920s, fundamentalists sought to impose creedal uniformity within the Northern Baptist Convention (NBC). Liberals succeeded in maintaining control over Northern Baptist governing boards, seminaries and other major agencies, but by 1933, fifty conservative congregations separated from the NBC to form the General Association of Regular Baptists. By 1948, the continuous exodus led to the formation of the Conservative Baptist Association of America.[17]

And finally, during the early years of the twentieth century, conservatives, operating from the same sense of opposition to modernism, withdrew from the Disciples of Christ to form a new denomination, the Churches of Christ. In this case, rather than forming a new religious union they insisted on maintaining an independent congregational polity, refusing even to establish denominational headquarters. Nevertheless, in 1927, yet another group of churches went their own way. This time the seceders traced their roots to Alexander Campbell, whose attempt in the 1820s to return Christianity to its more pure apostolic age led to the formation of the Disciples of Christ, also referred to as the Christian Church. They took the name the North American Christian Connection. As Edwin Gaustad and Leigh Schmidt commented, this was an ironic development for a religious body that was founded to heal the wounds in Christianity, prevent further separation, and even serve to reunify the Church.[18]

Fundamentalists and the "Great Reversal"

In Chapter 3, we discussed what is commonly referred to as the "Great Reversal" among conservative Christians during the early years of the twentieth century. The focus was on holiness believers and pentecostals. The years between 1917 and 1925 witnessed a dramatic change among fundamentalists, as well. On the one hand, fundamentalists, much like their fellow conservatives, warned against the tendencies of their more liberal brethren to accommodate developments in science, especially evolution, and higher criticism and to pursue the Social Gospel. Rather than withdraw from the world, however, for the first half of the 1920s, they engaged in "holy warfare to drive the scourge of modernism out of church and culture." Major causes of this declaration of holy warfare were the more aggressive and more radical forms of liberal theology that developed in this period and the fundamentalist response to World War I.[19]

The fundamentalist response to World War I occurred in stages. Many Americans first response to the outbreak of war in Europe in 1914 was not to get involved, a position taken by fundamentalists as well. Once the US entered the war, however, popular opinion shifted in the direction of patriotic support for the war, a shift that was much slower in coming for fundamentalists, who retained their general hesitancy to engage in any substantial political involvement. That more complicated response to the war was most pronounced among the premillennial wing of fundamentalism. The premillennialist fundamentalist response to the course of events was that what was happening was based on their reading of Scripture and was a sign that the end times were close. *The King's Business*, edited by Reuben Torrey, the leading premillennial journal, and seen by many as a continuation of *The Fundamentals*, consistently delivered this message and opposed the war, as did Arno C. Gaebelein, editor of the premillennialist journal, *Our Hope*. Gaebelein associated the events leading to war with what "every close student of prophetic portions of the Bible" would readily see as "the predicted end of this age." Even after the United States entered the war, Gaebelein continued to see it as a sign of the end times and published an article by Samuel Ridout, whose title posed the question "Should a Christian Go to War?" Ridout answered, no, insisting that "the very question well-nigh answers itself." Christians should separate themselves from the world and not set out to improve it. They should "render unto Caesar" what civil leaders command, as long as what they command does not conflict with God's commands. But in the event of war, prayer and other types of service are better than fighting, to wit he suggested clerical duties, ambulance service, and ministering to the wounded and dying.[20]

The premillennialist opposition to the war alarmed liberals, which in turn led to their fierce assault on premillennialist teaching, which precipitated the fundamentalist-liberal cultural war that played itself out in the 1920s.[21] The premillennialists responded by denying any disloyalty and by reiterating what they believed was the biblical basis for their views. They also fought back by arguing that German militarism was the result of German theology, which they tied to the higher criticism, which, along with Darwinian evolution and other forms of modernism, had become so influential in that country. It was these ideas, and the cultural crisis that bred them, that transformed fundamentalism into its classic form. Further, during the 1920s, the confrontation between fundamentalists and modernists was not only a theological debate, but also a cultural one, thereby making it an even more heated affair. Whereas to that point, premillennialists had not engaged in cultural issues (as much as they concerned them), in response to all of the challenges they then faced, theirs became a moral crusade first to make the war a godly cause and then to save the nation by returning it to Christian principles upon which, they believed, the nation had been founded.[22]

An important goal in the effort of fundamentalists to return the nation to Christian principles was their effort to drive liberals from the nation's major Protestant denominations. This effort peaked in the early 1920s. All of the leading churches felt the heat to some extent, but as noted earlier, the major battles were fought among the Baptists and Presbyterians in the North. In the South, religious conservatism went largely unchallenged, as religious and cultural conservatism had gone hand-in-hand in preservation of the Southern way of life since the end of the Civil War. Not so in the North where liberalism had made significant inroads. As the sides were so evenly matched and aggressive among Northern Baptists and Presbyterians, many feared that schism was inevitable. That did not happen but the battle opened up wounds that would not heal for many years.[23]

Among the Baptists, the fundamentalists were ready to take action when, in May 1922, the liberal preacher Harry Emerson Fosdick struck first with a sermon aptly titled, "Shall the Fundamentalists Win?" The sermon struck so responsive a chord that it was published in three journals – *The Christian Century*, *The Baptist*, and *The Christian Work* – and in a widely distributed pamphlet under the title *The New Knowledge and the Christian Faith*. Fosdick provided what were commonly accepted by both sides as the four central doctrinal tests of American fundamentalism, namely belief in biblically recorded miracles such as the virgin birth, the inerrancy of Scripture, Christ's atonement for mankind, and the premillennial Second Coming of Christ. Fosdick's approach to the first three was to contrast the fundamentalist positions on these various points with those of the "multitudes of reverent Christians" who saw natural historical processes as God's way of doing things, including conservatives. He made clear his belief that, whereas conservatives subscribed to this set of beliefs, where they parted company was in the conservative's "true liberality of spirit." Fundamentalists, in contrast, "essentially illiberal and intolerant," he insisted, intended to force those who did not agree with them on these basic tests out of the churches, when reasonable people reading the same Bible could reach different conclusions in these matters. What the churches needed more than ironclad creeds to which all must subscribe, he argued, striking a responsive chord among many who had grown tired, if not fearful, of where fundamentalism was headed, was "magnanimity and liberality and tolerance of spirit," which had been central to the Baptist church in the United States since its founding.[24]

The Northern Baptist Convention failed to act at its 1922 meeting because of its inability to agree on a creedal test of orthodoxy, the moderates insisting that more time and careful preparation was needed. William B. Riley, the chief organizer of the World's Christian Fundamentals Association in 1919, the main organization of the premillennial wing of the fundamentalist movement, tried to force the issue. He proposed that the convention adopt one of the traditional Baptist creeds, the New Hampshire Confession. But instead the body approved a simpler and historically more consistent statement: "The New Testament is the all-sufficient ground for our faith and practice, and we need no other statement." The effect of this defeat not only stalled the fundamentalist movement, but it also drove a wedge between the conservative and moderate members of the movement that prevented any future action. Conservatives joined Riley in forming the Baptist Bible Union, while the moderates continued to work within the larger body seeking consensus that would head off any further movement toward schism.[25]

Presbyterians followed a similar pattern. Fosdick's sermon, though intended for a Baptist audience, stoked the fire that continued to burn in the Presbyterian Church in the U.S.A. from the controversy over the Briggs affair that occurred thirty years earlier. Fosdick, though a Baptist, was serving as the associate pastor of the First Presbyterian Church of New York when he preached his controversial sermon. The sermon served to more fully convince conservatives of the need to bring liberal members back into the fold or expel them. Charles Macartney, pastor of the Arch Street Presbyterian Church in Philadelphia, led the charge by countering Fosdick's sermon with one titled, "Shall Unbelief Win?" arguing that Fosdick's "naturalistic alternatives" to fundamentalism diverged from traditional Christianity. Where

Fosdick and others were "blasting at the Rock of Ages," Macartney insisted, it was essential to "contend for the faith. Macartney led the Presbytery of Philadelphia to petition the General Assembly at its meeting in 1923 to condemn Fosdick's sermon and order the Presbytery of New York to assure that ministers within its jurisdiction, the First Church in particular, conform to orthodox Presbyterian doctrine.[26]

Conservatives failed in their efforts to elect William Jennings Bryan – already taking his antievolution campaign national – moderator of the General Assembly, but they succeeded in having the body condemn Fosdick's sermon, in ordering the Presbytery to take action against any further such laxness in doctrine, and in reaffirming the doctrinal declaration of 1910 and 1916. In the months that followed, the controversy reached new heights with publication of Princeton New Testament scholar John Gresham Machen's *Christianity and Liberalism* (1923). Although not of one mind with conservatives on all issues, Machen was uncompromising on the main points. "The great redemptive religion which has always been known as Christianity," he wrote in his opening sentence, "is battling against a totally diverse type of religious belief, which is only the more destructive of the Christian faith because it makes use of traditional Christian terminology." He went on to declare the teaching of the liberal wing of Presbyterianism "un-Christian," and "unscientific." Christianity, he insisted, was a religion based on facts, which were open to scientific investigation, as opposed to liberalism which "appeals to man's will" and on an "indefinite type of religious aspiration." The result, he predicted, if not stopped, would be a uniformity that would turn the nation into "one huge 'Main Street.'"[27]

Among the Presbyterians, as was the case among Northern Baptists, the liberals succeeded in blocking conservative attempts to reject them, not because they were able to persuade moderates that their form of Christianity was acceptable, but rather because of their successful appeal to the long-standing tradition among Presbyterians, as well as Baptists, of tolerance. The substance of this position was put forth in January 1924 by those who protested the General Assembly's decision in 1923 in what was known as the "Auburn Affirmation." The Affirmation, which gathered some 1,300 signatures before the 1924 Assembly, argued that the fundamentalist five-point declaration was not only extra-Biblical but also extra-constitutional, meaning that it was not included in the body's still authoritative Westminster Confession of Faith adopted in 1792. Therefore, although there may be disagreement over these extra-constitutional points, that same Confession made clear that the Presbyterian Church should be broad enough to include all those who held to that Confession's authoritative points and provide for some liberty in interpreting the central tenets of the Confession. Pushed toward a rejection of such tolerance, not only moderates but many conservatives broke ranks with the more militant conservatives and the coalition necessary for the fundamentalists to succeed fell apart. Neither the Presbyterian nor the Baptist Church would be divided, at least organizationally; the two sides would coexist.[28]

The Scopes trial

Some would argue that the fundamentalist-modernist culture war peaked in 1925, focusing intently on evolution and on the teaching of evolution in the schools in particular. William Jennings Bryan led the crusade, which came to a head in Dayton, Tennessee. Although it is often portrayed as a pitting of northern liberals against Bible-belt conservatives, the contest was more correctly a pitting of fundamentalists and liberals in the northern Protestant denominations.[29]

Two points need to be made here. First, by the 1920s and the start of what has been described as "a clash of cultures symbolizing the old versus the new, the conservative versus the liberal, and the religious versus the scientific," the impact of evolution on religious belief was greater than ever, resulting from advances in genetics, which not only served to provide evidence for the long sought-for mechanism that drove generational variation and natural selection, but that also began to drive out alternative explanations such as Lamarckian evolution and further call into question theistic evolution. What followed was that textbooks became more Darwinian. In his research on the subject, Edward Larson found one representative biology textbook, which featured a picture of Darwin and a subchapter titled "The Struggle for Existence and Its Effects." Another hailed Darwin for discovering "the laws of life," including the concept of organic evolution through natural selection. And Hunter's *Civic Biology*, the best-selling textbook in the field, and the text approved for use in the Tennessee public schools, credited Darwin for "the proofs of the theory on which we today base the progress of the world." Hunter, a teacher at DeWitt Clinton High School in New York, included sections on natural selection and genetics, for whose assistance he relied on faculty from nearby Columbia University, including America's leading geneticist Thomas Hunt Morgan.[30]

Second, evolution did not become a fighting matter for many fundamentalists until it became a required part of their children's publicly supported education. Relatively few American teenagers attended high school in the nineteenth century, even fewer attended in the rural South where public schools were slow to appear and where compulsory attendance was even slower to be required by law. All of that began to change in the twentieth century. The number of pupils enrolled in American high schools increased from about 200,000 in 1890 to nearly 2 million in 1920. Tennessee largely followed this trajectory, with its high school population numbering fewer than 10,000 in 1910 to more than 50,000 by the opening of the Scopes trial in 1925. This increase resulted from the larger number of, and therefore greater access to, secondary schools and Progressive-era school attendance laws that included teenagers. None other than Tennessee Governor Austin Peay, who signed his state's antievolution bill into law, boasted in his 1925 inaugural address that high schools had "sprung up throughout the state which are the pride of their communities." Dayton opened its first high school in 1906. At that point, fundamentalists, who for years were simply able to ignore those scientific developments that had been bolstering Darwinian evolution, increasingly found them in their children's textbooks.[31]

William Jennings Bryan – three-time presidential candidate, former Secretary of State, and champion of many liberal causes, including the direct election of senators and female suffrage – was among those concerned with the teaching of evolution in the public schools. Although outspoken on the entirety of the theory of Darwinian evolution, Bryan's major concern was with the idea that man descended from lower orders of life, as opposed to being the product of special, divine creation, which, he believed, undermined the ties between God and man upon which all virtues rested. This was central to his ardent opposition to those who applied Darwin's natural selection theory to Social Darwinism, or what by the 1920s became better known as eugenics. First proposed by Darwin's cousin, Francis Galton, in the 1860s as a means to accelerate beneficial human evolution, the idea attracted few followers until the turn of the century, at which point it too found its way into textbooks. The public campaign to impose eugenic restrictions on reproduction peaked in the twenties along with the antievolution crusade. By 1935, for example, thirty-fives states enacted laws to compel the sexual segregation and sterilization of certain persons viewed as eugenically unfit, particularly the mentally ill, intellectually limited, and habitual criminals. Hunter, once again, was typical in his assessment. In another of his popular textbooks, he referred to eugenics as "the science of improving the human race by better heredity," while in his *Civic Biology*, he explained: "If such people were lower animals, we would probably kill them off to prevent them from spreading," although he quickly added: "Humanity will not allow this, but we do have the remedy of separating the sexes in asylums or other places and in various ways preventing intermarriage and the possibility of perpetuating such a low and degenerate race."[32]

The legislatures of six states actively considered antievolution proposals during the spring of 1923, with Bryan offering his support. Only two met with any success, but momentum was building. In 1925, Tennessee enacted one of the strongest laws to date, making it illegal "to teach any theory that denies the story of the Divine Creation of man as taught in the Bible, and to teach instead that man had descended from a lower order of animal." Bryan gave several antievolution speeches in the state in 1924 and 1925. Billy Sunday led a crusade in Memphis during the 1925 state legislative session, and fundamentalist leader William Riley convened a national conference of the World's Christian Fundamentals Associated in Memphis on the eve of the legislative vote with Bryan as the featured speaker. What was to be known as the Butler Act, after John W. Butler, who introduced the legislation in the state House of Representatives, was adopted with little opposition, and that mostly from professors and administrators of nearby Vanderbilt University.[33]

The American Civil Liberties Union decided to challenge the Tennessee statute, not on the grounds that it constituted a government act to protect or promote religion, but rather that it represented a threat to freedom and individual liberty. As historian Samuel Walker has written, in response to restrictive measures adopted by Washington during World War I and to postwar anticommunist and antianarchist hysteria – the "Red Scare" – the ACLU was increasingly concerned with majoritarian ideology that the Butler Act was seen as representing and that they saw as inconsistent, or in conflict, with protections guaranteed by the First Amendment.[34]

Clarence Darrow, who stepped forward to join the defense, was America's best-known criminal defense lawyer and champion of anticlericalism. He was nominated for a seat in Congress in 1896, a contest he lost, but ironically, he spent most of his time campaigning for the Democratic Party ticket headed by William Jennings Bryan with whom he remained allied on a number of causes for many years. In a time when such activity was not popular, Darrow championed the cause of labor, even defending highly suspect labor leader Eugene V. Debs against criminal charges that arose out of the 1894 Pullman strike and defending two union leaders charged with murder in the blowing up of the *Los Angeles Times* building in 1911, a charge to which they ultimately confessed. By the 1920s, he had shifted his practice to criminal law and gained a reputation for defending disreputable individuals, some political radicals, and a few murderers, like two wealthy Chicago teenagers in the Leopold-Loeb Case, decided the year before the Scopes trial and often commented on in Dayton before and during the trial.[35]

More important here were Darrow's views on religion. Darrow biographer, Kevin Tierney, has concluded that Darrow regarded Christianity as a "slave religion," encouraging "acquiescence in injustice, a willingness to make do with the mediocre, and complacency in the face of the intolerable." In the tradition of Robert Ingersoll, and with whom Darrow was quite familiar, he called himself an agnostic, although some have concluded that he was effectively an atheist. Darrow argued that the concept of original sin and salvation only through divine grace was "a very dangerous doctrine," "silly, impossible and wicked." "It is not the bad people I fear so much as the good people," he once noted. "When a person is sure that he is good, he is nearly hopeless; he gets cruel – he believes in punishment." Further, as he stated on another occasion, in response to those who argued that civilization was possible only among a religious people: "The origin of what we call civilization is not due to religion but to skepticism. . . . The modern world is the child of doubt and inquiry, as the ancient world was the child of fear and faith."[36]

Darrow never dealt in any depth on evolution in his public addresses or writings, but he readily embraced its antitheistic implications. Thus, he welcomed the chance to challenge the antievolution crusade. When the Scopes trial was announced, and Bryan joined the prosecution, Darrow volunteered his services for the defense, *pro bono*. As Darrow showed no great concern for free speech in the case against Scopes, or even academic freedom, but rather made clear his intent to storm the fortress of revealed religion and religious intolerance, the ACLU was less than enthusiastic about Darrow's joining the team and tried, but failed, to remove him from the defense. Their goal was simply to challenge the constitutionality of the Tennessee law, not defend evolution. As the ACLU stated: "The attempts of education authorities to inject into public schools and colleges instruction propaganda in the interest of any particular theory of society to the exclusion of others should be opposed."[37]

In early May 1925, the ACLU issued a press release offering to defend any teacher willing to test the Tennessee antievolution statute in court. It explained that their lawyers believed it would be "a friendly test case" that would not cost the teacher his or her job. George Rappleyea, a New Yorker with a doctorate in chemical engineering, who had moved to Dayton, Tennessee, to manage area mines, ran across the news in the *Chattanooga Times*. Rappleyea opposed the law and saw the opportunity to strike it down, but he also convinced local leaders that bringing the case to Dayton, the Rhea County seat of some 1800 residents, would attract considerable publicity. When the others agreed, they summoned John T. Scopes to inquire as to his willingness to be their defendant. Scopes, a 24-year-old general science teacher and part-time football coach, was not the high school biology teacher, but he had been substituting for the actual teacher, actually conducting study sessions for upcoming student exams. He could not recall having actually taught evolution, but it was in the textbook he and the high school were using and that was approved by the state of Tennessee, Hunter's *Civic Biology*. When asked, however, he commented that no one could teach biology without teaching evolution. He agreed to be the test case, and the stage was set for the trial. Word went out, and within a matter of days, William Jennings Bryan offered his services – *pro-bono* – to the prosecution; Darrow's offer came almost immediately thereafter.[38]

The local leaders of Dayton were thrilled, but not the ACLU and the Governor of Tennessee and others, who feared that despite filling out the legal teams on both sides with several attorneys not wishing an antievolution spectacle, the trial would become a circus that would bring anything but favorable publicity to the city and state. Darrow made his sentiments known immediately: "Nero tried to kill Christianity with persecution and law. Bryan would block enlightenment with law. Had Mr. Bryan's ideas of what a man may do towards free thinking existed throughout history, we would still be banning and burning witches and punishing persons who thought the earth was round." Bryan responded: "Darrow is an atheist, I'm an upholder of Christianity. That is the difference between us. I never attempt to answer atheists, or those who argue for the sake of arguing, so will make no reply to Mr. Darrow's attack. The real issue is not what can be taught in public schools, but who shall control the education system."[39]

Whatever the intent of Darrow and Bryan coming into the trial, the prosecution ultimately decided to oppose the admission of expert testimony on the theory of evolution and focus on whether or not Scopes broke the law, the latter point not being contested by the defense. Darrow, however, insisted on contesting the decision, hoping to somehow provide a legal basis for appeal on the constitutionality of the law before the state supreme court. Bryan reconciled himself to the position, publicly stating that he had come to Tennessee to defend the rights of the people, but he took his case to the people and the press, taking every opportunity outside of court to make his position on evolution known. Before the trial began, he explained the significance of the trial to Dayton's Progressive Club: "The contest between evolution and Christianity is a duel to the death. . . . If evolution wins, Christianity goes . . . for the two cannot stand together." Darrow's intent was made clear in a comment he also made before the trial: "Scopes is not on trial. Civilization is on trial. Nothing will satisfy us but broad victory, a knockout which will have an everlasting precedent to prove that America is founded on liberty and not on narrow, mean, intolerable, and brainless prejudice of soulless religio-maniacs."[40]

The trial began on July 10, 1925. A jury was impaneled, which was a challenge for the defense as, at least of the start of the trial, most of the local inhabitants were in favor of the law, if not outright antievolutionists. Darrow settled for those who at least appeared to be open minded about the charges being brought, if not about evolution. All were church members, had little formal education, and were mostly middle-aged farmers living in Rhea County. As reporter H. L. Mencken reported, "The most Mr. Darrow could hope for was to sneak in a few men bold enough to declare publicly that they would have to hear the evidence against Scopes before condemning him."[41]

The matter of Darrow's bringing to the stand a long list of scientists and theologians who would testify that evolution and the Biblical account of creation were not necessarily contradictory was immediately challenged by the prosecution. Their position was that such testimony was irrelevant, as the matter at hand was whether or not Scopes, a public school teacher, had taught a doctrine prohibited by a Tennessee statute – namely by teaching that "mankind is descended from a lower order of animals . . . a theory which denied the story of divine creation of man as taught in the Bible." The state, the prosecution argued, had the right to determine what was taught in its public schools, as well as what was to be excluded. Scopes had the right to believe and even to espouse in public whatever he wished, but not to teach that which was excluded from the curriculum by the state, as he accepted his teaching position of his own free will.[42]

With the jury out of the courtroom, Darrow was allowed to begin calling his witnesses, who provided evidence for evolution, testified to its widespread acceptance among biologists, and argued that evolution did not necessarily contradict the account of creation in the Bible. But after only a handful of such witnesses and with the constant objections of the prosecution on the relevance of the testimony, Judge Raulston ruled out any further expert testimony in the case and ordered the testimony to that point to be expunged from the court record. Upon appeal from the defense, he did allow the defense to submit expert testimony to the court for the purposes of an appeal in the form of sworn affidavits or testimony to the court reporter. The defense had only one card left to play – an unorthodox one at that – and called Bryan to the stand as an expert on the Bible. The ardent protests of his fellow prosecutors notwithstanding, Bryan agreed. And thus, as the *Nashville Banner* reported, "began an examination which has few, if any, parallels in court history. In reality, it was a debate between Darrow and Bryan on Biblical history, on agnosticism and belief in revealed religion." At long last, and quite unexpectedly, both men would have their day in court. Judge Raulston moved the proceedings to the courthouse lawn to accommodate the expected crowd, which he feared might cause the floor of the second story courtroom to collapse.[43]

Darrow treated Bryan much as he would any hostile witness, focusing almost exclusively on Bryan's contention – implied if not explicitly stated – that the Bible was to be taken literally. Darrow forced Bryan to abandon, or at least compromise on, it by bringing up various stories from the Bible that if taken literally defied any rational literal reading, such as Jonah being swallowed and living inside a whale for three days; or Joshua making the sun stand still; or most damaging, that references to days in Genesis could mean days of longer than twenty-four hours, even of an indeterminate length. In sum, Darrow pressured Bryan into admitting that he interpreted the Bible, which was central to Darrow's point about evolution and Scripture. Despite the pleadings of his fellow prosecutors, Bryan refused to leave the stand, instead arguing that he was "simply trying to protect the word of God against the greatest atheist or agnostic in the United States." Addressing the press, he explained: "I want the papers to know I am not afraid to get on the stand in front of him and let him do his worst. The only purpose Mr. Darrow has is to slur the Bible, but I will answer his questions," to which Darrow objected, shouting: "I am examining your fool ideas that no intelligent Christian on earth believes." At that point, the judge adjourned the court for the day and Bryan did not return to the stand. When court reconvened the next day, Judge Raulston ruled that the exchange between Darrow and Bryan had added noting to the case and ordered it expunged from the record.[44]

With no more witnesses to call, the defense asked the judge to bring in the jury and to instruct them to find the defendant guilty. The judge accepted the suggestion, clearly wishing to bring the trial, which had clearly gotten out of hand, to an end. What the defense intended by this move was to deprive Bryan of the last chance to deliver his closing argument, and to avoid any chance of a hung jury, which would have hampered its plans to challenge the constitutionality of the law in a higher court. On behalf of the prosecution, Bryan acquiesced, noting that he would avail himself of the opportunity to give to the press, not the court, what were to be his closing remarks. The jury left the room and returned in nine minutes with a guilty verdict. Scopes addressed the court only briefly, asserting that he believed the statute to be unjust and pledged to continue to fight it in the name of academic freedom. The judge imposed the minimum fine of $100. Bryan remarked that the brief trial had raised a major cause, which like other major causes would "stir the world." Darrow responded: "I think this case will be remembered because it is the first case of this sort since we stopped trying people in America for witchcraft. We have done our best to turn the tide . . . of testing every fact in science by a religious doctrine."[45]

The Scopes trial did not end the antievolution crusade. To begin with, Scopes lost his case, the Tennessee law was upheld, and more than twenty antievolution statutes were introduced in state legislatures across the country over the next several years. The defense did appeal the verdict, and the Tennessee Supreme Court took up the case in May 1926. Both sides presented their cases, and the court took the matter under advisement for another seven months before issuing its opinion. When it did, the Court upheld the law, echoing the defense's position that the statute only applied to public employees acting in their official capacity, and therefore did not infringe on individual liberty. Scopes "had no right or privilege to serve the state except upon such terms as the state prescribed." Furthermore, the law "requires the teaching of nothing," and therefore "we are not able to see how the prohibition . . . gives preference to any religious establishment." However, the Court went on to overturn Scopes' conviction on the grounds that the trial judge, rather than the jury, inappropriately fixed the amount of the fine, and advised the Tennessee attorney not to seek further prosecution of the case. In sum, the law stood and Scopes no longer had a case to appeal further to the federal courts, even the US Supreme Court.[46]

Returning to the days immediately following the Dayton trial, Bryan put the finishing touches to his closing argument, which he did not have a chance to deliver. In some 15,000 words, he once again attacked Darwinian evolution as contrary to the Biblical account of creation. He charged its survival-of-the-fittest explanation for human development with destroying one's faith in God. He argued that as such it only encouraged the ideas of Social Darwinism, to which he was unalterable opposed and he believed was responsible for the destructive path Germany took just a few years earlier. And he insisted that belief in the theory would undermine any commitment to, and realistic hope for, meaningful social reform. Bryan immediately took to the antievolution campaign trail once again and, at least in the South, his reputation seemed hardly to have been tarnished by events in Dayton and his cross-examination by Darrow. As his most recent biographers have noted, those who supported him prior to the trial not only continued to do so after the trial, but pictured him as having valiantly defended the Bible against the "Great Agnostic." When Bryan died only days after the trial – on July 26 – he became a martyr to the cause.[47]

"God's Flapper": Aimee Semple McPherson

The fundamentalists as an organized force would live to fight another day, but in the meantime, their battle would be waged by some of the most colorful preachers in American history: Billy Sunday, who has already been discussed; Aimee Semple McPherson; and the Black preachers Daddy Grace and Father Divine, all of whom took the country by storm through the 1920s and 1930s.

"God's Flapper," Aimee Semple McPherson (see Figure 4.1) reached an even larger audience than Sunday, largely through the use she made of radio, stage, and film. As one writer has summarized it: "If the Scopes Trial was supposed to be fundamentalism's last stand, someone forgot to tell Aimee Semple McPherson. . . . Even after the trial . . . [she] acted and spoke as if the movement was in its ascendancy and poised for victory over American culture." As one of her contemporaries put it: "[The Jazz Age] was a time for petting and necking; for flasks and roadside taverns; for movie palaces and automobiles . . . and Aimee was determined to lead the people on a grand detour to Heaven." By the early 1920s, Los Angeles became McPherson's home base, where she built the Angelus Temple, one of the largest houses of worship in the nation, and founded her own International Church of the Foursquare Gospel, which even today counts some 50,000 churches and 6 million adherents. And finally, as one biographer put it: "By linking the old-time religion to the modern world," she "ushered pentecostalism into the mainstream of American culture."[48]

McPherson emerged from, and after straying a bit, returned to the pentecostal movement. She was introduced to pentecostalism in 1907 by her first husband, Robert Semple, an early convert to the movement, who led revival services in Canada, where he met Aimee Elizabeth Kennedy. The first influence in Aimee's religious life came from her mother, Minnie, an active member of the Salvation Army near Ingersoll, Ontario, Canada. But as Aimee later reported, at one point in her youth, she underwent a crisis of faith when she encountered evolution, an encounter she never forgot nor ceased to fight for the rest of her life. Under Semple's tutelage, at age 17, Aimee reconnected to God. She abandoned her mother's

Figure 4.1 Aimee Semple McPherson, God's Flapper

Source: Everett Collection Historical/Alamy Stock Photo

Salvation Army and embraced pentecostalism. She married Robert Semple, nine years her senior in 1908 and soon thereafter moved to Chicago where both worked as evangelists at the North Avenue Mission and were ordained by William Durham at the Full Gospel Assembly. It should be noted that, among pentecostals, ordination was recognition that the person was "called" by God, but although it did not rule it out, it did not confer any direct access to the ministry. However, Aimee could expect to preach and even provide leadership at camp meetings and revivals. It was also while she was in Chicago that Aimee realized that God had given her "the gift of interpretation," or that by God's speaking through her, she would be able to interpret the words of those speaking in tongues otherwise unintelligible to others. In 1910, Aimee and Robert joined the missionary field in China. As she would later relate in "The Story of My Life," she had a vision of "men clad in priestly robes and ministerial attire" smothering the "Book of light and wisdom," with their erroneous ideas, whereupon she was told by God to venture forth to recover the truth.[49]

Within months after taking up their mission in China, when Aimee was eight months pregnant, Robert Semple died. Following the birth of a daughter, Roberta, Aimee and daughter joined her mother and the Salvation Army in New York City. Aimee suffered a relapse in her sense of calling and in 1912 married Harold McPherson. She later recalled: "It was just at the time of my greatest perplexity, when I began to lose out spiritually and wander away from the Lord, and was longing to make a home for the baby, that I married again." Although apparently devoted to Aimee, McPherson, a businessman, did not share his wife's religious mission, which she recovered when, in 1913, she became seriously ill and believed she was going to die. After giving birth to a son, Rolf, Aimee separated, and eventually was divorced from her husband, returned to Canada and joined in the pentecostal camp meetings led by itinerant preachers. Aimee painted the words, '"Where will you spend eternity?" on the side of her car, and she and her mother hit the road soon crossing the border into the United States Northeast. They traveled all along the East Coast, through the Midwest, and in 1918 arrived in California, gaining a following at every stop along the way. McPherson's message was a combination of pentecostalism, including spiritual gifts of healing and speaking in tongues; Salvation Army methodology, "making a scene to attract an audience"; and fundamentalism, including an attack on modernism and evolution. She spoke out in support of America's entry into World War I, proclaiming, "We are in this war as soldiers of Jesus." But more broadly, her preaching was positive and nurturing, speaking more of the joys of heaven than Billy Sunday, with his negative criticism of culture and his focus on hell.[50]

Her days on the road having worn her down, and after a series of wildly successful revivals in Southern California, McPherson decided to build a church in Los Angeles dedicated, as she put it, to "the preaching of a Four-Square Gospel: Jesus the Only Savior; Jesus the Great Physician; Jesus, Baptizer with the Holy Spirit; Jesus, the Coming Bridegroom, Lord and King." The $300,000 Angelus Temple opened on January 1, 1923, preceded and announced by a float shaped like the temple in the Annual Tournament of the Roses Parade. McPherson explained that it was to be

> a great revival center to which thousands may come to find salvation, divine healing, the Baptism of the Holy Spirit, encouragement, rest, refreshing and enduement of power for service, and where the prospective evangelist and worker may come for practical train-ing in winning souls for Jesus.

With the opening of the Angelus Temple, historian William Cooper has written: "American revivalism had separated into two forms, both similar in message but different in style and setting. One was itinerate, the other institutionalized."[51]

As we have seen, McPherson was not the first female revivalist, or even the first female pentecostal revivalist. But she was the first to lead a major revival movement, which stirred up some controversy among more conservative members of the clergy, as did her commit-ment to divine healing and speaking in tongues. As has been true of American churches in general, more women than men attended Angelus Temple services – estimated at 66 percent of attendees. The first class of her Evangelical Missionary Training Institute, noted below, enrolled 68 women and only 31 men. McPherson focused most intently on the role of women in the pulpit after 1936, as part of her "Back to Pentecost" movement. "Sex has nothing to do with the pulpit, and pants don't make preachers," she insisted, fearing that the female gradu-ates of her Institute, who far outnumbered men, would be discriminated against. "It is brains, not sex, that make a preacher." As she was quoted in the *New York Times*, "It is only within the church that a definite prejudice against women exists. I intend to wage a fight to break this down." And fight she did, although as Edith Blumhofer has found, as the number of her branch churches grew, the percentage of female pastors declined by as much as 50 percent.[52]

McPherson, who became the first religious celebrity of the mass media era, made use of the new forms of radio and film, adopting various Hollywood techniques, and transformed her services into dramatic productions and pageants in which she played a leading role.[53] But she was particularly famous for her illustrated sermons, which included animals from the city zoo, like a camel trying to go through the eye of a needle, and a sheep used to illustrate the parable of the lost sheep. Described by some as vaudeville programs, one journalist observed: "In the show-devouring city, no entertainment compares popularity with that of Angelus Temple; the audience, whether devout or otherwise, concede it the best for the money (or for no money) in town." Her theatrics incurred the wrath of fellow revivalists, and with those of Billy Sunday led to the "Elmer Gantry" image of revivalism, taken from the Sinclair Lewis novel (1926) and movie (1960). The main female character, Sister Sharon Falconer, was patterned at least in part after McPherson, as "a promiscuous hypocrite, whose sexual cravings belie her spiritual authenticity."[54]

But McPherson also offered piety along with pageantry, as well as hope through a simple presentation of the Christian Gospel message. She organized her entire message into one "Declaration of Faith," which temple members were required to affirm: "We believe that the Holy Bible is the Word of the living God; true, immutable, steadfast, unchangeable." As one biographer has written: "She humanized Jesus, making him come to life as a real person who earnestly sought a relationship with every human being." She avoided the sectarianism that had marginalized many pentecostals, as well as any formal theology, in which she had little training. She officially joined the Assemblies of God in 1919 but did not affirm her relationship with this leading pentecostal association for fear of alienating her non-pentecostal followers. Whereas in her early years she defended the exuberance of those baptized in the Holy Spirit as manifestations that cannot be stifled without quenching the power of the Holy Spirit, she spoke out against the "wildness, hysteria, screaming" and other forms of "unseemly manifestations," that marked pentecostal services, as inconsistent with the workings of the Holy Spirit.[55]

Like most early pentecostals, McPherson was a premillennialist. She preached that human sinfulness was leading the world toward ultimate destruction, the Second Coming of Christ, and the millennium, or thousand-year reign of peace. Her goal was to save as many souls as possible before that happened and those not saved were lost forever. She explained: "The realization that Jesus is coming soon and that whatever is done must be done quickly has put a 'hurry up' in my soul to get the message to the greatest number of people in the shortest possible time by every available means." Jesus could, and did, transform those who believed – those who accepted him – and in the salvation of souls lay the restoration of America as God's chosen nation. As William Cooper has explained:

> America suffered immorality in the 20s, economic collapse in the 30s, and world war in the 40s. There were turbulent times and conservative God-fearing people were afraid. They felt helpless, overwhelmed by the onslaught of evil and the events surrounding them. More and more the talk of the last days and the end of the world came to the fore. Fundamentalism, mostly located in dispensationalism, had fled the scene, grown deeply pessimistic about this world, seeking only to rescue who they could from a sinking society and then removing them from the influences of evil.

McPherson, Cooper insists, "saw pentecostalism not merely as a rescue mission but . . . a pouring out of power in the last days to restore. Those with the power of God were not to be in retreat. They were on the march. They would attack the foe and win."[56]

In 1926, McPherson attracted thousands to her temple, The Church of the Foursquare Gospel, where some 8,000 underwent conversion in the first six months. Millions more followed her via radio, newsreels, her monthly magazine, *Bridal Call*, and the press, finding her way to the front page of America's biggest newspapers on average three times a week. She built and operated her own radio station (KFSG), established the Angelus Temple Training School to prepare evangelists to oppose the higher criticism, evolution, and modernism, so that "no power on earth or hell" could shake the students from "the Fundamental Doctrines," and she attracted unprecedented financial contributions along the way. All of this began to take its toll on McPherson, who decided – encouraged by her mother – that a European vacation was in order. McPherson returned to work later in the year 1926, but on May 18 took a break, went to the beach, and disappeared. Some feared she had drowned, but McPherson insisted that she had been abducted by two men and a woman, who lured her from the beach to their car to pray for a child. They bound, gagged, and forced ether upon her, held her for a time in California and then moved her to northern Mexico from where she escaped. Contributing to the various rumors as to her disappearance were receipts of a ransom note demanding $500,000 for her safe return; various threats on her life that had been received over the years; and a report that the wife of Kenneth Ormiston, former engineer of radio station KFSG, had told police that "a certain prominent woman" – McPherson, it was rumored – was responsible for his disappearance and for his suggestion that they divorce. When McPherson returned a month later, the Los Angeles district attorney empaneled a grand jury to look into the matter of her disappearance, but it could not find enough evidence to suppose that a kidnapping had taken place.[57]

Immediately following the kidnapping, McPherson sought to parlay the publicity she had attracted into stardom in Hollywood. And for a brief time, movie offers poured in from major studios, including Metro-Goldwin-Mayer and Universal Studios. Her rationale, she explained, was to see what film could do to further her religious mission. She incorporated a movie company, Angelus Productions, to record and distribute her services worldwide. But her intentions went beyond that when she prepared a script for a film based on one of her best-known sermons, "Story of My Life." In 1930, *Time* magazine announced that a film was indeed in the offing, titled *Clay in the Potter's Hands*. McPherson was featured in several newsreels, which attracted large audiences, but her awkwardness before the camera discouraged any of the studios from pursuing a feature film. Nevertheless, that she made such an effort alienated many of her followers. In 1931, when McPherson eloped with David Hutton – the marriage violating her own teaching that one should not remarry if a previous spouse was still alive, in this case McPherson – rumors circulated of her having affairs with various men and the two soon divorced. McPherson tried vaudeville, at which she failed miserably as well, and even more followers, including staff members, and her mother and daughter, seen by many as Aimee's heir apparent, abandoned her.[58]

Dozens of Foursquare Gospel Churches, which she founded, disassociated with her, which forced her in 1936 to announce that she was returning to her pentecostal revivalist roots, championing – and once again offering hope – to those ravaged by the Great Depression. She established a social welfare organization, renewed her commitment to racial justice, migrant families, and the needs of women and children, and reaffirmed her faith in pentecostalism. "Back to Pentecost" became her new motto, and she committed herself once again to reclaiming America as a Christian nation, engaging in national politics supporting Herbert Hoover and Franklin Roosevelt for the presidency and opposing radical Upton Sinclair in his bid for California governor, despite their common concern for the poor. Much as she had during World War I, she took to the road in a national revival wrapped in patriotism complete with pageants intended to return the nation "to the Faith of our Fathers." She opposed communism abroad and at home and, sparked by the Japanese attack on Pearl Harbor in 1941, portrayed as villains Adolf Hitler and the leaders of Japan. The war confirmed her belief, which she in turn informed the people, that God had specially chosen the United States to implement his will on earth. And it worked, as millions returned to her meetings.[59]

Her health not being strong for years, McPherson died on September 27, 1944. Officially, her death was ruled accidental due to a drug overdose complicated by kidney disease, but some suspected suicide. Thousands of the common people, whom she had attracted to her over the years and stuck with her until the end, flocked to her memorial service. Conspicuously absent were established religious leaders, but her church lived on. After her death, her son Rolf McPherson was named president of the International Church of the Foursquare Gospel and the church continued to grow. In 1993, four years after Rolf's retirement, the denomination reported 27,000 churches and meeting places in North America. Outside North America, the membership stood at more than 1.5 million.[60]

Daddy Grace and Father Divine

Of a similar evangelical preaching ilk as Sunday and McPherson were the Black preachers Daddy Grace and Father Divine. Getting their start in the roaring 1920s, they were often described as "jazzmen" or "celebrity" preachers. Grace – who actually insisted that he was of mixed parentage: African and Portuguese – and Divine provided the segregated African American community the same religious ferment and cult of personality as their white counterparts.[61]

Born Marcelino Manuel da Graca in 1881 (possibly 1884) in Brava in the Cape Verde Islands, Charles Manuel (Imanuel) Grace, or Daddy Grace as he came to be known, was nothing if not theatrical in his preaching. It is not clear when he arrived in the United States, although 1904 is most likely, and he and his family settled in New Bedford, Massachusetts. The Roman Catholic Church dominated the Portuguese Islands, and Grace and his family were baptized Catholic. But the Pentecostal Church of the Nazarene established a mission there in 1900, and his brother became a Nazarene pastor soon after he arrived in the United States. Upon his arrival, Daddy Grace left the Catholic Church but was rejected for a pulpit in a Massachusetts Nazarene Church. He remained in the holiness and pentecostal traditions, but he made his own way claiming that he received a commission to preach directly from God.[62]

Like McPherson, Grace was an innovative Christian evangelist, who saw himself as preparing the way for the Second Coming. But he also let it be known that by the power of the Holy Spirit, he could heal the ill or infirmed, raise the dead, and perform other miracles. His sister Jeannie (Eugenia) accompanied her brother on his missionary trips and testified that her brother had raised her from the dead. Others added similar reports, which were included in the United House of Prayers publications and picked up by the press. In 1926, the New Bedford *Standard Times*, quoted Grace as saying: "I am come as the power of the Gospel to heal the sick, cleanse the lepers, raise the dead, cast out devils. . . . [I] do these things in (Jesus) name."[63]

Grace was often subject to mockery by the press for his claims to fantastic powers, extravagance, and flamboyant style. One critic referred to him as "a brown-skinned P. T. Barnum," and he was continually rebuffed by other pastors, black and white, for much the same reasons. He nevertheless attracted a sizable following and grew quite wealthy over the course of his forty-year ministry, not only through the collection plate but also through the sales of healing-power products, stationery, tea, coffee, cookies, various cosmetics, and his *Grace Magazine*. He accumulated over forty mansions around the United States and in Havana, Cuba, filled with expensive furniture and works of art. He used much of that wealth to feed the poor, and even offered his ministers and elderly members a pension fund and small insurance plan. But he always traveled in style, chauffeured in a Packard, Pierce-Arrow, or Cadillac. And when he entered a city in his "gospel car," he and his entourage rode through the streets in their cars with loudspeakers announcing, "Daddy Grace is in town. Come one and all, and listen to the man of God."[64]

Although he urged his followers to be modest in their deportment – especially women – he wore brightly colored suits and had long flowing black hair. He sported a pointed beard and two to four inch long fingernails, painted red, of which he made much show. He built his first church, or House of Prayer, in 1919 in West Wareham, Massachusetts, but the center of his early activity was in the New Bedford House of Prayer, which he founded in 1921. From there, he added branches in Newark, New Jersey; Charlotte, North Carolina, and elsewhere along the East Coast, all incorporated under the United House of Prayer for All People in 1927. Their united purpose, as explained in the Church's Constitution and By-Laws, was to provide "places of worship and assembly where all people may gather to pray and to worship the Almighty God, irrespective of denomination or creed."[65]

Each of the Houses of Prayer featured a sanctuary on a raised platform called the "holy mountain," and on the "holy mountain" stood a chair on which sat Daddy Grace, when he was in town, or his local representative when he was not. Although his services were occasionally racially integrated – for which he was arrested in Virginia – they were overwhelmingly African American. With musical accompaniment provided by brass shout bands, they engaged in ecstatic worship, crying and falling to the floor, speaking in tongues, and even "walking the benches," or jumping from seat to seat in their desperate attempt to "come to the mountain" and offer themselves to Grace, whose touch, it was reported by one observer, was "sufficient to induce terrific contortion of the body or to produce a state akin to catalepsy." Grace often performed faith healings at these services, but over time, he encouraged his followers to believe that they would be healed because of their faith not because of his touch. Beyond its weekly services, the church hosted parades with marching bands and majorettes, annual festive convocations, and group baptisms – first on beaches and later by fire hoses in city streets.[66]

The signature ceremonies in the House of Prayer were the convocations, which occurred every summer, signaling the start of the church year. Based on Biblical references in Exodus 12:16 and Leviticus 23, the church encouraged all of its members to participate. It lasted several days and included guest speakers and mass baptisms of new members as well as those who wanted to renew their ritual purification. The high point in the ceremony was Daddy Grace's appearance, whereupon he would preside over the baptisms.[67]

Although he officially shunned the label denomination, Grace took the title of Bishop of the United House of Prayer, which he also insisted gave him ultimate authority over the church. His theology was simple: one God, one faith, one baptism, and one leader. Grace was clear that he believed that God only empowered one man at a time for divine leadership, going back to Moses and Jesus and forward to him. He insisted that salvation was possible only by grace, but since He created the world, God had given the authority to grant grace to specially chosen men, including Daddy Grace. He is alleged to have said at one point:

"If you sin against God, Grace can save you, but if you sin against Grace, God cannot save you." This, although he never actually claimed that he was God, nevertheless persuaded some – mostly his critics – that he was God's divine agent on earth, or even God, himself. His most serious researchers largely discount any such claim on Grace's part, suggesting that it was taken out of context or attributing it to one of the members of Grace's Church. One documented, more temperate statement has Grace writing: "The House of Prayer is God's Kingdom and the gateway to Heaven. All people must enter into His gates. For inside is salvation, but outside, there is damnation and death."[68]

Grace had his day in court. In 1934, Grace was charged with violating the Mann Act, which forbade transporting someone across state lines for illicit purposes. Originally intended to control prostitution, the case was brought by a House of Prayer member who charged that while traveling with Grace from Brooklyn to Philadelphia in 1932, he forced himself on her and she became pregnant. Although a jury found Grace guilty, it was subsequently determined that the child was not Grace's and upon appeal the charges were thrown out. The final ruling was largely based on a technicality involving jurisdiction, however, and that did not change the minds of many on both sides of the case concerning Grace's behavior. As with McPherson's supposed abduction, however, most of Grace's followers not only refused to abandon him but closed ranks in his defense.[69]

Daddy Grace's leadership of the United House of Prayer peaked during the 1930s and 1940s. Charlotte, North Carolina, became the church's stronghold, and although Grace continued to live in Brooklyn, he visited Charlotte often and it bustled with church activity. When he died in 1960, he left behind what became the United House of Prayer for All People of the Church on the Rock of the Apostolic Faith, whose member churches now number some 145 in 29 states with an estimated 27,500 to 50,000 members.[70] The church is more mainstream today and is governed by a General Assembly and an ecclesiastical court, the General Council. But the bishop continues to hold the power to select, ordain, and supervise all ministers and is trustee over all church property. As is often the case, Daddy Grace's successors had their dissidents, occasionally quarreling over succession to the position of bishop, which led to religious associations that have broken away from the mother church, such as the House of the Lord Pentecostal Church on the Mount and True Grace Memorial House of Prayer.[71]

Although more detailed accounts point to theological differences, Daddy Grace and Father Divine are often described as essentially similar figures, commonly labeled "celebrity," "exotic," "bizarre," or cult leaders considered divine, or messiahs. Some identify both Grace and Divine as leading charismatic or pentecostal sects.[72] Father Divine, founder of the International Peace Mission, had a following as large as Daddy Grace. Further, the truth of his origins are even more mysterious, a mystery he never made much of an attempt to clarify. Although he denied it, his legal name was probably George Baker. Where and when he was born is unknown for certain. Some point to Georgia around 1876 to freed African American slaves and sharecroppers where he experienced a degree of racial oppression that prepared the way for his stance on civil rights. Jill Watts, on the other hand, has found evidence that he was born in Maryland, where he experienced less racial discrimination and little resulting initial interest in leading any civil rights movement. A few others point to an island off the coast of South Carolina.[73]

Like Daddy Grace, Father Divine was influenced by pentecostalism. He attended the 1906 revival at Azusa, where he spoke in tongues. He started his preaching career perhaps as early as 1899 in a local Baptist Church, but in 1907, a traveling preacher by the name of Samuel

Morris spoke at Divine's church. At one point Morris proclaimed that he was "the Eternal Father," whereupon he was expelled from the congregation. Father Divine became Morris's first follower, adopted the title "The Messenger" and Morris became "Father Jehovia." By 1912, Father Divine determined that Father Jehovia was not God, insisting instead that he was, and he set out preaching across the South, which proved to be problematic.[74]

Father Divine attracted a following mostly comprised of African American women. He taught celibacy and gender equality and almost immediately came into conflict with local ministers. In 1913, he was arrested and served sixty days on a chain gang. In 1914, several of the husbands of his female followers joined forces with the local ministry to have him arrested for mental incompetence. He would be judged insane and placed in mental institutions on at least two occasions. In this case, however, being found mentally sound, the charges against Father Divine were dropped, and he left for the North. He took his ministry to Brooklyn, New York, where he formed a commune, populated almost exclusively by African Americans, wherein he insisted that members refrain from sex and excessive mixed gender interaction, alcohol, tobacco, and gambling and that they dress modestly, including men but especially women. Formerly known as the "Messenger," Divine adopted the name Reverend Major Jealous Divine – the title Major in recognition of his authority and Jealous taken from Exodus 20:5, "For I, the Lord your God, am a jealous God," and Exodus 34:14, "For the Lord, whose name is Jealous, is a jealous God." But to his followers he was more often referred to as Father Divine. His wife, Penninah – with whom Father Divine insisted his marriage was never consummated – became Mother Divine.[75]

In 1919, Father Divine and his flock moved to Sayville, Long Island, New York, where they became the first black homeowners in town and set up a lodging house and an employment bureau. His services, as well as his free weekly banquets, attracted large crowds mostly from Brooklyn and Harlem, which also attracted the attention of the police. Although like other evangelical preachers of his day, his was a spiritual mission, he also taught hard work, self-reliance, and social responsibility. He opposed smoking, drinking, and profane language, and advocated for his followers economic independence and racial equality. Further, he welcomed whites into his midst, and it was this last issue, as well as the crowds, that alarmed his white neighbors.[76]

Father Divine's crowds overwhelmed the small community of Sayville, and at one point, in November 1931, a mob of local neighbors surrounded Father Divine's meeting. Riot police reacted and told Father Divine and his followers that they had to disperse or be arrested. When they failed to disperse, eighty of his followers were arrested for disturbing the peace. At Divine's direction, 55 of the 80 pleaded guilty, and Father Divine paid their fines, whereupon they were released. But some did not, including Father Divine, who claimed the action was racially motivated and a trial was set. The episode was sensationalized in the New York City press, and he resolved to move back into New York City. He set up branches in various locations in New York and New Jersey, but the center of his activity was Harlem, where he formally adopted the title International Peace Movement. When Father Divine's trial finally took place on May 24, 1932, he was found guilty. The jury asked for leniency, but the judge ignored the request, accused Father Divine of being a "menace to society," and applied the maximum sentence for disturbing the peace – one year in prison and a $500 fine. When the judge died of a heart attack only a few weeks later, Divine reportedly commented: "I hated to do it." Divine served only about one month of his sentence before being released, and the conviction was overturned in January 1933. While in jail, Divine studied the founding documents of the United States – the Declaration of Independence, the Constitution, and the Bill of Rights – and when he was released, patriotism became an earmark of his crusade, as well.[77]

Father Divine's ministry flourished during his stay in Harlem. Basically, there were two types of members. There were those who subscribed to his teachings and attended services, but otherwise lived outside the inner circle of believers and their communes. The inner circle of believers made a more serious commitment to Father Divine. They lived "evangelically," renouncing the things of the world and moving into the movement's communes, where they lived in accordance with Father Divine's instructions. They disposed of, or committed, most of their worldly goods to the mission, worked only at jobs Father Divine directed, and lived separately and celibately, even if married. Divorce was taboo, which followed his insistence that those among his inner circle should not marry. The communal buildings, called "heavens," were intended to ease the financial burden on the poor by providing low-cost sleeping quarters and meals. At the ministry's peak, heavens were located across North America as well as in Europe. They brought in considerable revenue, which when combined with the church's very successful budget restaurants and clothing shops and a large number of commercial ads published in the Mission's weekly periodical, supported Divine well.[78]

As referred to earlier, the defining element in Father Divine's mission was his claim to be God's messenger, or God incarnate. As he proclaimed in 1931: "I will rule millions of homes and houses, for I am divine, and that is not merely a word, it is power." The mission's sacred text consisted of the preaching and teachings of Father Divine, gathered and published weekly in the periodical the *Spoken Word*, which first appeared in 1934 and was succeeded by the *New Day*. Father Divine taught that there would be no more prophets of God and that in him God had returned in person. He was the fulfillment of Biblical prophecies about the Second Coming, or Christ reborn. He would bring about heaven on earth, and only those who followed his teachings would be saved.[79]

Increasingly, during the Great Depression, black churches imparted "a moral sanction and institutional base crucial to movements for social progress and protest." Accordingly, although somewhat of a reluctant social leader to that point, Father Divine increasingly spoke out for the need to counter the racial and economic divide in America. A pronounced and vocal capitalist, he was opposed to welfare, social security, and credit, favoring economic self-sufficiency. In 1934, however, he went on record as being sympathetic to the Communist Party of America's positions on the disparate distribution of income and civil rights. He combined a faith in American Democratic principles with warning that the government strictly honor these principles or face massive resistance.[80]

Divine always insisted that he was not black, which was more of a statement opposed to such labels than a reflection of the facts of his birth. He insisted that race did not exist, that "God hath made of one blood all races of men," and that race was but a product of the mind. Negative thinking, he insisted had created race, and that perpetuated oppression and inequality. He also castigated those who identified themselves as black, contending that they were manifesting the derogatory qualities that society had assigned them. In 1935, however, in response to a riot in Harlem over the shooting of a black teenager, he became more overtly political in his actions. In 1936, in his "Righteous Government Platform," he called for an end to segregation, lynching, and capital punishment. He organized a Righteous Government Movement, which at its 1939 convention issued a platform that opposed school segregation. Among the platform's several planks were statements that called for "immediate legislation in every state . . . making it a crime to discriminate in any public place against any individual on account of race, creed, or color; abolishing all segregated neighborhoods in cities and towns . . . abolishing all segregated schools . . . and all segregated areas in churches, theatres, public conveyances, and other public places." Another plank called for legislation that would make it "unlawful for employers of skilled or unskilled, technical or professional help, to have different wage scales or salaries for what they termed different races, creeds or colors; or to discriminate in any way in the hiring of help." In 1940, he and his followers gathered some 250,000 signatures on an antilynching measure, which never made it through the New York legislature.[81]

Father Divine continued his civil rights activity in the 1950s, in 1951 publicly espousing the cause of reparations to be paid to the descendants of slaves. He continued to oppose segregation including housing at this point but failed to take a leading position in the burgeoning civil rights movement of the late 1950s and early 1960s, perhaps due to the infirmities of his old age or because of the movement's more radical posture.[82]

Finally, sounding a common theme noted throughout our discussion of these popular, but often suspect, preachers, Father Divine had his fair share of public scandals, most of which were brought about by his followers and publicly denounced by him, but that nevertheless were associated with him by the press and his critics. To cite just a few, in December 1936, one of his followers, John Hunt – a white millionaire from California – kidnapped a 17-year-old girl, named her Virgin Mary, had sexual relations with her, and announced that she would conceive by immaculate conception. The press made much of this, associating Hunt with Father Divine's movement, despite Divine's denunciation of their affair. In April 1937, a man was stabbed at a service at which Father Divine was present. At about the same time, Faithful Mary, one of Father Divine's better-known followers, proved not to be so faithful. She defected, formed her own short-lived commune, and publicly denounced Divine for defrauding his followers in order to live a lavish lifestyle and for illicit sexual activity. And in 1937, he was sued by a couple who had entered one of Father Divine's communes, entrusted their savings to the group, subsequently left the commune, and demanded the return of their money. In 1942, when their case was sustained by the courts in New York, Divine moved to Philadelphia, where his notoriety and resulting press coverage gradually subsided.[83]

Father Divine died in 1965. Succession problems followed, which Father Divine warned might happen when his followers no longer had a "God-in-a-body" with them. But for the majority of his followers, he was succeeded by his widow, Mother Divine, who insisted that Father Divine was still with them, if in spirit, and insisted on referring to him in the present tense. Interestingly, as the group will be mentioned in a later chapter, Mother Divine blocked an attempt by Jim Jones to take over the church in the early 1970s. Jones, who would later lead his Peoples Temple mass suicide, claimed to be the reincarnation of Father Divine – that the spirit of Father Divine passed into his body upon Divine's demise. In part due to the insistence on celibacy, but also on the loss of its charismatic leader, the International Peace Movement has few chapters left, mostly in Pennsylvania, and those are largely decentralized.[84]

Other popular religious figures

There were other popular religious figures in the 1920s and 1930s that should be mentioned briefly before moving ahead to the next chapter. Much like Daddy Grace and Father Divine, the first two represent a new generation of religious leaders, the last an undercurrent of anti-Semitism mentioned in an earlier chapter, but still very much alive. They are Marcus Garvey, Timothy Drew, and Charles Coughlin.

Garvey came to the United States from Jamaica in 1916. As a leader of the Black Nationalism and Pan-Africanism movements, he was part of a growing movement among African Americans who sought spiritual encouragement in a black, rather than a white, God. As a prelude to what would follow in the 1960s, he also preached a message of black superiority and unity under the banner of the Universal Negro Improvement Association, which at its height claimed 4 million members. His slogan was "One God! One Aim! One Destiny!" Garvey started the Negro Factories Association, which consisted of a series of manufacturing companies, and formed a steamship company, the Black Star Line, which engaged in trade and commerce between Africans in America, the Caribbean, South and Central America, Canada and Africa. Recalling a movement from the pre-Civil War years, he also proposed that his Black Star Line be used to resettle African Americans in Africa. In 1925, however, federal authorities charged Garvey with mail fraud and he was jailed. President Calvin Coolidge commuted his sentence after he served only two years, but Garvey never regained his prominence. He moved to London, where he died in 1940.[85]

Timothy Drew was born in 1886 in North Carolina. Better known as Noble Drew Ali, he preached a message of black pride by teaching that the true religion of blacks was Islam, the religion that many Africans experienced prior to their being enslaved in America. Christianity, he insisted, was the white man's religion, used by whites to oppress blacks. Rather than accept Christianity, even through black Christian denominations, African Americans needed to recognize their Moorish heritage. They were no longer to be called negroes, blacks, or colored but Asiatics, Moors, or Moorish Americans. To that end, in 1913, he established the Moorish Science Temple in Newark, New Jersey. Other temples followed in Pittsburgh, Detroit, in several southern cities, and Chicago, where he had his largest following. Ali met an unfortunate end, as well, when he died after a run-in with police in 1929.[86]

Father Charles Coughlin was cut from different cloth. Rather than offering a message of pride and hope, his was a message of hate. Coughlin, the "radio priest" from Royal Oak, Michigan, whose voice was at one point heard by 30 million Americans across the country, began his radio career by preaching for and then against President Franklin Roosevelt and his New Deal. In 1936, he formed the National Union for Social Justice and the newspaper, *Social Justice*, under whose banner he lent his considerable support and prominence to labor unions. But soon he began spewing increasingly virile anti-Semitism that resonated with that heard in the fascist regimes of Europe. In 1939, in the face of opposition within the Catholic Church hierarchy, his broadcasts were shut down. Silenced, Coughlin returned to being a parish priest in the National Shrine of the Little Flower Church in Royal Oak, from which he retired in 1966 and died thirteen years later.[87]

A final note on the Great Depression and religion

The Great Depression, which followed the boom years of the '20s, had a devastating effect on nearly all Americans and their institutions, including the churches and synagogues. Twenty-five percent of the workforce – or over 12 million people – found themselves jobless, penniless, and dependent on social services provided by charitable organizations. Protestant, Catholic, and Jewish churches alike, however, suffered as well on multiple levels. During the 1920s, many congregations invested heavily in new structures and incurred heavy debts in the process, only to struggle to meet those obligations and in many cases default in the 1930s. Similarly, many churches expanded their outreach social services only to be forced to cut back when they were most needed.

This no doubt contributed to yet another adverse effect of the depression. The devastating effects of the collapsed economy led to a lack of confidence, even despair, after years of optimism. Contrary to what might have been expected, however, there was no appreciable increase in the number of church-goers. The Lynds' classic *Middletown*, a study of small town America, helps explain this in its analysis of the years between 1925 and 1935. In brief, the character of church-goers remained pretty much the same, with middle-aged women in the majority and with few people of either gender under the age of 30.[88]

The only notable exceptions were gains in membership among those churches that historically attracted members from the lower classes. These included the holiness and pentecostal churches – the Nazarenes, the Assemblies of God, for example – "storefront" churches in the urban north, and adventist churches like Jehovah's Witnesses with their message of the imminent Second Coming. Clearly their missions, which focused more on a radical emotional conversion, personal salvation, and the end times rather than on the Social Gospel of the more moderate and liberal churches, had greater appeal in an age of disillusionment. This helps explain, of course, the continued appeal of figures such as Aimee Semple McPherson, Father Divine, Daddy Grace, and the other previously mentioned figures.[89]

For most other churches and synagogues, it was a time for a reappraisal of their public missions. Protestant, Catholic, and Jewish charities continued to do what they could – soup kitchens, temporary shelter, healthcare, etc. – but most were simply overwhelmed by the challenges of poverty and the services they faced in caring for their flocks. As noted earlier, they turned to government to take up a greater share of the burden. In time, as what some thought would be a temporary flagging of the economy turned out otherwise, some went so far as to call for a restructuring of the American economy and government to meet those needs. A few clergy became more pronounced in their socialist sentiment, although few ventured far in a communist direction. Instead, most Protestant churches called on Franklin Roosevelt to take a stand and supported his New Deal. They were joined by American Catholics, who were encouraged by Pope Pius XI's encyclical *Quadragesimo Anno* (On the Reconstruction of the Social Order) (1931) and its call for massive social reform. American Jews faced the same challenges and joined in the call, but they also faced the distractions posed by their fellow Jews abroad in Nazi Germany and elsewhere, as well as an uptick in anti-Semitism, which as noted earlier began in the 1920s. The coming of the Second World War would change things yet again.[90]

Summary

Chapter 3 focused on the impact of the higher criticism and Darwinian evolution on revealed religion. In this chapter we have continued that story into the "roaring" 1920s and the depression-era 1930s, discussing the increasingly aggressive stance in opposition to both developments taken by fundamentalists. We have highlighted some of the more prominent evangelical ministers of the day and examined the showdown that occurred between modernists and fundamentalists in the Scopes trial of 1925. To Clarence Darrow, lawyer for the defense, the trial was all about "preventing bigots and ignoramuses from controlling education of the United States." For William Jennings Bryan, who assisted the prosecution, it was about taxpayers determining what their children should be taught in nation's public schools. But more personally, and as we have seen he was not alone in this, Bryan feared the social effects of evolutionary theory – Social Darwinism – that emphasized survival of the fittest and that could be used to justify the ravages of military force he associated with pre-World War I Germany, as well as the unbridled pursuit of wealth closer to home. The coming of the

Great Depression encouraged the churches to continue their efforts to relieve the resulting and widespread pain as offered earlier as part of the Social Gospel Movement. Try as hard as they did, however, the churches realized that providing the level of help necessary to cope with the devastation was beyond them. They turned to insisting on more help from governmental offices, which was forthcoming under the New Deal.

Review questions

1   Explain the origins and basic tenets of fundamentalism.
2   How did fundamentalism differ from the holiness and pentecostal movements?
3   Compare and contrast the leading evangelical preachers of the 1920s and 1930s: Billy Sunday, Aimee Semple McPherson, Daddy Grace, and Father Divine.
4   What was at stake in the Scopes trial? How have the results been differently interpreted?
5   What were the distinguishing characteristics of the following religious leaders: Marcus Garvey, Timothy Drew, and Charles Coughlin?

Notes

1   Randall Balmer's discussion of terminology is in his *Mine Eyes Have Seen the Glory: A Journey into the Evangelical Subculture in America* (New York: Oxford University Press, 1989), ix–xii. For George Marsden's discussion of fundamentalism and evangelicalism, see his "Tremors of Controversy," an excerpt from his *Fundamentalism and American Culture*, included in Robert R. Mathisen, *Critical Issues in American Religious History*, 2nd edn. (Waco, TX: Baylor University Press, 2006), 562–9.
2   George M. Marsden, *Fundamentalism and American Culture: The Shaping of Twentieth-Century Evangelism, 1870–1925*, 2nd edn. (New York: Oxford University Press, 2006), 118–19; Ernest R. Sandeen, *The Roots of Fundamentalism: British and American Millenarianism, 1800–1930* (Chicago, IL: The University of Chicago Press, 1970), 188, 194–9.
3   Marsden, *Fundamentalism and American Culture*, 118–19; Sandeen, *The Roots of Fundamentalism*, 189; Michael Lienesch, *In the Beginning: Fundamentalism, the Scopes Trial, and the Making of the Antievolution Movement* (Chapel Hill: The University of North Carolina Press, 2007), 8.
4   Norman F. Furniss, *The Fundamentalist Controversy, 1918–1931* (New Haven, CT: Yale University Press, 1954), 13; Stewart G. Cole, *The History of Fundamentalism* (Hamden, CT: Archon Books, 1963), 34; Marsden, *Fundamentalism and American Culture*, 117.
5   Lienesch, *In the Beginning*, 11; Sandeen, *The Roots of Fundamentalism*, 203; see *The Fundamentals: A Testimony to the Truth*, 12 vols., ed. Reuben Archer Torrey and Amzi Clarence Dixon (Chicago: Testimony Publishing Co., 1910–1915). For more on *The Fundamentals*, see Marsden, *Fundamentalism and American Culture*, esp. 118–23, 194–201.
6   Lienesch, *In the Beginning*, 13; Marsden, *Fundamentalism and American Culture*, 120.
7   Sandeen, *The Roots of Fundamentalism*, 42.
8   *Millennial Harbinger*, April 1831, 167. Alexander Campbell, *Millennial Harbinger* (April 1831): 167. Campbell was not always consistent in his premillennial predictions. In June 1846, for example, he articulated what came close to a postmillennial vision after a trip into the American West, which so impressed him that he could not resist commenting on the glory of America's future and the likelihood that it would accomplish "the highest perfection our nature is capable of." Alexander Campbell, *Millennial Harbinger* (June 1846): 356. Sandeen, *The Roots of Fundamentalism*, 46–9.
9   Sandeen, *The Roots of Fundamentalism*, 50; See Leroy Edwin Froom, *The Prophetic Faith of Our Fathers: The Historical Development of Prophetic Interpretation*, 4 vols. (Washington, DC: Review and Herald, 1954), 4: 783.
10   Sandeen, *The Roots of Fundamentalism*, 55; Whitney, R. Cross, *The Burned Over District: The Social and Intellectual History of Enthusiastic Religion in Western New York, 1800–1850* (Ithaca, NY: Cornell University Press, 1950), 321.
11   Sandeen, *The Roots of Fundamentalism*, 60–4.

12 Sandeen, *The Roots of Fundamentalism*, 62, 71, 75, 208–32; Jon Butler, Grant Wacker, and Randall Balmer, *Religion in American Life: A Short History*, 2nd edn. (New York: Oxford University Press, 2011), 282–3, 322. For more on dispensationalism, see Timothy P. Weber, *Living in the Shadow of the Second Coming* (Chicago, IL: University of Chicago Press, 1987), 13–42. On Darby and Scofield, see Paul Boyer, *When Time Shall Be No More: Prophesy Belief in Modern American Culture* (Cambridge, MA: Harvard University Press, 1992), 86–100; Arno C. Gaebelein, "Fulfilled Prophesy a Potent Argument for the Bible," *The Fundamentals*, 11 (1915): 86.

13 Sandeen, *The Roots of Fundamentalism*, 206; Marsden, *Fundamentalism and American Culture*, 119–21. See, for example, Reuben Torrey, "The Certainty and Importance of Bodily Resurrection of Jesus Christ from the Dead," *The Fundamentals*, 5 (1910): 83, 104–5. Lienesch, *In the Beginning*, 21–4.

14 Sandeen, *The Roots of Fundamentalism*, 124–38; Lienesch, *In the Beginning*, 24–6; Marsden, *Fundamentalism and American Culture*, 122; George S. Bishop, "The Testimony of Scriptures to Themselves," *The Fundamentals*, 7 (1912): 43; Howard Crosby, "Preach the Word," *The Fundamentals*, 8 (1912): 108.

15 Lienesche, *In the Beginning*, 26; Robert E. Speer, "Foreign Missions or World-Wide Evangelism," *The Fundamentals*, 12 (1915): 74; Charles R. Erdman, "The Church and Socialism," *The Fundamentals*, 12 (1915): 112; Alexander White Pitzer, "The Wisdom of the World," *The Fundamentals*, 9 (1912): 23–5. For more on the debate between Darwinists and Protestant theologians, see Ronald L. Numbers, *The Creationists* (Berkeley: University of California Press, 1993), 37–8; Jon H. Roberts, *Darwinism and the Divine in America: Protestant Intellectuals and Organic Evolution, 1859–1900* (Madison: University of Wisconsin Press, 1988), 209–31; James R. Moore, *The Post-Darwinian Controversies: A Study of the Protestant Struggle to Come to Terms with Darwin in Great Britain and America, 1870–1900* (Cambridge, England: Cambridge University Press, 1979), 193–216.

16 Sandeen, *The Roots of Fundamentalism*, 206–7; Edwin S. Gaustad and Leigh E. Schmidt, *The Religious History of America*, rev. ed. (San Francisco, CA: HarperSanFrancisco, 2002), 292–3.

17 Gaustad and Schmidt, *The Religious History of America*, 293.

18 Gaustad and Schmidt, *The Religious History of America*, 155–6, 293–4.

19 Marsden, *Fundamentalism and American Culture*, 141.

20 Marsden, *Fundamentalism and American Culture*, 143–4; Arno C. Gaebelein, *Our Hope*, 23 (July 1916): 44. See also James M. Gray, *Prophesy and the Lord's Return* (New York: Fleming and Revell, 1917); James M. Gray, *Light on Prophesy* (New York: Fleming and Revell, 1918); Sandeen, *The Roots of Fundamentalism*, 233; Samuel Ridout, "Should a Christian Go to War?," *Our Hope*, 24 (September 1917): 165–9.

21 Marsden, *Fundamentalism and American Culture*, 146–7; Shirley Jackson Case, "The Premillennial Menace," *Biblical World*, 52 (July 1918): 16–17, 21; Sandeen, *The Roots of Fundamentalism*, 235–6.

22 Marsden, *Fundamentalism and American Culture*, 149–50.

23 Kenneth K. Bailey, *Southern White Protestantism in the Twentieth Century* (New York: Harper & Row, 1964), 44–71; Marsden, *Fundamentalism and American Culture*, 146–7.

24 It is worth noting that Fosdick also mentioned fundamentalist efforts to exclude "teaching modern biology" – read evolution – in the public schools, a subject he recently debated with William Jennings Bryan in the *New York Times*. Marsden, *Fundamentalism and American Culture*, 171, 307, FN 1; Butler, *Religion in American Life*, 327. For a complete text of "Shall the Fundamentalists Win?" see *The Christian Work*, June 10, 1922, 716–19; a substantial excerpt can be found in Mathisen, *Critical Issues in American Religious History*, 555–7.

25 Marsden, *Fundamentalism and American Culture*, 152, 172; Sandeen, *The Roots of Fundamentalism*, 233–69.

26 Clarence E. Macartney, "Shall Unbelief Win? An Answer to Dr. Fosdick," *The Presbyterian*, 92 (July 13, 1922): 8; Marsden, *Fundamentalism and American Culture*, 173. See Lefferts A. Loetscher, *The Broadening Church* (Philadelphia, PA: University of Pennsylvania Press, 1957); Charles Allyn Russell, *Voices of American Fundamentalism* (Louisville, KY: Westminster John Knox Press, 1976); Sandeen, *The Roots of Fundamentalism*, 233–69.

27 Marsden, *Fundamentalism and American Culture*, 174–5; John Gresham Machen, *Christianity and Liberalism* (New York: Macmillan, 1923), 2, 5, 7–8, 10–5, 47, 160.

28 Charles E. Quirk, "Origins of the Auburn Affirmation," *Journal of Presbyterian History*, 53 (1975): 120–42; Marsden, *Fundamentalism and American Culture*, 180.

29 Ronald L. Numbers, *Darwinism Comes to America* (Cambridge, MA: Harvard University Press, 1998), 23, 76; Lienesch, *In the Beginning*, 3.

30 Hankins, *Jesus and Gin*, 83–4; Peter J. Bowler, *Evolution: The History of an Idea* (Berkeley: University of California Press, 1984), 233; Moore, *The Post-Darwinian Controversies*, 73. Hunter's commentary on Darwin also reflected a decidedly anthropocentric and racist twist on the theory. In brief, Hunter argued that simple forms of life gradually gave rise to more complex forms, which not only led to humans but also to the Caucasian race as "finally, the highest type of all." Edward J. Larson, *Summer for the Gods: The Scopes Trial and America's Continuing Debate over Science and Religion* (Cambridge, MA: Harvard University Press, 1997), 13–4, 23–5; George William Hunter, *A Civic Biology* (New York: American, 1914), 194–6, 405.

31 On the Fundamentalist adoption of a "warfare model" versus one seeking accommodation, see Hankins, *Jesus and Gin*, 86–7; Larson, *Summer for the Gods*, 24.

32 Hankins, *Jesus and Gin*, 89; William Jennings Bryan, *In His Image* (New York: Fleming and Revell, 1922), 88; Larson, *Summer for the Gods*, 27; George W. Hunter and Walter G. Whitman, *Science in Our World of Progress* (New York: American, 1935), 486; Hunter, *A Civic Biology*, 263.

33 Lienesch, *In the Beginning*, 143.

34 Samuel Walker, *In Defense of American Liberties: A History of the ACLU* (New York: Oxford University Press, 1990), 21.

35 For more on Darrow, see Kevin Tierney, *Darrow: A Biography* (New York: Croswell, 1979); Clarence Darrow, *The Story of My Life* (New York: Grosset, 1932); Hankins, *Jesus and Gin*, 91.

36 Tierney, *Darrow*, 86; Darrow, *The Story of My Life*, 409; Clarence Darrow, "Why I Am an Agnostic," in Clarence Darrow, *Verdicts Out of Court*, ed. Arthur Weinberg and Lila Weinberg (Chicago: Quadrangle, 1963), 434, 436; Larson, *Summer for the Gods*, 71–2.

37 Larson, *Summer for the Gods*, 72, 74, 77, 107; Lienesch, *In the Beginning*, 144. Academic freedom had only recently become a concern at the collegiate level. The American Association of University Professors organized in 1913, largely in response to this concern.

38 Larson, *Summer for the Gods*, 88–90; Hankins, *Jesus and Gin*, 90–1; Lienesch, *In the Beginning*, 139, 142–3.

39 "Darrow Likens Bryan to Nero," *Nashville Banner*, May 18, 1925, 1; Bryant Harbert, "Darrow an Atheist, Is Bryan's Answer," (Memphis) *Commercial Appeal*, May 23, 1925, 1. See also Hankins, *Jesus and Gin*, 93; Larson, *Summer for the Gods*, 129; Lienesch, *In the Beginning*, 56, 156.

40 "Christianity Goes If Evolution Wins, Bryan Tells Dayton," *Chattanooga Times*, July 8, 1925, 1; "Bryan in Dayton, Calls Scopes Trial Duel to the Death," *New York Times*, June 8, 1925, 1; "Visitors Come on Every Train," *Nashville Banner*, July 9, 1925, 3; Hankins, *Jesus and Gin*, 92–3; Larson, *Summer for the Gods*, 143, 146; Lienesch, *In the Beginning*, 139, 150; W. C. Cross, "Bryan, Noted Orator, in Favor at Dayton," *Knoxville Journal*, July 10, 1925, 1; "Darrow Loud in His Protest," *Nashville Banner*, July 8, 1925, 1.

41 Larson, *Summer for the Gods*, 153–4; Henry Louis Mencken, "The Monkey Trial: A Reporter's Account," in *D-Days at Dayton: Reflections on the Scopes Trial*, ed. Jerry D. Tomkins (Baton Rouge: Louisiana State University Press, 1965), 38–9 (a reprint of a July 11, 1925 article by Mencken).

42 *The World's Most Famous Court Case: Tennessee's Evolution Case* (Trial Transcript) (Dayton, TN: Bryan College, 1990), 79–84, 112; Larson, *Summer for the Gods*, 161–2.

43 *The World's Most Famous Court Case*, 204–9; Larson, *Summer for the Gods*, 180–1; Ralph Perry, "Added Thrill Given Dayton," *Nashville Banner*, July 21, 1925, 2; "Dramatic Scenes in Trial," *New York Times*, July 21, 1925, 1.

44 Hankins, *Jesus and Gin*, 97–8; Larson, *Summer for the Gods*, 187–91; Lienesch, *In the Beginning*, 162–5; *The World's Most Famous Court Case*, 285, 299, 302, 304; Perry, "Added Thrill Given Dayton," 2; Darrow, *The Story of My Life*, 267; Arthur Garfield Hayes, *Let Freedom Ring* (New York: Liveright, 1928), 77.

45 Larson, *Summer for the Gods*, 191–3; *The World's Most Famous Court Case*, 306–8, 316–17.

46 As summarized by Larson, *Summer for the Gods*, 220–1; Hankins, *Jesus and Gin*, 100–1; Lienesch, *In the Beginning*, 169, 171.

47 The text of Bryan's closing remarks is included as a supplement in *The World's Most Famous Court Case*; Larson, *Summer for the Gods*, 197–206, 226–7; Lawrence W. Levine, *Defender of the Faith: William Jennings, The Last Decade, 1915–1925* (New York: Oxford University Press, 1965), 355;

Lienesch, *In the Beginning*, 168. The case has been represented as a triumph for the defense in Frederick Lewis Allen's *Only Yesterday: An Informal History of the Nineteen Twenties* (1931) and in 1960 in the film, *Inherit the Wind*, based on the Broadway play by Jerome Lawrence and Robert E. Lee written in 1955.

48 Hankins, *Jesus and Gin*, 107–8; Matthew Avery Sutton, *Aimee Semple McPherson and the Resurrection of Christian America* (Cambridge, MA: Harvard University Press, 2007), 271.

49 For Aimee's personal account of her first encounter with Robert Semple and her baptism by the Holy Spirit, see Aimee Semple McPherson, *This Is That: Personal Experiences, Sermons, and Writings of Aimee Semple McPherson, Evangelist* (1919, rpt. New York: Garland Publishing, 1985), 11, 36–57, see also 58–9, 68. William H. Cooper, Jr., *The Great Revivalists in American Religion, 1740–1944: The Careers and Theology of Jonathan Edwards, Charles Finney, Dwight Moody, Billy Sunday, and Aimee Semple McPherson* (Jefferson, NC: McFarland & Company, 2010), 145; Edith Blumhofer, *Aimee Semple McPherson: Everybody's Sister* (Grand Rapids, MI: W. B. Eerdman's, 1993), 3, 63, 68–9, 80; Sutton, *Aimee Semple McPherson*, 107–11.

50 McPherson, *This Is That*, 95–102, 345; Blumhofer, *Aimee Semple McPherson*, 3, 90, 125, 128; Sutton, *Aimee Semple McPherson*, 12–14; Cooper, *The Great Revivalists in American Religion*, 145–7.

51 Blumhofer, *Aimee Semple McPherson*, 161–8, 191, 238; Cooper, *The Great Revivalists in American Religion*, 149; Sutton, *Aimee Semple McPherson*, 7.

52 McPherson's emphasis on the "Bride of Christ," commonly perceived to be aimed at women, raised concerns among some that it discouraged, even harmed, traditional marriage, something she ardently denied as having anything but a metaphorical relationship with earthly marital union. Sutton, *Aimee Semple McPherson*, 55–7. For some of McPherson's early preaching on the "Bridal Call," Jesus as bridegroom, and the "wife . . . yearning for his return," see McPherson, *This Is That*, 513–23, 532–5. Blumhofer, *Aimee Semple McPherson*, 261; Sutton, *Aimee Semple McPherson*, 19, 34, 54, 207.

53 In 1930, Charlie Chaplin and McPherson met while vacationing in southern France. They become close friends and spent evenings discussing the overlap between acting and religion. Chaplin, who had attended several of McPherson's services, observed: "Half of your success is due to your magnetic appeal," and "half due to props and lights." (Quoted in Sutton, *Aimee Semple McPherson*, 74, 76; Blumhofer, *Aimee Semple McPherson*, 8.)

54 Sutton, *Aimee Semple McPherson*, 3–4, 36–7, 52, 71, 73, 145–8; Blumhofer, *Aimee Semple McPherson*, 6, 157, 262–3.

55 Sutton, *Aimee Semple McPherson*, 145–8; Blumhofer, *Aimee Semple McPherson*, 262–3.

56 For some of her earlier preaching on the Second Coming, see McPherson, *This Is That*, 7. Blumhofer, *Aimee Semple McPherson*, 181. In one of her early sermons, undated but done before 1919, she defined her "Four-Fold Message" as "Salvation, the Baptism of the Holy Spirit, Soon Coming of Jesus, and the Preparation of the Bride." McPherson, "The Four-Fold Message of the Hour," in her, *This Is That*, 629–33. Sutton, *Aimee Semple McPherson*, 41, 61; Cooper, *The Great Revivalists in American Religion*, 156–9.

57 Blumhofer, *Aimee Semple McPherson*, 3, 7, 247, 253, 256, 283–90, 299; Sutton, *Aimee Semple McPherson*, 53–4, 79; Cooper, *The Great Revivalists in American Religion*, 150–2. For a detailed account of the "kidnapping," see Sutton, *Aimee Semple McPherson*, 90–151.

58 Sutton, *Aimee Semple McPherson*, 152–67; Blumhofer, *Aimee Semple McPherson*, 7, 333.

59 Cooper, *The Great Revivalists in American Religion*, 153–5; Sutton, *Aimee Semple McPherson*, 170–3, 183–6, 212–13, 221–3, 227–8, 243, 259, 265.

60 Blumhofer, *Aimee Semple McPherson*, 8, 381–4; Sutton, *Aimee Semple McPherson*, 210–1.

61 Marie W. Dallam, *Daddy Grace: A Celebrity Preacher and His House of Prayer* (New York: New York University Press, 2007), 1; Hankins found that Grace "bristled" when referred to as a "negro" preacher, insisting that he was "colorless." Hankins, *Jesus and Gin*, 149, 152. Fauset reports that Grace not only refused to admit that he was African but also frequently patronized his African American followers, explaining that he chose to lead them because of their lowly state. Arthur Huff Fauset, *Black Gods of the Metropolis: Negro Religious Cults of the Urban North* (Philadelphia: University of Pennsylvania, 1944), 23.

62 The title "Daddy" was not uncommon among African American religious leaders and likely derived from its use in Africa as a term of respect. See Dallam, *Daddy Grace*, 1, 4, 5, 29–30, 35, 42; Hankins, *Jesus and Gin*, 150.

63 Dallam, *Daddy Grace*, 45–51.
64 Dallam, *Daddy Grace*, 2; Fauset, *Black Gods of the Metropolis*, 30; Hankins, *Jesus and Gin*, 149, 154–5.
65 Dallam, *Daddy Grace*, 1, 21, 25, 40, 90–6; Hankins, *Jesus and Gin*, 151–2; United House of Prayer for All People website: www.tuhopfap.org/index2.html
66 Dallam, *Daddy Grace*, 1, 6,7,63–74; Fauset, *Black Gods of the Metropolis*, 27, 29; For an analysis of the socio-economic composition of Daddy Grace's followers, see Dallam, *Daddy Grace*, 80–6.
67 Dallam, *Daddy Grace*, 140–8.
68 Hankins, *Jesus and Gin*, 157; Fauset, *Black Gods of the Metropolis*, 26; Dallam, *Daddy Grace*, 57, 87. See also Edward E. Curtis, IV and Danielle Brune Sigler, *The New Black Gods: Arthur Huff Fauset and the Study of African American Religions* (Bloomington: Indiana University Press, 2009); Danielle Brune, "Sweet Daddy Grace: The Life and Times of a Modern Prophet," Ph.D. diss. (Austin: University of Texas, 2002).
69 Dallam, *Daddy Grace*, 95–106; Hankins, *Jesus and Gin*, 155–6.
70 Church membership reporting is not required by law. It is self-reported and often inaccurate. Stanly Burgess and Edouard M. Van de Maas, eds., "United House of Prayer for All People, Church on the Rock of the Apostolic Faith." *The New International Dictionary of Pentecostal and Charismatic Movements* (Grand Rapids, MI: Zondervan, 2002); Stanly Burgess and Edouard M. Van de Maas, "United House of Prayer for All People," *Britannica Online Encyclopedia* (2008), www.britannica. com
71 Dallam, *Daddy Grace*, 3; Burgess and Van de Maas, "United House of Prayer for All People," (Britannica Online). See also "Charles Emmanuel Grace," www.britannica.com/EBchecked/topic/240465/Charles-Emmanuel-Grace. For a discussion of the problem of succession of bishops following Grace's death, see Dallam, *Daddy Grace*, 161–84.
72 See for example: Winthrop Hudson, *Religion in America* (New York: Scribner's, 1965), 353; Sydney Ahlstrom, *A Religious History of the American People* (New Haven, CT: Yale University Press, 1972), 1061; Catherine Albanese, *America: Religions and Religion* (Belmont, CA: Wadsworth, 1981), 145; Fauset, *Black Gods of the Metropolis*, 23; Jill Watts, by way of example, denies the black cult label for Father Divine, explaining that some of his followers where white, that his followers had a degree of authority regarding the direction of the mission, and that they could come and go as they wished. Jill Watts, *God, Harlem U.S.A.: The Father Divine Story* (Berkeley: University of California Press, 1992), x. On Daddy Grace, see Dallam, *Daddy Grace*, 107–12.
73 Fauset, *Black Gods of the Metropolis*, 55; Robert Weisbrot, *Father Divine and the Struggle for Racial Equality* (Urbana: University of Illinois Press, 1983), 3, 9–28; Watts, *God, Harlem U.S.A.*, xi, 224.
74 Clarence E. Hardy, III, "Faucet's (Missing) Pentecostals: Church Mothers, Remaking Respectability, and Religious Modernism," in *The New Black Gods: Arthur Huff Fauset and the Study of African American Religions*, ed. Edward E. Curtis and Danielle Brune Sigler (Bloomington: Indiana University Press, 2009), 26; Watts, *God, Harlem U.S.A.*, 26–30.
75 Faucet, *Black Gods of the Metropolis*, 55–6; Hardy, "Faucet's (Missing) Pentecostals," 15–30; Hankins, *Jesus and Gin*, 158–9.
76 Faucet, *Black Gods of the Metropolis*, 56; Watts, *God, Harlem U.S.A.*, 72–80.
77 Faucet, *Black Gods of the Metropolis*, 55; Kenneth E. Burnham, *God Comes to America: Father Divine and the Peace Mission Movement* (Boston: Lambeth Press, 1979), 10–1; Watts, *God, Harlem U.S.A.*, 72–97; Hankins, *Jesus and Gin*, 159–62.
78 Faucet, *Black Gods of the Metropolis*, 59–61, 64, 66.
79 Watts, *God, Harlem U.S.A.*, 72–97; Burnham, *God Comes to America*, 24–31; Faucet, *Black Gods of the Metropolis*, 56–7, 60, 62.
80 Weisbrot, *Father Divine and the Struggle for Racial Equality*, 3–5, 7; Watts, *God, Harlem U.S.A.*, xi.
81 Burnham, *God Comes to America*, 39–49; Appendix A; Watts, *God, Harlem U.S.A.*, xi, 40–9; Leonard Norman Primiano, "The Consciousness of Innovation in the Music of Father Divine's Peace Mission Movement," in *The New Black Gods: Arthur Huff Fauset and the Study of African American Religions*, ed. Edward E. Curtis and Danielle Brune Sigler (Bloomington: Indiana University Press, 2009), 107–9; Hardy, "Faucet's (Missing) Pentecostals," 26–7.
82 "Father Divine," *Encyclopedia Britannica Online* (2015), www.britannica.com/EBchecked/topic/166561/Father-Divine. For opposing views on Father Divine's role in the civil rights movement, see Weisbrot, *Father Divine and the Struggle for Racial Equality*; Watts, *God, Harlem U.S.*;

Nora L. Rubel, "'Chased Out of Palestine': Prophet Cherry's Church of God and Early Black Judaism in the United States," in *The New Black Gods: Arthur Huff Fauset and the Study of African American Religions*, ed. Edward E. Curtis and Danielle Brune Sigler (Bloomington: Indiana University Press, 2009), 49–69; Faucet, *Black Gods of the Metropolis*, 62.

83 Watts, *God, Harlem U.S.*, 147–50, 166–7.

84 On succession challenges, see Burnham, *God Comes to America*, 97–102; Faucet, *Black Gods of the Metropolis*, 62; Watts, *God, Harlem U.S.*, 173–5.

85 See Randall K. Burkett, *Garveyism as a Religious Movement: The Institutionalization of a Black Civil Religion* (Metuchen, NJ: Scarecrow Press and the American Theological Library Association, 1978); Edward David Cronon, *Black Moses: The Story of Marcus Garvey and the University Negro Improvement Association* (1969 and 2007, rpt. Madison: University of Wisconsin Press, 1955).

86 See Edward E. Curtis, IV, *Muslims in America: A Short History* (New York: Oxford University Press, 2009); Richard Brent Turner, *Islam in the African-American Experience* (Bloomington: Indiana University Press, 2003); Michael A. Gomez, *Black Crescent: The Experience and Legacy of African Muslims in the Americas* (New York: Cambridge University Press, 2005), 203–75.

87 See Donald Warren, *Radio Priest: Charles Coughlin, the Father of Hate Radio* (New York: Free Press, 1996); Alan Brinkley, *Voice of Protest: Huey Long, Father Coughlin, and the Great Depression* (New York: Vintage Books, 1983).

88 Robert Staughton Lynd and Helen Merrell Lynd, *Middletown in Transition: A Study in Cultural Conflicts* (New York: Harcourt Brace, 1937).

89 See Matthew Avery Sutton, *American Apocalypse: A History of Modern Evangelicalism* (Cambridge, MA: The Belknap Press, 2014), Ch. 8.

90 Jerald C. Brauer, *Protestantism in America: A Narrative History* (Philadelphia: Westminster Press, 1953), Ch. 17. See also Robert M. Miller, *American Protestantism and Social Issues, 1919–1939* (Chapel Hill: The University of North Carolina Press, 1958); David J. O'Brien, *American Catholics and Social Reform: The New Deal Years* (New York: Oxford University Press, 1968); Lee J. Levinger, *A History of the Jews in the United States* (Cincinnati: Commission on Jewish Education, 1949).

Recommended for further reading

Blumhofer, Edith. *Aimee Semple McPherson: Everybody's Sister*. Grand Rapids, MI: W. B. Eerdman's, 1993.

Boyer, Paul. *When Time Shall be No More: Prophesy Belief in Modern American Culture*. Cambridge, MA: Harvard University Press, 1992.

Furniss, Norman F. *The Fundamentalist Controversy, 1918–1931*. New Haven, CT: Yale University Press, 1954.

Ginger, Ray. *Six Days or Forever: Tennessee v. John Thomas Scopes*. New York: Oxford University Press, 1958.

Larson, Edward J. *Summer for the Gods: The Scopes Trial and America's Continuing Debate over Science and Religion*. Cambridge, MA: Harvard University Press, 1997.

Lienesch, Michael. *In the Beginning: Fundamentalism, the Scopes Trial, and the Making of the Antievolution Movement*. Chapel Hill: The University of North Carolina Press, 2007.

Marsden, George M. *Fundamentalism and American Culture: The Shaping of Twentieth-Century Evangelicalism, 1870–1925*, 2nd edn. New York: Oxford University Press, 2006.

Numbers, Ronald L. *The Creationists: The Evolution of Scientific Creationism*. Berkeley: University of California Press, 1993.

Sutton, Matthew Avery. *Aimee Semple McPherson and the Resurrection of Christian America*. Cambridge, MA: Harvard University Press, 2007.

Tierney, Kevin. *Darrow: A Biography*. New York: Croswell, 1979.

Chapter 5

Religion in post-World War II America, 1945 to 1960

The response to World War II

American entrance into World War II was gradual and resisted by many in power. Dark clouds appeared on the horizon as early as 1922, when Benito Mussolini and his Fascist Party took control of Italy. But momentum built in 1933 when the German parliament granted its new chancellor, Adolf Hitler, leader of the Nazi Party, dictatorial powers. Mussolini and Hitler established an alliance, which Japan soon joined, and all three pursued aggressive domestic and military policies at home and abroad. At the same time, the 1930s were marked by various antiwar conferences and agreements, heartily supported by most Americans, including its churches. Many continued to believe that American involvement in World War I was a mistake and that neutrality was the correct path. They campaigned to "Keep America Out of the War," the position initially taken by Franklin Delano Roosevelt and Congress. As late as 1937, a Gallup Poll found that nearly two-thirds of Americans continued to hold this position, but the nation and its leaders found themselves increasingly drawn into the war, indirectly by its support for England, for example, and directly with the bombing of Pearl Harbor in 1941.[1]

With its entrance into the war, the majority of Americans rallied in support of their country. Much as was the case in World War I, however, a few churches and some religious leaders continued to insist on their pacifist teachings, the Mennonites, Quakers, Seventh-Day Adventists, and Jehovah's Witnesses being the most notable. Dorothy Day, the influential Catholic leader, and her followers preached pacifism even after Pearl Harbor. One month after the United States entered the war, she wrote in the *Catholic Worker*:

> We are still pacifists. Our manifesto is the Sermon on the Mount, which means that we will try to be peacemakers. Speaking for many of our conscientious objectors, we will not participate in armed warfare or in making munitions, or by buying government bonds to prosecute the war, or in urging others to these efforts. But neither will we be carping in our criticism. We love our country and we love our President. We have the only country in the world where men of all nations have taken refuge from oppression. We recognize that while in the order of intention we have tried to stand for peace, for love of our brother, in the order of execution we have failed as Americans in living up to our principles.[2]

Some of those who opposed the war based on their religious beliefs were granted conscientious objector status and allowed to provide alternative services. Most churches that had hoped to avoid war, however, changed their position to explain that war was evil, but sometimes a necessary evil, and propounded a "just war" position on conducting the war. Basically just war theory requires that the response be a last resort, after all other options have been exhausted; that it be to a just cause; that it be proportionate; and that non-combatant casualties be avoided to the fullest extent possible. Some argued at the time that just war theory came into conflict with the Allied insistence on the Axis's unconditional surrender and its bombing of European and Japanese cities. Hoping to achieve a lasting peace in victory – that which had eluded the world in the wake of World War I and Wilson's plan to make the world safe for democracy – most churches and synagogues organized to support the American war effort by providing war-related services such as food, clothing, medical supplies, and other necessities, as well as over 8,000 chaplains that took their places in the front lines in Europe and Asia. Through denominational operations, and following the war through the interdenominational World Council of Churches, founded in 1948, they also provided relief aid to civilians displaced by the war.[3]

Clearly, the most devastating impact on believers during the war was the Holocaust. Although evidence began to surface as early as 1942, discovery of the horrors of gas chambers and mass burials in 1945 at Dachau and Auschwitz confirmed everyone's worst fears and caused many to rethink their ideas on man's humanity and God's relationship to man. Between 1936 and 1943, some 150,000 Jews fled central Europe for the United States. Millions more could not or would not leave, and they and other minorities met their end in Nazi concentration camps. Elie Wiesel, a native of Romania and an Auschwitz survivor, came to the United States, spoke of the Holocaust and in the process reflected on the dark side of humanity and the apparent "silence of God" in the face of this evil. "Man's betrayal matches God's silence. If we are moved by the dehumanization of the victim, we must be shocked by the dehumanization of mankind." Wiesel insisted that despair was not the answer, but: "It is the question, the question of questions. It is both man's way of questioning God and God's way of questioning man." And for this question, "there is no answer coming from either side." Nevertheless, he concluded, one must not cease to believe in God, but rather continue to question Him through such belief. Much as there is "no heart . . . as whole as a broken heart, no faith is as whole as a broken faith."[4]

Then, of course, there was the development of the atomic bomb. Upon his witnessing the first test explosion in New Mexico, J. Robert Oppenheimer, one of the scientists who led the American effort to create the bomb, reflected the conflicting emotions that greeted that momentous event. His first response to the immense mushroom cloud that rose into the air was to quote a passage from the *Bhagavad Gita*, the Hindu scripture: "If the radiance of a thousand suns were to burst into the sky, that would be like the splendour of the Mighty One." Moments later, a more sober reflection from the same text came to mind: "I am become Death, the shatterer of worlds." When these weapons were dropped on Hiroshima and Nagasaki, accounting for the combined deaths of 200,000 Japanese and the mortal wounding of up to another 100,000, another reminder to some of man's inhumanity was driven home. Most came to justify the use of the two atomic bombs as an appropriate response to Japanese atrocities during the war, while others supported it as the best way to end the war without causing the loss of an even greater number of people on both sides if a land invasion were to be undertaken. Roper Polls conducted in the years immediately following the war showed 75 percent of the American people approved of Truman's action, even though 65.6 percent of Americans expected another country to have the bomb within five years; 40.4 percent believed that the country would be the Soviet Union, and 38 percent anticipated a "big war" would happen in the next twenty-five to thirty years. Others, especially religious leaders, feared that America had descended to the same level of its enemies in making indiscriminate war on civilians.[5]

On August 10, 1945, the day after a second atomic bomb was dropped on Nagasaki, the President of the Federal Council of Churches and the chairman of its Commission on a Just and Durable Peace issued a statement on the precedent set by the United States by its use of atomic weapons: If "we, a professedly Christian nation, feel morally free to use atomic energy in that way, men elsewhere will accept that verdict. Atomic weapons will be looked upon as a normal part of the arsenal of war and the stage will be set for the sudden and final destruction of mankind. . . . We pray that our authorities may, in this difficult matter, find and follow the way of Christian statesmanship." On August 15, *The Christian Century* editorialized that, rather than celebrating, "we should now be standing in penitence before the Creator of the power which the atom has hitherto kept inviolate, using what may be our last opportunity to learn the lost secret of peace on earth."[6]

On August 20, a group of thirty-four clergy authored a column in the *New York Times* denouncing the bomb as "an atrocity of a new magnitude," stating that its "reckless and irresponsible employment against an already virtually beaten foe will have to receive judgment before God and the conscience of humankind. It has our unmitigated condemnation." They called upon President Truman to discontinue production of atomic bombs and to seek international agreements outlawing not only the new weapon but war itself. And finally, the Federal Council of Churches asked for a report on atomic warfare from its Commission on the Relation of the Church to the War in the Light of the Christian Faith. Twenty-two theologians signed their names to the report, which came out in March 1946. They wrote that "the surprise bombing of Hiroshima and Nagasaki was morally indefensible. . . . As the power that first used the atomic bomb under these circumstances, we have sinned grievously against the laws of God and the people of Japan." The commission went on to report that it felt compelled to reconsider its earlier approval of the carpet bombing of German and Japanese cities, as the dropping of the atomic bombs were simply part of the "whole system of obliteration attacks with explosives and fire bombs," and both kinds of "indiscriminate, excessive violence" had to be condemned. Richard Fagley, a member of the FCC's Commission concluded that the only alternative to the total world disaster atomic bombs forecast was "repentance and regeneration." "The fate of the world . . . in a literal sense, depends upon the ability of the moral and religious forces . . . to call men effectively to repentance, worship, and service."[7]

Arthur Compton, a Protestant lay religious leader saw things a bit differently, but closer to how the American public came to see it. In his 1946 essay, "The Moral Meaning of the Atomic Bomb," he argued that the moral obligation that the United Sates had inherited from World War II was "the responsibility to protect the world from a suicidal war," even if that meant going to war. "Most Americans," he asserted, "freely chose war with all its agony and evil rather than have their consciences bear the burden of refusing to share in protecting the world against great disaster." As historian Raymond Haberski has summarized the dilemma that underscored the consensus opinion: "The moral crisis of the early Cold War apparently offered two options: The protection of liberty or the abdication of responsibility. . . . In other words, the nation had moral authority and those who dissented from it were in moral jeopardy."[8]

A moral reckoning follows

On August 10, 1945, President Harry Truman spoke in a radio address of "the awful responsibility" that had descended on the American people. The awful responsibility of which he spoke was the possession of the atomic bomb. He gave thanks to God that the United States had come to possess it and not the nation's enemies. But, he added: "We pray that He may guide us to use it in His ways and for His purposes." As previously noted, the war had united most Americans in support of their government and against the common enemy. Henry Luce's pronouncement in 1941 of the "American Century" is perhaps the best known articulation of that vision. Luce marshalled support for American entry into the war by declaring that "it now becomes our time to be the powerhouse from which the ideals of [Western civilization] spread throughout the world and do their mysterious work of lifting the life of mankind from the level of beasts to what the Psalmist called a little lower than the angels."[9]

Similarly, when the war ended, the majority of Americans celebrated its triumphant end, but an influential few dared speak of what they saw as the spiritual crisis into which Americans had entered. Moreover, reflecting the mood of the nation and the role religion would play in postwar America, polls showed that when asked who did the most good for the country, religious leaders rose from third to first place between 1942 and 1947. They were not the leaders of any specific denominations, but rather, they represented an American civil religion that did what the churches could not do, unify a nation of multiple faiths under one common set of beliefs. Since the 1930s, American Protestant theologians had begun to concern themselves with, and emphasize, the ground that Christianity shared with Judaism, pointing out that Christianity grew out of Judaism or that the New Testament succeeded the Old Testament, or Hebrew Bible. Reinhold Niebuhr was a leader in this area of study, seeking "to strengthen the Hebraic-prophetic content of the Christian tradition." There were those who thought the idea undermined the uniqueness of each faith, but most Christians and Jews welcomed the idea. The hope was to realize "two harmonious minorities in an overwhelmed and menacing world," a goal that would become even more important in Cold War America.[10]

As explained by sociologist Robert Bellah in an influential 1967 essay, civil religion offered the American people something they could use in times of trial, namely a common heritage. It "incorporated the myths of the nation's past with the promise of the nation's unique position in the present to create meaning in a time of great distress." Although others would come to a different conclusion, Bellah insisted that "American civil religion is not the worship of the American nation but an understanding of the American experience in the light of ultimate and universal reality." Further, it was hoped that a civil religion would provide Americans a common creed that would not only unify them but also provide a means to evaluate their nation's actions.[11]

There were those who saw danger in such consensus. A. J. Muste, an influential Protestant layman described the situation in his influential book, *Not by Might*, published in 1947. "Thus it has fallen upon this 'Christian' nation, incessantly declaiming against the perpetrators of atrocities, and still doing so, to perpetuate the ultimate atomic atrocity – needlessly – and so to remove all restrain upon atrocity. That is the logic of the atrocious means. . . . With fatal precision the means in war become more destructive, both of physical life and of moral standards and spiritual values." "Has it come to this?" he asked. "The atomic bomb is the symbol of power to destroy and kill raised to demonic proportions. What shall be set against it? What shall overcome it?"[12]

Paul Tillich, another notable Protestant, in his influential book *The Courage to Be* (1952), pointed to change in Christianity in the postwar era, as well. But the individual who addressed it more directly, in political and ethical terms, and to a greater extent than just about anyone else, was Tillich's colleague at the Union Theological Seminary in New York, the Protestant theologian Reinhold Niebuhr. Niebuhr, who had been a socialist and pacifist during the 1920s, attracted national attention when he broke with his liberal Protestant brethren, abandoned his pacifism, and defended America's entrance into the war against Germany and Japan. As early as the 1930s, he became convinced that socialism and pacifism were based on the fallacy of human perfectibility and that they could not come to terms with the ineradicable reality of sin. He explained his change of heart in *Moral Man and Immoral Society*, which he published in 1932, only to have the course of international developments of the 1930s and 1940s underscore his assertions. In 1941, he founded the journal, *Christianity and Crisis*, in which he helped make the case for war. But at the same time, Niebuhr argued that "a simple Christian moralism is senseless and confusing. It is senseless when, as in the World War, it sought to uncritically identify the cause of Christ with the cause of democracy without a religious reservation." It was just as senseless when it sought to purge itself of this error by an uncritical refusal to make any distinctions between relative values in history. Niebuhr thereby challenged both absolute pacifism and patriotism for their tending to see the nation as simply a moral agent for good. He found no moral position to take in World War II, as both sides – indeed all humanity – were involved in guilt. But, he insisted, guilt should not paralyze Christians into inaction. God's grace frees a Christian to act, to devote himself "to the highest values he knows, to defend those citadels of civilization of which necessity and historic destiny have made him the defender." At the same time, Niebuhr added, that same grace would convince him of the ambiguity of even his best intentions and actions.[13]

The dropping of the atomic bomb made Niebuhr's argument at the same time more pressing and complicated. On March 6, 1946, a front-page article noted appeared in the *New York Times* that included a declaration made by the Federal Council of Churches that called the use of the atomic bomb on Japan "morally indefensible." Niebuhr was one of those who signed it. That prompted Harvard University's president to challenge him. James Conant argued that Niebuhr's support for America's war effort had lent ethical and moral legitimacy to the use of force including the bombing of enemy cities and even the use of the atomic bomb. Conant's challenge gave Niebuhr the opportunity to reexamine his position from the postwar perspective, which he did in a letter to Conant dated March 16.[14]

Central to Niebuhr's position was his questioning the use of immoral means (dropping the atomic bomb) to achieve moral ends. Echoing his position during the war, but applied to the atomic age, he explained that he believed that use of the atomic bomb in certain circumstances was morally justifiable and that included its use to defeat Japan. He explained that his support for the FCC statement was not intended to reverse that position but rather to remind people that our doing good did not remove the guilt we incurred in the process. "On the one hand," he wrote, "it seems to me there is too general a disposition to disavow guilt because on the whole we have done good – in this case defeated tyranny. I was ready to sign the report on the expression of guilt particularly because I thought it important from the Christian standpoint to admit the moral ambiguity of all righteous people in history, who are, despite the good they do, involved in antecedent and in marginal guilt." Put another way, Niebuhr did not object to America's use of the bomb, but rather its use without considering the implications of such an act.[15]

Niebuhr returned to the subject of the moral ambiguities of America's Cold War in 1952 in his best-known book, *The Irony of American History*. By then he felt the need to warn Americans against self-righteousness in their crusade against communism, which was commonly portrayed as their having been chosen by God to carry out God's will. He argued that Americans had seldom shown any kind of humility over the past several years and that they had demonstrated that there was nothing necessarily righteous in their emergence as a world superpower. Niebuhr wrote:

We take, and must continue to take, morally hazardous action to preserve our civilization. We must exercise our power. But we ought neither to believe that a nation is capable of perfect disinterestedness in its exercise, nor become complacent about particular degrees of interest and passion which corrupt the justice by which the exercise of that power is legitimized. Communism is a vivid object lesson in the monstrous consequences of moral complacency about the relation of dubious means to supposedly good ends.

But America was not immune to such complacency.[16]

Niebuhr's sense of guilt, or sin, became central to what came to be known as Christian realism. Christian realism has been described as "more than simple moral affirmation of America's special mission in world; it was rather a morally rigorous, complex, and tragic understanding of the difficult but ultimately defensible position of a nation that was forced to commit acts of extraordinary violence in order to protect its citizens and to defeat the monstrous systems that led to wars of catastrophic destruction." For those who were listening, and not tempted to take the easy road around the moral complexities of the age, it was hoped that religion would help clarify – at the same time that it made more complicated – what was at stake in the Cold War and how the United States should act as the world's preeminent military power. Put simply, religion was to check as well as justify the American exercise of power. As the Federal Council of Churches resolved in 1950: "We have no clever new political strategy to offer. But in sight of God we are persuaded that our desperate times call for a mighty and costly drive for the political and moral revival and uniting of the free world and beyond that for reconciliation." The nation did not have to wait long for a group of religious leaders to take up this call to arms.[17]

Billy Graham

Among the most prominent of those who answered the call to lead the nation in repentance and regeneration, catching the wave of resurgent evangelicalism, was Billy Graham. A North Carolina farm boy born in 1918 and raised in a Reformed Presbyterian Church with a Calvinist theology, Graham led a normal young person's life with interests in sports and young women. He aspired to become a professional baseball player, but after that failed to materialize, six days before he turned 16, he was converted by the traveling evangelist Mordecai Fowler Ham.[18]

Upon graduating from Wheaton College (Illinois), in 1943, Graham began his ministry at a small poor Baptist church near Chicago (Western Springs, IL). In a failed attempt to raise money for the church, he took on a weekly radio broadcast on a local Chicago radio station, but within two years, he gave up on that pastorate and became involved in the Youth for Christ movement. Graham rose quickly through the ranks of the Youth for Christ, but in 1947, with only a bachelor's degree in hand, he became the nation's youngest college president when he was appointed to head the evangelical Northwestern Schools in Minneapolis, Minnesota. He continued to travel the nation, however, and soon found that he could not do both and resigned his presidency to devote himself to his revival campaign. Graham's 1949 Los Angeles revival is commonly seen as the event that transformed him from an evangelical circuit star to a national celebrity.[19]

The revival began on September 25, just days after President Truman announced that the Russians had detonated their first atomic bomb, thereby eliminating America's sole possession of the largest weapon of mass destruction. Graham addressed the anxiety that development prompted, not only by once again imploring Americans to turn to God, but also tying their turning to God to preserving the special place of Western civilization in the world. Graham explained that America had been spared the ravages of war thus far because "God's people prayed," and as such, God had used, and could continue to "use America to evangelize the world." As became clear from recent world events, however: "An arms race, unprecedented in the history of the world, is driving us madly toward destruction! And I sincerely believe that it is in the providence of God that He has chosen this hour for a campaign – giving this city [Los Angeles] one more chance to repent of sin and turn to a believing knowledge of the Lord Jesus Christ." Los Angeles, indeed "the whole of America is becoming as wicked as the world of Noah's day," but "God is giving us a desperate choice," he explained, "a choice of either revival or judgment. There is no alternative. Judgment is coming just as sure as I'm standing here!"[20]

Originally planned for three weeks, the Los Angeles revival lasted eight weeks and attracted an estimated 350,000 attendees to the "canvas cathedral," about 4,200 of whom "made a decision for Christ." Further, a revival that attracted very little attention from the press at its opening became front-page news. But Graham's message, as effective and timely as it was, may not have brought about the attention it received without the assistance of two newspaper and magazine publishers – William Randolph Hearst and Henry Luce. The anticommunist Hearst was so taken by Graham's Los Angeles crusade that he sent a telegram to his editors, saying, "Puff Graham," in effect ordering his coast-to-coast newspapers to give Graham front-page coverage. Soon, banner headlines referencing Graham's crusade appeared in Hearst's *Examiner* and *Herald Express*. When he returned to the East Coast, Luce was persuaded by financier Bernard Baruch to attend one of Graham's crusades in Columbia, South Carolina, where he, too, was sold on the young evangelist. Graham would soon be able to count on the covers of Luce's *Time* and *Life* magazines, as well.[21]

Graham's most famous extended meeting took place in New York City's Madison Square Garden in 1957. The revival ran 16 weeks and attracted 2.4 million attendees and made 61,000 converts, or as Graham preferred to identify them, "inquirers." But the New York City revival was significant for another reason. It marked the point at which Graham's cooperation with mainline Protestants and Roman Catholics caused a rift that had been growing between Graham and many of those fundamentalists with whom he had been associated earlier. As Grant Wacker has argued:

> From that point forward, Graham, more than anyone else, both galvanized and exemplified a rapidly growing faction in American Protestantism. The new evangelicals, as they sometimes called themselves, affirmed most of the doctrinal corner stones that fundamentalists affirmed, but with less dogmatism and with little inclination to fall into arcane debates about how the world would end. They placed more emphasis on evangelism, social reform, and cooperation with other Christians.[22]

If Graham came out of a fundamentalist tradition, what brought him into the national limelight were his successes at gaining the support of mainline Protestants and the ear of the nation's secular leaders. His methods, his talent for publicity and for attracting the rich and powerful, and his ecumenism, were all built on a century of mainstream Protestantism. And many Americans, who had grown skeptical of mainstream liberal Protestantism, were ready to embrace what he offered. Graham was closely associated with the National Association of Evangelicals for United Action (NAE), the organizational arm of what came to be known in the 1950s as the New Evangelicalism. Although most of its members held membership in the Federal Council of Churches, which would become the National Council of Churches (NCC), the leadership of the NCC and the NAE were moving in different directions. Leaders of the NCC were focusing on institutionalizing ecumenism and saw the NAE as seeking to take control of the NCC and imposing its conservative evangelicalism on it.[23]

Graham, who during the early 1950s attended NAE conventions, was associated with that body and viewed with concern by leaders of the NCC. Seeking to bridge the divide, his breakthrough moment came in 1954 when Graham accepted an invitation to speak at New York's Union Theological Seminary, the citadel of liberal Protestantism. John Bennett, Union's dean of faculty, explained what happened in the *Union Seminary Quarterly*. He cited Graham's sincerity and magnetism, his verbal adroitness, and perhaps most importantly, the relief his audience felt that Graham was not as threatening as they had feared. Bennett observed that Graham was "breaking the pattern" of the crude, opportunist mercenary. Indeed Graham was seen as a model of propriety, and, Bennett explained, "many of us gained the strong impression that he can be used for highly constructive Christian purposes in the churches and in the nation." Bennett pointed out that Graham's uses of the Bible did not reflect a "hard Fundamentalism," that he used the word "ecumenical" several times in his remarks, and that he was "growing" in his social vision. He concluded:

> It is a fact that until his visit to Union I had classed him as a fundamentalist and socially reactionary evangelist and had dismissed him as a possible constructive force in the American Church. . . . [Following Graham's visit] when all is said, I believe that his coming to Union was a very good lesson for us. It may have helped us to realize more vividly, what we should have known from Church history, that God can work powerfully through men who do not meet all of our specifications.[24]

The 1950s witnessed Graham's move into various media enterprises, including radio, television, movies, book publishing, and journalism, all of which greatly enhanced his national profile. His *Hour of Decision* radio program debuted in November 1950 and in a little over a month enjoyed the largest audience of any other religious program in history. In 1951, he went into television with a Sunday night edition of *Hour of Decision*, which lasted until 1954. In 1957, he began to telecast live broadcasts from his crusades, the first coming from Madison Square Garden, New York City, and running fourteen successive Saturdays. Graham's film ministry, begun in 1951, eventually reached more than 100 million viewers through more than 30 feature-length films, commonly described as "religious melodramas whose climaxes turned on the principals listening to Graham's message" and choosing God. In 1952, he moved into the newspaper mass market with a daily syndicated column called "My Answer," which by 1954 appeared in 73 newspapers across the country with an estimated readership of 15 million. And in 1956 he started the evangelical periodical, *Christianity Today.*[25]

The 1950s also witnessed Graham's engagement with matters of political and social concern. He addressed the vital issues of the day, including teenage delinquency, marriage, divorce, crime, and alcoholism. But he also joined with the many who attacked communism, even supporting the charges of communists holding office at the highest levels of the nation brought by Senator Joseph McCarthy. Striking a similar note to that of McCarthy's Wheeling, West Virginia, speech, Graham warned of "over eleven hundred social-sounding organizations that are Communist or Communist-oriented in this country. They control the minds of a great segment of our people; the infiltration of the left wing . . . both pink and red into the intellectual strata of America" has gone so far that our "educational [and] religious culture is almost beyond repair." Such "Communists and left-wingers," he continued, constitute "a fifth column in our midst" that could sabotage the United States." They constituted "a cancer eating at the heart and core of the American way of life" – "subversive groups seek[ing] to destroy us . . . doing their deadly work in government, education, and even in religion."[26]

Graham also concerned himself with the civil rights movement. Prior to 1950, Graham fell in line with most Southern white preachers in abiding by local customs, which in nearly every case meant segregation. In 1951, he began to take a different road, signaled by his speech before the Southern Baptist Convention in which he took them to task for their discriminatory policy in Baptist schools. The following year at one of his crusades, he attacked segregation. In 1953, at a crusade in Chattanooga, Tennessee, he personally removed the rope separating the races, and after the *Brown v. Board of Education* decision was handed down by the US Supreme Court in 1954, he never again permitted segregation of his audiences and refused to conduct revivals in cities where integration was not allowed. Graham never engaged in or endorsed confrontational tactics becoming increasingly more prevalent during the 1950s, and his relationship with Martin Luther King, Jr. was never warm. On July 21, 1957, while in New York City, he was quoted in the *New York Herald Tribune* as saying:

> Certainly we need civil rights legislation. We should do all we can to make sure that no man's rights are limited because of his race or creed or color. But in order to establish race relations that conform to the Christian Principles on which our country was founded, we need love.[27]

During the summer of 1950, Graham visited President Truman in the White House, but it did not go well. Their meeting was awkward, as the President proved resistant to Graham's attempts to engage him in prayer and was angered when, following their meeting, Graham was asked by the press to talk about what went on during his meeting with Truman. Nevertheless, Graham established a foothold in the nation's capital, followed two years later by his holding a revival in Washington that included a religious service on the steps of the US Capitol and daily prayers at the Pentagon.[28]

In 1952, Graham met Dwight Eisenhower, whom he encouraged to run for President, even advising him to become a Presbyterian, as Eisenhower did not have any strong attachment to a particular denomination, which could prove to be a liability in any campaign. Immediately after Eisenhower's election, Graham announced in a sermon titled "Peace in Our Time" on his weekly radio show, *Hour of Decision*, that he had met with Eisenhower twice over the past year and that he was impressed by the national war hero. He spoke of Eisenhower's sincerity, humility, and grasp of world affairs: "I also sensed a dependence upon God. He told me on both occasions [of his visits] that the hope for building a better America lay in a spiritual revival." To this he added: "Another thing that encourages me about Mr. Eisenhower is that he is taking advice from some genuine born-again Christians." Graham assured his listeners that, as a result of the election, the American people could feel "a little more secure, realizing we have a man who believes in prayer at the helm of our government at this crucial hour."[29]

Immediately following his election, as he was preparing for his inaugural speech, Eisenhower invited Graham to visit with him. He told Graham that his victory made clear to him that he wanted to lend a higher spiritual quality to the nation's business, and he asked Graham to advise him on "bringing something spiritual, some spiritual note and tone, in the inauguration ceremony." Graham recalled that, with tears in his eyes, he said to the President: "General, you can do more to inspire the American people to a more spiritual way of life than any other man alive!" Thereafter Graham would be a regular visitor to the White House and spiritual confidant not only for Eisenhower but also for several Presidents yet to come, including Lyndon Johnson, Richard Nixon, Gerald Ford, Ronald Reagan, Bill Clinton, and both Bushes. Just as importantly, Graham's impact on American evangelism was so significant that, for the rest of the century, it was identified with him far more than anyone else.[30]

Other religious leaders in the American Cold War, anticommunist movement

Graham's preaching both appealed to and strengthened evangelical, as well as Roman Catholic, anticommunism. It also lent support to those who called into question liberal Protestant patriotism – the "pink fringe" – and their less strident opposition to communism and socialism during the 1930s. Although it is arguable that he was the most successful, Graham was not the only preacher with such a message. Others included Fred Schwarz, who created the Christian Anti-Communist Crusade in 1953; Billy James Hargis of the Christian Crusade; and Carl MacIntire of the American Council of Christian Churches. At a time when figures such as Niebuhr and organizations such as the National Council of Churches offered a more moderate response to communism, they offered clarity. As Schwarz later explained, to use just one example,

> My opposition to Communism was not based upon economics or politics but upon its false doctrines about God and man. . . . Communism had a doctrine of God – that God did not exist but that the idea of God had been projected into human consciousness by the universal existence of the Class Struggle; that it has a doctrine of Man – that man was a collection of atoms and molecules without soul or spirit and that all human ideas and emotions were derived from experiences provided by the economic environment; that it had a doctrine of Sin – that sin resulted from the experience provided by Capitalism; that it had a doctrine of Redemption – a Communist revolution; and that it had a doctrine of the future – that the Communist victory was inevitable due to the progressive nature of being. It also pointed out that it had a Creator – Karl Marx; a Messiah – Vladimir Lenin; a Pope – Joseph Stalin; and a devil – Leon Trotsky.[31]

Roman Catholic opposition to communism was long standing. In 1846, two years before Marx published his *Communist Manifesto*, Pope Pius IX promulgated an encyclical titled *Qui Pluribus: On Faith and Religion*, which provided the Church's first publically articulated objection to communism. He expanded on that condemnation in 1864, less than three months after Marx created the First International. That was followed by additional papal condemnations by Pope Leo XIII in 1878 and, in 1937, Pope Pius XII's *Divini Redemptoris* (Divine Redeemer), which pointed to its atheism as his fundamental objection to communism.[32]

Postwar American Catholics were particularly opposed to communism, perhaps even more so than most American Protestants and Jews, and they were supported by their contemporary Cold War Pope, Pius XII. Under his leadership and that of American Catholic bishops and other church leaders, the American Catholic Church was able to establish itself as both a formidable and uncompromising counterforce to communism. American bishops denounced communist oppression of Catholics in Eastern Europe, while in the late 1940s and 1950s the American Catholic press made anticommunism its number one concern. As a result of its anticommunist position, American Catholics ceased to be an immigrant church and took a major step toward overcoming their long-standing position in the eyes of American Protestants as incompatible in the Church's teachings with American democracy. In the leadership role it would come to play in American anticommunism, Catholics would be able to depict themselves champions of freedom and defenders of Christendom against its anti-Christian enemies.[33]

Among the leading American Catholic anticommunist Cold War crusaders were Archbishop Sheen, Cardinal Spellman, and John Courtney Murray. Jacques Maritain, however, deserves at least brief mention. His influence was more intellectual than the three other more public figures. A native of France and a Catholic convert, Murray ended up in America because of the Nazis, who overran France in 1940, accepting a professorship at Princeton University. In his collection of speeches published in *Reflections on America* (1958), he defended America against its European detractors who charged that the country was greedy or materialistic. While allowing that making money was central to the American way of life, he explained, Americans did so with a sense of moral responsibility and were generously philanthropic in pursuit of elevated ideals. Nowhere else in the world, he wrote, was there such an abundance of spiritual vitality. Harkening back to his book *Integral Humanism*, published twenty years earlier, he argued that the United States was the closest approximation in practice to the ideal form of society he outlined in that book. Maritain allowed that America had its problems – racial segregation and an unhealthy preoccupation with sex, in particular – but it also possessed "a certain hidden disposition that is Christian in origin, and appears to me as a kind of humble and remote reminiscence of the Gospel in the inner attitude of the people. Behind the façade of violence and callousness of modern life, this something of old, subtle Christian flavor lies, I think, deep in the soul of this country." Maritain recalled the history of America, with its people having migrated to avoid religious persecution, moral persecution, and poverty, and observed that in the optimistic American environment, "the tears and sufferings of the persecuted and unfortunate are transmuted into a perpetual effort to improve human destiny and to make life bearable; they are transfigured into optimism and creativity." Having established the United States as the leader in the free world, he concluded: "What the world expects from America is that she keep alive, in human history, a fraternal recognition of the dignity of man, in other words, the terrestrial hope of men in the Gospel."[34]

Of the three other Catholic leaders, Archbishop Fulton J. Sheen, "patriarch of the electronic church," reached the largest audience through radio and television and, as a result, was the most influential. In 1952, *Time* magazine, in a cover story on Sheen, recognized him as "perhaps the most famous preacher in the United States, certainly America's best-known Roman Catholic priest." Ordained a priest in 1919, Sheen earned a doctorate in philosophy from the Catholic University of Leuven in Belgium and became a highly regarded theologian. He taught at the Catholic University of America and for the entirety of his life in the ministry. Sheen's church sermons, whether they be in Peoria, Illinois, or in New York City, were given to capacity crowds. Sheen also published sixty-six books, including his best sellers, *Peace of Soul* (1949) and *Life of Christ* (1958), and scores of articles. While at Catholic University, from 1930 to 1950, Sheen began his career in the media hosting the radio program, *The Catholic Hour*, which by the close of its run had a weekly audience of 4 million on 150 stations. In 1951, he moved to television to host *Life Is Worth Living*, the first religious-oriented national television program. It ran until 1957 and drew 30 million weekly viewers, despite being scheduled to compete with the likes of Milton Berle and Frank Sinatra. Sheen's programs have been described as a combination of common sense, logic, and Christian ethics on such topics as Stalin and communism, psychiatry, patriotism, pain and suffering, angels, ethics, and many more. Reasons for Sheen's success on the airways were his rare combination of scholarly intellect and common touch, as well as his ability to connect with Catholic, Protestants, and Jews, alike.[35]

American involvement in World War II and the nation's Cold War consensus against communism following the war contributed significantly to Sheen's success. Sheen ardently supported American involvement in World War II, in one *Catholic Hour* radio broadcast calling the war not only a political struggle but also a theological one, referring to Adolf Hitler as the Antichrist. And similarly he saw the Cold War as "the final stage of degeneration of Western society," or as "Satan's answer to religion." As early as 1937, Sheen devoted six consecutive radio sermons to the subject of communism. After the war, in his sermon, "God and Country," Sheen declared: "We want to keep the United States a leader in the world and we believe that all God-believing people of the United States should unite to keep the country under Providence as the secondary cause [second to God's work on earth] for preservation of the liberties of the world."[36]

Critics of Sheen's preaching on communism have concluded that it was "righteous, inflexible, proselytizing, and paranoid." But some of those same critics have allowed that Sheen also was instrumental in developing a theological justification for resisting communism, presenting the conflict as a battle between good and evil and as part of a larger crusade to save Western Civilization. In his widely read book, *Communism and the Conscience of the West* (1948), Sheen wrote, "Communism is not to be feared just because it is anti-God, but because we are Godless, not because it is strong, but because we are weak, for if we were under God, then who could conquer us?" In February 1953, he took on Soviet leader Joseph Stalin. In a television broadcast on *Life Is Worth Living*, Sheen gave a dramatic reading of the burial scene from Shakespeare's *Julius Caesar*, substituting the names of prominent Soviet leaders for Caesar, Cassius, Marc Antony, and Brutus, concluding by saying, "Stalin must one day meet his judgment." A few days later, Stalin suffered a stroke and died, a coincidence not lost on his listeners and the public.[37]

Francis J. Spellman was educated at Fordham University in New York City. He graduated in 1911 and decided to study for the priesthood, whereupon Boston Archbishop William Henry O'Connell sent him off to study at the Pontifical North American College in Rome. Spellman was ordained a priest in 1916 and upon his return to the United States was assigned pastoral work in the Archdiocese of Boston. Cardinal O'Connell, a powerful figure in the American church hierarchy, took an apparent dislike to the young priest from the start, and the next few years have been referred to by one biographer as "Years of Bitterness" for the young priest. Although to be fair, Spellman proved not to be "a spiritual priest," as one biographer put it. His ambitions lay elsewhere, ambitions O'Connell largely frustrated.[38]

In 1925, with the help of some influential Boston Catholics, Spellman was named the first American attaché of the Vatican Secretariat of State. In that position, Spellman soon cultivated a positive relationship with influential figures in the Vatican, including Pope Pius XI, and became known among many influential American Catholics as the "American back-door to the Vatican." One special relationship Spellman developed was with Eugenio Pacelli, the papal ambassador, or nuncio, to Munich and then Berlin, who was destined to become the next Pope. In 1926, only one year after arriving in Rome, Spellman was elevated to the rank of monsignor. In 1932, the Pope appointed him Auxiliary Bishop of Boston, in which position he would serve under Cardinal O'Connell, but with the understanding that he would succeed him in that office.[39]

Upon his return to Boston, Spellman's years in Rome and the close ties he developed with the Vatican served him well, as church figures as well as politicians sought him out for his influence. Moreover, unlike during his early years in Boston, he was now treated as near royalty, with access to the highest levels of wealth and power, including the Kennedy family led by patriarch Joseph Kennedy. When his old friend, Cardinal Pacelli – the highest ranking Vatican figure ever to come to America – announced that he was going to visit the United States in 1936, President Franklin Roosevelt contacted Spellman seeking his assistance in arranging for Pacelli's visit to the White House. FDR's hope was that he could get Pacelli to silence Father Charles Coughlin, who in his popular radio program spoke increasingly well of Germany's Nazi leaders and policies, while blaming the nation's ills on Roosevelt, Jews, Communists, and "godless capitalists." Pacelli agreed, and with Spellman's help had Coughlin's radio program removed from the air.[40]

In 1938, Cardinal Pacelli was elected Pope Pius XII. The next year, the Pope appointed Spellman Archbishop of New York, a position he held until he died in 1967. He was named a cardinal in 1946. It was during his tenure as Archbishop of New York that Spellman secured national attention. Given the size of the Catholic population in New York City, and especially the political power of Irish Catholics, Spellman's influence on New York City politics was particularly strong. Even Mayor Fiorello La Guardia, who resented Spellman's meddling, was forced to deal with the Cardinal. Spellman's support for the President in his reelection bid in 1936, and his support for American involvement in World War II, led FDR in 1939 to make him the President's emissary to the Vatican. When the United States entered the war, he served as Apostolic Vicar for the US Armed Forces in which position he spent several Christmases with American troops abroad. Spellman became a close confidante of the President. He advised and assisted the President in establishing the US mission to the Vatican, and in 1943, FDR chose Spellman to act as his emissary to visit the leaders of sixteen countries in Europe, Africa, and the Middle East.[41]

Following the war, Spellman used his patriotic stance and the various resulting political connections to become involved in political affairs, earning his residence the name "the powerhouse." He hosted a long list of prominent figures, entertainers and political leaders, and in 1946, he instituted the Al Smith dinner, named after the American Catholic statesman who was elected Governor of New York four times and was the Democratic (and Catholic) presidential candidate in 1928. The dinner became a very popular annual fundraiser for the Catholic Charities of the Archdiocese, but it also became a political must event that attracted many prominent individuals. That he was successful in raising money can be seen in his spending more than a billion dollars on construction projects during his twenty-eight years in power, second only to New York City government as the biggest builder in the city.[42]

Spellman also shifted the focus of his Christian crusade to communism and the Soviet Union, in particular, at various points stating that "a true American can neither be a communist nor a communist condoner" and that "the first loyalty of every American is vigilantly to weed out and counteract communism and convert American communists to Americanism." Reflecting on the historical tension between the Catholic Church and Americanism, Spellman insisted that henceforth, the two would no longer be seen as mutually exclusive. When in 1947 the Knights of Columbus broadcast a series of programs to show the "truth about Communism," Spellman was often a guest. And he even became a comic book character, although in a serious vein, when the Catechetical Guild printed *Is This Tomorrow?* a color comic book that in one scene depicted a horde of crazed Communists who attacked St. Patrick's Cathedral and nailed Spellman to the front door. In 1948, some 2,800 guests in the Grand Ballroom of the Hotel Astor in New York City roared their approval when Spellman attacked Communism and warned that the war had not ended on V-J Day: "America is no safer from mastery by Communism than was any European country. There we witnessed the killing and enslavement of whole peoples by Communists, who, with the shedding of blood, became as if drunk with it!" Seconding the motion was the actual guest speaker for the night, President Harry Truman.[43]

Although in 1948 he shared the rostrum with President Truman, Spellman often made clear that he believed that the government was doing too little to combat communism in America and supported Senator Joseph McCarthy. In 1951, he praised Douglas MacArthur, whom Truman had just called home from Korea, where the popular general had led the fight against communist North Korea. In 1953, he went public defending McCarthy's investigations of supposed communist subversives in the federal government. The following year, Spellman warned of another Pearl Harbor and declared: "War to the hilt between communism and capitalism is inevitable." Known as the American Pope, Spellman's influence was unmatched in the United States by any other figure in the Catholic Church other than the Pope himself.[44]

If Sheen and Spellman "maneuvered American Catholics into the martial culture of the Cold War," as one historian has written, "John Courtney Murray helped justify that culture through Catholic thought." Serving very much as a public intellectual, and not merely a theologian, Murray provided an intellectual basis for the American church's patriotic anti-communism. That did not position Murray to share the popular limelight with Sheen and Spellman, but it did provide a much needed justification for those who needed or wanted it. In 1951, Murray addressed the need for the American Catholic Church to apply its principles to those of the nation. He wrote: "What therefore the Church must seek, and has sought, in every age is such a vital application of her principles, such an institutional embodiment of them, as will make them operative in particular temporal contexts." This had been the case throughout the Church's history, he pointed out, and it was necessary once again, as democracy in America

> offers to the Church as a spiritual power as good a hope of freedom as she has ever had; it offers to the Church as the Christian people a means, through its free political institutions, of achieving harmony between law and social organizations and the demands of their Christian conscience; finally, by reason of its aspirations toward an order of personal and associational freedom, political equality, civic friendship, social justice, and cultural advancement, it offers to the Church the kind of cooperation which she presently needs, and it merits in turn her cooperation in the realization of its own aspirations.[45]

Murray entered the New York province of the Society of Jesus in 1920. He studied at Boston College, where he received his bachelor's and master's degrees, thereafter continuing his studies at the Gregorian University in Rome, where he earned his doctorate in theology. He was ordained a priest in 1933, taught theology at the Jesuit theologate in Woodstock, Maryland, and served as editor of the Jesuit journal, *Theological Studies*, holding both positions until his death in 1967. As representative of the United States Conference of Catholic Bishops and consultant to the religious affairs section of the Allied High Commission during World War II, he helped draft the 1943 *Declaration on World Peace*, which set forth the principles upon which postwar reconstruction was to be erected. From 1958 to 1962, he served at the Center for the Study of Democratic Institutions in Santa Barbara, California, addressing the application of just war criteria to Soviet-American relations.

At the same time, Murray was a critic of American liberalism, in that if there was a threat to America, it was less a threat from the enemy abroad than it was from the enemy within. As he explained in the same *Time* article, the greater threat came from the children of the modern industrial state – those proponents of Enlightenment philosophy who were "engaged in the construction of a philosophy to put an end to all philosophy . . . to corrupt the inherited intuitive wisdom by which the people have always lived, and to do this not by spreading new beliefs but by creating a climate of doubt and bewilderment in which clarity about the larger aims of life is dimmed and the self-confidence of the people is destroyed." In this regard, Murray contributed to the discontent with American liberal Protestants, but it did not detract – and possibly even enhanced – the respect he gained among more conservative Protestant religious leaders and the general public. "Can we or can we not achieve a successful conduct of our national affairs, foreign and domestic," he asked in his *Time* interview, "in the absence of a consensus that will set our purposes, furnish a standard of judgment on polices, and establish the proper conditions for political dialog?" Could we do anything more than just survive in our battle with communism without "a new moral act of purpose"?[46]

Other prominent religious leaders of the 1940s and 1950s

Other prominent religious leaders of the 1940s and 1950s include Dutch Reformed pastor Norman Vincent Peale, Reform Rabbi Joshua Loth Liebman, and Catholic monk Thomas Merton. Peale popularized a "feel-good" message through his wildly successful books, *A Guide to Confident Living*, published in 1948 and *The Power of Positive Thinking*, which appeared in 1952 and sold over 2 million copies. Pastor of the Marble Collegiate Church on Fifth Avenue in New York City, he became the leading proponent of "Mind Cure," or positive thinking. Influenced by psychoanalysis, Peale took the position that you should believe in yourself. A "humble but reasonable" self-esteem, he argued, would lead to success – or self-realization – made possible by drawing on divine power, and it would lead to success in health, wealth, and happiness. "Christianity," Peale preached, "is a throbbing, pulsating, vibrant, creative energy, even in such manner as the sunlight is energy. . . . It is a deep therapy which can drive to the heart of a personality or of society . . . in breaking down infection centers, building up life centers, transforming, endowing with new energy." What people needed to do was to access that energy.[47]

Liebman, in his best-selling *Peace of Mind*, published in 1946, struck a similar chord to Peale's, offering another form of spiritual self-help. He believed that religion and psychiatry, notably psychoanalysis, had the same mission – to promote health and well-being. "The express purpose of religion is the achievement of the good life," he wrote, making clear that he did not mean material riches but, rather, "the good life." And psychoanalysis was a useful tool in achieving that end, although not a substitute for religion. Liebman did not limit his definition to any one religion. Rather, he explained that by religion he meant "the accumulated spiritual wisdom and ethical precepts dating from the time of the earliest prophets and gradually formulated into a body of tested truths for man's moral guidance and spiritual at-homeness in the universe." Religion, he insisted, taking a page from psychiatry, should be driven by the belief that peace of mind came from self-knowledge, not self-condemnation; to wit, he offered his own "ten commandments of a new morality," which replaced the "shalt nots" of the Hebrew Bible with a list of "shalts." Among Liebman's commandments were: "Thou shalt not be afraid of thy hidden impulses," "Thou shalt learn to respect thyself and then thou wilt love thy neighbor as thyself," and "Thou shalt transcend inner anxiety." And by facing up to private feelings of guilt and distress, "a new birth of confidence in life and in the God of life: could be achieved."[48]

Thomas Merton, a Trappist monk, poet, and social activist, was influential in postwar America, largely for his more than seventy books and many essays, but especially for his best seller, *The Seven Storey Mountain* (1948). He was also a student of comparative religions, dwelling extensively on Asian spirituality, authoring books on Zen Buddhism and Taoism. Merton was born in France, but his family moved to the United States in 1915. He attended three English boarding schools and was baptized in the Church of England, but as a young man, he considered himself an agnostic. He believed that all religions "lead to God, only in different ways, and every man should go according to his own conscience, and settle things according to his own private way of looking at things." In 1933, Merton entered Cambridge University's Clare College, but after a year of heavy drinking and womanizing, he returned to the United States. In 1935, he enrolled in Columbia University.[49]

Merton resisted much of the modern world. As he looked back at his early years, he observed: "I had refused to pay any attention to the moral laws upon which all our vitality and sanity depend. . . . I had at last become a true child of the modern world. . . . In devouring pleasures and joys, I had found distress and anguish and fear." Merton aspired to be a writer, but during the 1930s, while at Columbia, he engaged in socially radical politics, at one point joining the Young Communist League and became a pacifist. Merton detested the modern commercial world, but soon abandoned communism, and in 1938, while still in graduate school at Columbia, and after reading a book about Gerard Manley Hopkins' conversion to Catholicism, he converted to Catholicism. In 1941, he entered the Trappist monastery at Gethsemani, Kentucky. Trappists take vows of perpetual silence, communicate in a simple sign language, and sing Gregorian chants in their seven daily chapel visits, while also working their subsistence farms. Merton embraced the lifestyle and was ordained in 1947.[50]

Although he was ambivalent about his writing while a Trappist monk, fearing it would prevent him from fully integrating into the monastic community, Merton's abbot encouraged him to translate religious texts and to write biographies of the saints. He soon began to write poetry, which was collected into his first published book, *Thirty Poems* (1946), and two years later, he published his spiritual autobiography, *The Seven Storey Mountain.* Merton challenged the frenzy of American life and instead extoled contemplation. He criticized the growing secularism of American intellectuals and recommended the solace of the interior and spiritual life. Merton's best seller led to a rush of young men to join the Trappists, but perhaps more importantly, as historian Mark Massa found: "Merton legitimized the possibility of a sophisticated, accessible Catholic spirituality for a middle-class suburban constituency without really 'converting' them to the radical implications of Cistercian or Benedictine Spirituality."[51]

Religion, politics, and the Cold War

As previously noted, communism was not referred to simply as communism but as "atheistic Communism," and the majority of Americans – not just religious leaders – saw atheistic communism as a mortal threat to Christian America. According to a 1947 Gallup Poll, 72 percent of Americans believed that communists would destroy the Christian religion if they could. Another poll, taken two years later, had 77 percent denying that someone could be both a good Christian and a member of the Communist Party. Such a threat could only be successfully defeated by Christian America, and Christian America was to be led by the neo-evangelicals and their conservative allies. Liberal Christian leaders, on the other hand, found themselves under suspicion, even branded in some quarters, as communist sympathizers, if not outright Communists, fellow travelers in a conspiracy, perhaps unwillingly in some cases, to destroy America by weakening its religious or moral fabric, and therefore resistance. Very few liberal Protestant religious leaders were, or even had been, communists. But during the 1930s, some had enlisted in organizations dedicated to peace, international understanding, and social justice, where fellow members may have been communists or socialists, and although most had distanced themselves from such groups after the war, that personal history was enough to land them on a list of presumed subversives. In March 1953, the Chairman of the House Un-American Activities Committee let it be known that he intended to investigate several church groups and clergy on their various associations but had to back off when his comment ignited a firestorm of protest.[52]

Joseph McCarthy provided the most serious call to arms in his West Virginia speech of 1950, in which he announced that there were no fewer than 205 communists in the State Department. Soon he and others sought communists in every walk of life, but especially politics, higher education, and the film industry. In July 1953, John Brown Matthews, chief investigator for the House of Representatives probing "un-American activities," published an article in *The American Mercury*, "Reds and Our Churches," in which he reported that "the largest single group supporting the Communist apparatus in the United States today is composed of Protestant clergyman." He charged that the Communist Party had enlisted the support of at least 7,000 Protestant clergy as "party members, fellow-travelers, espionage agents, party-line adherents, and unwilling dupes," all of whom were serving a cause which aimed at "the total obliteration of Judeo-Christian civilization." He found the reason for this mass defection, or outright treason, in the Social Gospel. "Could it be," Matthews asked, "that these pro-Communist clergymen have allowed their zeal for social justice to run away with the better judgment and patriotism?"[53]

Among the prominent Protestant ministers to be named was the Methodist Bishop G. Bromley Oxnam. As president of the liberal-leaning Federal Council of Churches and then the World Council of Churches, he became a promising target for those seeking to undercut the socially active wing of American Protestantism. Although several Catholic and Jewish leaders, as well as Protestant clergy, denounced Matthews' charges, the House Un-American Activities Committee repeatedly accused Oxnam as either being a Communist or being used by the party to further their cause. When Oxnam demanded the opportunity, and was allowed, to defend himself before the committee, he testified that his Christian faith was unwavering and that he rejected both atheism and communism. He insisted that the American churches had "done more . . . to destroy the Communist threat to faith and to freedom than all investigating committees put together and chastised them for their use of "unverified and unevaluated material" to destroy people's lives by accusing them of being communists."[54]

But there were more moderate voices of anticommunism, perhaps most prominent being the two immediate postwar presidents, Harry Truman and Dwight Eisenhower. Neither Truman, a Baptist, nor Eisenhower, a Presbyterian, were particularly ardent in their respective faiths, but both made religion a key part of their Cold War policies, at a non-denominational/civil religion level. From the very start, as noted earlier, Truman made it clear that he understood the awful responsibility that had descended on him and the nation when he utilized the atomic bomb and at least at the moment was the sole possessor of the bomb. To counter those who would question his decision as well as America's ability to cope with the responsibility that followed, Truman recalled a long-standing belief in American exceptionalism, in this case based on the nation's Judeo-Christian tradition.

In his State of the Union address in January 1948, Truman defended the sacrifices the nation had made in World War II and projected a continued defense of those ideals into the Cold War. Truman described the United States as a great nation with great economic and military power, but he identified the source of that strength as spiritual. "We are a people of faith," he explained, and that provided the imperative for Americans to act in a world beset by "great questions, great anxieties, and great aspirations." The cost to America to fulfill its great challenges and aspirations would be considerable and require great sacrifice, but Americans would accept such sacrifices as long as they understood that

> it is our faith in human dignity that underlies these purposes. It is this faith that keeps us a strong and vital people. . . . Today the whole world looks to us for leadership. This is the hour to rededicate ourselves to the faith in mankind that makes us strong. This is the hour to rededicate ourselves to the faith in God that gives us confidence as we face the challenge of the years ahead.[55]

President Eisenhower never clearly defined his religious beliefs. Nevertheless, he continued Truman's furthering of America's civil religion. Like Truman he emphasized the need for a moral rationale that would unite the nation in its struggle against communism. Eisenhower's first significant talk on the nation's civil religion occurred in a speech before the Freedom Foundation on December 22, 1952, only one month after his election to office. He recalled an encounter with Soviet General Georgy Zhukov during World War II that clarified for him why the Soviets and Americans could not understand one another. Eisenhower believed that because Zhukov belonged to a political system that rejected religion – or that was comprised of what Eisenhower termed "the Bolshevik religion" – he would never be able to understand America, whose "form of government is founded in religion." "Our form of government has no sense unless it is founded in a deeply felt religious faith, and I don't care what it is. With us of course it is the Judeo-Christian concept but it must be a religion that all men are created equal." Given that religious faith, the nation was obligated to use its overwhelming power to carry out God's will, as best as they could understand it. That was America's mission.[56]

Eisenhower elaborated on this message in his first inaugural address, in which he began by asking Americans to pray. Indeed, he remains the only President to begin an inaugural address with a prayer – of his own composition, it is believed – in which he made frequent reference to "the Supreme Being" and used the word "faith" thirteen times in the course of his remarks. In one instance, he explained that "this faith is the abiding creed of our fathers. It is our faith in the deathless dignity of man, governed by eternal moral and natural laws. This faith defines our full view of life. It establishes, beyond debate, those gifts of the

Creator that are man's inalienable rights, and that make all men equal in His sight." He then reminded Americans of the sacrifice that faith required of them: "We must be ready to dare all for our country. For history does not long entrust the care of freedom to the weak or the timid. We must acquire proficiency in defense and display stamina in purpose. We must be willing, individually and as a nation, to accept whatever sacrifices may be required of us. A people that values its privileges above its principles soon loses both."[57]

On February 7, 1954, in a radio address made as part of the American Legion's "Back to God" program, Eisenhower encapsulated this idea of faith in God and the need for sacrifice in perhaps his best-known comment on the subject: In battle "there are no atheists in fox-holes . . . in a time of test and trial, we instinctively turn to God for new courage and peace of mind." But what might be seen as his culminating action occurred on Flag Day, June 14, 1954, when he signed a bill which inserted "under God" in the Pledge of Allegiance. By that signing, he explained, "We are affirming the transcendence of religious faith in America's heritage and future; in this way we shall constantly strengthen those spiritual weapons which forever will be our country's most powerful resource, in peace or in war." It was espe-cially important at that time, Eisenhower continued, given a world in which millions had been "deadened in mind and soul by a materialistic philosophy of life" and where all were "appalled by the prospect of atomic war." In particular, he pointed out that with this change in the pledge, the nation's school children would daily proclaim, "the dedication of our Nation and our people to the Almighty."[58]

The signing was quickly followed by acts of Congress in 1955 that required the phrase "In God We Trust" be placed on all US currency and in 1956 that made "In God we Trust" the nation's official motto. But the US Supreme Court set the stage in 1952 when Justice William O. Douglas wrote in the majority opinion in *Zorach v. Clauson*: "We are a religious people whose institutions presuppose a Supreme Being," although he later commented on the Edward R. Murrow radio show, *This I Believe*, that he saw America "drifting from the Christian faith . . . acting abroad as an arrogant, selfish, greedy nation interested only in guns and in dollars . . . not in people and their hopes and aspirations. We need a faith that dedicates us to something bigger and more important than ourselves or our possessions" – a civil religion.[59]

As Douglas's comment suggests, not everyone was yet convinced that all Americans had yet bought into the faith Truman and Eisenhower espoused. By the mid-twentieth century, Protestant domination of American society was being challenged by a dramatic increase in the number and power of Roman Catholics and Jews. Forced to share leadership, identify-ing a tradition in which all three could share – namely a Judeo-Christian tradition – not only served to unify these three groups for the first time in American history, but also provided a unified front to combat communism. It also could serve to exclude a growing number of newcomers, including Buddhists, Muslims, Hindus, and others. As Will Herbert wrote in his seminal *Protestant, Catholic Jew:* "American religion and American society would seem to be so closely interrelated as to make it virtually impossible to understand each without refer-ence to the other." The "American way of life," he explained included Protestants, Catholics, and Jews – "the religions of democracy."[60]

Some found the idea of a Judeo-Christian tradition flawed and even dangerous, in that it suggested a moral consensus between Christians and Jews that had never existed. Robert Gordis, for example, a Jew writing in 1956, described it as presenting "a cloudy, blurred image of an imaginary 'Judeo-Christian world view.'" In *We Hold These Truths*, the Catholic John Courtney argued that Protestantism, Catholicism, and Judaism were "radically different styles of religious beliefs, none of which "is reducible, or perhaps even comparable, to any of the others."[61] Civil religion's most prominent critic, however, was the distinguished Jewish intellectual, Will Herberg. Herberg described America's civil religion, which he referred to as "the American way of life," as having been built on a supposed Judeo-Christian tradition that emphasized the commonalities between both religious traditions, thereby providing unity for a nation of multiple faiths and ethnicities threatened by atheistic communism. He explained that it was based on "a spiritual structure, a structure of ideas and ideals, of aspirations and values, of beliefs and standards; it synthesizes all that commends itself to the American as the right, the good, and the true in actual life." This was the official religion of the nation, but "insofar as any reference is made to the God in whom all Americans 'believe' and of whom the 'official' religions speak, it is primarily a sanction and underpinning for the supreme values of the faith embedded in the American way of life. Secularization of religion could hardly go further." Herberg described civil religion as a religion that "validates culture and society, without in any sense bringing them under judgment. . . . Religion becomes, in effect, the cult of culture and society, in which the 'right' social order and the received cultural values are divinized by being identified with the divine purpose." This identification of religion with national purpose, he argued, generates a kind of national messianism that sees as the vocation of America to bring the American way of life, compounded almost equally of democracy and free enterprise, to every corner of the globe. "It sees God as the champion of America, endorsing American might." As a result, he concluded: "The God of judgment has died."[62]

The high point for religion in America

Postwar America proved to be the exception to the rule of secularization in the Western industrialized nations. As rates of church attendance and belief in God declined steadily throughout twentieth-century Europe, in America, they climbed higher. Despite, or perhaps because of, the challenges organized religion faced in the immediate post-World War II period, by most traditional measures, religion in America reached an all-time high in the 1950s. In part as the result of the need to reaffirm their allegiance to Christian America and opposition to the godless communist Soviet Union, Americans made public their commitment to God in an unprecedented manner.[63]

Billy Graham explained the great upsurge in religion in the 1950s: "The human mind cannot cope with the problems that we are wrestling with today. And when our intellectual leaders begin to admit that they don't know the answer, and that fact reaches the masses in the street, then they are going to run somewhere. They will turn to all sorts of escapisms. Some will turn to alcohol. Others will turn to religion in the want of security and peace – something to hold onto." And turn to religion they did. Church membership as a percentage of total population grew 8 percent between 1940 and 1950, more than in the three previous decades combined. In the next decade, it grew an additional fourteen points, from 55 to 69 percent of the national population – the highest ever recorded – leading some to believe the United States was experiencing its Fourth Great Awakening. Reported attendance at weekly services and contributions to churches and synagogues increased in a similar manner, as did church and synagogue construction, following a mass migration from the nation's cities to the suburbs. Money spent on church construction rose from $26 million in 1945 to $409 million in 1950 and to $1 billion in 1960. According to the 1957 US Bureau of the Census poll, 96 percent of Americans identified themselves with some religious tradition, whether or not they actually held any formal membership. Although new religions began to be identified, of a population of 120 million, an estimated 70 million Americans considered themselves Protestants, 30 million Roman Catholics, and 4 million Jewish. Only 4 percent indicated no religious identification.[64]

At the same time that religion appeared to flourish in America and influence nearly every aspect of American society and culture, the Supreme Court arose to challenge the influence of organized religion in America. The same flourishing of organized religion in America led inevitably to not only quarrels between denominations that believed their particular religious beliefs were being unfairly interfered with by others, but also by non-believers who argued that they too had rights guaranteed under the Constitution not to worship. It would be left to the Supreme Court to become the arbiter in such matters. But first, the court had to establish that it had the authority under the First Amendment to intervene in matters of religion, over-riding in many cases the authority of the states.

The Supreme Court takes up matter of religious freedom

Despite passage of the First Amendment to the United States Constitution at the very found-ing of the nation, for the next century-and-a-half, matters of religion, including free exercise of religion and separation of church and state, remained largely a state matter. As the word-ing of the amendment appeared to make clear, "Congress shall make no law respecting an establishment of religion, or prohibiting the free exercise thereof." No mention was made of the states, and except where their constitutions included similar provisions, the states were left alone to act as they wished in the matter. The few cases that arose that did involve the national government regarded religion in the territories – the case of Mormon polygamy, for example. That began to change in the 1940s with a handful of seminal Supreme Court cases that would lead to an avalanche of cases in the decades to follow.

The first case was decided in 1943. But in order to show how quickly and completely the court's position changed, we need to look at *Minersville School District v. Gobitis*, which preceded it by three years. In the Minersville case of 1940, the US Supreme Court took the first step in applying the First Amendment to the states, that is, that the states as well as the federal government were obligated to respect the individual's free exercise of religion and the separation of church and state. The case involved two public school Jehovah's Witnesses children, ages 10 and 12, who refused to salute the flag and recite the Pledge of Allegiance as part of a teacher-led activity. They did so on the grounds that such a practice violated their religious beliefs in idolatry, namely that it violated the commandment in Exodus: 20:3–5: "You shall not make yourself a graven image. . . . You shall not bow down to them or serve them." In that case, the Supreme Court ruled in favor of the school district, that the require-ment was constitutional. In the majority opinion, Justice Felix Frankfurter acknowledged that the Gobitis children were acting on the basis of their religious beliefs. But he also pos-ited that the US flag was critically important as a symbol of national unity, without which "there can ultimately be no liberties, civil or religious."[65]

Three years later, in *West Virginia State Board of Education v. Barnette*, the Court effec-tively reversed itself. Continuing to recognize the importance of fostering national unity "by persuasion and example," Justice Robert Jackson, writing for the majority (Frankfurter authored a dissenting minority opinion), raised the question of "whether under our Constitu-tion compulsion as here employed is a permissible means for its achievement." In his answer to this question he explained: "If there is any fixed star in our constitutional constellation, it is that no official, high or petty, can prescribe what shall be orthodox in politics, national-ism, religion, or other matters of opinion, or force citizens to confess by word or act their faith therein." He could find no exception to that rule in this case. In the decades to come, other religious minorities would successfully seek the Court's protection along similar lines including, by way of example, Orthodox Jews and Seventh-Day Adventists, who sought not to be precluded by law from doing business on the Christian Sabbath, Sunday, when their Sabbath was on Saturday. In 1963, in *Sherbert v. Verner*, the Court sided with a Seventh-Day Adventist who claimed that she had unfairly been denied unemployment benefits because she would not work on Saturday. As Justice William Brennan explained in the court's major-ity opinion, to hold otherwise would force the claimant "to choose between following the precepts of her religion and forfeiting benefits on the one hand, and abandoning one of the precepts of her religion in order to accept work on the other hand." Neither was an accept-able alternative.[66]

The other critical case, *Everson v. Board of Education of Ewing Township*, decided in 1947, applied the Establishment Clause of the First Amendment to the states and initiated a series of cases related to religion in the schools. *Everson* is important because it explicitly applied, for the first time, the Establishment Clause of the First Amendment to the states using the Incorporation Clause of the Fourteenth Amendment. That clause reads: "no state shall . . . deprive any person of life, liberty or property without due process of law" In *Ever-son*, the Supreme Court held that the establishment clause is one of those liberties protected by the due-process clause. The case arose from a New Jersey law that authorized public school districts to use public transportation to travel to and from school for which they would be reimbursed. In one township, children were reimbursed for using public buses to parochial school, raising the question of whether what some argued was the state's support of parochial schools constituted a violation of the separation of church and state. In his rul-ing for the majority, Justice Hugo Black used words that would echo throughout the years, whenever church and state cases reached the court: "The First Amendment has erected a wall between church and state. That wall must be kept high and impregnable. We could not approve the slightest breach." He went on to rule that the state of New Jersey had not breached the wall, but his statement as to the court's overall position in such cases ruled the day. It did not matter that the Fourteenth Amendment was adopted three years after the end of the Civil War, in 1868, specifically to provide African Americans, most of whom were recently freed from bondage, with citizenship. Neither did it matter that the phrase referring to the wall separating church and state cannot be found in the US Constitution or any of its amendments. Rather it came from a letter Thomas Jefferson wrote to the Danbury Baptist Association in 1802. As we will see in the next chapter and beyond, this case unleashed a torrent of cases for decades to come, not only on financial aid to parochial and other private schools, but also, and perhaps more heatedly, prayer and Bible reading in the schools.[67]

Religion and the civil rights movement

A final significant event involving American religion that began in the 1950s but would spill over into the 1960s was the civil rights movement. African Americans who had fought in World War II expected their lives in postwar America to be different for their sacrifices. Many white Americans agreed, including leaders like President Harry Truman, who advocated for federal laws that would bring greater equality to African Americans. In 1946, Truman signed an executive order establishing the President's Committee on Civil Rights, which issued a report, *To Secure These Rights*, that called for antilynching and antisegregation legislation as well as for laws guaranteeing voting rights and equal employment opportunities. In 1948, President Truman issued two executive orders declaring an end to racial discrimination in the federal government including the armed services. Truman's successor, Dwight Eisenhower, was less willing to take action, preferring a more gradual, voluntary approach. But even he saw the need to act when necessary as when he ordered the Arkansas National Guard to implement the court ordered desegregation of Little Rock's Central High School.[68]

Resistance was fierce, including a resurgence of the Ku Klux Klan. But African Americans took action to advance their cause, building on accomplishments from previous decades under the leadership of figures such as A. Philip Randolph, A. J. Muste, Bayard Rustin, and others. The National Association for the Advancement of Colored People was particularly effective in setting the stage for the 1950s civil rights movement. Founded in 1909, in the 1930s leadership of the NAACP fell to Charles Hamilton Houston and Thurgood Marshall. Houston and Marshall engaged in a series of legal actions that chipped away at the statutes that served as the basis for racial segregation and that had been in place since the Jim Crow Era at the close of the nineteenth century and sustained by the US Supreme Court decision, *Plessy v. Ferguson* (1896). These included college admissions, interstate bus transportation, and racially restrictive housing covenants. The landmark case, however, came in 1954 in the US Supreme Court case, *Brown v. Board of Education*, which led to the desegregation of the nation's public schools by denying the very premise of *Plessy*: "In the field of public education the doctrine of 'separate but equal' [taken from the 1896 case] has no place. Separate educational facilities are inherently unequal." Thirteen years later, Marshall would become the first African American US Supreme Court Justice.[69]

The majority of African Americans in the 1940s and 1950s belonged to evangelical Protestant churches; nearly two-thirds were Baptist and nearly one-third Methodist. Black churches served as "a refuge in a hostile white world." They offered fellowship and consolation but at the same time "aided the Negro to become accommodated to an inferior status." That changed in the late 1940s as black churches became the leading force among African Americans to advance their quest for equality. Black churches joined forces with sympathetic whites in organizations such as the National Council of Churches, but young African American clergy – including Martin Luther King, Jr.; Ralph David Abernathy; Andrew Young; Jesse Jackson; and others – started a more grass roots movement among themselves.[70]

The earliest leader of this grass roots civil rights movement was Martin Luther King, Jr. King was a black Baptist minister, but the movement he led came to involve people from a wide range of denominations, white and black, as well as many who had no strong religious convictions at all. King was born in Atlanta, Georgia, in 1929, the son and maternal grandson of ministers of that city's Ebenezer Baptist Church. A precocious young man, he entered Atlanta's Morehouse College at the age of 15. At first put off by the emotionalism of the religious worship he experienced, in his junior year, he renewed his faith and resolved to enter the ministry. Upon his graduation from Morehouse, he pursued his ministerial studies at the more liberal Crozer Theological Seminary in Chester, Pennsylvania. Graduating in 1951 as student body president and valedictorian, King went on to study for his Ph.D. in theology at Boston University. While at BU, King read the theology of Walter Rauschenbusch, Reinhold Niebuhr, and Paul Tillich. About Niebuhr King later commented: "My reading of the works of Reinhold Niebuhr made me aware of the complexity of human motives and the reality of sin on every level of man's existence. . . . I also came to see that the superficial optimism of liberalism concerning human nature overlooked the fact that reason is darkened by sin."[71]

Figure 5.1 Rosa Parks' Mug Shot

Source: World History Archive/Alamy Stock Photo

Already resolved upon his arrival at Boston University that his Christianity would be a force for social change, King studied Christian social teachings or the role of the church in bringing about social change and the non-violent protest and civil disobedience teachings of Mohandas "Mahatma" Gandhi. Armed with both, King hoped to oppose and ultimately defeat the nation's racist laws and practices. In 1954, he took a position as pastor of the Dexter Avenue Baptist Church in Montgomery, Alabama, where he almost immediately got caught up in a black-white confrontation that is seen by many as the start of the modern civil rights struggle. In 1955, Rosa Parks, (See Figure 5.1) a department store seamstress and NAACP activist, refused to give up her seat to a white passenger. Rosa was among four black passengers who were seated in the first row of the "colored" section, but who were told to move further back in the bus when the white section filled. Three complied; Rosa did not. The daughter of strong advocates for racial equality, Rosa had decided that she was tired of giving in to the segregationist policies that surrounded her. She was promptly arrested, which caused the city's African Americans to organize in her support. E. D. Nixon, head of the local chapter of the NAACP, called for a boycott of the city's buses. Originally intended to be one day – the day Rosa was to go to court – organizers decided that they would continue the action until the segregation of the city's buses was ended altogether. They formed the Montgomery Improvement Association and elected as their leader the new arrival in the city, the 26-year-old King. King accepted with the rallying cries that "it was ultimately more honorable to walk the streets in dignity than to ride the buses in humiliation" and providing the bridge between social activism and religion: "If we are wrong, the Constitution is wrong. If we are wrong, God Almighty is wrong. If we are wrong, Jesus of Nazareth was merely a utopian dreamer. . . . If we are wrong, justice is a lie."[72]

Years later, in 1967, at a time when some civil rights leaders questioned the effectiveness of King's non-violent resistance, King explained how he came to embrace non-violent resistance in Montgomery. He traced its origins to his encountering the idea while reading Henry David Thoreau's *On Civil Disobedience* (1849) in 1944 while at Morehouse College. He was taken by the courage Thoreau exercised in refusing to pay his taxes and going to jail rather than support the Mexican-American War, which would spread slavery into what would become the American Southwest. That was followed by his reading about the life and teaching of Mahatma Gandhi in his resistance to British colonial rule in India. "Before reading Gandhi," he wrote,

> I had believed that Jesus' 'turn the other cheek' philosophy and the 'love your enemies' philosophy could only be useful when individuals were in conflict with other individuals – when racial groups and nations were in conflict, a more realistic approach seemed necessary. But after reading Gandhi, I saw how utterly mistaken I was. During the days of the Montgomery bus boycott, I came to see the power of nonviolence more and more. As I lived through the actual experience of this protest, nonviolence became more than a useful method; it became a way of life.[73]

The Montgomery boycott soon took on a much larger meaning than the desegregation of city buses and attracted supporters from across the nation, black and white. It was met with fierce resistance, including attacks on the homes of both King and E. D. Nixon. King persisted in his non-violent resistance, and after more than a year, the protestors won. The city had little choice. The transit company was nearly broke. Downtown business suffered substantial financial losses, and the Supreme Court declared Alabama's bus segregation laws unconstitutional. The civil rights movement caught the nation's attention, and King would become its most visible leader. Historian Patrick Allitt has explained the advantage King had in leading the movement as a minister:

> He was able to appeal to white Americans in Bible language, a language that the majority of them understood, respected, and took seriously. He took Bible passages they knew well but applied them in jarringly immediate and contemporary ways to underscore his

belief that segregation was not simply unjust, nor simply tactless in view of the Cold War propaganda competition then being waged over the loyalties of postcolonial Africans, but sinful.[74]

In 1957, King, Ralph Abernathy, and sixty other ministers and civil rights leaders founded the Southern Christian Leadership Conference (SCLC). Leaders of the SCLC asked Black Americans "to accept Christian love in full knowledge of its power to defy evil. We call upon them to understand that non-violence is not a symbol of weakness or cowardice, but, as Jesus demonstrated, non-violent resistance transforms weakness into strength and breeds courage in the face of danger." Dedicated to coordinating the moral authority and power of the nation's black churches, the SCLC resolved to conduct non-violent protests to promote civil rights reform, beginning with voting rights for African Americans. King was elected the organization's first president, and during February 1958, the SCLC sponsored more than twenty mass meetings throughout the South to register black voters. In 1959, King visited Gandhi's birthplace in India, which served to increase his commitment to his non-violent approach to America's civil rights struggle. In 1960, he resigned from the Dexter Avenue Church and moved to Atlanta where he became co-pastor with his father at Ebenezer Baptist Church and devoted himself to the civil rights movement. As to Rosa Parks, she and her husband faced such strong retaliation that she decided to move to Detroit, Michigan. But she continued her activism and over the course of her remaining lifetime she won major awards such as the NAACP's Spingarn Medal, the Martin Luther King Jr. Award, the Presidential Medal of Freedom, and the Congressional Gold Medal.[75]

By 1960, some – but certainly not all or even a majority of – white clergy grew sympathetic to the African American led civil rights movement. A group of fifty-nine North Carolina preachers, black and white, responded favorably to the sit-in movement of 1960 with a statement that read, in part: "We feel that Christ would refuse no man good if he was hungry, no child education if he wanted to learn, and no person fellowship if he sought worship." Many North Carolina clergy, including some who were sympathetic to the movement, refused to sign the declaration fearing it would divide their congregations. But others refused because they remained convinced that segregation was religiously defensible and the civil rights movement wrong. Humphrey Ezell, a Southern Baptist minister, for example, argued in a 1959 book that segregation according to the "separate but equal" formula was the best way of assuring "the prosperity, the happiness and the divine blessing of both races." Their evidence in support of this position was much the same as that used by proslavery clergy prior to the Civil War, namely that God created racial segregation when he separated Shem, Japeth, and Ham, the sons of Noah, making Ham black and cursing him and his descendants.[76]

Summary

Much as was the case with World War I, when World War II broke out, the United States was reluctant to enter. During the 1930s, it had been among those nation's that participated in antiwar and disarmament conferences and agreements that it hoped would prevent the outbreak of another world war. The bombing of Pearl Harbor changed all that and the nation went to war with religious leaders propounding a "just war" rationale that both justified US entry into the war, but also insisted that military actions be proportionate and that non-combatant casualties be kept to a minimum. The dropping of the atomic bombs on Hiroshima and Nagasaki in 1945 caused some religious leaders to question that commitment, but such doubts were soon swept away. Americans had long believed that their nation had a unique, God-given role to play in the world to secure good, and the position America held at the end of the war appeared to provide an opportunity to do just that, an opportunity for which the nation was both destined and morally obligated to accept. The only force that stood in the way of the United States was the Soviet Union, and after a series of confrontations, the United States entered into a four-decade-long Cold War with "atheistic communism," which was acted out abroad and at home. On the home front, the Cold War led to the development of a civil religion around which the religiously diverse nation could rally, to an insistence on uniformity of thought and behavior, and to the high point for religion in American history marked by a soaring of church membership and attendance, "God talk," the adoption of largely Christian national symbols, and public prayer at nearly every opportunity. The chapter concluded with references to the start of two other developments that would gain the limelight in the 1960s and 1970s, namely the US Supreme Court's application of the incorporation clause of the Fourteenth Amendment to take under its purview interpretations of the First Amendment's clauses on the free exercise of religion and separation of church and state and the civil rights movement.

Review questions

1 How did the Japanese bombing of Pearl Harbor and the US bombing of Hiroshima and Nagasaki challenge religious leaders and their formulation of just war theory? How did they resolve those challenges?

2 How was the Cold War between the United States and the Soviet Union defined in religious terms? What impact did it have on the practice of religion in America?

3 Billy Graham became the preeminent religious leader in Cold War America. How did that happen? Explain his rise to fame.

4 The Roman Catholic Church was second to none in its opposition to communism and support of the United States in the Cold War. How did Archbishop Sheen, Cardinal Spellman, and John Courtney Murray provide leadership for the church in that regard?

5 The civil rights movement commonly associated with the 1960s had its start in the 1950s under the leadership of Martin Luther King, Jr. Explain how that happened.

Notes

1 Mary Beth Norton, David M. Katzman, David W. Blight, Howard P. Chudacoff, Fredrik Logevall, Beth Bailey, Thomas G. Peterson, and William M. Tuttle, Jr., *A People and a Nation: A History of the United States*, 7th edn. (Boston: Houghton Mifflin Company, 2005), 2: 724.

2 Dorothy Day, "Our Country Passes from Undeclared War to Declared War: We Continue Our Christian Pacifist Stand," *Catholic Worker* (January 1942): 1, 4; Patrick Allitt, *Religion in America since 1945: A History* (New York: Columbia University Press, 2003), 2.

3 Edwin Gaustad and Leigh Schmidt, *The Religious History of America: The Heart of the American Story from Colonial Times to Today*, rev. edn. (New York: HarperSanFrancisco, 2002), 329.

4 Gaustad and Schmidt, *The Religious History of America*, 333.

5 Oppenheimer is quoted in Allitt, *Religion in America since 1945*, 1; Mark Silk, *Spiritual Politics: Religion and America since World War II* (New York: Simon and Schuster, 1988), 27, 33.

6 The FCC statement was published in the *New York Times* on August 10, 1945; passage taken from the excerpt in Silk, *Spiritual Politics*, 23; The Editorial was published in *The Christian Century*, 62: 923; quote taken from Silk, *Spiritual Politics: Religion and America since World War II*, 224.

7 Silk, *Spiritual Politics*, 24–5; "Report of the Calhoun Commission" (1946), excerpt from Richard Fox, *Reinhold Niebuhr: A Biography* (San Francisco: Harper & Row, 1987), 224; Gaustad and Schmidt, *The Religious History of America*, 335.

8 Arthur H. Compton, "The Moral Meaning of the Atomic Bomb," in *Christianity Takes a Stand: An Approach to the Issues of Today*, ed. William Scarlett (New York: Penguin Books, 1946), 58, 63; Raymond Haberski, Jr., *God and War: American Civil Religion since 1945* (New Brunswick, NJ: Rutgers University Press, 2012), 15; see also Paul Boyer, *By the Bomb's Early Light: American Thought and Culture at the Dawn of the Atomic Age* (New York: Pantheon Books, 1985), 6. Roman Catholic leaders were divided on the matter, as well. See Silk, *Spiritual Politics*, 26; Haberski, *God and War*, 14; O'Brien quoted in John Bodnar, *The "Good War" in American Memory* (Baltimore, MD: John Hopkins University Press, 2010), 215.

9 Haberski, *God and War*, 11; Henry R. Luce, "The American Century," *Life* (February 1941): 61; Bodnar, *The "Good War" in American Memory*, 60–4.

10 Haberski, *God and War*, 12; Silk, *Spiritual Politics*, 45–8, 95.

11 Haberski, *God and War*, 13–14; Bodnar, *The "Good War" in American Memory*, 4; Robert N. Bellah, "Civil Religion in America," *Daedalus*, 96 (1967): see www.robertbellah.com/articles_5. htm; see also Robert N. Bellah, *The Broken Covenant: American Civil Religion in Time of Trial*, 2nd edn. (Chicago, IL: University of Chicago Press, 1993); O'Brien is quoted in Bodnar, *The "Good War" in American Memory*, 215.

12 Abraham Johannes Muste, *Not by Might* (New York: Harper, 1947), 18, 86; Haberski, *God and War*, 15.

13 Paul Tillich, *The Courage to Be* (New Haven, CT: Yale University Press, 1952); Allitt, *Religion in America since 1945*, 26; Reinhold Niebuhr, "Why the Christiana Church Is Not Pacifist," in *The Essential Reinhold Niebuhr, Selected Essays and Addresses*, ed. Robert McAfee Brown (New Haven CT: Yale University Press, 1986), 118; Haberski, *God and War*, 16–17.

14 Haberski, *God and War*, 17.

15 Haberski, *God and War*, 17–18.

16 Reinhold Niebuhr, *The Irony of American History* (1952; rpt. New York; Scribner, 1962), 5, 16; Allitt, *Religion in America since 1945*, 26–7.

17 Haberski, *God and War*, 17–19; see also Richard Wightman Fox, "Niebuhr's World and Ours," in *Reinhold Niebuhr Today*, ed. Richard John Neuhaus (Grand Rapids, MI; Eerdmans, 1989), 2; William Inboden, *Religion and American Foreign Policy: The Soul of Containment, 1945–1960* (New York: Cambridge University Press, 2008), 4; Federal Council of Churches, *The Christian Conscience and Weapons of Mass Destruction* (New York: Department of International Justice and Goodwill, 1950), 9, 22. For more on this emerging religious consensus on the relationship between God and nation in the early Cold War, see Robert Wuthnow, *The Restructuring of Religion* (Princeton, NJ: Princeton University Press, 1988), 54–70; Silk, *Spiritual Politics*, 54–86; and Jason W. Stevens, *God-Fearing and Free: A Spiritual History of America's Cold War* (Cambridge, MA: Harvard University Press, 2010), 29–63.

18 Grant Wacker, *America's Pastor: Billy Graham and the Shaping of a Nation* (Cambridge, MA: The Belknap Press, 2014), 5–8; Marshall Frady, *Billy Graham, a Parable of American Righteousness* (Boston: Little, Brown, 1979), 84–5; William McLoughlin, *Billy Graham, Revivalist in a Secular Age* (New York; Ronald House, 1960), 28–31.

19 McLoughlin, *Billy Graham*, 35–7, 40–2; Billy Graham, *Revival in Our Time* (Wheaton, IL: Wheaton College, 1950), 3; Silk, *Spiritual Politics*, 55; Wacker, *America's Pastor*, 5, 8–10; Frady, *Billy Graham*, 160–76; Allitt, *Religion in America since 1945*, 14; Carl F. H. Henry, *The Uneasy Conscience of Modern Fundamentalism* (Grand Rapids, MI: William B. Eerdmans Publishing Company, 1947); excerpt from Mathisen, *Critical Issues in American Religious History*, 639–40.

20 Frady, *Billy Graham*, 191; Russ Busby, *Billy Graham, God's Ambassador: A Lifelong Mission of Giving Hope to the World* (Alexandria, VA: Time-Life Books, 1999), 49; Graham, *Revival in Our Time*, 69–80; McLoughlin, *Billy Graham*, 47–8; Silk, *Spiritual Politics*, 64–7. On the Jeremiad, see Sacvan Bercovitch, *The American Jeremiad* (Madison: University of Wisconsin Press, 1978); Wacker, *America's Pastor*, 12–13; Frady, *Billy Graham*, 191–205.

21 Graham is quoted in William Martin, *With God on Our Side: The Rise of the Religious Right in America* (New York: Broadway Books, 1996), 29; see also Allitt, *Religion in America since 1945*, 14–16; Silk, *Spiritual Politics*, 54–6; Wacker, *America's Pastor*, 23; Frady, *Billy Graham*, 191–205, 241; McLoughlin, *Billy Graham*, 51, 56.

22 Wacker, *America's Pastor*, 14.
23 *Silk, Spiritual Politics*, 58–60.
24 John C. Bennett, "Billy Graham at Union," *Union Seminary Quarterly Review*, 9 (1954): 9–14; see also Silk, *Spiritual Politics*, 61–4.
25 Frady, *Billy Graham*, 225, 231; Wacker, *America's Pastor*, 15.
26 Frady, *Billy Graham*, 238–9; McLoughlin, *Billy Graham*, 83–7, 111–2.
27 Quoted in McLoughlin, *Billy Graham*, 92; and Wacker, *America's Pastor*, 16–17.
28 Frady, *Billy Graham*, 252–3.
29 McLoughlin, *Billy Graham*, 96–7.
30 McLoughlin, *Billy Graham*, 96; Frady, *Billy Graham*, 255–8; Martin, *With God on Our Side*, 31–3; Silk, *Spiritual Politics*, 68; Haberski, *God and War*, 23; Wacker, *America's Pastor*, 17, 306, 308; George M. Marsden, *Understanding Fundamentalism and Evangelicalism* (Grand Rapids, MI: W. B. Eerdmans, 1991), 6; see also Andrew S. Finstuen, *Original Sin and Everyday Protestants: The Theology of Reinhold Niebuhr, Billy Graham, and Paul Tillich in an Age of Anxiety* (Chapel Hill: University of North Carolina Press, 2009), 149, 151.
31 Allitt, *Religion in America since 1945*, 12–13, 24–5; Angela M. Lahr, *Millennial Dreams and Apocalyptic Nightmares: The Cold War Origins of Political Evangelicals* (New York: Oxford University Press, 2007), 35; Fred Schwartz, *Beating the Unbeatable Foe: One Man's Victory over Communism, Leviathan, and the Last Enemy* (Washington, DC: Regnery, 1996), 22, 43.
32 Timothy H. Sherwood, *The Preaching of Archbishop Fulton J. Sheen: The Gospel Meets the Cold War* (New York: Lexington Books, 2010), 55–6; Thomas C. Reeves, *America's Bishop: The Life and Times of Fulton J. Sheen* (San Francisco: Encounter Books, 2001), 30.
33 Silk, *Spiritual Politics*, 87–8; Patrick Allitt, *Catholic Intellectuals and Conservative Politics in America, 1950–1985* (Ithaca, NY: Cornell University Press, 1993), 2; Allitt, *Religion in America since 1945*, 21–3; Charles Morris, *American Catholics: The Saints and Sinners Who Built America's Most Powerful Church* (New York: Random House/Times Books, 1997), 229–30. It should be noted that there were some American Catholic leaders who were not entirely opposed to all aspects of communism, especially its social teachings. The American Communist Party was never large, but in the 1930s – in the midst of the Great Depression – it attracted a vocal and publicly visible group of communist sympathizers. Even as late as 1954, Catholic Worker Dorothy Day expressed admiration for its commitment to economic equality but not its atheism. "It is atheistic Communism which we oppose, but as for economic Communism – it is a system which has worked admirably in religious orders for two thousand years." Allitt, *Religion in America since 1945*, 20.
34 Jacques Maritain, *Reflections on America* (New York: Scribner's, 1958), 83, 85, 195; Allitt, *Religion in America since 1945*, 28–9.
35 Boris Chaliapin, "Microphone Missionary," *Time* (April 14, 1952): 72; Sherwood, *The Preaching of Archbishop Fulton J. Sheen*, 1, 12, 14, 16, 18, 53; "Radio Religion," *Time* (January 21, 1947). www.time.com/time/magazine/article/0,9171,934406,00.html; Mary A. Watson, "And They Said 'Uncle Fultie' Didn't Have a Prayer," *Television Quarterly*, 2 (Spring 1993): 16–21; Daniel Noonan, *The Passion of Fulton Sheen* (New York: Dodd, Mead, 1973), 56; Kathleen L. Riley, *Fulton J. Sheen: An American Catholic Response to the Twentieth Century* (Staten Island, NY: Alba House, 2004), 72; Mark S. Massa, *Catholics and American Culture: Fulton Sheen, Dorothy Day, and the Notre Dame Football Team* (New York: Crossroad, 1999), 90. See also Thomas C. Reeves, *America's Bishop: The Life and Times of Fulton J. Sheen* (San Francisco: Encounter Books, 2001); and Sheen's autobiography: Fulton J. Sheen, *Treasure in Clay: The Autobiography of Fulton J. Sheen* (Garden City, NY: Doubleday, 1980).
36 James Hennesey, *American Catholics: A History of the Roman Catholic Community in the United States* (New York: Oxford University Press, 1981), 280; Erwin D. S. Winsboro and Michael Epple, "Religion, Culture, and the Cold War: Bishop Fulton J, Sheen and America's Anti-Communist Crusade of the 1950s," *Historian* (Summer 2009): 212, 226; Sherwood, *The Preaching of Archbishop Fulton J. Sheen*, 6.
37 Sherwood, *The Preaching of Archbishop Fulton J. Sheen*, 6, 58; Fulton J. Sheen, *Communism and the Conscience of the West* (New York: Bobbs-Merrill, 1948), 55; Barbara Mikkelson and David P. Mikkelson, "Stalin for Time: Did Bishop Fulton Sheen Foretell the Death of Stalin?," Snopes.com (August 8, 2007). www.snopes.com/radiotv/tv/sheen/htm; Allitt, *Catholic Intellectuals and Conservative Politics in America, 1950–1985*, 340.

38 Cooney, *The American Pope*, 18, 19, 22.
39 Cooney, *The American Pope*, 30–49, 54–5.
40 Cooney, *The American Pope*, 67, 118–19.
41 Cooney, *The American Pope*, 103–8, 114, 129–30; "Odyssey for the Millennium," *Time* (June 7, 1943). www/time.com/time/magazine/article/0,9171,884953,00.htm
42 Peter Quinn, "New York's Catholic Century," *New York Times* (June 4, 2006). www.nytimes.com/2006/06/04/nyregion/thecity/04cath.html?fta=y; See also Cooney, *The American Pope*, 169–70, 175.
43 Cooney, *The American Pope*, 154–5; Donald F. Crosby, *God, Church and Flag: Senator Joseph R. McCarthy and the Catholic Church, 1950–1957* (Chapel Hill: University of North Carolina Press, 1978), 18.
44 Edward T. O'Donnell, "Spellman Leads Crusade Against Communism," *Irish Echo Online* (November 4–10, 2009). www.irishecho.com/newspaper/story.cfm?id=14219; Cooney, *The American Pope*, 154–5, 212–13, 220–1, 240, 231, 240; Haberski, *God and War*, 25–6.
45 Haberski, *God and War*, 27–8; John Courtney Murray, "The People of State Religion," *Theological Studies* 12 (June 1951): 160–7, excerpt in Mathisen, *Critical Issues in American Religious History*, 649–50. See also John Courtney Murray, *We Hold These Truths: Catholic Reflections on the American Proposition* (New York: Sheed and Ward, 1960); John Courtney Murray, *Religious Liberty: Catholic Struggles with Pluralism*, ed. John Leon Hooper (Louisville, KY: Westminster/John Knox Press, 1993); John T. McGreevy, *Catholicism and American Freedom: A History* (New York: Norton, 2003), 206; and "City of God and Man," *Time* (December 12, 1960). www.time.com/time/magazine/article/0,9171,871923,00.html
46 Haberski, *God and War*, 28–9; "City of God and Man," *Time* (December 12, 1960). www.time.com/time/magazine/article/0,9171,871923,00.html; Robert McElroy, "We Hold These Truths," *America* (February 7, 2005). www.americamagazine.org/content/article.cfm?article_id=3995
47 Allitt, *Religion in America since 1945*, 16, 18; Gaustad and Schmidt, *The Religious History of America*, 336–7; Norman Vincent Peale, *A Guide to Confident Living* (New York: Prentice Hall, 1948), 6, 58; Silk, *Spiritual Politics*, 34.
48 Joshua Loth Liebman, *Peace of Mind* (New York: Simon and Shuster, 1946), 12, 15, 202–3; Silk, *Spiritual Politics*, 334; Allitt, *Religion in America since 1945*, 16–17.
49 The title – *The Seven Storey Mountain* – refers to the seven levels of Dante's *Purgatory*. Mary R. Reichardt, *Encyclopedia of Catholic Literature* (Westport, CT: Greenwood Press, 2004), 2: 450; Thomas Merton, *The Seven Storey Mountain* (New York: Harcourt, Brace, 1948), 63–4, 108.
50 Merton, *The Seven Storey Mountain*, 163–4; William Henry Shannon, *Thomas Merton's Paradise Journey* (New York: Bloomsbury Academic, 2000), 268.
51 Massa, *Catholics and American Culture*, 56; Monica Furlong, *Merton: Biography* (San Francisco: Harper and Row, 1980), 263. See also William Henry Shannon, *Silent Lamp: The Thomas Merton Story* (New York: Crossroad, 1992); Jim Forest, *Living with Wisdom: A Life of Thomas Merton*, rev. edn. (Maryknoll, NY: Orbis Books, 1991); Thomas P. McDonnell, *A Thomas Merton Reader* (New York: Image Books, 1996); Christine M. Bochen, *Cold War Letters of Thomas Merton* (Maryknoll, NY: Orbis Books, 2006); William H. Shannon, *Passion for Peace: The Social Essays of Thomas Merton* (New York Crossroad, 1995).
52 Silk, *Spiritual Politics*, 88; Gaustad and Schmidt, *The Religious History of America*, 339.
53 John Brown Matthews, "Reds and Our Churches," *American Mercury* (July 1953): 13; Gaustad and Schmidt, *The Religious History of America*, 339.
54 Gaustad and Schmidt, *The Religious History of America*, 339; Silk, *Spiritual Politics*, 90.
55 Harry S. Truman, "Annual Message to the Congress of the State of the Union," American Presidency Project (January 20, 1949). www.presidency.ucsb.edu/ws/index.php?pid=13005#axzz1SfihUrw7. See also Harry S. Truman, "Inaugural Address" American Presidency Project (January 20, 1949). www.presidency.ucsb.edu/ws/?pid=13282; Haberski, *God and War*, 32; and Elizabeth Edward Spalding, *The First Cold Warrior: Harry Truman, Containment, and the Remaking of Liberal Internationalism* (Lexington: University Press of Kentucky, 2006), 205.
56 Miller is quoted in Paul Carter, *Another Part of the Fifties* (New York: Columbia University Press, 1987), 124; Eisenhower is quoted in Patrick Henry, "'And I Don't Care What It Is': The Tradition History of a Civil Religion Proof Text," *Journal of the American Academy of Religion*, 64 (March 1981): 41; Haberski, *God and War*, 36; Allitt, *Religion in America since 1945*, 31; Silk, *Spiritual Politics*, 40, 44.

57 Dwight D. Eisenhower, "Inaugural Address" American Presidency Project (January 20, 1953). www.presidency.ucsb.edu/ws/?pid=9600; see also Inboden, *Religion and American Foreign Policy*, 250; Allitt, *Religion in America since 1955*, 31.

58 Dwight D. Eisenhower, "Remarks Broadcast as Part of the American Legion 'Back to God' Program" American Presidency Project (February 7, 1954). www.presidency.ucsb.edu/ws/?pid=10119; Dwight D. Eisenhower, "Statement upon Signing Bill to Include the Words 'Under God' in the Pledge to the Flag," American Presidency Project. www.presidency.ucsb.edu/ws/?pid=9920; Among the earliest uses of the phrase "under God," was that of Abraham Lincoln in his Gettysburg Address – "That this nation under God shall have a new birth of freedom." For a brief history of the phrase, see Haberksi, *God and War*, 38–9; and Silk, *Spiritual Politics*, 96–7.

59 Haberksi, *God and War*, 39; James Hudnut-Beumler, *Look for God in the Suburbs: The Religion of the American Dream and Its Critics, 1945–1965* (New Brunswick, NJ: Rutgers University Press, 1994), 50, 52, 54; Allitt, *Religion in America since 1945*, 31; Silk, *Spiritual Politics*, 97.

60 Jon Butler, Grant Wacker, and Randall Balmer, *Religion in American Life: A Short History*, 2nd edn. (New York: Oxford University Press, 2011), 345–6.

61 Silk, *Spiritual Politics*, 50–2; Murray, *We Hold These Truths*, 124.

62 Will Herberg, "Judaism and Christianity: The Unity and Difference," in *Faith Enacted as History: Essays in Biblical Theology*, ed. Will Herberg (Philadelphia: Westminster Press, 1967), 51; Will Herberg, *Protestant, Catholic, Jew: An Essay in American Religious Sociology* (1955; ret. Chicago, IL: University of Chicago Press, 1983), 3, 75–7, 82–4, 89, 263–4. See also William Lee Miller, *Piety along the Potomac: Notes on Politics and Morals in the Fifties* (New York: Houghton Mifflin, 1963) and Martin E. Marty, *The New Shape of American Religion* (New York: Harper, 1959); Allitt, *Religion in America since 1945*, 31; John Paul Williams, *What Americans Believe and How They Worship* (New York: Harper and Row, 1952), 364–74.

63 Allitt, *Religion in America since 1945*, xi; Gaustad and Schmidt, *The Religious History of America*, 341.

64 Graham was quoted in *U.S. News and World Report* (August 27, 1954): 87; and in McLoughlin, *Billy Graham*, 94; Silk, *Spiritual Politics*, 38–9; Gaustad and Schmidt, *The Religious History of America*, 341; For a more detailed description of the American religious landscape in 1945, see Allitt, *Religion in America since 1945*, 5–12, 33; McLoughlin, *Billy Graham*, 22.

65 Gaustad and Schmidt, *The Religious History of America*, 351–2.

66 Gaustad and Schmidt, *The Religious History of America*, 352–4; Robert S. Alley, *The Constitution and Religion: Leading Supreme Court Cases on Church and State* (Amherst, NY: Prometheus Books, 1999), 428–36.

67 Gaustad and Schmidt, *The Religious History of America*, 363; Leonard W. Levy, *The Establishment Clause: Religion and the First Amendment* (New York: Macmillan, 1986), 123–4; Robert S. Alley, *The Supreme Court on Church and State* (New York: Oxford University Press, 1988), 38, 48; John E. Semonche, *Religion and Constitutional Government in the United States: A Historical Overview with Sources* (Carrboro, NC: Signal Books, 1985), 48.

68 Norton, *A People and A Nation*, 808–10.

69 Norton, *A People and A Nation*, 809–10.

70 Edward Franklin Frazier, "The Negro Church in America," in Edward Franklin Frazier, *The Negro Church in America* and Charles Eric Lincoln, *The Black Church since Frazier* (combined in one volume) (1963; rpt. New York: Schocken, 1974), 50–1.

71 Martin Luther King, Jr., "Pilgrimage in Nonviolence," in *Strength in Love* (1963; rpt. Philadelphia, PA: Fortress Press, 1981), 148. King wrote his dissertation on Paul Tillich and personalist theology. Allitt, *Religion in America since 1945*, 49.

72 Gaustad and Schmidt, *The Religious History of America*, 374–5; Allitt, *Religion in America since 1945*, 48; David Garrow, *Bearing the Cross: Martin Luther King, Jr. and the Southern Christian Leadership Conference* (1986; rpt. New York: Vintage, 1988), 24.

73 Taken from William Loren Katz, *Eyewitness* (New York: Ethrac Publications, 2000), 468–70; excerpted in Mathisen, *Critical Issues in American Religious History*, 703–4.

74 David Garrow, "Martin Luther King, Jr. and the Spirit of Leadership," *Journal of American History*, 74 (September 1987): 442; Gaustad and Schmidt, *The Religious History of America*, 374–5, 811; Allitt, *Religion in America since 1945*, 48–9. See also Martin Luther King, Jr., *Stride Toward Freedom: The Montgomery Story* (New York: Harper and Row, 1958).

75 Charles Eric Lincoln, "The Black Church Since Frazier," in Edward Franklin Frazier, *The Negro Church in America* and Charles Eric Lincoln, *The Black Church Since Frazier* (combined in one volume) (1963; rpt. New York: Schocken, 1974), 117. For more on King and the Southern Christian Leadership Conference, see Adam Fairclough, *To Redeem the Soul of America: The Southern Christian Leadership Conference and Martin Luther King, Jr.* (Athens: The University of Georgia Press, 1987). For more on Rose Parks, see her autobiography, *Rosa Parks: My Story* (New York: Dial Books, 1991) and Rosa Parks, *Quiet Strength* (Nashville, TN: Zondervan, 1995), which focuses on the role of religious faith in her life and activities. See also Ralph Abernathy, *And the Walls Came Tumbling Down* (New York: Harper and Row, 1989), 114; Allitt, *Religion in America since 1945*, 51.
76 North Carolina preachers are quoted in Allitt, *Religion in America since 1945*, 52, see also 53; Humphrey K. Ezell, *The Christian Problem of Racial Segregation* (New York: Greenwich Books, 1959), 23.

Recommended for further reading

Allitt, Patrick. *Catholic Intellectuals and Conservative Politics in America, 1950–1985.* Ithaca, NY: Cornell University Press, 1993.

Bellah, Robert N. *The Broken Covenant: American Civil Religion in Time of Trial*, 2nd edn. Chicago, IL: University of Chicago Press, 1993.

Branch, Taylor. *Parting the Waters: America in the King Years, 1954–63.* New York: Simon & Schuster, 1988.

Crosby, Donald F. *God, Church and Flag: Senator Joseph R. McCarthy and the Catholic Church, 1950–1957.* Chapel Hill: University of North Carolina Press, 1978.

Haberski, Jr. Raymond. *God and War: American Civil Religion Since 1945.* New Brunswick, NJ: Rutgers University Press, 2012.

Herberg, Will. *Protestant, Catholic Jew: An Essay in American Religious Sociology.* 1955; repr., Chicago, IL: University of Chicago Press, 1983.

Inboden, William. *Religion and American Foreign Policy: The Soul of Containment, 1945–1960.* New York: Cambridge University Press, 2008.

Merton, Thomas. *The Seven Storey Mountain.* New York: Harcourt, Brace, 1948.

Silk, Mark. *Spiritual Politics: Religion and America Since World War II.* New York: Simon and Schuster, 1988.

Wacker, Grant. *America's Pastor: Billy Graham and the Shaping of a Nation.* Cambridge, MA: The Belknap Press, 2014.

Chapter 6

Religion in an age of turmoil – the 1960s and 1970s

The presidential election of 1960

In some ways, the election of 1960 was a reprise of the Alfred E. Smith contest of 1928, the only other instance where a Roman Catholic ran for president on a major party ticket. Smith tried to focus his campaign on issues other than religious, but he was unable to overcome questions about his Catholicism. Smith's Republican opponent, Herbert Hoover, won in a landslide with 444 electoral votes to Smith's 87. By 1960, however, American Catholics constituted one-fourth of the population, and they were breaking loose from their centuries-old position of being subordinate to the Protestant majority and taking a more positive, dynamic, confident, and aggressive stance. The time was right for social, cultural, and historical reasons for the youthful, charismatic personality of John F. Kennedy. As noted in Chapter 5, a major contributing factor to this upward political mobility was the leading role American Catholics, including the Kennedys, played in the anti-Communist crusade of the 1940s and 1950s.[1]

Thus, although it is not surprising that Kennedy faced the "religious issue," especially as to the influence the Pope might have on decisions he would be called upon to make if he were to be elected, Kennedy was better positioned to respond. When questioned as to his Catholicism, Kennedy pointed out that the US Constitution prohibited the imposition of any religious test upon someone seeking federal office and that the government of the United States was not based on one-man rule, but rather provided a secure system of checks and balances between the three branches as well as the voters. Before the press and in September 1960 before the Ministerial Association in Houston, Texas, Kennedy insisted that should he become President he would uphold and defend the Constitution, including the First Amendment guarantees regarding freedom of religion and the separation of church and state: "Members of my faith abound in public office at every level . . . except the White House," he pointed out, and their performance in those offices had never been questioned on religious grounds. Nevertheless, recognizing that some level of bigotry likely remained, he concluded: "If that bigotry is too great to permit the fair consideration of a Catholic who has made clear his complete independence and his complete dedication to separation of church and state, we ought to know it."[2]

Kennedy faced his most formidable opposition from conservative evangelical Protestants. Some were open and aggressive in their opposition, while others, Billy Graham most notably, tended to work behind the scenes. On August 10, 1960, he sent a letter to Kennedy telling him that he would vote for Nixon "for several reasons, including a longstanding personal friendship," but that if Kennedy won Graham would work to unify the American people behind him and give Kennedy his "wholehearted loyalty and support." He also promised that he would not raise the "religious issue" during the campaign. Nevertheless, eight days later, Graham convened a gathering of evangelical ministers in Montreaux, Switzerland, ostensibly to focus on strategies for evangelization, but at which Norman Vincent Peale addressed those gathered on the threat posed by the Catholic Kennedy's candidacy.[3] Upon their return on September 7, Peale presided over a gathering of more than 150 mostly conservative Protestant ministers, several of whom had attended the Montreaux meeting, at the Mayflower Hotel in Washington, DC, to make clear what they saw as the problems that a Catholic presidency would pose for American democracy in general and for the constitutionally guaranteed separation of church and state in particular.[4]

Liberal Protestants and Jews were similarly skeptical, if less vocal, in raising questions as to the compatibility of what they saw as the Church's authoritarian system of control and American democracy. Protestant theologian John C. Bennett offered the following observation on electing a Catholic president in 1960: "The issue raised by the possibility of a Roman Catholic candidate for the Presidency is the most significant immediate problem that grows out of the confrontation of Roman Catholicism with other religious communities in the United States." Bennett allowed that there were two considerations behind this position that had substance. The first is that the traditional teaching of the Catholic Church was at variance with American conceptions of religious liberty and of church-state relations. Further, there was a fear that a Catholic President might be used by a politically powerful Catholic Church to give that church the preferred position to which, according to tradition, it believed itself entitled. That having been said, however, Bennett acknowledged that in 1960 there were few issues on which there is a specifically Catholic position and that on most major issues American Catholics were in accord with most non-Catholics. Further, "Catholic teaching has its better and more human side, and it is the repository of much wisdom that would stand a Catholic President in good standing."[5]

What is surprising is the amount of opposition Kennedy received from the Catholic Church's most prominent leaders. The Vatican directed the American bishops to stay out of the campaign of 1960, but there were ways for them to make their preference known without violating the letter of that directive. Cardinal Spellman, for one, appeared regularly in public with Nixon and in private made his views clear. And he was not alone. Of the three major Catholic leaders noted earlier, only one – Cardinal Cushing – supported Kennedy. Cardinals Sheen and Spellman opposed Kennedy either out of loyalty to Nixon – loyalty gained while Nixon was vice president, especially for his anticommunist stance – or out of their distrust of Kennedy as a "good Catholic," or both. Cardinal Cushing was among the strongest of Kennedy's supporters. Kennedy was Massachusetts' United States Senator, but just as importantly, his was the Archdiocese of Boston wherein the Kennedy clan gathered and exercised considerable influence. Cushing had officiated at John Kennedy's wedding, and when rumors circulated that Kennedy wasn't a good Catholic, Cushing offered to issue a statement denying the rumor. John Kennedy and his father declined Cushing's offer, not wanting the church closely identified with John's campaign.[6]

Although his victory over the Republican Richard Nixon was by a very slim margin of the popular vote, Graham and Cardinals Sheen and Spellman, as well as other prominent figures voiced their support for Kennedy. Kennedy did nothing to confirm his non-Catholic opposition concerns, but his success in office was also in large part the result of another major change, taking place simultaneously within the Roman Catholic Church itself. Two years before John Kennedy was elected President, Angelo Giuseppe Roncalli was elected Pope John XXIII. During his fewer than five years in office, the new Pope took the church in a radically new direction.[7]

In 1963, Pope John issued *Pacem in Terris* (Peace on Earth), which he addressed not only to the Roman Catholic community but also to "all men of good will." The encyclical began with a recognition of basic human rights, including the right of all people "to honor God according to the sincere dictates" of their own consciences. He urged the world's governments to provide a "charter of fundamental human rights . . . drawn up in clear and precise terms and that it be incorporated in its entirety in the constitution" of that nation. Only as "an equal natural dignity" was recognized as the fundamental right of all people could powerful nations begin to treat other nations in terms of their "equal natural dignity as well."[8]

Pope John XXIII, who was named "Man of the Year" for 1962 by *Time* magazine, is best known, however, for convening Vatican II, the first such major church conclave in nearly one hundred years. On October 11, 1962, more than 2,000 bishops from around the world gathered in Rome. Pope John would not live long enough to adjourn the meeting some three years later, but Vatican II dramatically changed the course of the Roman Catholic Church, distancing itself from its long held antimodernist position. A leading figure at Vatican II was the Jesuit theologian John Courtney Murray. Murray introduced to the Council the "Declaration on Religious Liberty," generally called the "American document" not only because of the home of its author but also because of its position on religious freedom, which had become closely associated with the United States. Following considerable debate, Murray hailed passage of the Declaration as bringing "the church at long last abreast of the consciousness of civilized mankind." The "Declaration on Religious Liberty" stated: "Truth cannot impose itself except by virtue of its own truth, as it makes its entrance into the mind at once quietly and with power. . . . No merely human power can either command or prohibit acts of this kind."[9]

The civil rights and black power movements

With the passing of "the torch to a new generation of Americans" in pursuit of a "New Frontier," as Kennedy put it in his inaugural speech, still other changes were in the offing, some unanticipated and even more challenging. Among those challenges was the civil rights movement. Its postwar phase having begun in the 1950s, the movement gained strength in the 1960s. And for the first few years of the decade, it continued to be led by African American religious leaders who remained faithful to King's non-violent resistance. On February 1, 1960, four college students staged a sit-in at an all-white Greensboro, North Carolina lunch counter, and from Greensboro sit-ins spread rapidly. Within a year more than 70,000 Americans – white and black – engaged in similar protests expanding the goal from desegregating lunch counters to challenging all "white only" and "colored only" Jim Crow facilities throughout the South. They formed the Student Nonviolent Coordinating Committee (SNCC), which, although a separate organization capably led by John Lewis, assumed a non-violent approach similar to King's. As explained in its "Statement of Purpose": "We affirm the philosophical or religious ideal of non-violence as the foundation of our purpose, the presupposition of our faith, and the manner of our action. Non-violence as it grows from the Judaeo-Christian tradition seeks a social order of justice permeated by love." The larger movement, however, continued to be led by African American religious leaders, especially

King's Southern Christian Leadership Conference, whose volunteers were required to sign a commitment card to non-violence.[10]

In March 1960, King contributed a seminal article in *The Christian Century*'s "How My Mind Has Changed" series. He acknowledged that he had been a "thoroughgoing liberal," until he read Reinhold Niebuhr, whereupon he concluded that "liberalism had been all too sentimental concerning human nature and that it leaned toward a false idealism" when it came to man's true sinfulness: "Any religion that professes to be concerned about the souls of men and is not concerned about the slums that damn them, the economic conditions that strangle them, and the social conditions that cripple them is a spiritually moribund religion awaiting burial." Acknowledging the debt he owed Mahatma Gandhi, King offered:

> As I delved deeper into the philosophy of Gandhi, my skepticism concerning the power of love gradually diminished, and I came to see for the first time that the Christian doctrine of love operating through the Gandhian method of nonviolence was one of the most potent weapons available to oppressed people in their struggle for freedom.[11]

In May 1961, members of the Congress of Racial Equality (CORE), also a non-violent civil rights organization, formed a group called the Freedom Riders. Led by James Farmer, they organized a bus ride through the South to demonstrate that despite Supreme Court rulings, desegregation of interstate buses and bus stations had not yet occurred. They were met along the way by white gangs who attacked the riders and firebombed one bus, all of which made the national media and provoked a national outcry that persuaded President Kennedy to send federal marshals to Alabama to protect the Freedom Riders. In 1963, King and the SCLC organized a campaign in Birmingham, Alabama, that he hoped would bring about a confrontation large enough to take the civil rights movement to the next level. He was right. Under orders of Police Commissioner Eugene "Bull" Connor, the marchers were met with high-powered hoses and police dogs. When all of this was captured on television, President Kennedy was once again forced to act, in this case urging that Birmingham's business and political leaders to negotiate a settlement with the marchers.

It was the white opposition to King's Birmingham protest that prompted one of his most eloquent responses. Eight Alabama clergy – Protestant, Catholic, and Jewish – wrote in the *Birmingham News* that they sympathized with King's message, but that they considered his march "unwise and untimely," as well as tainted by the presence of outsider agitators. King responded in his "Letter from Birmingham Jail." He reminded them that, much as Paul left his village of Tarsus and carried the gospel throughout the Greco-Roman world, "so am I compelled to carry the gospel of freedom beyond my own home town." As to those who argued that it was untimely and urged him to wait, he responded: "Perhaps it is easy for those who have never felt the stinging darts of segregation to say, 'Wait,' . . . [But] there comes a time when the cup of endurance runs over, and men are no longer willing to be plunged into the abyss of despair." King explained that he was "greatly disappointed with the white church and its leadership" for their failure to support the bus boycott, some even becoming "outright opponents, refusing to understand the freedom movement and misrepresenting its leaders." But he crediting those white clergy whose support for the movement had "carved a tunnel of hope through the dark mountain of disappointment," and urged those who were holding back to follow their example.[12]

That led to the much heralded March on Washington, (see Figure 6.1) where on August 28, 1963, a quarter of a million people, white, black, and from all walks of life, listened to King's most famous speech. In that speech King mixed biblical references (from the Book of Isaiah,

Figure 6.1 Martin Luther King's March on Washington
Source: Pictorial Press Ltd/Alamy Stock Photo

in particular), images of segregated life in the South, and passages from the Declaration of Independence. To those assembled he offered three dreams:

(1) I have a dream, that one day this nation will rise up and live out the true meaning of its creed – we hold these truths to be self-evident, that all men are created equal. . . .

(2) I have a dream that one day on the red hills of Georgia, the sons of former slaves and the sons of former slave-owners will be able to sit down together at the table of brotherhood. . . .

(3) I have a dream that one day every valley shall be exalted, every hill and mountain shall be made low, the rough places will be made plain and the crooked places will be made straight and the glory of the Lord shall be revealed and all flesh shall see it together. . . .

He concluded:

When we allow freedom to ring . . . we will be able to speed up that day when all of God's children – black men and white men, Jews and Gentiles, Protestants and Catholics – will be able to join hands and sing in the words of the old Negro spiritual, "Free at last! Free at last! Thank God Almighty, we are free at last!"

In 1964, King won the Nobel Peace Prize, but already the civil rights movement was coming apart as, in the face of repeated acts of violence against protesters, an increasingly outspoken number of civil rights leaders were losing faith in King and coming to believe that non-violence was no longer the answer.[13]

In 1966, a group of young black clergy met in Harlem and formed the National Committee of Negro Churchmen (to become the National Conference of Black Churchmen). They wrote the "Black Power Statement" and published it as a full-page advertisement in the *New York Times* on July 31. The statement criticized the non-violent approach of the civil rights movement by arguing that as long as the nation's African Americans were powerless, its dependence on the transforming power of Christian love was "a distorted form of love, which in the absence of justice becomes chaotic self-surrender." In 1969, the Interreligious Foundation for Community Organization commissioned James Forman, a former Student Nonviolent Coordinating Committee organizer, to write a report on the black community and the responsibilities of the white churches. The result was "The Black Manifesto." In addition to its Marxist rhetoric, it included a demand that reparations of half a billion dollars ("fifteen dollars per nigger") be paid by white churches and synagogues to the black community in compensation for centuries of oppression in which they had participated, and it threatened mayhem if the churches did not pay.[14]

Forman became a spokesman for "The Black Manifesto," and James Cone, author of *Black Theology and Black Power* (1968) and a faculty member at the Union Theological Seminary, a leader in the new black theology movement. But the most prominent figure among the more radical black religious leaders was Malcolm X. Born Malcom Little and a high school dropout at age 15, he became a petty street criminal and was sent to prison, where he joined the Nation of Islam. Upon his release from prison in 1952, he attended Detroit's Black Muslim Temple Number 1 and chose to replace Little with the letter "X" in his name to show that his real name had been stolen from his ancestors by their owners, when they were slaves.[15]

The Nation of Islam, its followers known at Black Muslims, was founded in 1930 by Wallace Fard Muhammad in Detroit. Soon after he founded the Temples of Islam, he chose as his assistant Elijah Poole, who renamed himself Elijah Muhammad, took over leadership of the Nation of Islam in 1934, and declared himself "Prophet" and the last "Messenger of God." Located in the ghettos of the North, the Nation of Islam insisted on running its own schools, businesses, and mosques. They emphasized sobriety, including abstinence from alcohol, tea, coffee, tobacco, and pork, as well as thrift, personal rectitude, and social responsibility. This appealed to many poor urban blacks, including Malcolm X, who by the early 1960s became the chief emissary for the Black Muslims. Malcolm X had no patience for King's ideal of desegregation. Instead, he argued that "the only solution to America's race problem is complete separation of the two races." He compared Elijah Muhammad to Moses and Jesus in that as religious leaders they were despised by the higher classes of their times. In 1961, he told a group of students at Harvard Law School that the only way whites could avert a catastrophe was to give blacks their own country to start their own civilization on land set aside from the United States. "This is God's plan. This is God's solution. . . . Otherwise Americans will reap the full fury of God's wrath for her crimes against our people. As your Bible says, 'He that leads into captivity shall go into captivity; he that kills with the sword shall be killed by the sword.'"[16]

In 1964, Malcolm X took a *hajj* (pilgrimage) to the Muslim holy city of Mecca, where he met Muslims from around the world, who impressed him with their lack of racial bias. When he returned to the United States, he distanced himself from the Nation of Islam, denounced its black supremacy teachings, and questioned other doctrines that varied from mainstream Islam. He took a new name, El-Hajj Malik el-Shabazz, and founded the Moslem Mosque, Inc. Shortly thereafter his home on Long Island was firebombed and on February 21, 1965, while giving a speech at the Audubon Ballroom in upper Manhattan, three men in the audience shot him to death. Many believe that his assassins were members of the Nation of Islam, who believed he had betrayed their cause. (Elijah Muhammad denied that he played any role in the killing.)[17]

With the rise of more extreme, non-religious groups such as the Black Panthers and leaders like Stokely Carmichael, the African American struggle for equality became dominantly secular. And among white churches, although many religious leaders continued to support the civil rights movement, they were outnumbered by lay people who acted independently of the churches, for the most part, and from a more humanist than religious framework.

The United Farm Workers movement

The civil rights movement, along with its theology of liberation and demands of African Americans for social justice, drew in other minorities as well, including Hispanics. Their numbers reached 4 million by 1960, accounting for over 4 percent of America's total population and one-quarter of American Catholics. Eighty percent of Mexican Americans lived in urban centers largely abandoned by whites, like San Antonio, Los Angeles, El Paso, and Chicago, commonly in squalid conditions, but migrant farm workers, whose ranks swelled beginning in the mid-1960s, found life just as challenging. A burgeoning population of younger newly arrived Mexican immigrants sparked a renaissance in Mexican consciousness, a growth of cultural nationalism, and a fight for social justice.[18]

A key player in the Mexican American movement for social justice for migrant workers was the Catholic layman Cesar Chavez, who emerged not only as a union and civil rights leader, but also as a symbol for the Chicano movement, as it came to be known. Chavez was born to a Mexican American family in Yuma, Arizona, in 1927. His father belonged to farm labor unions, and Chavez himself was a member of the National Farm Labor Union. In the 1940s, the family moved to San Jose, California, where Caesar met Father Donald McDonnell, who tutored him in *Rerum Novarum*, Pope Leo XIII's encyclical that supported labor unions and social justice, to which Chavez added reading about Saint Francis of Assisi and Mahatma Gandhi. In 1962, Chavez moved to Delano, California where he and Dolores

Huerta began to organize the National Farm Workers Association (NFWA) (later the United Farm Workers), which by 1965 had 1,700 members.[19]

In 1965, Chavez led migrant workers in a strike against the grape growers in California's San Joaquin valley. The strike began in September when the Filipinos in the Agricultural Workers Organizing Committee (AWOC) struck the grape growers of the Delano area for higher wages and better working conditions. Within days, the rank and file of the National Farm Workers Association (NFWA) voted to join the Filipinos, and Chavez emerged as the central figure in the strike. Drawing on the imagery of the civil rights movement, insisting on non-violence, using mass mobilizing techniques – including a march on Sacramento in 1966 – Chavez attracted large numbers to the cause. He originated the slogan, *Sí, se puede* ("Yes, one can"), which Barack Obama adopted as his presidential campaign slogan in 2008.[20]

For five years, Chavez expanded the strike throughout most of California, taking on major growers of grapes and lettuce. The press coverage he received attracted major figures such as Robert Kennedy and Coretta Scott King, wife of Martin Luther King, as well as a cover story in March in *Time* magazine. The public rallied to Chavez's cause calling for a national consumer boycott of table grapes involving millions of Americans, which ended only when he finally won. Chavez not only achieved his immediate goals for wages and working conditions, but also the NFWA's position as the principal union of migrant farm workers and passage of California's Agricultural Labor Relations Act in 1975 (the first of its kind in the nation), which promised to ensure justice for the state's farm workers.[21]

Chavez is seen as "a unique breed of social reformer whose basis for action is derived from his mystical encounters with God." He is shown to have incorporated religious leaders of various faiths in his movement, as well as pilgrimages, fasts, rituals, and symbols with decidedly Mexican Catholic origins. Vigils and Catholic masses were held in the fields. The UFW's theme song, "De Colores," was taken from the Catholic *cursillo* movement, and the Virgen de Guadalupe was present at nearly every meeting, procession, and march.[22]

Historian Ronald Wells has explained: "Chavez was a Christian, and, unlike some other prior secular leaders, his faith guided his life in a transparent way that ordinary *campesinos* (farm workers) could understand. No one had to tell them why the march to Sacramento was called a pilgrimage or that it should culminate on Easter." The United Farm Workers march to the state capitol in Sacramento in 1966, a 300-mile trek that began with about 300 walking behind an image of the Virgin of Guadalupe, by journey's end swelled to several thousand. The leaders' choice for the slogan of the march, appropriate to the cause and the holy season of lent in which it took place, was: "*Peregrination, Penitencia, Revolution*" (Pilgrimage, Penitence, Revolution). The pilgrimage ended on Good Friday, and a rally, begun with a Catholic mass, took place at the capital on Easter Sunday.[23]

The Protestant contribution to the migrant workers' cause was led by the Migrant Ministry, an ecumenical Protestant group affiliated with the National Council of Churches and dedicated to serving the needs of the California farm workers. Among the speakers that concluded the Sacramental march, for example, was the Reverend Chris Hartmire, director of the California Migrant Ministry. He told those assembled that Chavez regularly thanked the churches for their support, but that "he really shouldn't have to," as "standing with oppressed people ought to be as natural as breathing or singing hymns. It should be part of our daily life, unexceptional and uncontroversial." Included in the *Time* magazine cover story noted earlier, Chavez noted that when the California Migrant Ministry first approached him and the WFU, he was leery, "since we were Catholics and they were

Protestants." However, even while some Catholic priests held back in their support, members of the California Migrant Ministry stepped forward: "They had developed a very clear conception of the Church. It was called to serve, to be at the mercy of the poor, and not to try to use them."[24]

Native Americans

Another group that rose up to demand their civil rights and liberties in the turbulent 1960s and 1970s was Native Americans. Native Americans were among the nation's poorest minority group with 40 percent of their people living below the poverty line. Their unemployment rate was ten times the national average, and their life expectancy was just forty-four years, a third less than the average for all Americans. Yet, beginning in 1960, although conditions did not improve all that much, the Native American population grew dramatically. The number of Native Americans in the United States in 1900, which in pre-Columbian years reached into the millions, hit its low point at 237,196. By 1950, they numbered 357, 499, and by the end of the century, nearly 2 million.[25]

The reversal of the decline in the Indian population was paralleled by a similarly dramatic renaissance in American Indian culture, what anthropologists term "ethnogenesis." By 1960, the Native American renaissance gave rise to a new spirit of Indian nationalism led by new more militant organizations such as the National Indian Youth Council formed in 1961, which initiated the use of the phrase "Red Power," and the American Indian Movement (AIM), formed by a group of Chippewas in Minneapolis in 1968. Initially, AIM was started to protest police brutality, but it soon expanded its purview to include Indian sovereignty, treaty issues, and spirituality. Founded by Dennis Banks, Clyde and Vernon Bellecourt, and other young Native Americans, and soon to include Russell Means, AIM initially participated in the Rainbow Coalition, organized by civil rights leaders, and was welcomed by Martin Luther King, Jr., Malcolm X, and Robert Kennedy.[26]

In November 1969, in what is often cited as the start of the Red Power Movement, 200 Native Americans, including members of AIM, seized the abandoned federal penitentiary on Alcatraz Island in San Francisco Bay and occupied it for nineteen months to draw attention to conditions of the nation's Indian reservations, which they suggested mirrored those at the abandoned prison. The following year another group of Native Americans established a settlement at Mount Rushmore to assert Indian claims to the Black Hills. In October 1972, AIM led a March along the "Trail of Broken Treaties" from Seattle to Washington, DC, where it seized the offices of the Bureau of Indian Affairs and demanded the restoration and honoring of past treaties between various tribes and the United States. That was followed in February 1973 by AIM's takeover of the town of Wounded Knee, South Dakota, on the Pine Ridge Reservation, the site of the 1890 massacre of 300 Sioux by the US Army cavalry. The occupation lasted 71 days and resulted in the deaths of 1 Indian and 2 FBI agents. All of this led to various responses by government agencies such as the Indian Education Act of 1972, which gave Indian parents greater control over their children's schools; the Indian Health Care Act of 1976, intended to improve healthcare for Native Americans; and a series of Supreme Court and state court cases, that protected traditional Native American rights and awarded tribes payments to compensate for the seizure of Indians lands by whites in violation of treaty agreements.[27]

Two contrasting, yet complementary, and representative religious developments in this era of Native American activism were the Indian Ecumenical Conference and the struggles of the Native American Church for the free exercise of Indian religion. The first Indian Ecumenical Conference was held on the Crow Reservation in Montana in August 1970. Forty-seven tribes were represented, most of the delegates being Christian ministers or Native American ceremonial leaders. Those assembled agreed that Native American religious life must be a furthering of the historical continuity of time honored Indian values and that both modern Indian ceremonies and Indian Christianity could be mutually supportive and cooperatively integrated. Among the twelve resolutions they adopted were calls for self-determination for Indian communities in religious matters, an end to the desecration of formerly Indian lands still held sacred by them, and the return of relics and other sacred items once owned by Native Americans but taken from them and placed in museums. Its participants were optimistic that it would be a "pivotal moment in the history of interfaith cooperation" but that optimism began to dissipate after 1974 as differences in their pursuit of this goal produced divergent outcomes and a rift between Christian and Native groups, led especially by younger members.[28]

The Native American Church was at the center of the Native American movement for religious freedom. Although most Native Americans were Christian, by 1960, the NAC was the largest indigenous religious movement in the United States, counting about 25 percent of Native Americans among its followers, and the most influential form of Pan-Indianism. It fought for Plains Native Americans' access to sacred lands no longer theirs and the right to use peyote in their religious ceremonies, which raised the question of whether the use of an illegal drug in the exercise of religion could be accommodated under the law.[29]

The Native American Church, incorporated in 1918, which came to embrace a mix of traditional and Christian beliefs as well as the sacramental use of peyote, spread rapidly throughout the many Indian tribes in the United States. In the 1950s, as part of the growing cultural renaissance among Indians, the church broke into two major bodies: the original body, which became officially known as the Native American Church of the United States, and the break-away Native American Church of North America, which allowed only Native Americans to participate in its ceremonies. The Native American Church faced challenges from the start, from missionaries who denied that the NAC was an acceptable mix of Christian and traditional beliefs, and federal Indian agents and state, and local officials who opposed allowing adherents' the use of peyote. The NAC made little headway in regaining access to former tribal lands, but it was able to stave off legislation that would have impaired their use of peyote. In the 1960s, however, NAC encountered the passage of new or expanded federal policies and laws regarding drug use, including peyote.[30]

Courts in states such as Arizona and California ruled in favor of Native Americans, but when other states persisted in their outlawing of peyote, Congress decided to lend its support to the Native American Church's push for greater autonomy with passage of the Indian Self-Determination and Education Assistance Act of 1975 and in 1978 with the American Religious Freedom Act (ARFA). The ARFA made it federal policy "to protect and preserve for American Indians their inherent right of freedom to believe, express, and exercise the traditional religions of the American Indian . . . including but not limited to access to sites, use and possession of scared objects, and the freedom to worship through ceremonials and traditional rights."[31]

In 1990, however, in *Employment Division v. Smith*, the US Supreme Court ruled in favor of the State of Oregon and against Native Americans. Alfred Smith and Galen Black, co-workers and both members of the Native American Church, were fired from their jobs and denied unemployment benefits for participating in ceremonies of the NAC in which peyote was used. Both defended their use under the First Amendment's free exercise of religion clause and the American Indian Religious Freedom Act. The Oregon courts ruled in their favor, but the US Supreme Court overturned the Oregon court ruling. In its majority opinion, the Supreme Court stated that the plaintiffs could be fired and denied unemployment benefits because by using peyote they had violated the state's criminal law. Of more far-reaching consequence was the basis of the majority opinion, which had the potential of broader and longer-term repercussions by reversing the basis for earlier free exercise decisions. In brief, Justice Anthony Scalia, who wrote for the majority, reversed the finding in *Sherbert v. Verner* (1963), arguing that, despite the precedent set by earlier Court decisions, the state did not have to prove a "compelling interest" when a valid and neutral law of general applicability burdened the free exercise of religion.[32]

The decision was so hotly contested that it prompted the development of the Native American Religious Freedom Project, which attracted not only nearly every Indian tribe in the country but also a wide array of non-Native American religious leaders that opposed the change in the "compelling interest" precedent. Congress stepped in and passed the Religious Freedom Restoration Act of 1993 and the following year adopted the American Indian Religious Freedom Act Amendments. Congress made reference to the Supreme Court's ruling but then restated its earlier position that:

> Notwithstanding any other provision of the law, the use, possession or transportation of peyote by an Indian who uses peyote in a traditional manner for bona fide ceremonial purposes in connection with the practice of a traditional Indian religions is lawful and shall not be prohibited by the United States or by any state.[33]

Congress' action notwithstanding, the Supreme Court once again ruled unconstitutional the Religious Freedom Restoration Act, as applied to the states in *City of Boerne, Texas v. Flores*, decided in 1997. The Court ruled that, in its application to the states, the Religious Freedom Restoration Act was not a proper exercise of Congress's enforcement power. However, the Court let the act's authority in federal matters stand, and as of this writing, twenty states have passed similar acts that apply its protections to their state and local governments.[34]

Women's rights

The women's rights movement of the 1960s and 1970s raised questions that challenged the most fundamental assumptions and most basic institutions of Western civilization, not just the United States, including the churches and their biblical traditions concerning women. It might be argued that the movement – also known as the Women's Liberation Movement, the Feminist Movement, or the Second Wave of the Feminist Movement (the first wave being the suffrage movement at the turn of the century) – began in 1963 with publication of *The Feminine Mystique* by Betty Friedan, a critique of middle-class women and their discontent. Friedan encouraged women to seek new roles and responsibilities and their own personal identities rather than have them defined by a male-dominated society. The Civil Rights Act of 1964 outlawed discrimination on the basis of gender, as well as race, and in 1966, twenty-eight professional women, including Friedan, established the National Organization for Woman (NOW). The movement, however, reached its height in the early 1970s. In 1972, journalist Gloria Steinem founded *Ms.* magazine, which became the popular organ of the movement. In the same year, Congress approved the Equal Rights Amendment to the US Constitution. It declared: "Equality of rights under the law shall not be denied or abridged by the United States or by any State on account of sex." And in 1973, the Supreme Court in *Roe v. Wade* held that a woman had considerable autonomy over her pregnancy, especially during the first trimester. All of these victories, however, brought about a powerful reaction that stopped the ratification process of the Equal Rights Amendment three states short of the required 38 states and caused the movement to stagnate, which in turn led it to fragment into moderate and radical components.[35]

The abortion issue became the most heated issue among religious groups, as most took sides in what some have described as a "religious war." The Supreme Court recognized the many factors that go into one's position on a women's right to abortion, including "one's religious training," and it took into consideration the various friends-of-the-court briefs, in religious circles largely pitting conservative Protestant denominations and the Roman Catholic Church, against more liberal mainstream Protestants and Jews. Largely avoiding the issue of determining the philosophical or religious point at which human life begins, however, the Court took into consideration scientific current knowledge as to the point at which a fetus is viable outside the womb. The Court ruled that during the first trimester, the decision must be left to the judgment of the pregnant woman and her doctor. During the second trimester, "states may promote their interests in the mother's health by regulating abortion procedures related to the health of the mother." And during final trimester pregnancies, "states may promote their interests in the potentiality of human life by regulating or even prohibiting abortion, except when necessary to preserve the life or health of the mother."[36]

These issues involved women who were religious and not, while those more intently religious addressed topics such as gender-inclusive language and symbols, the development of Christian feminist spirituality and ritual, and the demands of women to enter the ministry. By way of one example, for centuries Jewish and Christian prayers, liturgies, and hymns had used the male pronoun for God and for the people of God ("Faith of Our Fathers," for example). Feminists of the 1960s challenged that practice as symbolically constructing male power and privilege and underscoring patriarchal domination and sexist exclusion, rendering women invisible. As feminist theologian, Rosemary Radford Ruether argued: "Women, more than any other group, are overwhelmed by a linguistic form that excludes them from visible existence." Sallie McFague observed that it was not merely the use of male pronouns and images, but rather the entire patriarchal image of God and the church that resulted in the marginalization of women. In seeking to revise language, however, feminists ran into considerable opposition from men and women who were unwilling to give up what they considered to be a biblical tradition.[37]

As to the progress of women in assuming positions of leadership in churches and synagogues, the flash point became demands for women's ordination. The Congregationalists were among the first of the major denominations to ordain a woman, Antoinette Brown, which it did in 1853. Pentecostal and holiness churches allowed female preaching for decades, and in Christian Science, female leaders outnumbered males. The Presbyterians voted to ordain women in 1953 and in 1954 ordained its first woman minister. But that was not the case among the majority of religious groups, and when it was attempted, the resistance was considerable. Advocates of male-only leadership pointed to several passages in the Bible to support their position. In 1 Timothy 2:11–12, for example, Paul stated: "During instruction a woman should be quiet and respectful. I give no permission for a woman to teach or to have authority over a man. A woman ought to be quiet, because Adam was formed first and Eve afterwards, and it was not Adam who was led astray, but the woman who was led astray and fell into sin." Advocates for equal rites for women in their religious bodies, had their own scriptural passages to cite in their favor, including Paul's letter to the Galatians 3:38: "There is no such thing as Jew or Greek, slave or freeman, male or female, for you are all one in Christ Jesus."[38]

By way of examples of developments in the 1960s and 1970s, when the Episcopal Church in 1976 ruled that women could be ordained priests, several churches broke away to form a separate diocese. "Most of the reasons the church gave for ordaining women," the separatists explained, "are on a sociological plane, not a theological plane." They further argued that equality between the sexes did not imply identity of function for the sexes. The Episcopal Church persisted in ordaining women and in 1989 elected is first female bishop, Barbara Harris. Women's ordination among Lutherans varied by group. By the late 1960s, three of the larger Lutheran bodies held an Inter-Lutheran Consultation on the Ordination of Women. By 1970, two of the three approved such ordination, while the third – the more conservative Lutheran Church – Missouri Synod – did not. And Jews responded in a similar manner. Reform Judaism ordained its first woman rabbi in 1972 and Reconstructionists followed two years later. Conservative Jews voted against it in 1974 only to reverse themselves in 1983. Orthodox Jews remained opposed.[39]

The Southern Baptist Convention stepped back from its earlier approval of women's ordination. The Convention began ordaining women in 1964 and by the mid-1980s had ordained over 400 women. By that time, however, an increasingly conservative leadership began to oppose the policy. At its annual meeting in 1984, the conservatives had their way and the Convention declared that women should not assume a role of authority over men, and therefore were to be excluded from the ministry. Two years later, the Convention's Home Mission Board voted not to grant funds to any church that employed a woman pastor, and the Southern Baptist seminaries purged their tenured faculty ranks of women.[40]

Similarly the Roman Catholic leadership denied women ordination in the face of considerable opposition. In 1972, the Leadership Conference of Women Religious organized, representing about 90 percent of all women religions (nuns) in the country. Two years later, the Conference voted to support "the principle that all ministries in the Church be open to women and men as the Spirit calls them," and that "women [should] have active participation in all decision-making bodies in the Church." In 1975, the Conference added that in its treatment of women, "the mainstream of tradition within the Catholic Church . . . is one of the most oppressive of all religious superstructures." In 1976, hundreds of Catholic women organized a Women's Ordination Conference to protest "a priesthood that is elitist, hierarchical, racist, [and] classist." It called for equal rights for women, insisting that "what is central to the historical Jesus is his humanity and not his maleness." The following year, however, the Vatican released its *Declaration on the Question of the Admission of Women to the Ministerial Priesthood*, which took the position that as Christ and his apostles were male, and as there is no evidence in the early church that the ministry was to include females, ordination was not to be allowed.[41]

Finally, the women's movement also developed a feminist theology, which went far beyond inclusive language and ordination. In general, as there were variations, feminist theology focused on "displacing androcentrism (male-centeredness) and finding the deeper truths in Christianity that centuries of patriarchy (male domination) and misogyny (women hating) had obscured." Carol Christ and Judith Plaskow have divided feminist theologians into two groups: reformists and revolutionaries. Both groups agreed that religious traditions of Judaism and Christianity were patriarchal and oppressive and that change was necessary. Where they differed was in the former's commitment to work within their traditions to bring about that change, and the latter's belief that both traditions were irredeemable and that the best option was to seek a new source of spiritual experience.[42]

Rosemary Ruether, one of the earliest and most distinguished feminist theologians and who refused to leave the church, has written:

> This exclusion of women and its justifications result in a systematic distortion of all the symbols of Christian theology by patriarchal bias. The imagery and understanding of God, Christ, human nature, sin, salvation, church, and ministry were all shaped by a male-centered, misogynist world-view that subordinated women and rendered them non-normative and invisible.

Nevertheless, she was among those who believed that women could find a "usable past" within Judaism and Christianity and, that once rid of male-centered distortions in both traditions, women could begin to create a non-sexist theology. Phyllis Trible, lent her support to what Ruether was suggesting by pursuing a reinterpretation of biblical stories by using a "hermeneutics of suspicion," which meant a rereading and reinterpretation of the Bible mindful of the patriarchal assumptions that lay behind previous interpretations. She wrote: "Over the centuries . . . translators and commentators have ignored such female imagery, with disastrous results for God, man and woman."[43]

Early feminist theologians were mostly white and middle class. Although they considered themselves oppressed by a male-dominated church hierarchy, various minorities felt the need to further reassess things from their own largely different perspective. Black women theologians used the term "womanist," a term invented by novelist Alice Walker to differentiate themselves; Latin American women chose "mujerist." Both built their theology on their oppression by other races, men and women. Still others abandoned the whole idea of trying to reconfigure the Judeo-Christian tradition in order to empower women, concluding that the entire tradition was so androcentric that it could never provide women with the liberation they sought. Theologian Mary Daly staked out that position in 1972 in *Beyond God the Father*, wherein she concluded that women's power had been stolen by men and sanctified by the leaders of the Judeo-Christian religions, from whose grip women must rescue it. Until them, it was a hopeless task to look for the feminine within the Christian God.[44]

The environmental movement

An enhanced concern for the environment began to gain momentum in the 1960s, and that attracted many who approached it from a theological perspective. The larger movement is often dated to publication of Rachel Carson's *Silent Spring* in 1962, which detailed the harmful effects of the indiscriminate use of pesticides. The movement at first emphasized the threats of world overpopulation, chemical hazards, urban decay, and suburban sprawl. In response, in 1964, the Faith-Man-Nature group, a consortium of theologians and conservationists, formed out of the National Council of Churches. They set as their goal to explore the religious dimensions of environmental issues, "to understand man's relationship with nature in light of religious faith and to spell out ethical imperatives for the conservation of natural resources." In 1967, it published *Christians and the Good Earth* followed in 1969 by *A New Ethic for a New Earth*. The basic message of these documents was that the earth and its resources are gifts of God, which humans have abused, and that it was their moral responsibility to God to assume stewardship or to care for God's good earth.[45]

The relationship of theology to the modern ecological crisis became an even more intense issue of debate in 1967 with publication of the article in *Science*, "The Historical Roots of Our Ecological Crisis," by Lynn White, Jr. White argued that Americans in the Judeo-Christian tradition had exploited the natural world partly because, according to the Hebrew Bible in Genesis 1:28, God had authorized Adam to "have dominion over the fish of the sea, over the birds of the air, and over every living thing." This, White explained, implied that the natural world was devoid of any connection to God and thereby provided people with a model of human dominion over nature that had led to environmental devastation.[46]

The first Earth Day was celebrated on April 22, 1970, the same year that the Environmental Protection Agency became a department of the federal government. The celebration included teach-ins on pollution and recycling and other topics of environmental concern. Religious institutions offered substantial support for the event, especially the National Council of Churches which added its official endorsement. That these messages struck home among those seeking a theology of ecology is attested to by the proliferation of publications on that subject that followed. By way of examples, on October 7, 1970, the *Christian Century* devoted an entire issue to what it termed the "environmental crisis." John B. Cobb published *Is It Too Late? A Theology of Ecology* (1972); Matthew Fox, *Creation Spirituality* (1988); and Sallie McFague, *Models of God: Theology for an Ecological, Nuclear Age* (1989).[47]

In 1990, the Pope John Paul II devoted his New Year's message to the issue, which prompted the American Catholic bishops to issue a pastoral letter, "Renewing the Earth," which was followed two years later by the United States Catholic Conference establishing an environmental justice program. American Jews joined in by the end of the 1990s. Ellen Bernstein founded Shomrei Adamah (Keepers of the Earth) promoting environment education among American Jews. And Michael Smart, a Jewish environmental educator, urged Jews to rethink the meaning of wilderness: "The Torah was given to us in the wilderness. . . . Wilderness is the place where Jews freed their hearts from slavery and prepared themselves for the promised land."[48]

And so too did many conservatives. The Interfaith Council for Environmental Stewardship, a neoconservative group that drew its members from conservative Protestants, Catholics, and Jews, distinguished between what they considered genuine environmental hazards, like poor pollution, and those they thought were inflated, such as species loss and global warming. Further, whereas many of the more extreme elements of the environmental movement looked askance at science and technology as sources of help, some even writing both off as threats to the environment, the Interfaith Council continued to believe that both were essential to saving the environment. In February 2000, in its Cornwall Declaration, the Council stated:

> Human beings are called to be fruitful, to bring forth good things form the earth, to join with God in making provision for our temporal well-being, and to enhance the beauty and fruitfulness of the rest of the earth. Our call to fruitfulness, therefore, is not contrary to but mutually complementary with our call to steward God's gifts.[49]

Gay rights

The Gay Rights Movement was yet another contentious issue involving the churches, which arose in these tumultuous decades. As was the case with the previously mentioned equal rights movements, the Gay Rights Movement had its roots much earlier. Looking at the period from the end of World War II, there were gay and lesbian organizations such as the Mattachine Society, formed in 1950 and named after a medieval group whose members performed in masks evoking the masked lives of gay Americans, and the Daughters of Bilitis, named after love poems between women, that had worked for equal rights since its founding in 1955. Nevertheless, as late as the 1960s, homosexuality was identified as a mental disorder by the American Psychiatric Association. Consensual sexual relations between people of the same sex were still illegal in nearly every state. Gay couples could not marry, adopt children, or receive partnership benefits, and they were often excluded from other equal rights groups such as NOW, which expelled its lesbian officers in 1970.

Widely seen as the symbolic start of the Gay Rights Movement is the New York City Police raid of the Stonewall Inn, a Greenwich Village gay hangout, on June 28, 1969. Although nothing new, this time, inspired by what was happening among other groups seeking equal treatment, the patrons resisted arrest and were soon joined by hundreds more from throughout the city. By the next morning, peace had been restored, but signaling what was to come, someone borrowed from the civil rights movement and spray painted on a Village wall, the phrase "Gay Power." The Gay Rights (or Gay Liberation) Movement, which by 1973 included about 800 gay organizations, set as its goals gay pride and equal rights. Some fought to be accepted into heterosexual society, others sought a separate lifestyle, and still others struggled for both – inclusion and identity. All rallied behind a call for homosexuals to come "out of the closet."[50]

As was the case with other equal rights movements, the churches played a significant role in the Gay Rights Movement, both for and against the movement. At least at the start, many religious groups, Jewish and Christian alike, saw homosexuality as a sin. The Southern Baptist Convention was not atypical, although perhaps more public, when it declared that "even the desire to engage in a homosexual relationship is always sinful, impure, degrading, shameful, unnatural, indecent, and perverted." Many that took an ardent position in opposition in the 1960s and 1970s, however, tempered their remarks by the close of the century, *Christianity Today*, the journal for evangelicals, being a case in point. Whereas in 1973 it insisted that it was morally wrong to even "show compassion toward the homosexual," as it "confirms the sinner in his wicked ways," some three decades later it condemned the harassment of homosexuals: "Something is deeply wrong if a Christian suffers ostracism after admitting to struggles with same-sex attraction."[51]

Even before the Stonewall Riot, some religious leaders sought to provide support for gays and lesbians. In 1964, for example, sympathetic clergy created the San Francisco Council on Religion and Homosexuality. In 1969, the United Church of Christ issued a declaration in favor of full civil rights for homosexuals, and other liberal Protestant churches soon followed suit. And when the AIDS epidemic struck in the early 1980s – which evangelical Southern Baptist preacher Jerry Falwell pronounced "a lethal judgement of God on the sin of homosexuality" – these same churches and others offered their help in awareness campaigns and support groups.[52]

Most notable among early leaders was Troy Perry, an openly gay minister. In October 1968, he gathered a group of worshippers in his Los Angeles home, inaugurating a gay and lesbian Christian fellowship. In 1972, his influential autobiography, *The Lord Is My Shepherd and He Knows I'm Gay* (1972), which told the story of his early years as a pentecostal and Baptist preacher leading up to the revoking of his ministerial license as a result of his homosexuality, helped define the Gay Rights Movement in religious circles. It also served as a manifesto for a new ministry that he hoped would create a transformed church that would welcome gay and lesbians into its midst. Soon, what Perry started became a national movement and included the founding of the Universal Fellowship of Metropolitan Community Churches (UFMCC), led by gay ministers, offering gay wedding ceremonies, and supporting gay rights.[53]

Much like feminist theologians, gay theologians adopted a hermeneutic of suspicion in their interpretation of the Bible, seeking to remove what they saw as homophobic translations and commentaries that had been adopted over the centuries and to emphasize Christ's love for all humanity regardless of their sexual orientation. But the two issues that dominated the conversation in the religious community for gays and lesbians were ordination and denominational blessings of same-sex marriage. In the matter of ordination, some denominations, such as Reform Jews and Unitarian-Universalists moved quickly toward acceptance. Others, like Southern Baptists and the Roman Catholic Church remained opposed.[54]

The Episcopal Church, much as it had in the ordination of women, moved slowly. In 1979, the Episcopal Church's General Convention passed a resolution against openly gay priests, but in 1990, Assistant Bishop Walter Righter of Newark, New Jersey, ordained openly gay Barry Stopfel as a deacon. One year later, Bishop John Spong, Righter's superior, who endorsed Righter's action and supported gay rights, ordained Stopfel to the priesthood. In 1995, Righter was tried for heresy, but the case was dismissed as Episcopal doctrine did not specifically ban gay ordination, and from then on, the church followed a policy of permitting each bishop to decide policy for his or her own diocese. Conservative Jews took a different approach. They were willing to ordain gays to the rabbinate, but mindful of the divisions such actions brought about in other religious bodies, it urged all rabbis to be quiet about their sexual orientation, noting that "publicly acknowledging one's homosexuality . . . can have grave professional consequences."[55]

Consideration of solemnizing marriages proved divisive as well. By the 1990s, Reform and Reconstructionist Jews, Unitarians, the United Church of Christ, and Episcopalians agreed to it. Other denominations refused, including Southern Baptists, Jehovah's Witnesses, Mormons, Orthodox Jews, and Catholics, while in a few cases clergy in those bodies disregarded their governing bodies' rules and conducted gay weddings. United Methodist minister Jimmy Creech is among the best known of this group. In the late 1980s, Creech became a local leader of the Raleigh, North Carolina, Religious Network for Gay and Lesbian Equality. Among the Network's various causes was recognition of same-sex unions, which Creech took on as his own cause, despite the General Conference of the United Methodist Church having voted against the ordination of homosexuals in 1988 and against the celebration of union ceremonies for gay couples in 1996. In 1997, Creech conducted "a holy union ceremony" for a lesbian couple at a Methodist Church in Omaha, Nebraska, which resulted in his being summoned to a church trial, which initially acquitted him but two years later reversed its position when Creech continued to perform such ceremonies. In protest against Creech's punishment, ninety-six other Methodist clergy gathered to celebrate another lesbian wedding in Sacramento, California. But Creech remained stripped of his ministerial credentials among Methodists, whereupon he moved to the UFMCC.[56]

The antiwar movement and the churches

The free exercise of religion has often included an individual's seeking to exercise his or her right to oppose war, or his or her participation therein, on the grounds of personally held religious beliefs. Such instances have commonly proved contentious, pitting individual rights against the authority of the state to conduct war and call upon its citizens to defend the nation. We have seen examples of this earlier in our discussion of the World Wars, but no war proved more contentious in this matter than the Vietnam War. Although American military involvement in Vietnam dates to the early 1950s, it reached its height in the mid-1960s, which also marked an escalation of young men refusing to register for the draft or accept conscription into the armed forces.

Until the mid-1960s, the anticommunist consensus that had developed in America justified for many involvement in the Vietnam War to prevent the spread of communism. The mood of the nation began to change when President Lyndon Johnson began a rapid escalation of American involvement in the war. That religious, as well as political, issues underscored opposition to the war became apparent when mainline Protestant religious leaders began to take the position that South Vietnam's leaders had proven to be brutal, authoritarian, and untrustworthy of American support. In April 1964, A. J. Muste's Fellowship of Reconciliation published an open letter to President Johnson protesting the increased bombing of North Vietnam and the introduction of additional American combat troops in South Vietnam, signed by 2,500 ministers, priests, and rabbis. But soon thereafter the protest grew more extreme and shocking. In March 1965, Alice Herz, a Jew, immolated herself on a Detroit Street to protest the war. On November 2, Norman Morrison, a Quaker, did the same on the steps of the Pentagon, followed one week later by Roger LaPorte, one of Dorothy Day's Catholic Workers, on the steps of the United Nations building in New York City.[57]

In the midst of these antiwar suicides, an ecumenical group of religious leaders decided it was time to make their voices heard. A group of Protestants, Catholics, and Jews organized Clergy Concerned About Vietnam, which was soon changed to Clergy and Laity Concerned About Vietnam (CALCAV). Its founders were the Lutheran pastor Richard Neuhaus, the Jesuit priest Daniel Berrigan, and Rabbi Abraham Heschel. Heschel explained the goals of the organization simply as organizing the nation's churches and synagogues against the war by providing greater focus for religious protests. Just as importantly, CALCAV tried to encompass those who may have been uneasy about American's involvement in the war but still believed that America was God's chosen country. To that end, CALCAV sought to condemn the Vietnam War as an isolated, even aberrant, event that if addressed in a moral fashion would not adversely affect the nation's moral standing in the long run. Michael Novak reflected the position of many in the group when he wrote:

> Many of us who loved our country are sad to see its flag carried in this war. We might be as brave as anyone else in other wars, and as eager to leap to the defense of the values dear to our nation. But in regard to this war many have felt, from year to year, increasing shame. It is not in order that our flag might be carried in wars like this that men of the generations before us suffered and died for liberty, for bravery, for justice.[58]

An increasing number of religious leaders made their antiwar positions known. But a few took more direct action, the best known of whom were the brothers Daniel and Philip Berrigan. Daniel, a Jesuit (Society of Jesus) priest, and Philip, a Josephite (Society of Saint

Joseph), publicly encouraged resistance to the military draft and led by example. On October 27, 1964, Philip Berrigan and three others entered the offices of the Selective Service Board in Baltimore and threw pints of his and his friends' blood over its files. He had alerted the press beforehand, and they were there to take pictures of the incident. In a written statement, "The Baltimore Four" explained that the act was intended to protest the pitiful waste of American and Vietnamese blood in Indochina. The four were arrested, but the next May, before they would stand trial, Philip and Daniel, who had just returned from a much publicized "peace-mission" to Hanoi, North Vietnam, and seven others broke into the Selective Service Office in Catonsville, Maryland, and used homemade napalm – used by Americans in bombings in Vietnam – to burn some 600 files. Once again the press was alerted in time for the photo opportunity. And in the statement of "The Catonsville Nine," all of whom were Catholic, they explained:

> We confront the Roman Catholic Church, other Christian bodies, and the synagogues of America with their silence and cowardice in the face of our country's crimes. We are convinced that the religious bureaucracy in this country is racist, is an accomplice in this war, and is hostile to the poor."

They were arrested, jailed, censured by their ecclesiastical superiors, and ordered to distance themselves from further antiwar activity, an order both ignored.[59]

The Berrigan brothers did not act alone. To cite just two other examples, William Sloane Coffin organized church services at which draft-age men turned in their draft cards to him, a rabbi, and a Catholic priest, for which Sloan was arrested. Some liberal churches became sanctuaries for draft resisters and deserters, shielding them from arrest. And as might be expected, these protest actions were met with dramatically opposed reactions. One fundamentalist critic commented: "The sad spectacle is that in some cases church leaders – clergymen – who have long since departed from the authority of the Bible as God's Word, are leading in this rebellion against the laws of our land." Lay theologian William Stringfellow provided an opposing perspective, comparing their protests to those of Jesus: "I say that Jesus was, according to the testimonials of the gospels, a criminal; not a mere nonconformist, not just a protester, more than a militant, not only a dissident, not simply a dissenter, but a criminal" in his opposition to the state and to ecclesiastical authorities. In such of his activities, "Jesus was the most dangerous and reprehensible sort of criminal."[60]

As the nation entered a new decade and the war began to wind down – a peace agreement being signed in January 1973 – many on both sides of the war paused to reflect on the tumult of the past several years. Some concluded that the nation was in need, once again, of a "moral reckoning" or at least a better understanding of the toll the Vietnam War had taken on the "patriotic piety" that had reigned supreme in the United States in the immediate post-World War II era. In 1972, historian Sydney Ahlstrom observed that the "crisis of the present decade finds America's patriotic piety more seriously endangered than ever before," thus causing a kind of national nervous breakdown. "Nearly all Americans now have reason to wonder if the 'mystic chords' of memory and affection are still audible."[61]

The antiwar movement also prompted the question as to on what religious grounds it was lawful to refuse to serve in the military called to fight in the Vietnam War, or to obtain conscientious objector status? During the early years of the war, one had to be a member of a denomination whose pacifist doctrines were well established, like the Mennonites, Moravians, or Quakers. Could it be made available to a member of a religious organization that had not established itself as pacifist? Were one's personally held religious beliefs that were not associated with a particular faith sufficient? Could one seek exemption from fighting in a particular war, as opposed to all wars? The answers to these questions may have begun at the local draft board level, but inevitably, they ended up before the United States Supreme Court.

Basic to the Court's actions in the series of cases that came its way was its interpretation of the Congress's language employed in the Universal Military Training and Service Act of 1948 and the Selective Service Act of 1967 and its application to matters of individual conscience. In 1965, in *United States v. Seeger*, the court sought to interpret that passage wherein Congress limited exemption from the military draft to "those persons who by reason of their religious training and belief are conscientiously opposed to participation in war in any form." The court considered three cases involving claims of conscientious objectors, which raised the meaning of the phrase "religious training and belief" as it related to "an individual's belief in a relation to a Supreme Being involving duties superior to those arising from any human relation, excluding political, sociological, or philosophical views or a merely personal moral code." The court held that the term "Supreme Being" meant "the concept of a power or being, or a faith, to which all else is subordinate or upon which all else is ultimately dependent." And from that definition, it established that the test that qualified a person for an exemption is whether the individual holds "a sincere and meaningful belief that occupied in the life of its possessor a place parallel to that filled by the God of those admittedly qualifying for the exemption." In that particular case, the court concluded all of the plaintiffs satisfied this test for conscientious objector status.[62]

There were no dissenting judges in *Seeger*, but five years later, in *Welsh v. United States*, some members of the court began to demure. The case raised the question as to how broadly the term conscience could be applied. Did a person's appeal for conscientious objector status have to have a religious base? Welsh specifically indicated that his objection was not rooted in religious belief. He responded, "No" where the questionnaire asked if he believed in a supreme being, whereupon an appeal board rejected his application and the appeal process began, which raised further questions along the way: Could a person object to a particular war, or must it be to all wars? And how and where was the line to be drawn between the requirements of national interest and the protections of free exercise of religion? In a 5 to 3 decision, the court ruled that people should be exempted from military service if their "consciences, spurred by deeply held moral, ethical, or religious beliefs, would give them no rest or peace if they allowed themselves to become a part of an instrument of war."[63]

In 1971, the court equivocated even further. In *Gillette v. United States*, the court addressed the limits to which dissent could be applied by someone seeking conscientious objector status. In this case, the plaintiffs claimed exemptions from military service because of their conscientious objection to participation in the Vietnam conflict, as an unjust war. They also challenged the law as it was construed to cover only objectors to all wars, as violating the Free Exercise and Establishment of Religion Clauses of the First Amendment. One of the two plaintiffs further based his objection on the grounds of religious objection to what he as a Catholic referred to as "unjust killings." The court ruled against the plaintiffs, holding that the exemption for those who oppose "participation in war in any form" applies only to those who oppose participating in all wars and not to those who object to participation in a particular war, even if the latter objection is religious in character. It also found that the selective service acts did not violate the Establishment Clause of the First Amendment. In presenting the opinion of the court in its 8 to 1 decision, Justice Thurgood Marshall observed that the nation had to be careful to see that those drafted for military service are not chosen "unfairly or capriciously," or else "a mood of bitterness and cynicism might corrode the spirit of public service." Unfortunately that mood of bitterness and cynicism had already set in.[64]

"New" religious movements

The United States has been a religiously diverse nation from its founding, but that diversity reached new heights after 1965, largely, but not exclusively, because of the proliferation of different indigenous religious groups but also due to the increased number of immigrant religions neither Western nor Christian. The Immigration and Naturalization Act of 1965 abolished an earlier quota system dating to the 1920s that was based on national origin and favored those nations already represented in the United States, mainly Western European countries.[65]

In 1965, Americans of Asian ancestry made up less than 1 percent of the nation's total population. By 2000, the percentage reached roughly 3 percent. Many were Protestant or Catholic, but many more brought their Asian faiths with them, including Buddhists, Taoists, Confucians, Muslims, Hindus, Jains, and Sikhs. By 2000, Hinduism, the third largest of the world religions after Christianity and Islam, counted more than 1 million adherents and 200 temples and sites in the United States. Sikhs and Jains accounted for 80 temples and centers, and 60 temples and centers, respectively. Similarly, the number of Buddhists began to grow dramatically in the 1960s and 1970s, with Nichiren Shoshu and then Soka Gakkai International-USA leading the way attracting both Asian immigrants and American converts. Tibetan and Japanese Buddhists introduced new forms in the 1970s in the Rocky Mountain Dharma Center in Boulder, Colorado. Among Asian religions, Buddhism's attractiveness to Americans was second to none, especially among the cultural elite and the young. That particular part of the movement began in earnest in the 1950s among writers of the Beat Generation and into the 1960s among those of the counterculture. Today, Soka Gakkai International-USA clams between 100,000 and 300,000 members and estimates that only one-quarter of its members are Asian.[66]

These Asian religions not only established themselves among the many existing Western religions, but they also inspired creative variations among countercultural spiritual seekers, who were disillusioned with traditional Western religions. For example, since the 1960s, Hinduism inspired such diverse movements as the Transcendental Meditation of the Maharishi Mahesh Yogi, who arrived in the United States in 1959 with teachings based on the Indian spiritual books, the *Upanishads*, and the ashram of Bhagwan Shree Rajneesh in Antelope, Oregon, in the 1980s. Similarly Hindu meditation and chanting became central to the International Society for Krishna Consciousness (Hare Krishnas as believers were known), which became popular in the US during the 1990s. All three of these groups had significant numbers of Americans.[67]

Hindus and Buddhists were not universally welcomed, of course. Nativist resistance raised its head from time to time. And so it was among the other large immigrant religious group, the Muslims, who experienced even more deep seated and heated opposition. Although present in America in small numbers from its colonial period, the final three decades of the twentieth century saw the greatest expansion of Muslims in America. From 1967 to 1997, approximately 2.8 million people immigrated to the United States from areas of the world with significant Muslim populations. Because the government does not require people to reveal their religious affiliation, it is not known exactly how many of these immigrants were

Muslims. One demographer estimates that 1.1 million were Muslim and that of them about 327,000 came from Arabic-speaking countries in North Africa and the Middle East and approximately 316,000 from South Asia, the rest from scattered locations around the globe. Estimates of the number of Muslims in the country at the end of the century vary, but it most likely hovered around 5 million, an estimated 40 percent of whom were African Americans. The number of Islamic centers, mosques, and schools reached about 1,000.[68]

Although much smaller, other groups of foreign origin – occasionally described as "Asian spirituality in American dress" – deserve brief mention here, as they became popular in the closing decades of the twentieth century. The appeal of each to Americans during that period is readily apparent. First there was Baha'i, which was founded in the nineteenth century in Persia by Baha'u'llah. From there, the religion spread into Europe and America. By the best estimates, the number of Baha'i in the United States was 150,000 by the end of the twentieth century.[69]

The Bhagwan Shree Rajneesh, an Indian from the Jain tradition, created an ashram (spiritual community) in Poona, India, where unlike most other such movements, he encouraged members not to renounce the material world, but rather to seek holiness within it through meditation and ritual dancing. Members wore orange robes and a string of 108 wooden beads, and carried pictures of the Bhagwan. He moved to the United States in 1981 and bought a 64,000-acre ranch near Antelope, Oregon, which he named Rajneeshpuram. Some 5,000 followers, mostly Americans, soon joined him and engaged in building a community that blended spiritual and hedonistic fulfillment. The Bhagwan's open display of his great wealth, which included ninety-three Rolls-Royces, got him into some difficulty. But it should also be noted that he encouraged the homeless and beggars to join him.[70]

By one account, 184 new religious organizations were founded in the 1960s. Many were inspired by Asian beliefs, but others were not. One such movement, the Jesus Movement (its members variously known as the Jesus People or Jesus Freaks), which consisted of several similar but independent groups, did not reject Christianity but instead embraced it and sought to transform it in such manner as to make it more compatible with the 1960s, or some would say hippie, lifestyle. There was the Haight-Ashbury Living Room, a storefront ministry and coffeehouse run by evangelist Ted Wise, and the Berkeley Episcopal priest, Richard York, who led a Christian Hippie Happening on the Feast of the Blessed Virgin Mary, involving religious rituals; rock music; foot washing; and balloons labeled "love," "peace," and "Mary."[71]

One of the larger, more formally organized, and at times highly controversial groups associated with the Jesus Movement, was the Children of God, founded in 1968 by a former Baptist minister, David Berg. Composed largely of hippies, it called for a spiritual revolution and a return to the faith of the early Christians. Their sackcloth vigils, enthusiastic demonstrations against the evils of war and injustice, and active missionary efforts attracted considerable media coverage and press. By 1977, there were reportedly 741 Children of God communities in 73 countries. But in the following year, reports of serious misconduct on the part of several of its leaders persuaded Berg to disband the Children of God and reorganize as the Family and soon thereafter the Family International.[72]

Still another group of new religions in this period were those commonly grouped under the heading New Age religions, including Arica, a human potential movement founded in 1968 by Bolivian-born Oscar Ichazo and incorporated in the United States in 1971; EST, or Erhard Seminars Training, intended "to transform one's ability to experience living so that the situations one had been trying to change or had been putting up with, clear up just in the process of life itself"; Raelism, a UFO religion founded in 1974 by Claude Vorilhon, who believed that life on Earth was scientifically created by a species of extraterrestrials; and the Church Universal and Triumphant, founded in 1975 by Elizabeth Clare Prophet, who claimed to be in constant communion with God and whose doctrine, Path of Personal Christhood, taught that one's salvation could be found through a one-on-one relationship with God.[73]

Wicca, also referred to as witchcraft, combined several ancient and twentieth-century concepts. Highly decentralized with an array of beliefs and rituals, some common elements include the worship of both a god and goddess; among Dianic Wiccans, the goddess rules supreme. Reference is often made to the ritual practice of magic or casting spells, but most practitioners prefer to define it as the ability to influence the forces of nature and insist such abilities are to be used only for positive ends. Wicca is commonly confused with Satanism, which neither subscribes to the tenets of Wicca nor, despite what its name implies, encourages the worship of Satan in the Judeo-Christian sense of doing the will of Satan in the world. This common misperception led to the "Satanic Panic," of the 1980s with its numerous high-profile revelations of "satanic activities," many including children, which either proved to be groundless or unrelated to the Church of Satan. Rather, as most notably practiced in the Church of Satan, founded by Anton LaVey in San Francisco in 1966, it is best understood as a hedonistic, social Darwinistic, and mostly libertarian belief system, which encourages its followers to seek personal success in whatever area they choose without regard to the dictates of society. It values meritocracy but does not encourage doing harm to others.[74]

The anticult movement

The appearance of so many new religious groups in so short a period of time caused considerable alarm in many quarters, testing yet again as had happened many times in American history, the limits of religious freedom and pluralism. What resulted was the rise of an anticult network in the 1970s that challenged these new religions in various ways and heightened vigilance on the part of authorities as to violations of the law of which any of these new movements might be guilty. Some of the anticult groups, assuming that members were being brainwashed, abducted family members and friends and engaged deprogrammers to allow them to think "independently." One such group was the Citizens' Freedom Foundation, established in 1974, later called the Cult Awareness Network. Some of these cases proved highly controversial. In several cases, however, these new religious groups played into the fears held by many Americans.[75]

One of the most extreme of such episodes was the mass suicides in 1978 of over 900 followers of Jim Jones in Jonestown, Guyana. Jones founded the People's Temple Full Gospel Church in Indianapolis, Indiana, in 1955 and in 1965 moved the group to Redwood Valley, California, and then to San Francisco. The People's Temple combined an intense pentecostal Christianity with a racially inclusive communal lifestyle and socialist orientation dedicated to racial justice. As such it shared much with the counterculture and civil rights movement of the period. But Jones became increasingly more extreme in his claims – that he could raise people from the dead, and that he was the embodiment of God, for example – more authoritarian in his governance, and his religious vison more apocalyptic and paranoid. In 1977, when the *San Francisco Examiner* published a series of articles critical of Jones, and Jones became convinced that California authorities were going to investigate Peoples Temple, he moved it to Guyana, in South America. In November 1978, California Congressman Leo Ryan and others flew to Guyana to investigate the compound. When Ryan attempted to leave, taking with him fourteen members who wanted to return to the United States, Jones had Ryan and four others killed. The same day, Jones led the over 900 of the commune's numbers to commit suicide by drinking cyanide-poisoned Kool Aid. As Jones told his followers: "The time has come for us to meet in another place."[76]

The Jonestown massacre was followed in the early 1980s by charges brought against Sun Myung Moon, leader of the Unification Church. Moon, a Korean Christian, in his book, *The Divine Principle* (1957), foresaw the coming of the "Lord of the Second Advent," which his followers concluded, with the not-so-subtle encouragement of their leader, was the Reverend Moon. Founded in South Korea in 1954, church missionaries arrived in the United States in 1959 followed by Moon's moving there in 1971. Within a few years, he attracted thousands of followers, as well as the critical attention of deprogrammers and the press. In 1982, Moon was found guilty of income tax evasion and was forced to leave the country. In 1994, Moon declared that the era of the Unification Church had ended and inaugurated The Family Federation for World Peace and Unification.[77]

The next major alarm for the anticult forces was sounded in Waco, Texas, in 1993, when government authorities, investigating charges of child abuse and other alleged crimes, surrounded the Branch Davidian compound but were held at bay. Negotiations with the leader David Koresh stretched on for 51 days at which point federal agents laid siege to the compound, which caught fire and caused the death of 74 members, including 21 children.[78]

The anticult movement, or even wider sense of concern on the part of the general public, continued to raise alarms as to many of the new religious movements. Some successfully defended themselves, but many were forced to break up and flee the country. A few leaders were jailed for various offenses, and other groups pulled back with a much lower public profile. For these and other reasons, mostly because their appeal was short-lived, many of the new religious movements that formed in the 1960s and 1970s did not survive. But some that were really new only in their late arrival in the United States continued to flourish, further changing the religious landscape, Hinduism, Buddhism, and Islam being the most notable of this group. In the 1980s, however, conservatives struck back.

Summary

The 1960s proved to be revolutionary, as just about every aspect of life in America – social, cultural, political, economic, and religious – was challenged by one segment of the population or another. It was not, as commonly assumed, an entirely youth-oriented movement, but rather one that engaged several different entities including the young and old, African Americans, Mexican Americans, feminists, gay rights advocates, Native Americans, environmentalists, advocates for new religious movements, and still others. The 1960s began with the election of the nation's first Roman Catholic President, who announced that "the torch [of leadership] had been passed to a new generation." That new generation would lead the civil rights movement to a more extreme, less clergy guided, Black Power Movement. It would energize Catholic and Protestant religious leaders to support the United Farm Workers Movement led by the Cesar Chavez. It would gain control of a renewed Native American civil rights movement that largely through the Native American Church fought for self-determination in many areas, including religion. It would provide a new generation of leaders who would continue the fight for women's and gay rights, take up the cause of environmentalism, oppose US involvement in the Vietnam War, and turn their backs on traditional Western religions and seek greater spiritual satisfaction in new religious movements. As pointed out in this chapter, all of the preceding reforms involved significant religious involvement and challenges to the dominant, mainstream religions in America. By the end of the 1970s, however, the major American denominations remained in place, if shaken, only to then face the counterforce of conservative reaction.

Review questions

1   The 1960s and 1970s have been described as revolutionary. Why and how does that term apply to religion?
2   The Roman Catholic Church's ardent anticommunism in the 1950s, the Presidential Election of 1960, and Vatican II are often credited with ushering in a new era for Catholics in America. Explain why that was the case.
3   The civil rights movement began in the 1950s, but it escalated and changed in the 1960s and 1970s. How did it change and how did that change affect the role of religion in that movement?
4   From the many "revolutionary" movements of the 1960s and 1970s, select three and explain the role religion played in each.
5   Discuss the various "new" religious movements of the 1960s and 1970s, how they came about, and their impact on the American religious landscape.

Notes

1   Martin E. Marty, *Modern American Religion: Under God Indivisible, 1941–1960* (Chicago: University of Chicago Press, 1996), excerpt from Robert R. Mathisen, *Critical Issues in American Religious History: A Reader*, 2nd rev. edn. (Waco, TX: Baylor University Press, 2006), 650–66.
2   Edwin Gaustad and Leigh Schmidt, *The Religious History of America: The Heart of the American Story from Colonial Times to Today*, rev. edn. (New York: HarperSanFrancisco, 2012), 344; Jon Butler, Grant Wacker, and Randall Balmer, *Religion in American Life: A Short History*, 2nd edn. (New York: Oxford University Press, 2011), 364–5; Patrick Allitt, *Religion in America: since 1945* (New York: Columbia University Press, 2003), 66; Mark Silk, *Spiritual Politics: Religion and America since World War II* (New York: Simon and Schuster, 1988), 123–4.
3   Grant Wacker, *America's Pastor: Billy Graham and the Shaping of a Nation* (Cambridge, MA: The Belknap Press, 2014), 207–8; Marshall Frady, *Billy Graham, a Parable of American Righteousness* (Boston: Little, Brown, 1979), 442–3; Billy Graham, *Just As I Am: The Autobiography of Billy Graham* (San Francisco: HarperSanFrancisco, 1997), 391.
4   Shaun Casey, *The Making of a Catholic President: Kennedy vs. Nixon 1960* (New York: Oxford University Press, 2009), 135–44, 375, note 33; Gaustad and Schmidt, *The Religious History of America*, 363–4; Wacker, *America's Pastor*, 100, 208; Graham, *Just As I Am*, 392; For an example of an anti-Kennedy statement that came out during the campaign, see James Pike, *A Catholic in the White House* (Garden City, NY: Doubleday, 1960).
5   John C. Bennett, "A Roman Catholic for President?," *Christianity and Crisis*, 20 (March 7, 1960): 117–19.
6   John Cooney, *The American Pope: The Life and Times of Francis Cardinal Spellman* (New York: Times Books, 1984), 255–6, 266–7, 278–80; Allitt, *Religion in America*, 65–6. Martin Marty described Kennedy as "spiritually rootless and politically almost disturbingly secular: Lawrence Fuchs, *John F. Kennedy and American Catholicism* (New York; Meredith, 1967), 168.
7   Gaustad and Schmidt, *The Religious History of America*, 345. See Paul Johnson, *Pope John XXIII* (Boston: Little, Brown, 1974).
8   Gaustad and Schmidt, *The Religious History of America*, 345–6.

9 Gaustad and Schmidt, *The Religious History of America*, 347–8; Butler, *Religion in American Life*, 366–71; Silk, *Spiritual Politics*, 123. See also Vincent Yzermans, *American Participation in the Second Vatican Council* (New York: Sheed & Ward, 1967).

10 Silk, *Spiritual Politics*, 111–15; Martin Luther King, Jr., *Why We Can't Wait* (New York: New American Library, 1964), 59, 61; John C. Bennett, "Two Revivals," *Christianity and Crisis* (December 28, 1959), 192; "Constitution of the Student Nonviolent Coordinating Committee, Originally Adopted in 1960 and Revised in 1962," in *Nonviolence in America: A Documentary History*, ed. Staughton Lynd (New York: Bobbs – Merrill Co., 1966), 398–9.

11 Martin Luther King, Jr., "Pilgrimage to Nonviolence," *The Christian Century*, 77 (March 14, 1960): 41.

12 Martin Luther King, Jr., "Letter from Birmingham Jail," reprinted in Milton C. Sernette, ed., *Afro-American Religious History: A Documentary Witness* (Durham, NC: Duke University Press, 1985), 431, 441–3.

13 King is quoted in David Garrow, *Bearing the Cross: Martin Luther King, Jr. and the Southern Christian Leadership Conference* (1986; rpt. New York: Vintage Books, 1988), 283–4. For a more detailed analysis of King's speech, see Allitt, *Religion in America*, 54–5. On incidents of violence, see Allitt, *Religion in America*, 55; and Leonard Dinnerstein, *Antisemitism in America* (New York: Oxford University Press, 1994), 192.

14 National Conference of Black Churchmen, "Black Power Statement," July 31, 1966, in *Black Theology: A Documentary History, 1966–1979*, ed. Gayraud Wilmore and James H. Cone (Maryknoll, NY: Orbis Press, 1979), 24, 27; James Forman, "The Black Manifesto," in *Black Theology*, ed. Wilmore and Cone, 82–4; Allitt, *Religion in America*, 112–13.

15 James Cone, "The White Church and Black Power," *Black Theology and Black Power*, ed. James Cone (1969), reprinted in Wilmore and Cone, *Black Theology*, 117. See also James Cone, *A Black Theology of Liberation* (Philadelphia: Lippincott, 1970), 59–60; Alex Haley, *Autobiography of Malcolm X* (1964; rpt. New York: Ballantine Books, 1978), 195.

16 Butler, *Religion in American Life*, 374; Haley, *Autobiography of Malcolm X*, 165–6; Allitt, *Religion in America*, 56–8; For the complete list of Black Muslim demands see Charles Eric Lincoln, *Assuring Freedom to the Free*, ed. Arnold M. Rose (Detroit, MI: Wayne State University Press, 1964), excerpt from Mathisen, *Critical Issues in American Religious History*, 699–701. For more on the Nation of Islam, see also Michael A. Gomez, *Black Crescent: The Experience and Legacy of African Muslim in America* (New York: Cambridge University Press, 2005), 276–330.

17 George Breitman, ed., *Malcolm X Speaks: Selected Speeches and Statements* (1965; rpt. New York: Pathfinder, 1989), 113. Malcolm X is quoted in George B. Tindall and David E. Shi, *America: A Narrative History* (New York: Norton, 1996), 153–4; Spike is quoted in Silk, *Spiritual Politics*, 128–30. See also William Stringfellow, *My People Is the Enemy: An Autobiographical Polemic* (New York: Holt, Rinehart and Winston, 1964), 139; Gomez, *Black Crescent*, 331–75; Edward E. Curtis, IV, *Muslims in America: A Short History* (New York: Oxford University Press, 2009), 64–6, 78–9. For more on the Black Muslim experience, see Edward E. Curtis, IV, *Black Muslim Religion in the Nation of Islam, 1960–1975* (Chapel Hill: University of North Carolina Press, 2006); Robert Dannin, *Black Pilgrimage to Islam* (New York Oxford University Press, 2002); and Richard Brent Turner, *Islam in the African-American Experience*, 2nd edn. (Bloomington: Indiana University Press, 2003).

18 Rodolfo Acuna, *Occupied America; A History of Chicanos*, 3rd edn. (New York: Harper & Row, 1988), 298–9, 320, 354.

19 "Cesar Chavez Grows Up." www.americaslibrary.gov/aa/chavez/aa_chavez_growup_1.html; "The Story of Cesar Chavez." www.ufw.org/_page.php?inc=history/07.html&menu=research; Rick Tejada-Flores, "The Fight in the Fields – Cesar Chavez and the Farmworkers Struggle." www.pbs.org/itvs/fightfields/cesarchavez.html; Acuna, *Occupied America*, 325, 355; Miriam Pawell, *The Crusades of Cesar Chavez: A Biography* (New York: Bloomsbury Press, 2014), 27–9.

20 Acuna, *Occupied America*, 325.

21 Chavez actively opposed the Bracero program, which began during World War II and ended in 1964, by which the US and Mexico entered into an agreement to allow Mexican workers to enter the US temporarily to fill unskilled labor positions. He saw this as a threat to his unionization activities among resident Mexican Americans. For the same reason, he also discouraged illegal immigration from Mexico; or when they were already in the United States, he tried to dissuade them from

taking farm workers' jobs at lower wages or as strike breakers. Acuna, *Occupied America*, 261–8, 326–7; Richard W. Etulain, *Cesar Chavez: A Brief Biography with Documents* (New York: Palgrave Macmillan, 2002), 18; Gregory Dunne, *Delano* (New York: Farrar, Straus & Giroux, 1967), 51, 144–8; Ronald B. Taylor, *Chavez and the Farm Workers* (Boston: Beacon Press, 1975), 157, 287. See also Sam Kushner, *Long Road to Delano* (New York: International Publishers, 1975), and Susan Ferriss and Ricardo Sandoval, *The Fight in the Fields: Cesar Chavez and the Farmworkers Movement* (New York: Harcourt Brace & Company, 1997).

22 Stephen R. Lloyd-Moffett, "The Mysticism and Social Action of Cesar Chavez," in *Latino Religions and Civic Activism in the United States*, ed. Gaston Espinoza, Virgilio Elizando, and Jesse Miranda (New York: Oxford University Press, 2005), 35–6; Pierrette Hondagneu-Sotelo, "Religious Reenactment on the Line," in *Religion and Social Justice for Immigrants*, ed. Pierrette Hondagneu-Sotelo (New Brunswick, NJ: Rutgers University Press, 2007), 124, 131, citing John C. Hammerback and Richard J. Jensen, *The Rhetorical Career of Cesar Chavez* (College Station: Texas A & M University Press); Alan J. Watt, *Farm Workers and the Churches: The Movement in California and Texas* (College Station: Texas A & M University Press, 2010), 2–3, 82–8.

23 Ronald A. Wells, "Cesar Chavez's Protestant Allies: The California Migrant Ministry and the Farm Workers," *Journal of Presbyterian History*, 87 (Spring/Summer 2009): 7, 14; Chavez is quoted in Winthrop Yinger, *Cesar Chavez: The Rhetoric of Nonviolence* (Hicksville, NY: Exposition Press, 1975), 33.

24 Hondagneu-Sotelo, "Religious Reenactment on the Line," 135; Watt, *Farm Workers and the Churches*, 5, 27–30, 117–21, and elsewhere in passing; Pat Hoffman, *Ministry of the Dispossessed: Learning from the Farm Workers Movement* (Los Angeles: Wallace Press, 1987), viii; Sydney D. Smith, *Grapes of Conflict* (Pasadena, CA: Hope Publishing Company, 1987), 2. Hartmire is quoted in Wells, "Cesar Chavez's Protestant Allies," 8; The *Time* magazine story on Chavez was reprinted on April 8, 1968, and can be found here: www.americanrhetoric.com/speeches/cesarchavezspeech mexicanamerican&church.htm

25 Joane, Nagel, *American Indian Ethnic Renewal: Red Power and the Resurgence of Identity and Culture* (New York: Oxford University Press, 1996), 5.

26 Nagel, *American Indian Ethnic Renewal*, 6, 10; Peter Matthiessen, *In the Spirit of Crazy Horse: The FBI's War against the American Indian Movement* (New York: Penguin Group, 1992), 28, 34; Dennis Banks and Richard Erdoes, *Ojibwa Warrior: Dennis Banks and the Rise of the American Indian Movement* (Norman: University of Oklahoma Press, 2004), 62–4; Paul Chaat Smith and Robert Allen Warrior, *Like a Hurricane: The Indian Movement from Alcatraz to Wounded Knee* (New York: The New Press, 1997), 127–48.

27 Nagel, *American Indian Ethnic Renewal*, viii; Smith and Warrior, *Like a Hurricane*, 20–35, 149–68, 194–268; "Twenty Points" (American Indian Movement Website). www.aimovement.org/ archives/index.html; Matthiessen, *In the Spirit of Crazy Horse*, 55, 256–7, 446–51, 464. For more on AIM, see Rex Weyler, *Blood of the Land; The Government and Corporate War against the American Indian Movement* (New York: Random House, 1982).

28 Vine Deloria, Jr., *Custer Died for Your Sins: An Indian Manifesto* (New York: Macmillan, 1969), 2, 101–242, 167, 243, 246, 248, 263; James Treat, *Around the Sacred Fire: Native Religious Activism in the Red Power Era, a Narrative Map of the Indian Ecumenical Conference* (New York: Palgrave Macmillan, 2003), 152–3, 257–90; Vine Deloria, Jr., *God is Red: A Native View of Religion* (Golden, CO: North American Press, 1992), 54.

29 Smith and Warrior, *Like a Hurricane*, 10; Gaustad and Schmidt, *The Religious History of America*, 371.

30 Omer C. Stewart, *Peyote Religion: A History* (Norman: University of Oklahoma Press, 1987), 128–209, 213–38; Carolyn N. Long, *Religious Freedom and Indian Rights: The Case of Oregon v. Smith* (Lawrence: University Press of Kansas, 2000), 11–6; Catherine L. Albanese, *America: Religions and Religion*, 4th edn. (Belmont, CA: Thomson Wadsworth, 2007), 35.

31 Long, *Religious Freedom and Indian Rights*, 17–20; Gaustad and Schmidt, *The Religious History of America*, 371–2; "*People v. Woody*," in Mathisen, *Critical Issues in American Religious History*, 742–5; David H. Getches, Charles F. Wilkinson, and Robert A. Williams, *Cases and Material on Federal Indian Law*, 5th edn. (Eagan, MN: West Group, 1998), 764; Brian Edward Brown, *Religion, Law, and the Land: Native Americans and the Judicial Interpretations of Sacred Land* (Westport, CT: Greenwood Press, 1999), 6–7; N. Bruce Duthu, *American Indians and the Law*

(New York: The Penguin Group, 2008), 110; Francis Paul Prucha, *The Great Father: The United States Government and the American Indians* (Lincoln: University of Nebraska Press, 1985), II: 1127; Albanese, *America*, 37.

32 Albanese, *America*, 37. The case brought by Galen Black, Smith's coworker – *Black v. Employment Division* – was joined with *Employment Division v. Smith* and heard simultaneously and covered by the same decision. Huston Smith, *Why Religion Matters: The Fate of the Human Spirit in An Age of Disbelief* (New York: Harper Collins, 2001), 124; Paul W. Kahn, *Putting Liberalism in Its Place* (Princeton, NJ: Princeton University Press, 2005), 76.

33 Smith, *Why Religion Matters*, 126–7; Long, *Religious Freedom and Indian Rights*, 203–50; 103 D Cong., US Government Printing Office, Washington, DC: *1994 Congressional Record 10* (1994); or 103rd Congress, H.R. 4155, Library of Congress Website. http://thomas.loc.gov/cgi-bin/query/z?c103:H.R.4230.Enr

34 Long, *Religious Freedom and Indian Rights*, 251–76; Robert S. Alley, *The Constitution and Religion: Leading Supreme Court Cases on Church and State* (Amherst, NY: Prometheus Books, 1999), 515–35. National Conference of State Legislatures, "State Religious Freedom Acts." www.ncsl.org/research/civil-and-criminal-justice/state-rfra-statutes.aspx

35 Betty Friedan, *The Feminine Mystique* (New York: W. W. Norton, 1963).

36 For a more detailed summary of the Court's decision, see www.lawnix.com/cases/roe-wade.html. See also N.E.H. Hull and Peter Charles Hoffer, *Roe v. Wade: The Abortion Rights Controversy in American History*, 2nd edn. (Lawrence: University Press of Kansas, 2010).

37 Gaustad and Schmidt, *The Religious History of America*, 385–7; Allitt, *Religion in America since 1945*, 122; Sally McFague, *Models of God: Theology for an Ecological Nuclear Age* (Philadelphia, PA: Fortress Press, 1987), 169; Susan Hill Lindley, *You Have Stept Out of Your Place: A History of Women and Religion in America* (Louisville, KY: Westminster Press, 1996), 428.

38 Allitt, *Religion in America since 1945*, 122–3.

39 Gaustad and Schmidt, *The Religious History of America*, 388–92; Allitt, *Religion in America since 1945*, 123–5. Harris, who was also African American, was ordained Bishop Saffragan of the Episcopal Diocese of Massachusetts on February 11, 1989.

40 Gaustad and Schmidt, *The Religious History of America*, 389.

41 Quoted in Rosemary Ruether, "Entering the Sanctuary: The Roman Catholic Story," in *Women of Spirit: Female Leadership in the Jewish and Christian Traditions*, ed. Rosemary Ruether and Eleanor McLaughlin (New York: Simon and Schuster/Touchstone, 1979), 375; Lindley, *You Have Stept Out of Your Place*, 429; Allitt, *Religion in America since 1945*, 126–7.

42 Allitt, *Religion in America since 1945*, 127; Lindley, *You Have Stept Out of Your Place*, 426; Carol Christ and Judith Plaskow, *Womanspirit Rising: A Feminist Reader in Religion* (New York: HarperCollins, 1979), 1–18. See also Anne M. Clifford, *Introducing Feminist Theology* (Maryknoll, NY: Orbis, 2001) and Judith Plaskow and Carol P. Christ, eds., *Weaving the Vision: New Patterns in Feminist Spirituality* (San Francisco, CA: Harper & Row, 1989).

43 Rosemary Ruether, "Christian Feminist Theology," in *Daughters of Abraham: Feminist Thought in Judaism, Christianity, and Islam*, ed. Yvonne Y. Haddad and John L. Esposito (Gainesville: University of Florida Press, 2001), 66–7; Rosemary Ruether, *Sexism and God Talk* (Boston: Beacon, 1983), 136; Phyllis Trible, "Feminist Hermeneutics and Biblical Studies," in *Feminist Theology: A Reader*, ed. Ann Loades (Louisville: Westminster/John Knox, 199), 25. See also Phyllis Trible, *God and the Rhetoric of Sexuality* (Philadelphia, PA: Fortress, 1978), 95–9; as well as Elizabeth Johnson, *She Who Is: The Mystery of God in Feminist Theological Discourse* (New York: Crossroad, 1992) and Elisabeth Schussler Fiorenza, *Jesus: Miriam's Child, Sophia's Prophet: Critical Issues in Feminist Theology* (New York: Continuum, 1994).

44 Alice Walker, *In Search of Our Mothers' Gardens* (San Diego: Harcourt Brace Jovanovich, 1983), xi–xii; Lindley, *You Have Stept Out of Your Place*, 426–7. For an example of a womanist who was critical of black male liberation theology, see Delores S. Williams, *Sisters in the Wilderness: The Challenge of Womanist God-Talk* (Maryknoll, NY: Orbis Books, 1993), 179–99. See also Jacquelyn Grant, *White Women's Christ and Black Women's Jesus: Feminist Christology and Womanist Response* (Atlanta, GA: Scholars Press, 1989); and Ada Maria Isasi-Diaz and Yolanda Tarango, *Hispanic Women: Prophetic Voice in the Church* (San Francisco, CA: Harper & Row, 1988); Allitt, *Religion in America since 1945*, 131, summarized from Mary Daly, *Beyond God the Father: Toward a Philosophy of a Women's Liberation* (1973; rpt. Boston: Beacon, 1985), 195–6.

45 Roderick Frazier Nash, *The Rights of Nature: A History of Environmental Ethics* (Madison: The University of Wisconsin Press, 1989), 102; Evan Berry has argued that "the roots of environmentalism grew in religious soil" in his *Devoted to Nature: The Religious Roots of American Environmentalism* (Berkeley: University of California Press, 2015), 4.
46 Lynn L. White, Jr., "The Historical Roots of Our Ecological Crisis," *Science*, 155 (March 10, 1967): 1203–7.
47 Gaustad and Schmidt, *The Religious History of America*, 401. See also Francis A. Schaeffer, *Pollution and the Death of Man* (1970; rpt. Wheaton, IL: Crossway, 2011); Allitt, *Religion in America since 1945*, 225; Robert B. Fowler, *The Greening of Protestant Thought* (Chapel Hill: University of North Carolina Press, 1995), 43.
48 Patrick Allitt, "American Catholics and the Environment," *Catholic Historical Review*, 84 (1998): 277; Russell Chandler, "Religions Join the Crusade to Save Earth from Pollution," *Los Angeles Times* (April 19, 1990): A3; Allitt, *Religion in America since 1945*, 220–1.
49 Michael Barkey, ed., *Environmental Stewardship in the Judeo-Christian Tradition: Jewish, Catholic, and Protestant Wisdom on the Environment* (Grand Rapids, MI: Acton Institute, 2000), xiv.
50 Mary Beth Norton, David M Katzman, David W. Blight, Howard P. Chudacoff, Fredrik Logevall, Beth Bailey, Thomas G. Paterson, and William M. Tuttle, Jr., *A People and a Nation: A History of the United States*, 7th edn. (Boston: Houghton Mifflin Company, 2005), 2: 867. Annual (Gay) Pride Parades, held in late June recall the Stonewall Riot, as it is known. For more on the Gay Rights Movement, see John D'Emilio and Estelle Freedman, *Intimate Matters: A History of Sexuality in America*, 3rd edn. (Chicago, IL: University of Chicago Press, 2012) and Marc Stein, *Rethinking the Gay and Lesbian Movement* (New York: Routledge, 2012).
51 "Walking in Truth" (editorial), *Christianity Today* (September 4, 2000): 46–7; Allitt, *Religion in America since 1945*, 236.
52 Allitt, *Religion in America since 1945*, 234–6.
53 Gaustad and Schmidt, *The Religious History of America*, 383–4; Allitt, *Religion in America since 1945*, 234.
54 See, for example: Robert Goss, *Jesus Acted Up: A Gay and Lesbian Manifesto* (San Francisco, CA: HarperSanFrancisco, 1993), 85; Allitt, *Religion in America since 1945*, 235–8.
55 Allitt, *Religion in America since 1945*, 238–9; Gary D. Comstock, *Unrepentant, Self-Affirming, Practicing: Lesbian/Bisexual/Gay People within Organized Religion* (New York: Continuum, 1996), 14.
56 Allitt, *Religion in America since 1945*, 238; Gaustad and Schmidt, *The Religious History of America*, 385.
57 Raymond Haberski, Jr., *God and War: American Civil Religion since 1945* (New Brunswick, NJ: Rutgers University Press, 2012), 64, 67.
58 Allitt, *Religion in America since 1945*, 101–2; Silk, *Spiritual Politics*, 148–50; Haberski, *God and War*, 66. Novak is quoted in Mitchell K. Hall, *Because of Their Faith: CALCAV and Religious Opposition to the Vietnam War* (New York: Columbia University Press, 1990), 34–55.
59 Sharon Erickson Nepstad, *Religion and War Resistance in the Plowshares Movement* (New York: Cambridge University Press, 2008), 48; Hennesey, *American Catholics*, 319; Shawn Francis Peters, *The Catonsville Nine: A Story of Faith and Resistance in the Vietnam Era* (New York: Oxford University Press, 2012), 35; Nepstad, *Religion and War Resistance in the Plowshares Movement*, 48; Francine du Plessix Gray, *Divine Disobedience: Profiles in Catholic Radicalism* (New York: Knopf, 1970), 77, 124–5, 175, 189, 199; Bernard V. Brady, *Essential Catholic Social Thought* (New York: Orbis Books, 2008), 27; Daniel Berrigan, *To Dwell in Peace* (San Francisco: Harper & Row, 1987). See also Murray Polner and Jim O'Grady, *Disarmed and Dangerous: The Radical Lives and Times of Daniel and Philip Berrigan* (New York: Basic Books, 1997) and Jerry Elmer, *Felon for Peace* (Nashville, TN: Vanderbilt University Press, 2005).
60 Allitt, *Religion in America since 1945*, 104–5; William Stringfellow and Anthony Towne, *Suspect Tenderness The Ethics of the Berrigan Witness* (New York: Holt, Rinehart and Winston, 1971), 22; Silk, *Spiritual Politics*, 152–3.
61 Sydney E. Ahlstrom, "Requiem for Patriotic Piety," *Worldview* (August 1972): 10–1; Haberski, *God and War*, 83–5.
62 Law School Case Briefs, "*United States v. Seeger* Case Brief," www.lawschoolcasebriefs.net/2013/04/united-states-v-seeger-case-brief.html
63 Oyez, "*Welch v. United States*," www.oyez.org/cases/1960-1969/1969/1969_76

64 Findlaw, "*Gillette v. United States*," http://caselaw.findlaw.com/us-supreme-court/401/437.html
65 For more on the growing diversity in this period see Diana L. Eck, *A New Religious America: How a "Christian Country" Has become the World's Most Religiously Diverse Nation* (San Francisco, CA: HarperSanFrancisco, 2001) and R. Stephen Warner and Judith G. Wittner, eds., *Gatherings in Diaspora: Religious Communities and the New Immigration* (Philadelphia, PA: Temple University Press, 1998).
66 Gaustad and Schmidt, *The Religious History of America*, 413–16. See David K. Yoo, ed., *New Spiritual Homes: Religion and Asian Americans* (Honolulu, HI: University of Hawaii Press, 1999); Allitt, *Religion in America since 1945*, 141–2; Albanese, *America*, 212–14, 218–23. See Raymond Brady Williams, *Religions of Immigrants from India and Pakistan: New Threads in the American Tapestry* (Cambridge, MA: Harvard University Press, 1988). See also Jack Kerouac, *The Dharma Bums* (1958; rpt. New York: Penguin, 1976), 97–8, and Richard Hughes Seager, *Buddhism in America* (New York: Columbia University Press, 1999).
67 Gaustad and Schmidt, *The Religious History of America*, 414; Albanese, *America*, 215–18; Allitt, *Religion in America since 1945*, 140, 145; Jacob Needleman, *The New Religions: The Teachings of the East* (1970; rpt. New York: Pocket Books, 1972), 133.
68 Curtis, *Muslims in America*, 1–24, 38–9, 47–63, 67–73, 81, 86–9, 91, 122. See Allan D. Austin, *African Muslims in Antebellum America: A Sourcebook* (New York: Garland, 1984), and Sylviane A. Diouf, *Servants of Allah: African Muslims Enslaved in the Americas* (New York: New York University Press, 1998); Albanese, *America*, 209–10; Gaustad and Schmidt, *The Religious History of America*, 420. See Jane I. Smith, *Islam in America* (New York: Columbia University Press, 1999). See also Richard Brent Turner, *Islam in the African-American Experience* (Bloomington: Indiana University Press, 2003), and Robert J. Allison, *The Crescent Obscured: The United States and the Muslim World, 1776–1815* (New York: Oxford University Press, 1995).
69 Manfred Hutter, "Baha'is", in *Encyclopedia of Religion*, ed. Lindsay Jones, 2nd edn. (Detroit, MI: Macmillan Reference US, 2005), 2: 737–40. See Peter Smith, *An Introduction to the Baha'i Faith* (Cambridge, UK: Cambridge University Press, 2008); Albanese, *America*, 212.
70 Allitt, *Religion in America since 1946*, 146.
71 Allitt, *Religion in America since 1946*, 133–5.
72 Allitt, *Religion in America since 1946*, 133–7. See *The Origins of a Movement: From "The Children of God" to "The Family International."* www.thefamily.org/dossier/statements/origins.htm; William Sims Bainbridge, *The Endtime Family: Children of God* (Albany: State University of New York, 2002) and John Gordon Melton, *The Children of God, "The Family"* (Berkeley, CA: Signature Books, 2004).
73 Gaustad and Schmidt, *The Religious History of America*, 424.
74 This information is summarized from various sources, which include: Margot Adler, *Drawing Down the Moon: Witches, Druids, Goddess-Worshippers and Oher Pagans in America Today* (1979; rpt. Boston: Beacon Press, 2005); Raymond Buckland, *Witchcraft from the Inside: Origins of the Fastest Growing Religious Movement in America*, 3rd edn. (St. Paul, MN: Llewellyn Publications, 2002); Janet Farrar and Steward Farrar, *The Witches' Goddess: The Feminine Principle of Divinity* (London: Robert Hale Publishing, 1987); and James Lewis, *Witchcraft Today: An Encyclopedia of Witchcraft, Wiccan, and Neopaganism* (Greenwood, CT: ABC-CLIO, 1999). See Blanche Barton, *The Church of Satan: A History of the World's Most Notorious Religion* (New York: Hell's Kitchen Productions, 1990); Chis Mathews, *Modern Satanism: Anatomy of a Radical Subculture* (New York: Praeger Publishers, 2009); Anton Szandor LaVey, *The Satanic Rituals* (New York: Avon Books, 1972); and the official Church of Satan website: www.churchofsatan.com
75 Allitt, *Religion in America since 1946*, 144–5. For an examples of anti-cult literature, see Ted Patrick and Tom Dulack, *Let Our Children Go* (New York: Dutton, 1976).
76 Gaustad and Schmidt, *The Religious History of America*, 423; Allitt, *Religion in America since 1946*, 138–9. See John R. Hall, *Gone from the Promised Land: Jonestown in American Cultural History* (New Brunswick, NJ: Transactions Books, 1987); David Chidester, *Salvation and Suicide* (Bloomington: University of Indiana Press, 1988); and Marshall Kilduff and Ron Javers, *The Suicide Cult* (New York: Bantam Books, 1978).
77 Summarized from Eileen Barker, *The Making of a Moonie: Choice or Brainwashing?* (Oxford, UK: Blackwell's, 1984); George Chryssides, *The Advent of Sun Myung Moon: The Origins, Beliefs and Practices of the Unification Church* (London: Macmillan Professional and Academic Ltd., 1991); and Massimo Introvigne, *The Unification Church* (New York: Signature Books, 2000).

78   See James D. Tabor and Eugene V. Gallagher, *Why Waco? Cults and the Battle for Religious Freedom in America* (Berkeley: University of California Press, 1995).

Recommended for further reading

Branch, Taylor. *Pillar of Fire: America in the King Years, 1963–65.* New York: Simon & Schuster, 1998.

Curtis, Edward E. IV. *Black Muslim Religion in the Nation of Islam, 1960–1975.* Chapel Hill: University of North Carolina Press, 2006.

Daly, Mary. *Beyond God the Father: Toward a Philosophy of a Women's Liberation.* 1973; repr., Boston: Beacon, 1985.

Deloria, Vine Jr. *Custer Died for Your Sins: An Indian Manifesto.* New York: Macmillan, 1969.

Ferriss, Susan and Ricardo Sandoval. *The Fight in the Fields: Cesar Chavez and the Farmworkers Movement.* New York: Harcourt Brace & Company, 1997.

Grant, Jacquelyn. *White Women's Christ and Black Women's Jesus: Feminist Christology and Womanist Response.* Atlanta, GA: Scholars Press, 1989.

Haberski, Raymond Jr. *God and War: American Civil Religion Since 1945.* New Brunswick, NJ: Rutgers University Press, 2012.

Haley, Alex. *The Autobiography of Malcolm X.* New York: Grove Press, 1965.

Nagel, Joane. *American Indian Ethnic Renewal: Red Power and the Resurgence of Identity and Culture.* New York: Oxford University Press, 1996.

Silk, Mark. *Spiritual Politics: Religion and America Since World War II.* New York: Simon and Schuster, 1988.

Chapter 7

An equal and opposite reaction

Conservative retrenchment
in the 1980s and 1990s

The resurgence of evangelical Protestantism

Although it is also often referred to as the New Religious Right or simply the Religious Right, for our purposes we will use the term New Christian Right. The movement did include some Roman Catholics and Jews when addressing certain issues – abortion and homosexuality, for example – but it was dominated by evangelical Protestants. The evangelical right has been with us for at least two centuries, if not longer, periodically surfacing in reaction to particular causes (e.g. the Social Gospel and evolution) and just as often receding into the background and working behind the scenes. But it has never gone away, largely because its causes continually resonate with a sizable segment of the population. Moreover, the periodic resurgences have shared at least three common characteristics: Each has been dependent on the prominent role played by popular preachers who have effectively used the mass media available to them in their day. Second, again for their day, these campaigns have been sophisticated in their organization. And finally, they have found themselves – for better and worse – joined at the hip with politicians who were sympathetic to the cause or seeking to expand their voter base.[1]

The rise of the New Christian Right began with the presidential candidacy of the born-again evangelical Jimmy Carter in 1976. In 1979, a Gallup Poll found that, not only did more than 80 percent of those polled believe Jesus Christ was divine, but that as many as one in three adults polled had experienced a religious conversion and almost half believed in the inerrancy of the Bible. Other studies found that the "electric church," on which the New Christian Right would rely, consisted of 1300 radio and television stations that claimed audiences of up to 130 million and profits of from $500 million to billions. To this mix was added the appearance of large numbers of "Bible-carrying political activists," who beginning in early 1980 were seen in ever-increasing numbers at party caucuses, campaign rallies, and party conventions. By all measures, the merging of these various forces produced a powerful and influential social, cultural, and political activism.[2]

Contradicting what the media has often portrayed as its being a populist uprising, historians of the movement have found it to be much more of a top-down phenomenon. They have found that those responsible for the rise of the New Christian Right and its leadership were a mix of conservative politicians and conservative, mostly evangelical, ministers. That is not to say that the New Christian Right was not a mass movement, as the leadership was successful in mobilizing a large number of followers. Although the numbers vary, some leaders claimed that New Christian Right numbered as many as 50 million Protestants; 30 million "morally conservative" Catholics; and millions of Mormons, Orthodox Jews, and others. Others estimated that those truly committed to the movement numbered no more than hundreds of thousands but that the number varied over time as various issues came to the fore. Even if the lower numbers are closer to reality, however, its organization was formidable.[3]

Various studies have found that members of the New Christian Right were largely living in the rapidly expanding cities and suburbs of the New South, described as "the broad crescent called the Southern Rim: beginning at Virginia Beach, Virginia (home of Pat Robertson's Christian Broadcasting Network); passing through Jerry Falwell's Lynchburg, in western Virginia; and Jim and Tammy Bakker's Charlotte, North Carolina, extending on through the Bible Belt heartland to the urban frontier of the Southwest and ending in Southern California. They had only recently arrived there from smaller towns and rural areas to take advantage of the booming employment opportunities, and they were struggling to maintain rural and small town values in an increasingly urban and secular society. They tended to have college degrees, or least some college education, and were employed mostly in middle- and lower-level clerical and service positions. They saw themselves as economic conservatives, committed to free market principles and limited social services, and they were antiunion.[4]

Leaders of the New Christian Right chose a moralistic rather than an economic approach by which they hoped to lure economically marginal people away from Democratic economic liberalism – betting on moral commitments trumping economic interests. They concentrated on highly charged issues such as abortion and homosexuality, which they addressed in terms of good and evil, and characterized those for and against their position as the forces of God and forces of the devil. They targeted political office holders and candidates who, according to their "moral report cards," did not subscribe to the movement's positions on such issues, and issued "Christian action manuals" by which voters could attack them. As Paul Weyrich instructed his operatives: "Frame [these issues] in such a way that there is no mistaking who is on the right side and who is on the wrong side. Ultimately, everything can be reduced to right and wrong." Weyrich admitted that "they're emotional issues, but," he added, "that's better than talking about capital formation."[5]

Jerry Falwell (see Figure 7.1) was born again as a teenager, and after graduating from Bible Baptist College in Missouri in 1956, he and thirty-five other dissidents separated from a Southern Baptist church and organized an independent congregation. He began a radio program and started an all-white Christian high school, Liberty Baptist College, and his television ministry, the *Old-Time Gospel Hour*, which by 1980 was being watched by an estimated 4 million people every week. In these early years of his ministry, Falwell adhered to the traditional Baptist principle of separating religion from politics. What he perceived as the moral deterioration of the nation in the late 1960s and 1970s, however, changed his mind.[6]

By 1979, Falwell concluded: "Americans must no longer linger in ignorance and apathy. We cannot be silent about the sins that are destroying this nation. . . . We must turn America around or prepare for inevitable destruction." To that end, he dedicated the Moral Majority, an interfaith conservative organization, to restoring Judeo-Christian morality in America. He made clear that secular humanism was the enemy, and he pledged to "encounter the enemy face-to-face and one-on-one bring them under submission to the gospel of Christ, move them into the household of God, put up the flag, and call it secured."[7]

Falwell's Moral Majority set the tone for much of what followed on the conservative, evangelical right. It led the charge for most of the 1980s, as Falwell made clear that the movement could, and would, be led from the pulpit. Under Falwell's leadership evangelicals

Figure 7.1 Jerry Falwell, Leader of the Moral Majority

Source: Keystone Pictures USA/Alamy

aligned with the GOP in what was to be "one of the most consequential political alliances in twentieth century American politics." And although Falwell shut down the Moral Majority in 1989, its impact on American political party alignment continued. The successor to the Moral Majority, formed in the same year as its demise, was the Christian Coalition, founded by televangelist Pat Robertson. The Christian Coalition focused on educating the electorate by disseminating information in print, on television, and on the radio on issues of concern to the Christian right and getting out the vote. By the mid-1980s, about 20 percent of Americans identified with the New Christian Right, and by the year 2000, the Christian Coalition could claim to be the flagship of the religious right.[8]

The Christian Coalition had several partners in its efforts, including, but not limited to, Focus on the Family founded in 1977 by James Dobson. That concern with the traditional family was important to many in the New Christian Right is suggested by Paul Weyrich's (co-founder of the Moral Majority) comment in 1980:

> What is behind the thrust against the traditional family values? Well, first of all, from our point of view, this is really the most significant battle of the age-old conflict between good and evil, between the forces of God and forces against God, that we have seen in our country. We see the antifamily movement as an attempt to prevent souls from reaching eternal salvation, and as such we feel not just a political commitment to change this situation, but a moral and, if you will, a religious commitment to battle these forces.

Among the threats to the family Dobson and Weyrich identified were homosexuality, the Equal Rights Amendment, abortion, and pornography. Other groups similarly aligned were the Concerned Women of America, led by Beverly LaHaye, and the Promise Keepers, founded in 1990 by college football coach Bill McCartney. The former was the right's response to the feminism of the past two decades – promoting "Bible-based family values." The latter emphasized the need for men to reclaim their family obligations. Together they would move the New Christian Right into a formidable position from which to influence politics in America.[9]

Appearance of megachurches

The rise of the New Christian Right was facilitated by the increase in the number of evangelical associated megachurches. These churches were notable not only for their size but also for the services they provided their parishioners. It was also the case that these new megachurches tended to appear in the rapidly growing suburbs of sunbelt cities – Miami, Atlanta, Dallas, Houston, Phoenix, and San Diego, for example – to which evangelicals were moving in large numbers. These new megachurches were often referred to as "Christian life" centers, as they provided experiences for all members of the family in a myriad of ways including not only various religious ceremonies and schools, but also gymnasiums, dining halls, shops selling Christian-themed gifts, Bible study, and small group meetings and therapy sessions tailored to participants' particular needs and interests.[10]

Most megachurches reflected a "feel-good" evangelism and featured charismatic preachers. They were decidedly high tech, targeting a younger population whose needs differed from those of their parents. Moreover, many were non-denominational, or perhaps affiliated with a denomination but welcoming to just about anyone regardless of their individual affiliation. As one megachurch planner explained: "Denominations don't count much anymore. We see that clearly in the new congregations that don't carry any denominational affiliations, while the old-line denominations get a smaller and smaller slice of the pie." The largest megachurch of this period, founded in 1975 by the Reverend Bill Hybels, was Willow Creek Church in South Barrington, Illinois. By 1995, it was drawing between 15,000 and 20,000 people to its Saturday and Sunday services. By 2000, it had a staff of 500 and 6,000 volunteers. Hybels hung a sign in his office that read: "What is our business? Who is our customer? What does the customer consider value?" taken from business management expert Peter Drucker, with whom Hybels was acquainted. When asked about his business-like approach, Hybels responded that such an approach was fine as long as the motive was spreading the gospel.[11]

Megachurches were not universally accepted. Liberal Christians dismissed them as shallow, commercialized, and vulgar. Even evangelicals warned that megachurches were in danger of creating "McChurch" or "Church-lite" environments, "therapeutic places, emphasizing how to feel good rather than how to confess to ones sinfulness and face up to the stern teaching of the Bible."[12]

Scandals and the New Christian Right

As we have seen, scandals among religious leaders did not originate in the closing decades of the twentieth century, but what occurred were nonetheless setbacks for the New Christian Right. The three that attracted the most headlines were among the most prominent evangelicals and televangelists Jim Bakker, Jimmy Swaggart, and Oral Roberts. Jim Bakker and his wife, Tammy, both associated with the Assemblies of God, first began to attract a following in the 1960s hosting shows on Pat Robertson's Christian Broadcasting Network (CBN). Tammy offered a religious puppet show for children; Jim hosted a chat show, *The 700 Club*. One of Jim Bakker's prominent themes was his "prosperity theology," which taught that money, comfort, and success, rather than something to be shunned, were all signs of God's favor, to wit he quoted the biblical passage from 3 John 1:2: "Beloved, I wish above all things that thou mayest prosper and be in good health, even as thy soul prospereth." This presumed that you were pleasing God, which his listeners could demonstrate by giving to Bakker's ministry, in support of which he cited Luke 6:38: "Give, that it may be given to you."

In 1972, Bakker and his wife left CBN. After a brief stay at Trinity Broadcasting Network in California, they moved to another television ministry, Praise the Lord (PTL), in Charlotte, North Carolina. They soon rose to leadership positions and expanded their reach by adding airtime from dozens of stations across the country. They built Heritage USA, a 2,300-acre evangelical theme park, in South Carolina, which consisted of hotels, condominiums, pools, shops, a water park, conference centers, and an amphitheater, as well as chapels and a home for single mothers. The mixture of fun and faith attracted several million visitors each year. But Heritage USA proved costly, as did the Bakkers' lavish lifestyles, and although their income was considerable, they were living beyond their means. When their financial records proved problematic, journalists published exposés of alleged fraud. Stories followed about Tammy's drug addiction and Jim's sexual affair with a 19-year-old church secretary. Bakker called on Jerry Falwell to take over PTL temporarily, but Falwell found the situation so bad that he was forced to freeze and sell various assets. That was followed by further allegations that Bakker had frequented prostitutes and had a homosexual encounter. As Falwell commented at that point: "It is doubtful that the cause of Jesus Christ has ever suffered a greater tragedy than during the past several weeks." PTL filed for bankruptcy. Jim Bakker went on trial for wire fraud, mail fraud, and conspiracy and was convicted and sentenced to forty-five years in prison, although he served six.[13]

At the same time that the Bakkers met their demise, in 1987, so too did Jimmy Swaggart. Swaggart had a large television audience in more than a hundred foreign countries, a school, and a college. And by the mid-1980s, he was drawing an estimated half million dollars a day in revenue. Journalist Lawrence Wright described his sermons as "wild tirades . . . delivered as [he] waves his Bible overhead, his baritone voice rising into shrieks or falling into breathless whispers but always demanding, insinuating, taunting – an untamed, irresistible performance. He kneels, he struts, he dances, he sings, he bursts into tears; then he abruptly rains laughter on the thousands of worshippers waving their arms before him. Suddenly he breaks into the incantatory language of the Holy Spirit" and speaks in tongues. But then Swaggart was photographed with a prostitute, and like Bakker, he too fell from grace with the same church secretary. In his case, however, not having legal charges to face, Swaggart confessed to his "moral failure" to his congregation and tearfully begged their forgiveness. Although not with the influence he once had, with their forgiveness, he was able to remain in the pulpit suffering only a three-month suspension from the Assemblies of God, the denomination to which he belonged.[14]

Finally, also in 1987, there was the case of Oral Roberts. Roberts was a Tulsa, Oklahoma, evangelist and faith healer who also had a television empire. On January 3, 1987, on his show *Expect a Miracle*, his tearful wife at his side, he announced that God was going to "call him home" unless his supporters contributed $8 million to provide fellowships for students at the Oral Roberts University medical school. He set the date at March 6 but later changed it to March 31. He went into isolation in the university's steel-and-glass prayer tower where he fasted and prayed awaiting the outcome. Although denounced widely in the press, more than $9.1 million rolled in, and Roberts's life was spared. He returned to the air, thanked his listeners, and added that he needed to raise that same amount of money every year.[15]

The New Christian Right and politics

"If you want to know whom American voters are for, ask what they believe, that is, in the religious sense of belief. For nothing – not economic status, not region, not even race – divides American voters as starkly as their religious beliefs." So wrote Michael Barone in his review of voting patterns in the elections of 1992 and 1994. The best example – the most dramatic religious-political commitment – Barone could find in those elections was among born-again Christians, or the New Christian Right.[16]

As has been noted, the success of the New Christian Right depended on its political ties with a major political party and its selecting like-minded candidates for national, as well as state and local offices. Encompassing a quarter of the population of the United States, or some 50 million people who considered themselves born again in 1976, its involvement at the national level had been largely limited since the Scopes trial. In retrospect, the Republican Party was the most obvious vehicle for the New Christian Right's political ambition, but establishing ties with that party was not as direct as one might expect. As previously noted, the resurgence of evangelical Protestantism began with the election of Jimmy Carter to the presidency. Indeed, in the midst of the campaign, *Newsweek* declared 1976 the "year of the evangelical," followed a few months later by Carter being recognized as *Time* magazine's "Man of the Year." The presidential campaign pitted Carter against incumbent, Republican Gerald Ford of Michigan, who assumed the office upon the resignation of Richard Nixon. Although both were religious in their own ways, the credentials of the Republican Episcopalian Ford paled in comparison to Carter's in the eyes of the evangelical right. Carter's openness about his faith and his religious commitments convinced many that he was moral, good, and trustworthy, something most could not find in the Republican Richard Nixon, who had just resigned the presidency.[17]

Although an evangelical, Carter held a more socially liberal perspective than conservatives who had shunned politics, thereby providing a rationale for his seeking political office. As Carter's biographer Peter Bourne explained:

Carter conceptualized politics as a vehicle for advancing God's kingdom on earth by alleviating human suffering and despair on a scale that infinitely magnified what one individual could do alone. His most frequent prayer was that his life be meaningful in the enhancement of God's will and in the lives of fellow human beings.

Further, although he made clear that he would be a strong defender of the First Amendment's separation of church and state and promised never to use "political office to force my religious convictions on someone else," he failed to see how faith could not play a role in his politics. Carter explained how he had become disillusioned with the nation, which had fallen short of its promise. But he remained hopeful that redemption was possible because Americans were a people of faith: "We've got a good country, the greatest on earth. Richard Nixon hasn't hurt our country; even Vietnam and Cambodia haven't hurt our system of government. . . . It's still clean and decent, the basis on which we can ask difficult questions, correct our nation's shortcomings, but we've got to keep searching." And finally, "America is learning God is not automatically on its side, and in the eyes of God, we're no better than anyone else."[18]

Carter had some notable achievements during his term in office, such as the Camp David Accords between Israel and Egypt, but those were overshadowed by the nation's economic problems, dramatic rise in oil prices, and the Muslim-led overthrow of the American-supported Shah of Iran and capture of the American embassy and its sixty-six inhabitants, who were held captive until he left office. Moreover, members of the New Christian Right failed to see that he had made any progress toward turning the tide of immorality sweeping the nation. By way of example, although he personally opposed abortion, he had not challenged his party's pro-choice position. Neither had he sought to limit, if not dismantle, what the New Christian Right saw as the Supreme Court's erecting a higher wall of separation of church and state, which involved such issues as prayer in the schools. And finally on July 15, 1979, sensing he had made little progress in his revival of Americans' faith in their country and in themselves, Carter began to speak about American "paralysis, stagnation, and drift" and its "crisis of confidence" – a "crisis that strikes at the heart and soul and spirit of our nation."[19]

The election of 1980 pitted Carter against former California governor Ronald Reagan. Once again, on the face of it, Reagan's religious credentials, at least as far as conservatives were concerned, paled in comparison to Carter's. Divorced and having spent most of his working life in Hollywood as an actor, he was raised in the Disciples of Christ and attended a denominational college, but thereafter had been inconsistent in his church membership and attendance. Nevertheless, he had built a political career during the 1960s as an anticommunist and social conservative who denounced that decade's "hippy culture," making his first, but failed, runs for the presidency in 1968 and 1976. In 1980, through his numerous public pronouncements and symbolic gestures, he was successful in rallying the New Christian Right around him, turning some leading evangelicals – like Jerry Falwell – against Carter. Recalling the words of the Puritan leader, John Winthrop, Reagan pictured America as "city upon a hill" for all the world to see, and in contrast to Carter, who focused on humility and contrition, represented optimism and refused to put any limits on what a people of faith could accomplish.[20]

During the campaign and while in office, Reagan continually called for a national spiritual revival. In what was a first in such a venue, he called for a moment of silent prayer at the 1980 Republican National Convention. He continually chastised the US Supreme Court for its "misinterpretation" of the First Amendment's provision for the separation of church and state. As president, he presided over National Prayer Breakfasts and addressed various religiously conservative groups such as the National Association of Evangelicals. In 1982, he proposed a constitutional amendment that would restore and protect prayer in the public schools. In 1984, on the anniversary of *Roe v. Wade*, he proclaimed the National Sanctity of Human Life Day, explaining that abortion had denied to the unborn "the first and most basic human rights, and we are infinitely poorer for this loss." His best-known speech, however, came on March 8, 1983, before the annual convention of the National Association of Evangelicals in Orlando, Florida. It was in that speech that he famously labeled the Soviet Union the "Evil Empire" – the "focus of evil in the modern world" – and solidified his appeal to evangelists.[21]

In the election of 1984, Reagan, by then the darling of the New Christian Right, had no difficulty disposing of Democrat Walter Mondale, whose insistence on keeping religious matters out of the campaign caused him to be branded in the religious right publication the *Presidential Biblical Scorecard*, "unchristian." Mondale also chose as his running mate Geraldine Ferraro, a Roman Catholic woman who explained that although she was personally opposed to abortion, she supported *Roe v. Wade*, alienating both Catholics and conservative evangelicals. Reagan and his running mate George H. W. Bush walked off with 80 percent of the white evangelical vote. In time, leaders of the New Christian Right grew somewhat disillusioned with Reagan, who, despite his continued rhetoric and symbolic gestures, failed to take on in any meaningful ways those issues they held dear and which would cause a loss of support among more moderate voters. Nevertheless, and despite the scandal-plagued year of 1987, the evangelical momentum encouraged two ministers to run for the presidency in 1988, civil rights veteran Jesse Jackson on the Democratic side and Pat Robertson on the Republican. Both were Baptists, but on opposite ends of the liberal-conservative continuum.[22]

Robertson's campaign started off well with strong showings in the Iowa caucuses and primaries in Michigan and Hawaii. But then his campaign faltered. The press revealed that Robertson's son has been born only ten weeks after his wedding; that his father, as a US Senator, had pulled strings to prevent his son from being drafted to serve in the Korean War; and that financial irregularities appeared in his ministry. Mostly, however, Robertson's defeat was the result of his inability to hold together the coalition that had characterized the New Christian Right since its inception. During the Republican primary in 1988, Falwell and many fundamentalists swung their support to George H. W. Bush, and evangelicals to Jack Kemp, while still others withdrew their participation in the Republican primaries altogether.[23]

Jesse Jackson, making his second run for the Democratic nomination – the first in 1984 – did not fare any better. Jackson was widely known for his civil rights activity, serving early on with Martin Luther King, Jr. In 1971, he created Operation PUSH (People United to Save Humanity), and in the early 1980s he founded the Rainbow Coalition comprised of poor blacks, whites, and other minorities. Jackson was an effective speaker on political issues as well as in the pulpit. But he carried certain liabilities as he tried to move from the pulpit into national politics. First, and most obviously, he had no experience in elected office on which to run. Second, many associated him with Louis Farrakhan of the Nation of Islam and Farrakhan's advocacy of black racial purity. And finally, Jackson's skills as a preacher failed to serve him well as a politician, as they were quite different, even repelling many voters.[24]

The New Christian Right in the post-Reagan years into the twenty-first century

The Republican and Democratic Party nominees in 1988 were Vice President George H. W. Bush and Massachusetts Governor Michael Dukakis. Bush's ties to the religious right were helped by his association with Reagan and the ardent support of Jerry Falwell and other leaders on the right. As he proclaimed on Loyalty Day in 1989, faith demands "more than civic pride; it also requires constant loyalty to the principles upon which our country was founded," that founders had sacrificed to secure – "the God-given rights and freedom of the American people." On the other hand, Dukakis struggled to establish any strong commitment to conservative religious issues. For example, during the campaign Bush capitalized on Dukakis's decision while governor of Massachusetts to ban compulsory flag salutes in the public schools, even though the decision was consistent with recent US Supreme Court decisions. And when in the summer of 1989, in *Texas v. Johnson*, the Court handed down a decision that defended a person's right to burn the American flag and many Americans, but especially conservatives, called for a constitutional amendment to overturn it, Bush seized upon the movement to make it his own. But perhaps the final blow was Dukakis's prison furlough program as governor, which had resulted in the release of a convicted murderer who upon his release committed a rape and assault.[25]

Bush carried the day. His first term in office, however, failed to convince his conservative religious supporters that they had made the right choice, and he went down to defeat in 1992. This run of Republican Presidents, who had successfully won over the New Religious Right, proved less than satisfying for most evangelicals. Moreover, the fall of the Berlin Wall and collapse of the Soviet Union in 1989–1991 also deprived conservatives of the unifying cause that had served them well for decades, the Cold War and the challenge of "atheistic communism." The New Christian Right fell somewhat into disarray, divided politically and unclear as to its political future. When Jerry Falwell announced the closure of the Moral Majority in 1989, proclaiming that its goal had been achieved – "The religious right is solidly in place" – some saw it instead as recognition of defeat, while others believed that the New Christian Right "claimed victory and withdrew, turning toward a more particularistic and pietistic concern with their own churches and their own souls."[26]

This is not to say, and most observers did not imply, that the various segments of the New Christian Right had grown silent. Indeed, each focused on those causes which interested them most – the Equal Rights Amendment, AIDS, sex education, the teaching of evolution – but many questioned whether the movement would rally again on the national scene behind any political candidate. Bush hoped to leverage victory in the Gulf War into a renewed sense of patriotism and pride in the nation and its place in the world. But not all religious leaders agreed. As reported in the *New York Times* in February 1991, leaders of more than twenty major Protestant and Orthodox Christian denominations, as well as 15 Roman Catholic bishops, voiced opposition to the war and called for a cease-fire.[27]

Indeed a little over a year after the war ended, a Gallup Poll reported that 84 percent of the people surveyed were dissatisfied with the state of the nation. Conservative Republican leader Patrick Buchanan seized on that low point on the first night of the 1992 Republican National Convention to declare a new war – a cultural war – in which Bush, who was nominated for a second term, played little part: "Friends, this election is about more than who gets what. It is about who we are. It is about what we believe and what we stand for as Americans. . . . There is a religious war going [on] in this country. It is a cultural war, as critical to the kind of nation we shall be as the Cold War itself. For this war is for the soul of America."[28]

When Arkansas Democrat Bill Clinton won the Democratic nomination in 1992, despite whatever misgivings conservatives may have harbored about Bush, they pulled out all the stops in opposing Clinton. Clinton, a baby boomer and a child of the 1960s, considered himself a "new Democrat." He was elected on a platform that was more centrist that any of his liberal Democratic predecessors, while exhibiting a personal pro-choice stance on abortion and sympathy for the aspirations of gays and lesbians. As early as the Republican National Convention, Randall Terry, founder of the radical anti-abortion organization Operation Rescue, pronounced that a vote for Clinton – a Southern Baptist – amounted to a sin in the eyes of God. Clinton nevertheless carried the day, and his social policies once in office were more socially progressive than the Religious Right could tolerate, thereby further encouraging evangelical opposition.[29]

Within months, Clinton's liberalism came to the fore in his first major policy decision, namely to lift the military's ban on gay men and women in the military. Although somewhat of a compromise in that gays could serve as long as they did not let it be known that they were gay – thus the name "don't ask, don't tell" – this policy placed Clinton into the thick of the culture wars and in opposition to the Religious Right, a position in which he would remain for the rest of his time in office, but that more directly set the stage for the sweeping victory of Republicans in the mid-term elections of 1994. With the support of the Christian Coalition, rallying behind Representative Newt Gingrich's "Contract with America" – which essentially included many of the issues championed, but not realized by, Reagan and George H. W. Bush – Republicans wrested solid control of both houses of Congress.[30]

Despite the political setback, Clinton managed to be reelected in 1996 and salvage some of his vision in his second term, but he could not rise above the culture wars that divided the nation. Neither did his "inappropriate relationship" with White House intern, Monica Lewinski, which led to his impeachment (the Senate failed to convict him). Clinton finished his second term in office, and with the start of the new century – and of the new millennium – the nation returned to the polls once again, and the New Christian Right threw its support behind Republican candidate George W. Bush.

Although it had been common practice for candidates for office and elected Presidents to incorporate biblical rhetoric into their public comments, Bush was among the most accomplished, leading one contemporary observer to comment: "No other President has so clearly perceived his calling in such epic biblical terms." Another argued that he was "the most outwardly religious president in the nation's history." For example, in the aftermath of 9/11, he quoted from the books of Psalms, Matthew, and Romans. At one point, Bible in hand, he explained: "This is the only handbook you need." Others, however, have argued that his biblical references notwithstanding, and although a deeply religious individual, the association of Bush with the conservative evangelical right was incorrect. Jacques Berlinerblau, for example, has found that when one actually reads through Bush's major addresses there are relatively few biblical references. Moreover, Bush never justified a policy by reference to a biblical text, and when he did cite Scripture, it was usually "as a means of celebrating the republic's finest virtues."[31]

Nevertheless, Bush's biblical rhetoric helped get him elected to the highest office in the land – twice – against Democratic opponents Al Gore, who actually might have tackled religious issues in a thoughtful manner but did not, and John Kerry. Neither made any serious attempt to give anyone but religious liberals and moderates any reason to vote for them.

However, it did not shield him from intense criticism from the left and right in the closing years of his administration, precipitated by more worldly events such as the war in Iraq and the failure to deal adequately with Hurricane Katrina.[32]

Although the New Christian Right, or even the conservative religious right generally, did not play a leading role in any organized form in the elections of 2008 and 2012, they remained an important force among the electorate. Candidate Obama learned from the Bush years and the elections of 2000 and 2004 that, if he was going to win over at least some of the conservative religious base, or at least not lose any of the party's moderates, it was necessary to reference the Bible in his talks, albeit sparingly and appropriately. In June 2006, he pointed to its importance: "If we don't reach out to evangelical Christians and other religious Americans and tell them what we stand for, Jerry Falwells and Pat Robertsons will continue to hold sway." To do this, Obama engaged in a complex balancing act, on the one hand portraying himself as a man of faith but also distancing himself from any extreme positions.[33]

That Obama was successful was in no small part due to the missteps and lack of appeal to the religious right of his two Republican challengers. Given his personal views and public pronouncements on matters such as right to life, intelligent design, and gay marriage, for example, John McCain, a Southern Baptist, should have had more appeal to the religious right. And he certainly realized he needed their support. But he had weaknesses in his record – such as when he co-sponsored the McCain-Feingold Act of 1999, which limited the power of Christian broadcasters to endorse candidates for office – as well as "flip flops" on abortion and a reluctance to take strong stands on conservative religious issues in Congress. Further, he often grew testy when pressed on these matters by the right. As historian Jon Butler has put it, "For the first time in decades, arguably since Jimmy Carter," the Democratic candidate "was more comfortable talking about his faith than the Republican nominee, who expressed some confusion about whether he was a Baptist or an Episcopalian." And to put it succinctly, that Mitt Romney, the 2004 candidate, was a member of the Church of Jesus Christ of Latter-day Saints, proved unsurmountable to the Christian right.[34]

While still a junior senator from Illinois, Barack Obama, a member of the liberal United Church of Christ, came to understand the role of belief in his life and was willing to tackle theological questions in a reasoned and even detached manner. And by the time he became a candidate for office, the brief challenge posed by his association with the outspoken Reverend Jeremiah Wright notwithstanding, he was effective in delivering that message. In his book, *The Audacity of Hope* (2006), Obama wrote: "The Democratic Party has become the party of reaction. . . . In reaction to religious overreach, we equate tolerance with secularism, and forfeit the moral language that would help infuse our policies with a larger meaning." Elsewhere in the same book, he continued, "Not every mention of God in public is a breach in the wall of separation" and "Secularists are wrong when they ask believers to leave their religion at the door before entering the public square." And finally, he wrote: "What our deliberative, pluralist democracy does demand is that the religiously motivated translate their concerns into universal, rather than religion-specific values. It requires that their proposals must be subject to argument and amenable to reason." To this he added, importantly, that when he read the Bible, he did it "with the belief that it is not a static text, but the Living Word," and that he "must be continually open to new revelations." To these might be added an example of his confidence from a 2006 address in which, rather than simply playing to the Right, he chastised those people whose interpretations of Scripture were sectarian and simplistic: "So before we get carried away, let's read our Bibles. Folks haven't been reading their Bibles."[35]

As of this writing, it is too soon to offer a definite analysis of voting patterns in the 2016 presidential election, or the impact of various religious beliefs as associated with the candidates on the outcome. Nevertheless, initial data suggest some reasonable assumptions.

First of all, it was striking how little time was spent during the presidential debates on religious matters. Nevertheless, preliminary studies of voting patterns suggest that religion played a major role in the outcome. They point to highly segmented voting patterns along conventional lines. A Pew Research Center exit poll, for example, revealed that little changed in the political alignments of US religious groups. Those who supported Republican candidates in recent elections, such as white Protestants (58 percent to 39 percent), white born-again or evangelical Christians (81 percent to 16 percent), and white Catholics (60 percent to 37 percent) supported Donald Trump. Groups that traditionally backed democratic candidates, including African Americans (88 percent to 8 percent), Hispanics (79 percent to 18 percent), Jews (71 percent to 24 percent), and those who report that they are unaligned with any particular religious body (68 percent to 26 percent) sided heavily with Hillary Clinton.[36]

How the thrice-married, casino-building, reality television host Donald Trump, who was not known for any strong religious association, as compared to the church-going United Methodist, Sunday school teacher, and, as Senator, regular attendee at weekly prayer breakfasts, attracted such overwhelming support from evangelicals has been attributed to evangelicals' deep dislike for Clinton, for her abortion rights advocacy, but also for her ties to the culture wars of the 1990s and the involvement of her husband, President Bill Clinton. In contrast, the overwhelming vote for Clinton among Hispanics – Trump receiving the lowest level of votes on record for any presidential candidate – despite a growing political conservatism among Hispanics, has been attributed to the hostility Trump showed toward Hispanics during the campaign.[37]

The premillennialist dilemma

Never absent among conservative evangelicals, premillennialism became visible once again during the 1970s and 1980s, perhaps due, at least in part, to President Reagan's characterization of the Soviet Union and the enhanced threat of nuclear war. One of the best-selling books of the 1970s was Hal Lindsey's premillennialist novel, *The Late, Great Planet Earth*, published in 1970, which appealed to non-premillennialists as well. That was followed in 1972 by *A Thief in the Night*, a popular movie on the same theme directed by the evangelical Donald W. Thompson. The film opened with a woman awakening to a news bulletin on the radio:

> To say that the world is in a state of shock this morning would be to understate the situation. . . . Suddenly and without warning literally thousands, perhaps millions of people just disappeared. The few eyewitness accounts of these disappearances have not been clear, but one thing is certainly sure: Millions who were on the earth last night are not here this morning.

She soon discovers that her husband is among those who are missing and that she has been left behind.[38]

Thomson estimated that between one-quarter and one-half of the American population had seen the movie by 1980 and that as a result had been born again. And he followed his success with *A Thief in the Night*, a series of movies on the horrors of life for those left behind to suffer the Tribulation, including *A Distant Thunder* (1978), *Image of the Beast* (1980), and *Prodigal Planet* (1983). When historian Randall Balmer asked Thompson's partner, Russell Doughten, whether the films were scaring people into embracing Jesus, he responded: "Anybody who seriously reads the prophetic books on Revelation . . . will be scared. There is some pretty heavy stuff in those prophecies. If you take seriously what's being said there, it's frightening, and it ought to be," to which he added: "If they get into the kingdom through being scared, that's better than not making it at all."[39]

The millennial expectation continued into the 1990s and even accelerated as the year 2000 approached and evangelicals believed they saw signs revealed in the Book of Revelation. An Associated Press poll taken in 1997 revealed that about 26 million American Christians (one in four) expected to witness the return of Christ in their own lifetime. Moreover, it was widely predicted that the advent of the year 2000 (referred to as Y2K) would bring about widespread failures in computer systems leading to severe economic damage, the collapse of world systems, and other apocalyptic events. Some evangelicals, like Jerry Falwell, seized on this prediction as a sign of the end times. Indeed, so many prophetic groups sprung up in the late 1990s that two institutes, the Millennium Watch Institute in Philadelphia and the Center for Millennial Studies at Boston University, set up to identify and track them.[40]

Many who believed the end times would begin with the new millennium, also believed that the decisive event would occur in Jerusalem. They flocked to Jerusalem as the day drew near, exhibiting what the Israeli police dubbed the "Jerusalem syndrome," wherein people who saw themselves as biblical characters roamed the streets dressed in bedsheets, declaiming Scripture or preaching ecstatically. About a hundred Americans settled on the Mount of Olives, which they expected would be the place where Christ would reappear. Another group was led by a minister from Denver, Monte Kim Miller. Miller had been active in the anticult movement in the 1980s, but then he gathered to him his own group of 100–200 followers called Concerned Christians. Miller claimed to be in direct communication with God and that God spoke through him warning his followers that the end times would begin with a catastrophic earthquake in Denver on October 10, 1998. God, through Miller, instructed the group to give up their worldly possessions and follow him to Jerusalem before October 10. The earthquake did not occur, but about seventy-five of his followers turned up a month later in Jerusalem – without Miller. It turned out that Miller told his followers that he was one of two prophets identified in Revelation 11; that he would die in a gun battle in the streets of Jerusalem on December 31, 1999; that three days later he would be resurrected; and that his resurrection would trigger the Second Coming. Israeli police monitored the Concerned Christians and when they learned that they planned to provoke a gun battle in the streets of Jerusalem, the police arrested and deported fourteen of them. Miller never reappeared.[41]

The greatest success at the general public level was achieved by fictional accounts of the end times in the *Left Behind* series of novels by Tim LaHaye and Jerry Jenkins, which sold tens of millions of copies. As noted earlier, LaHaye was one of the founders of the Moral Majority, and his wife, Beverly, the founder of Concerned Women for America. The series consisted of sixteen novels, the first of which appeared in 1995 under the title *Left Behind*, the last, *Kingdom Come*, in 2007, all of which centered on a conflict between members of the Tribulation Force and the Global Community, led by Nicolae Carpathia, the Antichrist. The hero is Rayford Steele, an airline pilot whose devout wife and son have mysteriously disappeared, along with millions of others. Steele realizes what has happened and only gradually is successful in convincing his skeptical daughter that the missing were taken up by the Rapture and that he and his daughter are among those left behind. Steele also believes that they can still be saved by accepting Christ into their lives, but in the meantime, they must live through the catastrophic end times. They join the Tribulation Force, a group of fellow believers who not only face the various natural disasters predicted in Revelations, but also must fight Carpathia, who through the United Nations is out to unite the world under one government and one religion. To date, the series has been adapted into a series of four films: *Left Behind: The Movie* (2000), *Left Behind II: Tribulation Force* (2002), *Left Behind: World at War* (2005), and a readaption aimed at a more mass market *Left Behind*, starring Nicholas Cage, released in 2014.

The premillennialist perspective posed a dilemma for those who also claimed allegiance to the New Christian Right. If the world was about to come to an end, what did it matter who became president? Why engage in politics? And why seek to make the world better, if those whom God had chosen would be raptured only when the condition of the world had reached its lowest point and the tribulation begun? Theologian Francis Schaeffer addressed that issue in his book and film series, *How Should We Then Live?* (1976) and in his subsequent book, *The Great Evangelical Disaster* (1984), which urged evangelicals to concentrate more on rescuing the world from moral decay and dwelling less on the end times. Schaeffer argued that, "in their failure to do this in the past, they had permitted the country to fall into the hands of God's enemies [who have] destroy[ed] our culture and the Christian ethos that once shaped our country."[42]

Major issues for the New Christian Right: abortion

The rank-and-file of the New Christian Right were concerned with many social and cultural issues, some more important than others. Abortion was one issue that was critical to the New Christian Right and that allowed for collaboration with Roman Catholics. Until 1973, legal access to abortion was a state-by-state matter, with battles fought at the local level, if at all, as in some states legalizing abortion was not even considered. But in 1973, in *Roe v. Wade*, it became a national issue, and the ruling became the law of the land. In reaching its decision, the US Supreme Court addressed two issues, which served as the basis of the opposing sides in the case: (1) whether a woman's constitutional guarantee to privacy gave her the right to an abortion under the Ninth Amendment and (2) whether fetal life was constitutionally protected under either the Fifth or Fourteenth Amendment. In his majority opinion – it was a 7 to 2 decision – Justice Harry Blackmun came down on the side of a woman's right to privacy. Although the Roman Catholic and most pro-lifers' position was that life began at inception, beyond that, there was little agreement as to when human life begins, whereupon he put aside pro-lifers' use of medical testimony to argue for the personhood of the fetus.[43]

Having undercut the pro-life argument, however, Blackmun continued to address limits that still might be imposed on abortion, allowing that at some point, the state might have a "compelling interest" in protecting fetal life. The result was a three-part ruling wherein during the first trimester women had an unrestricted right to an abortion. During the second trimester – which would take the fetus up to the point of viability – the states could place restrictions on abortion, but only for purposes of protecting a woman's health. And during the final trimester, states would have the option to ban abortions, as long as they made exceptions for cases in which abortion was needed to protect a woman's life or health.[44]

Although immediate widespread protests would suggest otherwise, various public opinion polls taken at the time pointed to a deeply and evenly divided populace. A Gallup Poll taken shortly after Roe, for example, indicated that 47 percent of those polled supported the decision, and 44 percent were opposed. Further, in contrast to the official Roman Catholic position, and despite growing opposition among conservative evangelicals, abortion did not become a national political issue for the latter group for another several years, when it was joined with other issues such as prayer and Bible reading in public schools, pornography, the Equal Rights Amendment, the teaching of evolution in the public schools, and IRS rulings that denied tax-exempt status to any organization that engaged in racial discrimination, which included some conservative evangelical schools like Bob Jones University. That occurred in the late 1970s, when, as discussed earlier, the New Christian Right organized to oppose President Jimmy Carter, who though born again, refused to publicly oppose abortion and to support Republican candidate Ronald Reagan, who voiced support for all of these issues. Single-issue political action committees appeared, such as the National Pro-Life PAC and the Life Amendment PAC, which though founded by a conservative Roman Catholic couple, attracted the support of Paul Weyrich, a leader of the New Christian Right. From that point on, anti-abortion, or pro-life, became the defining issue of the New Christian Right.[45]

The creation of Operation Rescue in 1987 signaled the emergence of evangelicals in the anti-abortion/pro-life movement. Taking a page from earlier protest movements, Randall Terry trained volunteers in non-violent resistance and stationed them at the entrances to clinics where abortions were performed, making it difficult for women seeking abortions to enter. Volunteers worked to have women reconsider and directed them to counseling centers where the option of giving birth was emphasized with the alternative of adoption. When confronted by police, the volunteers did not resist arrest, but instead prayed and sang as they were taken off to jail. The first major operation – involving a coalition of evangelicals and Catholics – took place in New York City in 1988. Later that summer, a similarly large demonstration was held in Atlanta, coinciding with the Democratic National Convention, where they were met by a sizable force of pro-choice counterprotesters. The result was mass arrests and considerable national press coverage. Such press in some cases served to discourage some key figures and groups from continuing to support Operation Rescue. The Catholic collaboration, for example, began to break down as its leaders recoiled from the mass-arrest strategy and its potential for violence. Closer to home, Jerry Falwell, who made headlines by appearing at the Atlanta demonstration and handing Terry a check for $10,000, subsequently began to distance himself in the face of a legal counteroffensive launched by pro-choice groups charging it with racketeering, intimidation, and conspiracy. The counteroffensive also served to fragment leadership of Operation Rescue, which became more intense when Terry was imprisoned and suffered a nervous breakdown.[46]

The Equal Rights Amendment

Another hot-button issue was the Equal Rights Amendment. The National Organization of Women and other feminist groups revived the Equal Rights Amendment to the US Constitution, which was first introduced to Congress in 1923. With this new initiative, it received the two-thirds approval necessary from Congress rather handily in 1972 and was sent out to the states for ratification. Soon thereafter, however, the amendment, which sought to eliminate discrimination against women in employment and other venues, got caught up in the growing anti-abortion movement and other anti-feminist activities and began to face considerable resistance at the state level as it approached the required three-quarter state approval. In this instance, conservative women led the opposition, the most visible and active figure being the Roman Catholic Phyllis Schlafly. The proposed amendment read: "Equality of rights under the law shall not be denied or abridged by the United States or by any state on account of sex." Schlafly's approach was to attack this rather general wording by pointing out what she argued were its implications, namely that it violated nature by seeking to reorganize society as though gender differences did not exist. For the sake of expanding opportunities for women, the ERA would deny women the legal protections they had long enjoyed, including exclusion of women from combat assignments in the military. Schlafly took her forces into the field as each state took up ratification, at first slowing the process and then stopping it altogether as states began to withhold ratification.

Conservative evangelicals did not necessarily disagree with liberals, including feminists, that gender relations were not as they should be. Where they disagreed was in their understanding of the reasons for the situation and possible solutions. They were guided by Scripture, such as Paul's decree: "Wives, be subject to your husbands, as to the Lord. For the husband is the head of the wife as Christ is the head of the church. . . . As the church is subject to Christ, so let wives also be subject in everything to their husbands" (Ephesians 4: 22–25). But they also placed limits on the authority of men, insisting that their authority was not to be arbitrary. Once again, they referenced Scripture and Paul's directive to men, "Husbands, love your wives as Christ loved the church and gave himself up for her," and elsewhere, "Live considerately with your wives, bestowing honor on the women as the weaker sex, since you are joint heirs of the grace of life."[47]

Joining forces with Schlafly was Beverly LaHaye, who wrote a series of evangelical women's advice books, which counseled women to find strength in their faith rather than joining forces with feminists in attacking what the latter described as patriarchal domination, thereby finding greater fulfillment as a wife and mother. Central to LaHaye's case was that the nuclear family, which she believed was being threatened by feminists, but was a divinely sanctioned principle of social organization. To that end, LaHaye founded Concerned Women for America, which claimed a million members by the late 1980s. In his book, *Mine Eyes Have Seen the Glory*, historian Randall Balmer included an interview with a member of the Iowa branch of Concerned Women that encapsulated the organizations perspectives, which at times seemed contradictory in their both supporting the submission and empowerment of women:

> I think women are the key to turning this nation around. I firmly believe that this is why Satan went to Eve, not Adam. . . . I firmly believe that the role of a woman today is to nurture our next generation. She has the power within her hands to either make or break a nation. . . . The secret to a woman's role, I believe, is authority and being submissive. And I feel that just as God asked the woman to bear children because He knew that she wouldn't want to put up with a pregnant man for nine months or He knew that a man could not tolerate the pain of having a child, God also asked her to be submissive, which is one of the hardest things that a woman is asked to do. But therein comes real peace.[48]

The Promise Keepers

Allied with the Concerned Women of America in their campaign to maintain traditional Christian family values was the Promise Keepers, founded in 1990 by college football coach Bill McCartney. If Concerned Women was the conservative women's response to the feminism of the past two decades, the Promise Keepers was the conservative men's response, emphasizing the need for men to reclaim their family obligations. It was a non-denominational organization for Christian men who believed that too many men were failing to play their biblically ordained role as strong husbands and fathers. It urged men to return to Christ, confess their sins, and take responsibility for their wives and children.[49]

Bill McCartney gained national attention in the 1960s and 1970s as a successful college football coach, especially with the University of Colorado. He was paid well for his success, and he and his family lived well, economically at least. But he regretted the toll his career with its heavy work schedule, punctuated by heavy drinking and an extramarital affair, had taken on his family. Already known as a motivational speaker and a member of the Fellowship of Christian Athletes, McCartney resigned his coaching job in 1994 and assumed control of the Promise Keepers. Soon McCartney and the Promise Keepers were filling stadiums with men, largely Christian, for two-day rallies that were part old evangelical-style camp meetings, chanting, traditional hymns, and prayers for forgiveness and part pep rallies. The first was held in 1991 at the University of Colorado, and by 1996 – with the help of national advertising – its membership topped 1 million. Men joining the movement signed on to a required "Seven Promises," by which they committed to

> honoring Jesus Christ through worship, prayer and obedience to God's Word in the power of the Holy Spirit . . . pursuing vital relationships with a few other men, understanding that he needs brothers to help him keep his promises . . . practicing spiritual, moral, ethical and sexual purity . . . building strong marriages and families through love, protection, and Biblical values . . . supporting the mission of his church by honoring and praying for his pastor and by actively giving his time and resources . . . reaching beyond any racial and denominational barriers to demonstrate the power of Biblical unity . . . [and] influencing his world, being obedient to the Great Commandment (Mark 12: 30–31) and the Great Commission (Mathew 28: 19–20).[50]

McCartney denounced racism as a collective sin and encouraged blacks to join the Promise Keepers. Many of the group's leaders were African American, but by the mid-1990s, about 85 percent of the entire membership was middle-class white men, and most of them from evangelical churches. McCartney opposed feminism to the extent that it challenged traditional family life. But he and organization leaders explained that although they believed that men should lead their families, they should not do so as tyrants, but rather as Jesus taught. Moreover, the Promise Keepers opposed pornography and adultery, a position which not only gained favor among conservative evangelical women but even led to the creation of women's auxiliary groups such as Suitable Helpers, Heritage Keepers, and Chosen Women. That did not placate feminist groups. In 1997, Patricia Ireland, president of the National Organization of Women, described the Promise Keepers as "a feel-good form of male supremacy with dangerous political potential." She noted that McCartney had sponsored an antigay rights amendment in Colorado, had referred to lesbians and gays as "stark raving mad," had spoken at Operation Rescue meetings, and had urged the Promise Keepers men to "take back the nation for Christ." Further, she challenged McCartney's claim that the movement was non-political, pointing to the endorsements of such figures as Jerry Falwell, Pat Robertson, and Billy Graham and asking how it could be possible to not have political ties with a staff of 450 and a budget of more than $97 million.[51]

Promise Keeper rallies served to convince liberals, religious or not, and many moderates, that it constituted yet "the third wave of the religious right's assault on American Democracy and values," after the Moral Majority and the Christian Coalition. But it was not opposition from the left that brought a halt to the Promise Keepers movement. Once again, it was finances, although this time minus scandals or mismanagement. The immediate cause was the decision not to charge entrance fees for stadium events. Other contributing factors included the repetitive nature of the rallies, which discouraged many men from continuing to attend, while it failed to attract new constituencies; the organization's opposition to denominationalism; and the absence of a solid theological foundation, which took its toll on evangelical supporters. But, although its numbers dropped considerably, and it cut its staff accordingly, the Promise Keepers did stabilize and live on into the twenty-first century.[52]

Prayer in the schools

Prayer in the schools, or more specifically school-led prayer and/or Bible reading in the public schools, was among the most contested points in the cultural wars of the 1980s and 1990s. Its roots, however, lay in the 1960s. In fact, the sides taken in the matter were pretty much determined by 1963 and changed little thereafter. Adoption of the First Amendment to the United States Constitution, which addressed matters related to religious establishment and the free exercise of religion, occurred in 1791, but those same matters remained largely with the states. As the wording of the amendment made clear, "*Congress* shall make no law respecting an establishment of religion, or prohibiting the free exercise thereof." That began to change in the 1940s when the United States Supreme Court extended the reach of the First Amendment to the states via the incorporation clause of the Fourteenth Amendment.

Court cases brought challenging prayer in the schools were by-and-large based on interpretations of the first part of the first sentence of the First Amendment: "Congress shall make no law respecting an establishment of religion." To some this clause was intended to ensure federal government neutrality between religious factions but not opposition to religion. To others it was intended to distance government from issues of religion in every possible way, to erect a wall separating church and state. These conflicting positions became central to the debates concerning prayer in the schools.[53]

As the reader will recall, the first major case was *Everson v. Board of Education* (1947). In that decision, the Supreme Court provided the definition of the Establishment Clause and its relationship to state and federal law. Justice Hugo Black wrote for the majority (the italics are mine and used for emphasis):

> The "establishment of religion" clause of the First Amendment means at least this: Neither *a state* nor the Federal Government can ... pass laws which aid one religion, aid all religions, or prefer one religion over another. Neither can force nor influence a person to ... profess a belief or disbelief in any religion. ... Neither *a state* nor the Federal Government can, openly or secretly, participate in the affairs of any religious organizations or groups and vice versa. In the words of Jefferson, the clause against establishment of religion by laws was intended to erect a "wall of separation between Church and State."[54]

In *McCollum v. Board of Education of Champaign, Illinois* (1948), the court applied the definition arrived at in *Everson* to declare religious instruction in the public schools unconstitutional. The ruling dealt with laws that permitted clergy to give religious instruction in the public schools during the regular hours set aside for secular teaching. It did not address prayer and/or Bible reading, but it did offer some important and related commentary on the nature of public schools. In a concurrent opinion, Judge Felix Frankfurter wrote: "Designed to serve as perhaps the most powerful agency for promoting cohesion among a heterogeneous democratic people, the public school must keep scrupulously free from entanglement in the strife of sects," and that requires "strict confinement of the state to instruction other than religious, leaving to the individual's church and home indoctrination in the faith of his choice." Dismissing the argument that students were not compelled to attend religious instruction classes in the schools, Justice Hugo Black wrote for the court:

> Here not only are the state's tax-supported public school buildings used for the dissemination of religious doctrines, the state also affords sectarian groups an invaluable aid in that it helps to provide pupils for the religious classes through use of the state's compulsory public school machinery. This is not separation of Church and State.[55]

Four years later, in *Zorach v. Clauson*, the court heard its second religious instruction case deciding whether to extend the *McCullom* ruling. The court sustained New York's program of releasing students from school on written request of parents so that they could attend religious centers of their choice for instruction off campus. The sectarian instructors were required to take attendance and report the results to the students' homeroom teachers, and students who did not take part in the program remained in school for study hall. In this instance, the court saw no coercion and no violation of the Establishment Clause. The clause, Justice William O. Douglas wrote for the court, "is absolute: there cannot be the slightest doubt that the First Amendment reflects the philosophy that Church and State should be separated." Nevertheless, he continued, it "does not say that in every and all respects there shall be a separation of Church and State." If the separation were absolute, he reasoned, government and religion would be "aliens to each other – hostile, suspicious, and even unfriendly." In the case at hand, the public schools did no more than "accommodate their schedules to a program of outside religious instruction." Douglas offered the following explanation by which the court would be guided:

> We are a religious people whose institutions presuppose a Supreme Being. We guarantee the freedom to worship as one chooses. We make room for as wide a variety of beliefs and creeds as the spiritual needs of men may deem necessary. . . . When the state encourages religious instruction or cooperates with religious authorities by adjusting the schedule of public events to sectarian needs, it follows the best of traditions. For it then respects the religious nature of our people and accommodates the public service to their spiritual needs. To hold that it may not would be to find in the Constitution a requirement that the government show a callous indifference to religious groups. That would be preferring those who believe in no religion over those who do believe. . . . But we find no constitutional requirement which makes it necessary for government to be hostile to religion and to throw its weight against efforts to widen the effective scope of religious influence.[56]

A key decision concerning prayer in the schools came in *Engel v. Vitale*, decided in 1962. Ten years earlier, the New York State Board of Regents voted to recommend the reading of a prayer in the public schools at the start of each day. The prayer was: "Almighty God, we acknowledge our dependence upon Thee, and we beg Thy blessing upon us, our parents, our teachers and our Country." Parents of ten pupils in the public schools of New Hyde Park,

Long Island, which had adopted the prayer, brought suit. Two of the parents were Jewish, one was a member of the Ethical Culture Society, one was a Unitarian, and one was a non-believer. The group insisted that use of this official prayer was contrary to the beliefs, religions, or religious practices of themselves and their children. This was not the first time that a challenge was brought against prayer in the schools, but it was the first challenge heard at the federal level. Moreover, earlier cases challenged the prayers or Bible readings because they were too sectarian – too Protestant – and because the Bible employed was usually the King James Version. The complaint of the Hyde Park families went beyond that. They charged that the prayer violated the Establishment Clause of the First Amendment, because it was "composed by governmental officials as part of a government program to further religious beliefs."[57]

The State of New York composed the prayer in an attempt to create a non-sectarian prayer, thereby requiring of the court a broader, more encompassing, ruling, namely on the constitutionality of organized teacher-led prayer in the public schools. Echoing earlier court rulings, Justice Black explained for the court that the Establishment Clause "must at least mean that in this country it is no part of the business of government to compose official prayers for any group of American people to recite." Neither its denominational neutrality nor the fact that the participation in the saying was voluntary freed the prayer from the reach of the First Amendment. Under the Establishment Clause government could not influence the prayers said by any citizens. Further, placing "the power, prestige and financial support of government" behind a particular form of religious observance, he insisted, tends to coerce religious minorities to conform.[58]

This was a turning point in the court of public opinion. If people were concerned prior to *Engel*, their objections were fairly muted, largely because most did not believe, or held out hope, that it would not happen, that the Supreme Court would declare organized prayer and/or Bible reading unconstitutional. The court's ruling in *Engel*, both in terms of what it actually decided and what many feared it forecasted, changed all of that. To be sure, some welcomed the decision. The American Civil Liberties Union hailed the case as a milestone in the separation of church and state. The Anti-Defamation League of B'Nai B'rith called the ruling "a splendid reaffirmation of a basic American principle," adding that it provided "another safeguard for freedom of religion in the United States." Dean Kelly, Director of the National Council of Churches' Department of Religious Liberty, said: "Many Christians will welcome the decision. It protects the religious rights of minorities and guards against the development of 'public school religion' which is neither Christian nor Judaism but something less than either." Others, if not pleased, acquiesced, some holding out that that matter might still be resolved in favor of prayer.[59]

For many others, however, the decision ignited a firestorm of protest. Roman Catholics and conservative Protestants led the charge. James Francis Cardinal McIntyre of Los Angeles pronounced the decision "positively shocking and scandalizing to one of American blood and principles. . . . The court presumes to deny the children of God in our schools the opportunity to speak to the Creator, the lawmaker, the Preserver of Mankind. This decision puts shame on our faces, as we are forced to emulate [Soviet leader] Mr. Khrushchev." And, after declaring his own shock and disbelief, Billy Graham described the decision as "another step toward secularism in the United States" and a "most dangerous trend": "Followed to its logical conclusion, prayers cannot be said in Congress, chaplains will be taken from the armed forces, and the President will not place his hand on the Bible when he takes the oath of office."[60]

Various sources estimated that, at that point, about 30 percent of all public schools practiced some form of morning exercise that usually included the Lord's Prayer, and that between 40 and 50 percent used Bible reading. So challenges to these practices were expected to follow. In fact, two cases involving those vary situations were already on the way to the Supreme Court, *School District of Abington Township v. Schempp* and *Murray v. Curlett*. In *Abington Township*, Edward Schempp and his wife Sidney, both Unitarians, filed suit on behalf of their children, challenging a Pennsylvania law that required the reading of at least ten verses from the Bible. The Schempps also complained about group recitation of the Lord's Prayer in the Abington Senior High School, but that was not covered by the challenged statute. The Bible reading was conducted over the school's public address system or in the classrooms. Students were permitted to select and read any passages from the Bible, or to use any version of the Bible, but the school district had provided the school with the King James Version. No comments were made during the exercise, and students with written permission from their parents were not required to participate. Insisting that they were religious, the Schempps nevertheless protested that the doctrines conveyed by a literal reading of the Bible were "contrary to the religious beliefs which they held and to their familial teaching."[61]

In *Murray v. Curlett*, Madalyn Murray, a publically pronounced atheist and founder of American Atheists (originally Society of Separationists), brought a suit on behalf of her son William, challenging a 1905 Baltimore school board rule requiring each school day to start with Bible reading or the Lord's Prayer or both. Whereas the Schempps studiously avoided the press and the public as well as they could, Murray (soon to become O'Hair) brought suit only after protesting to officials, stirring up media attention, and encouraging her son to conduct a strike that kept him out of school for eighteen days, which attracted extensive media coverage. The US Supreme Court merged the two cases and made a single decision covering both.[62]

On June 17, 1963, the US Supreme Court rendered its verdict. By an 8 to 1 margin, the court declared unconstitutional the Pennsylvania and Maryland laws requiring Bible reading and prayer recitation in the public schools because they violated the Establishment Clause of the First Amendment. It explained that such a violation occurs by any government sponsorship of religion in the public schools, regardless of whether a showing of coercion exists. As Justice Tom C. Clark put it for the court, for a law to be valid, "There must be a secular legislative purpose and a primary effect that neither advances nor inhibits religion." Clark added that the state might not establish a religion of secularism, in the sense of opposing religion or showing hostility to it, thus preferring irreligion, but neutrality demanded of the state extended to believers and non-believers alike, without the state being the adversary of one against the other.[63]

Clark wrote: "Since the [Pennsylvania] statute requires the reading of the 'Holy Bible,' a Christian document, the practice . . . prefers the Christian religion." Moreover, the record demonstrates to the court that the state intended "to introduce a religious ceremony into the public schools of the Commonwealth." He added: "Nothing we have said here," should be construed to preclude the study of the Bible or religion in the public schools, "when presented objectively as part of a secular program of education." But the court did not find that to be the case in Pennsylvania. And to the anticipated argument that by its ruling the majority was being denied its will, Clark responded that the purpose of the free exercise clause was to protect the minority from the pressure of the majority.[64]

Clark then took up the argument that "religion has been closely identified with our history and government," a position recognized by the court in earlier decisions. In *Engel*, the court found that "the history of man is inseparable from the history of religion." In *Zorach*, it recognized that "we are a religious people whose institutions presuppose a Supreme Being." And Clark agreed that the Founding Fathers "believed devotedly that there was a God and that the unalienable rights of man were rooted in Him," to wit he added that traditions abound over the nation's history of various supporting traditions such as chaplains providing prayer at the opening of Congress and oaths of office that mentioned God. He continued: "That is not to say, however, that religion has been so identified with our history and government that religious freedom is not likewise as strongly imbedded in our public and private life." That insistence on religious freedom had resulted from "the most telling of personal experiences in religious persecution suffered by our forebears," and it was "indispensable" in a country with such "diversity of religious opinion."[65]

Although the decision should have come as no surprise to anyone who had been following previous Supreme Court rulings, the public response to the *Abington Township/Murray* decision was even more vociferous than that which followed *Engel*. Once again, mainstream Protestants and Jews accepted the decision and even welcomed it. The National Council of Churches asserted that the decision served as a reminder that the "teaching for religious commitment is the responsibility of the home and the community of faith . . . rather than the public schools. Neither the church nor the state should use the public school to compel acceptance of any creed or conformity to any specific religious practice." Such a practice "endangers both true religion and civil liberties."[66]

On the other hand, Mark Murphy, vice president of Citizens for Educational Freedom, echoed the sentiments of many when he charged that the decision established "Godless schools" and was "another step toward the elimination of God from all public American life." Monsignor John Voight, secretary for education of the Roman Catholic Archdioceses of New York, admitted that the decision came as no surprise, but continued:

> I deeply regret the court action. I say this for two reasons: One, because it will bring about the complete secularization of public education in America, which to me represents a radical departure from our traditional and historical religious heritage; and, two, because it completely disregards parental rights in education and the wishes of a large segment of America's parents, who want their children to participate in these practices in public schools.

And once again, Billy Graham was "shocked," arguing that

> prayers and Bible reading have been a part of the public school life since the Pilgrims landed at Plymouth Rock. Now a Supreme Court in 1963 says our fathers were wrong all those years. . . . In my opinion, it is the Supreme Court that is wrong. At a time when moral decadence is evident on every hand, when race tension is mounting, when the threat of Communism is growing, when terrifying new weapons of destruction are being created, we need more religion not less.[67]

Some critics opted to take action to restore prayer in the public schools. Several states and localities adopted laws that provided prescribed prayers that students could voluntarily recite in school. All were challenged in court and ruled unconstitutional. In *Reed v. Van Horen*, the court ruled that such an activity not only had to be voluntary but it had to take place outside the regular school day. And there were calls for a constitutional amendment to "restore the original intent of the First Amendment" and prayer in the schools. Francis Burch, the attorney who represented the city of Baltimore in *Murray*, started a group called the Constitutional Prayer Foundation, which won the immediate support of former President Eisenhower and the governors of several states. Constituents besieged their congressmen with mail, and in April, May, and June 1964, the US House Judiciary Committee held 18 days of hearings to evaluate more than 145 resolutions proposing 35 different constitutional amendments, the Becker Amendment being the most prominent. None of the proposed amendments met the two-thirds majority vote required to make it out of Congress.[68]

In the 1990s, opponents of *Abington Township* and *Murray* shifted their focus slightly to protect prayer at school-sponsored extracurricular activities, which also were challenged in the courts. *Lee v. Weisman* (1992) and *Santa Fe Independent School District v. Doe* (2000) took up challenges to public prayers at graduation ceremonies and at high school athletic events in which the Supreme Court ruled such practices unconstitutional. Where they have had some success is when they challenged the courts under the Free Exercise of Religion Clause, arguing that students' expressing religious views even through prayer cannot be forbidden unless such activity can be shown to cause disruption in the school. As a result, students are allowed to pray in schools as long as the prayers are not officially sponsored by the school and are not disruptive.[69]

As if the decision alone was not sufficient to set off the at times bitter controversy surrounding the place of prayer in the school, and where the Schempps shunned the limelight despite their victory in court, Madalyn Murray basked in the spotlight of the public and media attention opponents and the press were only too willing to give her. Speaking from the front steps of the Supreme Court, she vowed, and over the next thirty years as leader of American Atheists, delivered in going beyond school prayer and Bible reading to challenge just about every instance where she believed the Establishment Clause or her free exercise of irreligion was being violated. To list just a few such cases, Murray (O'Hair), challenged in court the tax-exempt status of the churches, the clause "under God" in the pledge of allegiance, NASA's allowing Colonel Frank Boorman to pray on national television and radio on Christmas Eve in 1968 while orbiting the moon, President Nixon for holding weekly religious services in the White House, nativity displays on government grounds, opening prayers in Congress, oaths of office that included reference to God, etc. Although she lost in nearly every case (the nativity case being a notable exception, though not entirely of her own doing), she always attracted considerable attention and became ground zero for the culture wars that followed. Indeed, in its June 19, 1964, issue, *Life* magazine declared Murray "The Most Hated Woman in America."[70]

Creationism versus evolution

Court decisions reached in the 1960s prohibiting prayer and Bible reading in the nation's public schools served as a warning to antievolutionists that the continued teaching of the biblical account of creation would soon run afoul of First Amendment provisions for the separation of church and state, as well. The battle over the teaching of evolution in the nation's public schools largely receded from the national scene after the Scopes trial. The trial did not result in the immediate revocation of any of the many state laws that outlawed the practice, and antievolution forces took their fight to the state and local level, where they continued to be successful. But the issue surfaced once again at the national level during the 1980s. This time antievolutionists armed themselves with what they maintained was a scientific theory that explained the creation of the world and its current state. They called it creation science. Armed with this "science," proponents argued that there was no reason not to teach it in the public schools along with evolution.

What triggered the effort to have creation science taught in the public schools was the US Supreme Court's 1968 decision in *Epperson v. Arkansas*, which overturned laws opposed to the teaching of evolution in the nation's public schools dating to *Scopes*. What further prompted the issue was the nation's attempt to revamp its science curricula in the wake of the Soviet launch into orbit of *Sputnik* in 1957. Fundamentalists saw this coming and were already preparing their alternative approach. That began in 1961 with publication of *The Genesis Flood* by Henry Morris, an engineering professor at Virginia Polytechnic Institute, and John Whitcomb, a theologian. Rather than an original piece of work, Morris and Whitcomb provided an update of George McCready Price's *The New Geology*, published in 1923, which sought to reestablish the inerrancy of the Bible and the Genesis story of creation by arguing that the Earth's geological strata was the result of a massive flood that occurred 5,000 years ago, rather than the accumulation of sedimentation over millions of years.[71]

The Institute for Creation Research in San Diego flooded the market with information on creation science, targeting K-12 school teachers, state legislators, and school board members. They insisted that theirs was a scientific explanation for creation that was every bit as valid as evolution. Prominent scientists came out in opposition to creation science. Liberal ministers largely stayed out of the dispute, continuing to believe that the biblical account of creation could be reconciled with evolution. But fundamentalists seized on the new theory as an opportunity to circumvent recent Supreme Court decisions and keep this key piece of their mostly Christian belief in the schools. In the early 1980s, Arkansas and Louisiana passed laws that required equal time for evolution and creation science in science classes, hoping to avoid a First Amendment showdown. Nevertheless, the American Civil Liberties Union sued Arkansas in 1981, charging the state with covertly introducing religion into the science curriculum. In what is often referred to as "Scopes 2," but officially known as *McLean v. Arkansas Board of Education*, a federal court ruled for the ACLU. A federal judge found fault with creationist methodology, whereby he concluded that it was not a science: "While anybody is free to approach a scientific inquiry in any fashion they choose, they cannot properly describe the methodology as scientific, if they start with the conclusion and refuse to change it regardless of the evidence developed during the course of the investigation." Arkansas did not appeal the case, so the ACLU next turned to Louisiana, whose statute did not mention God, thereby possibly avoiding a First Amendment ruling. Once again, the judge sided with the ACLU, but the state appealed the decision, which ended up before the US Supreme Court. No doubt helped by the seventy-two Nobel Prize Winners in the natural sciences that signed an *amicus curiae* (friend of the court) brief denouncing creation science, in *Edwards v. Aguillard* (1987), the Supreme Court upheld the lower court decision by a vote of 7 to 2.[72]

In the 1990s, antievolutionists moved on to intelligent design. Basic to this concept is the existence of what is termed "irreducible complexity" in nature, which can only be attributed to an intelligent designer, an idea introduced by chemist Charles Thaxton in the 1980s and promoted by biochemist Michael Behe and mathematician William Dembski. Neither Behe nor Dembski insisted on a theistic creator. On that point, unlike most intelligent design proponents, they were agnostic. Further, supported by the Discovery Institute in Seattle, proponents argued that intelligent design can be responsible for small changes in various forms of life, while evolution cannot account for the large-scale differences that became entirely new species and for the origin of life. Basic to this strategy was assuming the role of questioners, "picking away at evolution, piece by piece" in an attempt to discredit evolution by pointing to parts of the theory for which direct evidence was still missing and largely theoretical. Armed with such evidence, antievolutionists pushed for alternative approaches.[73]

In Dover, Pennsylvania, eleven families sued their school board over its decision in October 2004 to require school teachers to read the following statement (in part) before ninth grade biology classes: "Because Darwin's theory is a theory, it continues to be tested as new evidence is discovered. The theory is not a fact. Gaps in the theory exist for which there is no evidence." It referred students to an intelligent design textbook, *Of Pandas and People*, available in the school library, and encouraged students to "keep an open mind" in the matter. The Pennsylvania ACLU and Americans United for Separation of Church and State filed a lawsuit in what became *Kitzmiller v. Dover Area School District*. And in a similar case, a suburban Atlanta school district (Cobbs County) voted to place stickers on each science book with the statement: "This book contains material on evolution. Evolution is a theory, not a fact, regarding the origins of living things. This material should be regarded with an open mind, studied carefully and critically considered."[74]

In November 2005, the people of Dover voted out of office those members of their school board who had supported the required classroom statement. On December 20, 2005, a US district judge ruled that intelligent design failed to meet the definition of being a science and that it constituted "a strong endorsement of a religious view" thereby violating the Supreme Court's precedent against the teaching of creationism in public schools. In January 2006, the Dover schools board rescinded the measure. In the matter of the textbook stickers in Cobb County, the school board ordered the stickers removed after a federal court in *Selman v. Cobb County School District* (2006) ordered the school district to remove them.[75]

As they had in the past, New Christian Right activists neither accepted nor openly challenged the court but rather campaigned for seats on local school boards hoping to influence curricula and textbooks to prevail on the basis of local rule or control of public education. Some chose to withdraw their children from the public schools either putting them in private religious schools, which were immune from First Amendment restrictions, or home schooling. Religious academies and home schooling spread rapidly during the 1960s through the 1980s. By the mid-1980s, they were educating more than a million children per year. Although the motives of those who chose to home school their children varied, a 1995 survey found that 90 percent of home-schooling families had religious motives. More specifically, 84 percent agreed that the Bible is the inspired word of God and literally true; 81 percent agreed that eternal life is a gift of God, predicated on belief in Jesus Christ; and 93 percent agreed that Satan was at work in the world. As to evangelicals and the general public and their views on evolution – in a 2006 survey, 76 percent of evangelicals continued to believe that living things have always existed in their current form, as compared to 32 percent of mainline Protestants and 31 percent of Roman Catholics.[76]

Summary

If the 1960s and 1970s can be characterized as revolutionary, the 1980s can be seen as counter-revolutionary. Those who found the 1960s and 1970s upsetting blamed liberal leadership in the nation's political, social, cultural, and religious arenas. Their counter-revolution would begin with the presidential candidacy of Jimmy Carter in the 1970s but reached its peak under President Ronald Reagan in the 1980s. It would be led by conservative evangelicals, commonly referred to as the New Christian Right. Their overall goal was to redeem the United States as a Christian nation by rolling back the liberal agenda from previous years. What success they had was in part due to the appeal of their message, but it was also due to their effective use of the mass media, their sophisticated organization, and their political collaboration.

Review questions

1   Some have argued that given the upheaval that marked the 1960s and 1970s, there was bound to be "an equal and opposite reaction" in the years that followed, as indeed there was. Describe that reaction.
2   What was the overarching goal of the New Christian Right, and what specific issues did it focus on in order to attain that goal?
3   Who were the leading religious figures in the New Christian Right during the final quarter of the twentieth century?
4   Describe the relationship between the New Christian Right and national politics from 1976 to the present.
5   How and why did premillennialism attract such a following in the closing years of the twentieth century, and how did that pose a dilemma for the more politically involved members of the New Christian Right?

Notes

1   Michael Lienesche, *Piety and Politics in the New Christian Right: Redeeming America* (Chapel Hill: University of North Carolina Press, 1993), 1, 4–7; "Old" Christian Right generally refers to the conservative religious crusade against liberalism and modernism in the half-century following the Civil War. Steve Bruce, *The Rise and Fall of the New Christian Right: Conservative Protestant Politics in America 1978–1988* (Oxford, UK: Clarendon Press, 1988), 25–49, 68–80, 85–90. Smith is quoted in Mark Silk, *Spiritual Politics: Religion and America since World War II* (New York: Simon and Schuster, 1988), 160, 165. Walter Capps, *The New Religious Right: Piety, Patriotism, and Politics* (Columbia: University of South Carolina Press, 1990), 3, 8–9, 89–126, especially 97–9. See also Kevin P. Phillips, *Post-Conservative America* (New York: Vintage, 1982); and Peter Beinert, "Battle for the Burbs," *The New Republic* (October 19, 1998): 25–9.
2   "The Christianity Today – Gallup Poll: An Overview," *Christianity Today* (December 21, 1979): 12–19; William Martin, "The Birth of a Media Myth," *Atlantic* (June 1981): 7–16; Lienesche, *Piety and Politics in the New Christian Right*, 1–3. For additional, contradictory estimates on the number of religious conservatives, as well as information pointing to their considerable diversity, and the size of the "electric" church's following, see Jeffrey K. Hadden and Anson Shupe, *Televangelism: Power and Politics on God's Frontier* (New York: Henry Holt and Company, 1988), 142–59; and Jeffrey K. Hadden and Charles E. Swann, *Prime Time Preachers: The Rising Power of Televangelism* (Reading, MA: Addison-Wesley, 1981), 164–5.
3   For information on the role played in the formation of the New Christian Right by lay figures like Paul Weyrich, Howard Phillips, Richard Viguerie, and others, see Lienesche, *Piety and Politics in the New Christian Right*, 8. Frances Fitzgerald, "A Disciplined, Charging Army," *New Yorker* (May 18, 1981): 53.
4   James L. Guth, "The Politics of the Evangelical Right: An Interpretive Essay," Paper presented to the American Political Science Association Annual Meeting (September 1981): 8–15, quoted in Lienesche, *Piety and Politics in the New Christian Right*, 10–11. Grant Wacker, "Searching for Norman Rockwell: Popular Evangelicalism in Contemporary America," in *The Evangelical Tradition in America*, ed. Leonard I. Sweet (Macon, GA: Mercer University Press, 1984), 289–315; Fitzgerald, "A Disciplined, Charging Army," 65–74, 120. For more on the New South, see Grant

Wacker, "Uneasy in Zion: Evangelical in Postmodern Society," in *Evangelism and Modern America*, ed. George Marsden (Grand Rapids, MI: William B. Eerdmans Publishing, 1984), 17–28; Kenneth D. Wald, *Religion and Politics in the United States*, 3rd edn. (Washington, DC: Congressional Quarterly, 1997), 238; Beinert, "Battle for the Burbs," 25–6.

5 Weyrich is quoted in George G. Higgins, "The Profile Movement and the New Right," *America* (September 13, 1980): 108; Pamela Johnson Conover, "The Mobilization of the New Right: A Test of Various Explanations," *Western Political Quarterly*, 36 (November 1983): 632–49; Louis J. Lorentzen, "Evangelical Lifestyle Concerns in Political Action," *Sociological Analysis*, 41 (Summer 1980): 144–54.

6 Patrick Allitt, *Religion in America since 1945: A History* (New York: Columbia University Press, 2003), 151; Frances Fitzgerald, *Cities on a Hill: A Journey through Contemporary American Cultures* (New York: Simon and Schuster, 1986), 129.

7 Jerry Falwell, *Listen America* (New York: Doubleday, 1980), 18–19; Capps, *The New Religious Right*, 31.

8 Falwell is quoted in George Vecsey, "Militant Television Preachers Try to Wield Fundamentalists Christians' Political Power," *New York Times* (January 21, 1980): A21, and Bill Keller, "Evangelical Conservatives Move from Pews to Polls," *Congressional Quarterly Weekly Report* (September 6, 1980): 2630. Capps, *The New Religious Right*, 52; Edwin Gaustad and Leigh Schmidt, *The Religious History of America: The Heart of the American Story from Colonial Times to Today*, rev. edn. (New York: HarperSanFrancisco, 2004), 403.

9 Weyrich is quoted in James Moffett, *Storm in the Mountains: A Case Study of Censorship, Conflict, and Consciousness* (Carbondale: Southern Illinois University Press, 1988), 191.

10 Dolly Paterson, "Churches and the Essential Few," *St. Petersburg Times* (August 31, 1991): 2E. For more on the "southernization of American religion" and its influence on the New Christian Right, see Mark A. Shibley, *Resurgent Evangelicalism in the United States: Mapping Cultural Change since 1970* (Columbia: University of South Carolina Press, 1996), chs. 1, 2, and 8.

11 George Cornell, "Today's Megachurches Able to Offer Younger Christians More Programs," *Memphis Commercial Appeal* (January 5, 1991): A10; see also Gustav Niebuhr, "Large Suburban Sanctuaries Are Using Country Music, Videos, and Whatever Else It Takes to Reach the Unchurched Masses," *Lakeland Ledger* (April 22, 1995): C1, and Angela Winter, "Young Adults Make Leap of Faith to Nondenominational Megachurches," *Baltimore Sun* (March 27, 1994): K1. "What Is Our Business?" *Wilmington Star-News* (April 18, 1995): A1; see also Allitt, *Religion in America since 1945*, 228–9, and John Wilson, "Not Just Another Megachurch," *Christianity Today* (December 4, 2000). www.christianitytoday.com/ct/2000/december4/8.62.html. See also Bellevue Baptist Church in Cordova, Tennessee: Robert Kerr, "Rev. Rogers Rolls On," *Memphis Commercial Appeal* (September 29, 1991): E1.

12 Allitt, *Religion in America since 1945*, 192, 230; David F. Wells, *No Place for Truth: Or Whatever Happened to Evangelical Theology?* (Grand Rapids, MI: Eerdmans, 1993). See also Joel Gregory, *Too Great a Temptation: The Seductive Power of America's Super Church* (Fort Worth, TX: Summit Group, 1994), and Stewart M. Hoover, "The Cross at Willow Creek: Seeker Religion and the Contemporary Marketplace," in *Religion and Popular Culture in America*, ed. Bruce David Forbes and Jeffery H. Mahan (Berkeley: University of California Press, 2000), 145–59.

13 Allitt, *Religion in America since 1945*, 193. Falwell is quoted in Capps, *The New Religious Right*, 137. For an overview of the ministry of Jim Bakker, see Charles Shepard, *Forgiven: The Rise and Fall of Jim Bakker and the PTL Ministry* (New York: Atlantic Monthly Press, 1989); Hunter James, *Smile Pretty and Say Jesus: The Last Great Days of PTL* (Athens: University of Georgia Press, 1993); and Gary Tidwell, *Anatomy of a Fraud: Inside the Finances of the PTL Ministries* (New York: Wiley, 1993).

14 Lawrence Wright, *Saints and Sinners* (New York: Knopf, 1993), 52; Capps, *The New Religious Right*, 180.

15 Victoria Sacket, "Oral Roberts Bucks Eternity," *New York Times* (March 30, 1987): A19. For a broader perspective on the entirety of this scandal-ridden period, see Wells, *No Place for Truth*.

16 Michael Barone, "Faith in Numbers," *National Review*, 48 (October 14, 1996): 56–8.

17 Capps, *The New Religious Right*, 11; Jon Butler, Grant Wacker, and Randall Balmer, *Religion in American Life: A Short History*, 2nd edn. (New York: Oxford University Press, 2011), 402; Allitt, *Religion in America since 1945*, 154; Raymond Haberski, Jr., *God and War: American Civil*

Religion since 1945 (New Brunswick, NJ: Rutgers University Press, 2012), 103–5; Gaustad and Schmidt, *The Religious History of America*, 405–6.

18 Peter G. Bourne, *Jimmy Carter: A Comprehensive Biography from Plains to Post-Presidency* (New York: Scribner, 1997), 178; Haberski, *God and War*, 105; Betty Glad, *Jimmy Carter: In Search of the Great White House* (New York: Norton, 1980), 333–4. See also Jimmy Carter, "Acceptance Speech at the Democratic National Convention," American Presidency Project (July 15, 1976). www.4president.org/speeches/carter1976acceptance.htm

19 Jimmy Carter, "National Prayer Breakfast Remarks," American Presidency Project (January 27, 1977). www.presidency.ucab.edu/ws/?pid=7189; Bourne, *Jimmy Carter*, 419–20, 445; Jimmy Carter, "Crisis of Confidence Speech," American Presidency Project (July 15, 1979). www.presidency.ucsb.edu/ws/?pid=32596; see also Kevin Mattson, *"What the Heck Are You Up to Mr. President?" Jimmy Carter, America's "Malaise," and the Speech That Should Have Changed the Country* (New York: Bloomsbury, USA, 2009), 20–1, 80, 144; Haberski, *God and War*, 111–2, 116; Butler, *Religion in American Life*, 402.

20 Haberski, *God and War*, 117, 121–4; Butler, *Religion in American Life*, 404; John Patrick Diggins, *Ronald Reagan: Fate, Freedom, and the Making of History* (New York: Norton, 2007), 27, 31, 41; Kiron K. Skinner, Martin Anderson, and Annelise Anderson, eds., *Reagan in His Own Hand: The Writings of Ronald Reagan That Reveal His Revolutionary Vision for America* (New York: Touchstone, 2001), xv, 227.

21 Gaustad and Schmidt, *The Religious History of America*, 406; Allitt, *Religion in America since 1945*, 155; Haberski, *God and War*, 126; Ronald Reagan, "Remarks to the Annual Convention of the National Association of Evangelicals, Orlando, Florida," American Presidency Project (March 8, 1983). www.presidency.ucsb.edu/ws/?pid=41023.

22 Gaustad and Schmidt, *The Religious History of America*, 407.

23 Randall Balmer, *Mine Eyes Have Seen the Glory: A Journey Into the Evangelical Subculture of America* (New York: Oxford University Press, 1999), 135; Allitt, *Religion in America since 1945*, 196; George Wills, *Under God: Religion and American Politics* (New York: Simon and Schuster, 1990), 80; Capps, *The New Religious Right*, 15–18, 176, 180–4; Lienesche, *Piety and Politics in the New Christian Right*, 17; W. Craig Bledsoe, "Post Moral Majority Politics: The Fundamentalist Impulse in 1988," Paper presented to the American Political Science Association Annual Meeting (September 1990): 13, quoted in Lienesche, *Piety and Politics in the New Christian Right*, 17; Kenneth D. Wald, "Ministering to the Nation: The Campaigns of Jesse Jackson and Pat Robertson," in *Nominating the President*, ed. Emmett H. Buell, Jr. and Lee Sigelman (Knoxville: University of Tennessee Press, 1991), 119–49.

24 Michael McTighe, "Jesse Jackson and the Dilemmas of a Prophet in Politics," *Journal of Church and State*, 32 (Summer 1990): 585; Wills, *Under God*, 242–3; McTighe, "Jesse Jackson and the Dilemmas of a Prophet in Politics," 594.

25 "Bush Interview with Robert Sherman, American Atheist News," George H. W. Bush Library Archives. http://robsherman.com/advocacy/bush/thirdfax.pdf; George Bush, "Proclamation 5962, Loyalty Day," American Presidency Project (April 28, 1989). www.presidency.ucsb.edu/ws/?pid=23510; George Bush, "Remarks Announcing the Proposed Constitutional Amendment on Desecration of the Flag," American Presidency Project (June 30, 1989). www.presidencyucsb.edu/ws/?pid=17232

26 Allitt, *Religion in America since 1945*, 147, 198; Sidney Blumenthal, "All the President's Wars," *New Yorker*, 68 (December 28, 1992/January 4, 1993): 62; Robert Wuthnow, *The Restructuring of American Religion: Society and Faith since World War II* (Princeton, NJ: Princeton University Press, 1988), 210–13, 242, 257; Kim A. Lawton, "Whatever Happened to the Religious Right?," *Christianity Today* (December 1989): 47; Lienesche, *Piety and Politics in the New Christian Right*, 19; Bruce, *The Rise and Fall of the New Christian Right*, 172–5. See also Michael D'Antonio, *Fall from Grace: The Failed Crusade of the Christian Right* (New York: Farrar, Straus, and Giroux, 1989).

27 George Bush, "State of the Union Address," American Presidency Project (January 28, 1992). www.presidency.ucsb.edu/ws/?pid=20544; Haberski, *God and War*, 161; Michael Barone, "Seeking Comfort," *U.S. News and World Report*, (January 28, 1991): 19; Kenneth Walsh, "Bush's 'Just War' Doctrine," *U.S. News and World Report* (February 4, 1991): 55; Jeffrey L. Shelter, "Holy War Doctrines," *U.S. News and World Report* (February 11, 1991): 55; George Weigel, "The Churches

and War in the Gulf," *First Things* (March 1991). http://firstthings.com/article/2007/10/003-the-churches-war-in-the-gulf-28; Richard John Neuhaus, "Just War and This War," *Wall Street Journal* (January 29, 1991): A18.

28 Haberski, *God and War*, 167; Patrick Buchanan, "Speech at the 1992 Republican National Convention – Known as "The Culture War Speech," (August 17, 1992). http://buchanan.org/blog/1_992-republican-national-convention-speech-148. For more on America's culture wars, see James Davison Hunter, *Culture Wars: The Struggle to Control the Family, Art, Education, Law, and Politics in America* (New York: Basic Books, 1992); and Andrew Hartman, *A War for the Soul of America: A History of the Culture Wars* (Chicago, IL: The University of Chicago Press, 2015).

29 Bruce, *The Rise and Fall of the New Christian Right*, 194.

30 Gaustad and Schmidt, *The Religious History of America*, 410; William Schneider, "Stealth Strategy for the Religious Right?," *National Journal*, 27 (May 1995): 1314. See also Matthew C. Moen, "School Prayer and the Politics of Life-Style Concern," *Social Science Quarterly*, 65 (December 1984): 1065–71. For more on the "Contract with America" presented through documents related to that event, see www.udel.edu/htr/American/Texts/contract.html

Wade Clark Roof, *A Generation of Seekers: The Spiritual Journeys of the Baby Boom Generation* (San Francisco, CA: Harper Collins, 1993). For more on Clinton, see William J. Clinton, "Remarks at Georgetown University," American Presidency Project (July 6, 1995). http://presidency.ucsb.edu/ws?pid=51584; William J. Clinton, "Remarks on International Security Issues at George Washington University," American Presidency Project (August 5, 1996). www.presidency.ucsb.edu/ws/?pid=53161

31 Jacques Berlinerblau, *Thumpin' It: The Use and Abuse of the Bible in Today's Presidential Politics* (Louisville, KY: Westminster John Knox Press, 2008), 3, 72, 78; Adelle Banks, "Is Bush an Evangelical?," Religion News Service (April 13, 2005). www.beliefnet.com/story/165/story_1html; Dana Stevens, "Oh God," *Slate* (April 29, 2004). www.slate.com/id/2099698; "Bush on God," *St. Petersburg Times* (January 16, 2005): A5; Tony Campolo, "The Ideological Roots of Christian Zionism," *Tikkun*, 20 (January/February 2005): 20. See also Tony Judt, "America and the World," *New York Review of Books* (April 10, 2003). www.nybooks.com/articles/16176; and Kevin Phillips, *American Theocracy: The Peril and Politics of Radical Religion, Oil, and Borrowed Money in the 21st Century* (New York: Viking, 2006), 261; George W. Bush, "Presidential Address to the Nation, September 11, 2001," in *"We Will Prevail": President George W. Bush on War, Terrorism, and Freedom*, ed. George W. Bush (New York: Bloomsbury Academic, 2003), 3; George W. Bush, "Presidential Proclamation Declaring National Day of Prayer and Remembrance for the Victims of the Terrorist Attacks, September 13, 2001," in *"We Will Prevail": President George W. Bush on War, Terrorism, and Freedom*, ed. George W. Bush (New York: Bloomsbury Academic, 2003), 4; George W. Bush, "Remarks by the President from Speech at the National Day of Prayer and Remembrance Ceremony, the National Cathedral, Washington, DC," (September 14, 2001) in *"We Will Prevail": President George W. Bush on War, Terrorism, and Freedom*, ed. George W. Bush (New York: Bloomsbury Academic, 2003), 7.

32 Crock is quoted in: Berlinerblau, *Thumpin' It*, 74, see also 84, 103. The reference to the public square and leaving religious beliefs at the public door comes from Richard John Neuhaus, *The Naked Public Square: Religion and Democracy in America* (Grand Rapids, MI: Eerdmans, 1986). See also Mark Sounder, "A Conservative Christian's View of Public Life," in *One Electorate under God: A Dialogue on Religion and American Politics*, ed. Eugene Joseph Dionne, Jean Bethke Elshtain, and Kayla Meltzer Drogosz (Washington, DC: Brookings Institute, 2004), 21.

33 Obama is quoted in David Kirkpatrick, "Consultant Helps Democrats Embrace Faith and Some in Party Are Not Pleased," *New York Times* (December 26, 2006): A10; Berlinerblau, *Thumpin' It*, 104.

34 Butler, et al., *Religion in American Life*, 436; Berlinerblau, *Thumpin' It*, 120–4. On McCain, see for example: David Brody, "McCain Says He Needs Evangelicals to Win," CBN News (March 19, 2007). www.cbn.com/CBNews/122005.aspx; Matt Stearns "McCain Reaching Out to Christian Conservative Base," *McClatchy Newspapers* (June 10, 2007). www.mcclatchydc.com/homepage/story/16589.html; Frank Bruni, "McCain Apologizes for Characterizing Falwell and Robertson as Forces of Evil," *New York Times* (March 2, 2000). http://www.nytimes.com/2000/03/02/us/2000-campaign-arizona-senator-mccain-apologizes-for-characterizing-falwell.html On Romney, see Hugh Hewitt, *A Mormon in the White House: 10 Things Every American Should Know About Mitt Romney* (Washington, DC:

Regenery, 2007), passim; Robert Rudy, "Public Views of Presidential Politics and Mormon Faith," *Pew Forum* (May 16, 2007). http://pewforum.org/docs/?DocsID=213; Amy Sullivan, "Mitt Romney's Evangelical Problem," *Washington Monthly* (September 2005). www.washingtonmonthly.com/features/2005/0509.sullivan1.html

35 Berlinerblau, *Thumpin' It*, 103–4; Barack Obama, *The Audacity of Hope: Thoughts on Reclaiming the American Dream* (New York: Crown, 2006), 39, 218–21, 234; Barack Obama, "'Call to Renewal' Keynote Address," (June 28, 2006). http://obama.senate.gov/speech/060628-call_to-renewal/

36 Pew Research, "How the Faithful Voted, A Preliminary 2016 Analysis." www.pewresearch.org/fact-tank/2016/11/09/how-the-faithful-voted-a-preliminary-2016-analysis/; Washington Post, "In Record Numbers Latinos Voted Overwhelmingly Against Trump, We Did the Research." www.washington-post.com/news/monkey-cage/wp/2016/11/11/in-record-numbers-latinos-voted-overwhelmingly-against-trump-we-did-the-research/?utm_term=.4daf38fd8982. The difference between the total of both figures and 100 percent is the result of votes cast for third-party candidates.

37 Washington Post, "Exit Polls Show White Evangelicals Voted Overwhelmingly for Donald Trump." www.washingtonpost.com/news/acts-of-faith/wp/2016/11/09/exit-polls-show-white-evangelicals-voted-overwhelmingly-for-donald-trump/?utm_term=.0c641d6eca2e; Washington Post, "In Record Numbers Latinos Voted Overwhelmingly Against Trump, We did the Research." www.washingtonpost.com/news/monkey-cage/wp/2016/11/11/in-record-numbers-latinos-voted-overwhelmingly-against-trump-we-did-the-research/?utm_term=.4daf38fd8982; Think Progress, "The Explosive Growth of Evangelical Belief in Latinos Has Big Political Implications." https://thinkprogress.org/the-explosive-growth-of-evangelical-belief-in-latinos-has-big-political-implications-c71a9a0a5009#.s1609wlpk

38 Balmer, *Mine Eyes Have Seen the Glory*, 58; Catherine L. Albanese, *America: Religions and Religion*, 4th edn. (Belmont CA: Wadsworth, 2002), 240.

39 Balmer, *Mine Eyes Have Seen the Glory*, 63.

40 Adam Perlman, "Time Has Come for the Millennium Center," *Boston Globe* (January 2, 1999): A1; Allitt, *Religion in America since 1945*, 246–9.

41 Allitt, *Religion in America since 1945*, 248. Among the few sources of information on Miller, see www.religioustolerance.org/dc_conc.htm

42 Allitt, *Religion in America since 1945*, 155. Francis Schaeffer, *The Great Evangelical Disaster* (Westchester, IL: Crossway, 1984), 23; Francis Schaeffer, *A Christian Manifesto* (Westchester, IL: Crossway, 1981), 61–2. Also Capps, *The New Religious Right*, ch. 3.

43 For more on the Catholic opposition to *Roe v. Wade*, see Kristin Luther, *Abortion and Politics of Motherhood* (Berkeley: University of California Press, 1984), 196–7; Allitt, *Religion in America since 1945*, 160–2; Butler, *Religion in American Life*, 403; Randall Balmer, "The Real Origins of the Religious Right," *Politico.com* (May 27, 2014). www.politico.com/magazine/story/2014/05/religious-right-real-origins-107133; Daniel K. Williams, *Defenders of the Unborn: The Pro-Life Movement before Roe V. Wade* (New York: Oxford University Press, 2016), 210–12.

44 Allitt, *Religion in America since 1945*, 160–2; Butler, *Religion in American Life*, 403; Williams, *Defenders of the Unborn*, 202.

45 Williams, *Defender of the Unborn*, 207, 234; Luther, *Abortion and Politics of Motherhood*, 196–7; Allitt, *Religion in America since 1945*, 160–2; Butler, *Religion in American Life*, 403; Balmer, "The Real Origins of the Religious Right." For more on the battle over abortion, see Johanna Schoen, *Abortion after Roe* (Chapel Hill: University of North Carolina Press, 2015).

46 Patrick Allitt has argued that, in part, the Catholic retreat was due to the threat of having its tax-exempt status challenged: Allitt, *Religion in America since 1945*, 164. For more on Operation Breakthrough and the abortion controversy, see also Luther, *Abortion and Politics of Motherhood*, and Melton, *The Churches Speak on Abortion*, noted earlier, as well as James Risen and Judy L. Thomas, *Wrath of Angels: The American Abortion War* (New York: Basic Books, 1998).

47 Allitt, *Religion in America since 1945*, 164–6. For more on the clash over the ERA and feminist programs, see Susan Faludi, *Backlash: The Undeclared War against American Women* (New York: Crown, 1991).

48 Balmer, *Mine Eyes Have Seen the Glory*, 120. See also Stephen Clark, *Man and Woman in Christ: An Examination of the Roles of Men and Women in Light of Scripture and the Social Sciences* (Cincinnati, OH: Servant Books, 1980), and Edward Hinson, *The Total Family* (Carol Stream, IL: Tyndall House, 1980).

49 Gustav Niebuhr, "Men Crowd Stadium to Fulfill Their Souls," *New York Times* (August 6, 1995): A1; Allitt, *Religion in America since 1945*, 242.
50 Bill McCartney, *Sold Out: Becoming Man Enough to Make a Difference* (Nashville, TN: Word, 1999); Promise Keepers official website http://Promisekeepers.org; Ken Abraham, *Who Are the Promise Keepers? Understanding the Christian Men's Movement* (New York: Doubleday, 1997); Albanese, *America; Religions and Religion*, 249–50.
51 Laurie Goodstein, "For Christian Men's Group, Racial Harmony Starts at the Local Level," *New York Times* (September 29, 1997): A12; Michael Janofsky, "Women on the Rally's Edge, Mirror Divided View of Groups," *New York Times* (October 5, 1997): A24; Patricia Ireland, "A Look at Promise Keepers," *Washington Post* (September 7, 1997): C3. See also Dane S. Clausen, ed., *Standing on the Promises: The Promise Keepers and the Revival of Manhood* (Cleveland, OH: Pilgrim, 1999); Allitt, *Religion in America since 1945*, 244.
52 Frank Rich, "Thank God I'm a Man," *New York Times* (September 25, 1996): A21; Allitt, *Religion in America since 1945*, 246.
53 Leonard W. Levy, *The Establishment Clause: Religion and the First Amendment* (New York: Macmillan, 1986), ix.
54 Levy, *The Establishment Clause*, 123–4; Peter Irons, *God on Trial: Landmark Cases from America's Religious Battlefields* (New York: Penguin, 2007), 21–4.
55 Levy, *The Establishment Clause*, 144–5; Robert S. Alley, *The Supreme Court on Church and State* (New York: Oxford University Press, 1988), 73, 3–4; Irons, *God on Trial*, 24–5.
56 John E. Semonche, *Religion and Constitutional Government in the United States: A Historical Overview with Sources* (Carrboro, NC: Signal Book, 1985), 51–2; Alley, *The Supreme Court on Church and State*, 183; Levy, *The Establishment Clause*, 146; Irons, *God on Trial*, 26–7.
57 Levy, *The Establishment Clause*, 147; Anthony Lewis, "Ruling Is 6 to 1/Suit Was Brought by 5 L: I. Parents against Education Board," *New York Times* (June 26, 1962): 17; Roy R. Siler, "Majority Opinion by Justice Black," *New York Times* (June 26, 1962): 16; Irons, *God on Trial*, 29–30.
58 Lewis, "Ruling is 6 to 1," 17; Semonche, *Religion and Constitutional Government in the United States*, 60; "Majority Opinion by Justice Black," 16–17; "Concurring Opinion by Justice Douglas," *New York Times* (June 26, 1961): 16; Irons, *God on Trial*, 29–30. See also Bruce J. Dierenfield, *The Battle over School Prayer: How Engle v. Vitale Changed America* (Lawrence: University Press of Kansas, 2007); and Adam Laats, "Our Schools, Our Country: American Evangelicals, Public Schools, and the Supreme Court Decisions of 1962 and 1963," *Journal of Religious History*, 36 (September 2012): 319–34.
59 Alexander Burnham, "Edict Is Called a Setback by Christian Clerics – Rabbis Praise It," *New York Times* (June 26, 1962): 1, 17; Fred M. Hechinger, "Challenges Are Predicted," *New York Times* (June 26, 1962): 1, 17.
60 Burnham, "Edict Is Called a Setback by Christian Clerics," 17; Levy, *The Establishment Clause*, 148; Leo Pfeffer, *Church, State, and Freedom*, rev. edn. (Boston: Beacon Press, 1967), 466–9; Alley, *The Supreme Court on Church and State*, 194.
61 Lewis, "Ruling is 6 to 1," 1; Irons, *God on Trial*, 30–1; "Text of Supreme Court's Decision on School Prayers and Bible Reading," *New York Times* (June 18, 1963): 28.
62 William Murray later became a born-again evangelist and opposed his mother's activities on behalf of atheists. For more background on the life and activities of Madalyn Murray O'Hair, see Bryan F. Le Beau, *The Atheist: Madalyn Murray O'Hair* (New York: New York University Press, 2003).
63 "Text of Supreme Court's Decision on School Prayers and Bible Reading," 28; Levy, *The Establishment Clause*, 149; Alley, *The Supreme Court on Church and State*, 204. The Court further refined its position in *Lemon v. Kurtzman* in 1971. In that decision, which established what came to be known as the "Lemon Test," it stated that, in order to be constitutional under the Establishment Clause, any practice sponsored by the state must adhere to three criteria: It 1) must have a secular purpose, 2) neither advance nor inhibit religion, and 3) not result in an excessive entanglement between government and religion: www.oyez.org/cases/1970-1979/1970/1970_89; Irons, *God on Trial*, 34–6; Levy, *The Establishment Clause*, 149.
64 "Text of Supreme Court's Decision on School Prayers and Bible Reading," 28.
65 "Text of Supreme Court's Decision on School Prayers and Bible Reading," 28.

66 James P. Moore, Jr., *One Nation under God: The History of Prayer in America* (New York: Doubleday, 2005), 361; George Dugan, "Churches Divided with Most in Favor," *New York Times* (June 18, 1963): 29.

67 Hechinger, "Challenges Are Predicted," 17; Dugan, "Churches Divided with Most in Favor," 29; "Billy Graham Voices Shock over Decision," *New York Times* (June 18, 1963): 17. In 2011, a study showed that 65 percent of Americans continued to support the reintroduction of school prayer. www.usnews.com/news/articles/2013/01/03/study-catholic-protestant-support-for-in-school-prayer-falls

68 Hechinger, "Challenges Are Predicted," 1; Madalyn Murray O'Hair, *An Atheist Epic: The Complete Unexpurgated Story of How Bible and Prayers Were Removed from the Public Schools in the United States* (Austin, TX: American Atheist Press, 1970), 305. See, for example: *Stein v. Oshinsky* (1965) and *DeSpain v. Dekalb County Community School District* (1966). Le Beau, *The Atheist*, 96–7; Lienesche, Redeeming America, 168; Alley, *The Supreme Court on Church and State*, 204; Moore, *One Nation under God*, 361–4.

69 Oyez, "*Lee v. Weisman.*" www.oyez.org/cases/1990-1999/1991/1991_90_1014; Oyez, "*Santa Fe Independent School District v Doe.*" www.oyez.org/cases/1990-1999/1999/1999_99_62; Irons, *God on Trial*, 145–59; J. D. Torr, "Preface," to *Does Separation of Church and State Threaten Religious Liberty?* ed. J. D. Torr [Current Controversies: Civil Liberties] (San Diego, CA: Greenhaven Press, 2003).

70 Janes Howard, "Madalyn Murray: The Most Hated Woman in America," *Life* (June 19, 1964): 91–2, 94; See also Le Beau, *The Atheist*; and Ann Rowe Seaman, *America's Most Hated Woman: The Life and Gruesome Death of Madalyn Murray O'Hair* (New York: Continuum, 2007).

71 Ronald L. Numbers, "Creationism Science 1859," in *Science and Religion: A Historical Introduction*, ed. Gary Bergner (Baltimore, MD: Johns Hopkins University Press, 2002), 283; Allitt, *Religion in America since 1945*, 181. John C. Whitcomb, Jr., and Henry M. Morris, *The Genesis Flood* (Philadelphia, PA: Presbyterian and Reformed Publishing Co., 1961); George Price, *New Geology* (Mountain View, CA: Pacific Press, 1923). See also Raymond Eve and Francis B. Harrold, *The Creationist Movement in Modern America* (Boston: Twayne Publishers, 1991); Peter J. Bowler, *Monkey Trials and Gorilla Sermons: Evolution and Christianity from Darwin to Intelligent Design* (Cambridge, MA: Harvard University Press, 2007); and Roland M. Frye, *Is God a Creationist: The Religious Case against Creation Science* (New York: Scribner's, 1983).

72 On *McLean*, see www.npr.org/templates.story/story.php?storyId=4726786. Reginald Stuart, "Judge Overturns Arkansas Law on Creationism," *New York Times* (January 5, 1982). www.nytimes.com/1982/01/06/us/judge-overturns-arkansas-law-on-creationism.html. On *Edwards*, see www.oyez.org/cases/1980-1989/1986/1986_85_1513; Edward Larson, *Summer for the Gods: The Scopes Trial and America's Continuing Debate over Science and Religion* (Cambridge, MA: Harvard University Press, 1997), 259; Lienesche, *Piety and Politics in the New Christian Right*, 207–12, 215–16.

73 Lienesche, *Piety and Politics in the New Christian Right*, 219–22; Bowler, *Monkey Trials and Gorilla Sermons*, 211–17. See Michael Behe, *Darwin's Black Box: The Biological Challenge to Evolution* (New York: Free Press, 1996); William A. Dembski, *The Design Inference: Eliminating Chance through Small Probabilities* (Cambridge, UK: Cambridge University Press, 1998); and Robert T. Penrock, *Tower of Babel: The Evidence against the New Creationism* (Cambridge, MA: MIT Press, 1998).

74 Irons, *God on Trial*, 287, 290, 299, 316. "Federal Evolution Trial Beings," *Kansas City Star* (September 27, 2005): A4; "Witness: Assertion Isn't Science," *Kansas City Star* (September 29, 2005): A3; David Klepper, "Evolution Wins Round in U.S. Court," *Kansas City Star* (December 11, 2005): A1. Percival David and Dan H. Kenyon, *Of Pandas and People: The Central Question of Biological Origins* (Mesquite, TX: Haughton Publishing Company, 1989). "Court Reviews Ruling against Textbook Stickers," *Kansas City Star* (December 15, 2005): A13.

75 Jill Lawrence, "Intelligent Design Backers Lose in PA," *USA Today* (November 10, 2005): A1; Bryan F. Le Beau, "Science and Religion: A Historical Perspective on the Conflict over the Teaching of Evolution in the Schools," *Radical History Review*, 99 (Fall 2007): 197–8; Phil Berardelli, "Evolution Stickers Gone for Good in Cobb Country," *Science*, (December 20, 2006). http://news.sciencemag.org/education/2006/12/evolution-stickers-gone-good-cobb-county; Lienesche, *Piety and Politics in the New Christian Right*, 234.

76 Allitt, *Religion in America since 1945*, 185–9; Mitchell Stevens, *Kingdom of Children: Culture and Controversy in the Home-schooling Movement* (Princeton, NJ: Princeton University Press, 2001), 12. See also Susan D. Rose, *Keeping Them Out of the Hands of Satan: Evangelical Schooling in America* (New York: Routledge, 1988). Pew Research Center for the People and the Press poll, discussed in Robert Lee Hotz, "Laws of Nature," Sunday Book Reviews, *Los Angeles Times* (July 30, 2006): R3; Laura Sheehan, "The Problem with God: An Interview with Richard Dawkins" (November 11, 2005). www.beliefnet.com/story/178/story_17889.html; Nichols D. Kristof, "The Hubris of the Humanities," *New York Times* (December 6, 2005). http://query.nytimes.com/gst/fullpage.html?res=9B00E2DB1331F935A35751C1A9639C8B63; Le Beau, "Science and Religion, 195–9.

Recommended for further reading

Alley, Robert S. *The Supreme Court on Church and State*. New York: Oxford University Press, 1988.

Balmer, Randall. *Mine Eyes Have Seen the Glory: A Journey Into the Evangelical Subculture of America*. New York: Oxford University Press, 1999.

Bowler, Peter J. *Monkey Trials and Gorilla Sermons: Evolution and Christianity from Darwin to Intelligent Design*. Cambridge, MA: Harvard University Press, 2007.

Eve, Raymond and Francis B. Harold. *The Creationist Movement in Modern America*. Boston: Twayne Publishers, 1991.

Faludi, Susan. *Backlash: The Undeclared War against American Women*. New York: Crown, 1991.

Hunter, James Davison. *Culture Wars: The Struggle to Control the Family, Art, Education, Law, and Politics in America*. New York: Basic Books, 1992.

Le Beau, Bryan F. *The Atheist: Madalyn Murray O'Hair*. New York: New York University Press, 2003.

Lienesch, Michael. *Piety and Politics in the New Christian Right: Redeeming America*. Chapel Hill: University of North Carolina Press, 1993.

Lindsey, Hal and Carole C. Carlson. *The Late Great Planet Earth*. Grand Rapids, MI: Eerdmans, 1970.

Silk, Mark. *Spiritual Politics: Religion and America Since World War II*. New York: Simon and Schuster, 1988.

Chapter 8

Whither religion in the twenty-first century?

The changing American religious landscape

As we have seen, diversity has been a common theme in the history of religion in America and its ever expanding and inclusive "sacred canopy." Yet, in the midst of the notable changes addressed in previous chapters, especially in the nation's religious diversity, much remains the same. To begin with, as anthropologist of religion Diana Eck wrote in 2001 in her book *A New Religious America:* "We the people of the United States now form the most profusely religious nation on earth." Although subject to some debate over how to measure religiosity and the reliability of survey data based on self-reporting, nearly all surveys of Americans' religiosity for the past several decades have reached the same conclusion. While other developed nations – those in Europe most notably – have become increasingly secularized, the United States has remained highly religious.[1]

Although religious diversity since 1965 can largely be attributed to immigration from non-Western and non-Christian countries, it has also been the result of an ongoing church-sect process whereby larger, more mainstream denominations continually lose their ability to serve the needs of all their adherents leading to a spinoff of new religious organizations, or sects. And this process, which we have seen in our earlier historical account, has been attributed to America's commitment to the free exercise of religion. As Roger Finke and Rodney Stark have put it: "The sect-church process is always under way, and the less regulated the religious economy, the more rapidly and thoroughly the process will occur." This religious economy helps explain the diverse paths of belief in Europe and America and counters the still widely held belief that pluralism weakens faith, which, at least in the United States, is not supported by the evidence. Although other factors in America may enter into it, such as the well-documented propensity of many Americans to constitute what Wade Clark Roof calls "a quest culture," continually seeking greater meaning in one's spiritual life, the evidence suggests that religious monopolies lead to indifference.[2]

The US Census does not ask Americans about their religious affiliations. Therefore, there are no official government statistics on the subject. Some denominations keep their own membership data, but they do so using different criteria, making any comparisons difficult.[3] Most students of American religious affiliations rely on national polling surveys, which have provided useful and often surprising information. For example, many observers anticipated that there would be a spike in religious commitment in the wake of 9/11. In fact, despite anecdotal comments about a surge in church attendance and Bible sales, at least to judge by polling data, 9/11 did not prompt any discernible and lingering change in Americans' religious beliefs or behavior. It did elicit some changes in their perspectives on moral truths,

God's active engagement with the world, and the existence of Satan. Comparing the results from polls conducted in October and early November 2001 to July and mid-August 2002, the Barna Group found that there was little to no lasting change in the percentage of Americans who considered themselves Christian, or Muslim, for that matter; in those who made a personal commitment to Jesus Christ, or were "born again"; in church attendance; in Bible reading; in contending that the Bible is accurate in all that it teaches; or in time spent praying. What changes did occur were that after 9/11 fewer adults – 22 percent – claimed that they believed in the existence of absolute moral truth down from 38 percent at the start of 2000. Those who believed that God was "the all-powerful, all-knowing perfect Creator of the universe who still rules the world" dropped from 72 percent one month before 9/11 to 68 percent one month after, while the percentage of those who strongly disagreed with the statement that "Satan/the devil is not a living being but is just a symbol of evil" increased from 23 percent to 28 percent.[4]

Pollster George Barna offered his observations on this data:

> After the attack, millions of nominally churched or generally religious Americans were desperately seeking something that would restore stability and a sense of meaning to life. Fortunately, many of them turned to the church. Unfortunately, few of them experienced anything that was sufficiently life-changing to capture their attention and their allegiance. They tended to appreciate the moments of comfort they received, but were unaware of anything sufficiently unique or beneficial as to redesign their lifestyle to integrate a deeper level of spiritual involvement. Our assessment is that churches succeeded at putting on a friendly face but failed at motivating the vast majority of spiritual explorers to connect with Christ in a more intimate or intense manner.[5]

Although the numbers vary, polls conducted throughout the first decade and a half of the twenty-first century continually pointed to a slow, but steady, decline in some measures of religiosity. On December 16, 2013, for example, Harris Interactive published a report – "Americans' Belief in God, Miracles and Heaven Declines" – in which it offered comparisons between its polling data collected between 2005 and 2013. It showed that, while a strong majority of American adults continued to believe in God, that percentage had declined over the intervening eight years from 82 percent to 74 percent. Similarly, the percentage of adult Americans who believed in heaven dropped from 75 percent to 68 percent, that Jesus is God or the Son of God from 72 percent to 68 percent, in the resurrection of Jesus Christ from 70 percent to 65 percent, in the survival of the soul after death from 69 percent to 64 percent, in the devil and hell from 62 percent to 58 percent, and that the New and Old Testament represent the word of God from 55 percent to 49 percent and 54 percent to 48 percent, respectively. The same polling data indicated a decline among Americans in their certainty that there is a God from 66 percent in 2005 to 54 percent in 2013. While the percentage of those who believed that God observes but does not control what happens on Earth declined from 50 percent to 37 percent, the percentage of Americans who believed that God controls what happens on Earth remained steady at 29 percent. And finally, while those who reported that they were very religious or somewhat religious declined from 21 percent to 19 percent and 49 percent to 40 percent, respectively, those self-described as not very religious remained steady at 10 percent, and those who reported that they were "not at all religious" increased from 12 percent to 23 percent. Consistent with most other polls, the likelihood that those questioned would report believing in any of the above increased with age, Millennials being least likely to believe, older Americans accounting for the largest percentage of believers, the range between the youngest and the oldest categories varying from 13 to 19 percent.[6]

The most detailed and current reports on Americans' religiosity appeared in 2015. The Pew Research Center compared polling data gathered in 2014 to that of 2007, and Gallup provided an overview from 1992 to 2013. The Pew report (see Table 8.1) was appropriately titled "America's Changing Religious Landscape" and descriptively subtitled: "Christians Decline Sharply as Share of Population; Unaffiliated and Other Faiths Continue to Grow." Its findings were consistent with most other and earlier surveys. A closer analysis of the numbers, however, provides some important nuances to these conclusions. Perhaps most importantly, it should be noted that Pew's survey shows that the United States continues to have more Christians than any other country in the world, with 7 out of 10 Americans identifying with some Christian denomination.[7]

Nevertheless, the percentage of adults (ages 18 and older) who described themselves as Christians in the Pew poll dropped by nearly 8 percentage points since 2007, from 78.4 percent to 70.6 percent. The drop was driven by declines among mainline Protestants by 3 percentage points. Mainline Protestants, which would include the United Methodist Church; the American Baptist Churches, USA; the Evangelical Lutheran Church in America; the Presbyterian Church (U.S.A.); and the Episcopal Church – constituting essentially the "founding religions" of America – dropped from about 41 million members in 2007 to an estimated 36 million in 2014. This decline has been documented for several decades. Somewhat new, the evangelical Protestant share of the US population also decreased but only by 1 percent. And in terms of the number of adherents, as opposed to percentage of the adult population, churches in the evangelical Protestant tradition – including the Southern Baptist Convention, the Assemblies of God, Churches of Christ, the Lutheran Church – Missouri Synod, the Presbyterian Church in America, and many non-denominational congregations – gained 2 million adherents and remained fairly stable as a percentage of the adult population at just over 25 percent. As a result, evangelicals now constitute 55 percent of all Protestants, as

Table 8.1 "America's Changing Religious Landscape"

Population*	2007 (%)	2014 (%)
Christians	78.4	70.6
Non-Christians	4.7	5.9
Unaffiliated	16.1	22.8
Atheist	1.6	3.1
Agnostic	2.4	4.0
"Nones"**	12.1	15.8
Millennials	25.0	35.0
Men	20.0	27.0
Women	13.0	19.0
College graduates	17.0	24.0
Less than college	16.0	22.0

* Adults 18 and over
** No particular religious affiliation

Source: PEW Research Center, May 2015

compared to 51 percent in 2007. A significant change is that the share of evangelical Protestants who identify with Baptists denominations has declined from 41 percent to 36 percent, while their share identifying with non-denominational churches has grown from 13 percent to 19 percent.[8]

Over the same time period, but continuing a pattern seen for over a decade, the percentage of Americans who reported to Pew that they were religiously unaffiliated – describing themselves as atheist, agnostic, or more commonly "nothing in particular" – jumped from 16.1 percent to 22.8 percent. In 2007, there were roughly 19 million unaffiliated adults in the United States; by 2014, that number increased to 56 million. That would make them more numerous than Roman Catholics and mainline Protestants and second in size only to evangelical Protestants. Pew found that whites were more likely than blacks and Hispanics to identify as religiously unaffiliated. Men, at 27 percent, accounted for a 7 percent increase since 2007. They outnumbered women in this category, but women were closing ranks with 19 percent unaffiliated, up from 13 percent seven years earlier. "Nones" constituted 24 percent of all college graduates, up from 17 percent in 2007, but adults with less than a college degree followed closely at 22 percent, an increase of 6 percent over the same time period. But perhaps most importantly the "nones," or religiously unaffiliated were comparatively young. As the survey found, as the number of unaffiliated Millennials (born between 1981 and 1996) reached adulthood, the median age of unaffiliated adults dropped to 36, down from 38 in 2007 and far lower than the general adult population's median age of 46. By way of comparison, the median age of mainline Protestant adults rose from 50 to 52 and of Catholic adults from 45 to 49 over the seven years. The Pew Research Center refers to this as "generational replacement," meaning that as Millennials enter adulthood, they continue to display lower levels of religious affiliation than older generations.[9]

To that point, the Pew Center found that 36 percent of Millennials (those between 18 and 24) were religiously unaffiliated, as were 34 percent of older Millennials (ages 25–33). Further, fewer than 60 percent of Millennials identified with any branch of Christianity, compared with 70 percent or more among older generations. Just 16 percent of Millennials were Catholic, 11 percent mainline Protestant, and 20 percent evangelical Protestant. However, the polling data also indicated that generation replacement was not the only reason religious "nones" were growing at the expense of Christians. People in older generations were becoming increasingly unaffiliated as well. About one-third of older Millennials (people in their late 20s and early 30s) reported that they had "no religion," up 9 percentage points since 2007, when that same group ranged between ages 18 and 26. Nearly 25 percent of generation Xers (born between 1965 and 1980) reported that they had no particular religion, up 4 percentage points in seven years. And finally, although only slightly, baby boomers were more likely to identify as "nones." Related to this population, although the number of inter-religious marriages had grown across the board – up to just short of 40 percent among those who had married since 2010, as compared to 19 percent before 1960 – nearly 20 percent of all marriages since 2010 had included an unaffiliated spouse marrying a Christian, as compared to just 5 percent before 1960.

In a similar vein, Pew found that many Americans, especially mainstream Protestants, continued be "seekers," or often change their religious affiliation – sometimes more than once in their lifetime – for various reasons but commonly to find a denomination that better satisfies their spiritual needs. Among the data Pew cited are that of all Protestants they polled 34 percent had a religious identity different from the one in which they were raised, which was 6 percentage points above the level in 2007. If taken into consideration movement from one Protestant denomination to another, that figure increases to 42 percent. As one might expect, switching among "nones" is more pronounced than with any other group, but to a large extent, that switching is toward the ranks of the unaffiliated. Put succinctly, Pew shows that, for every person who has moved from being raised unaffiliated to a religion, more than four have moved in the other direction. Pew found that overall 85 percent of American adults were raised Christian, but nearly 25 percent of those raised Christian no longer identified with Christianity. Put another way, former Christians represented 19.2 percent of adults in America. Pew also found that Catholicism has been losing more adherents through switching than it has been gaining. Nearly one-third of American adults say they were raised Catholic, but among that group, 41 percent no longer claimed that identity. What that means is that nearly 13 percent of American adults are former Catholics; only 2 percent have converted to Catholicism from another religion. Although not as dramatically, historically black Protestant denominations have lost members through religious switching, while evangelical Protestants have broken even.[10]

Not surprisingly given the change in immigration law since 1965, the Pew Research Center reports that over the same time period – from 2017 to 2014 – the share of Americans who identify with non-Christian faiths has increased from 4.7 percent to 5.9 percent, with the largest increase among Muslims followed by Hindus. The percentage of Muslims among adults increased from .4 percent in 2007 to .9 percent in 2014. The percentage of Hindus rose from .4 percent to .7 percent. Roughly 15 percent of those surveyed in 2014 were born outside the United States, and two-thirds of them are Christians, including 39 percent who were Catholic. Just over 10 percent of immigrants identified with a non-Christian faith. However, again to keep things in perspective, immigration over the past half-century, as has been true throughout American history, has led to changes among American Christians. Non-Hispanic whites now account for smaller shares of mainline Protestants, Catholics, and evangelical Protestants, whereas Hispanics have grown significantly as a share of all three religious groups. Racial and ethnic minorities now make up 41 percent of Catholics (up from 35 percent in 2007), 14 percent of mainline Protestants (up from 9 percent), and 24 percent of evangelical Protestants (up from 19 percent).

The Gallup Poll, "Historical Trends," provided an even longer-term perspective, from the early 1990s to 2013 or 2014, in some cases, once again showing, not only where attitudes remained the same, but more so where they changed over the twenty-year period, and what if any influence 9/11 appears to have had. One area where Americans were consistent was in their reporting that religion was very important in their lives, varying only two percentage points from 58 percent to 56 percent between 1992 and 2013. But when those polled were asked what their religious preferences were, the percentage of those who reported "none" doubled, from 8 percent to 16 percent. When asked how much confidence they had in organized religion, those that expressed "none" to "very little" increased from a combined 10 percent to 23 percent; those that ventured that they had either a "great deal" or "quite a lot" of confidence in organized religion dropped from 62 percent to 42 percent. How about the influence of organized religion? Between 2001 and 2015, the percentage of those polled who were either "satisfied" or "very satisfied" dropped from 64 percent to 53 percent, while those who were "somewhat" or "very dissatisfied" increased from 32 percent to 39 percent. When those who were dissatisfied were asked whether they wanted organized religion to have more influence, roughly the same percentage in 2001 and 2015 wanted more (between 8 percent and 10 percent); those who wanted less increased from 12 percent to 22 percent.

Finally, 78 percent of those polled by Gallup in 2013 expressed that religion was either "very" or "fairly important" in their lives, down from 87 percent in 1992. Twenty-two percent said it was "not very important" versus 12 percent in 1992. When asked if they thought religion was increasing its influence in American life or losing its influence, 21 percent said it was increasing its influence, 76 percent thought it was losing influence, as compared to 27 percent and 63 percent, respectively, earlier. Among those polled in 2013, 59 percent responded that they were members of a church or synagogue, down from 70 percent in 1992. Forty-one percent reported that they were "born-again" or "evangelical Christians," up from 36 percent twenty-one years earlier. In 2013, 56 percent thought religion could answer all or most of today's problems, down from 62 percent in 1994. When asked if they believed in God or a "universal spirit," 94 percent said yes in 1976; 86 percent, in 2014. Twenty-eight percent believed that the Bible was the actual word of God, 47 percent that it was the inspired word of God, and 21 percent "fables or legends," as compared to 38 percent, 45 percent, and 13 percent, respectively, in 1976. And finally, although the report did not offer any comparative data, in 2013, when asked if it would be positive or negative if more Americans were religious, 75 percent said it would be positive; 17 percent thought it would be negative.[11]

America and secularization: decline of mainline Protestant churches

In 1965, Harvard theologian Harvey Cox predicted that the United States would become a more secular society. Two years later, sociologist Thomas Luckmann anticipated a de-institutionalization of American religious behavior, which would legitimize individuals' retreat into their private spheres and subjective autonomy. In the 1980s, students of secularization in the United States combined both of these ideas into one, more nuanced explanation wherein they found secularization to be more structural than psychological. And, as we have seen, over the past several years, there has been a slow, but gradual and continuous, increase among those disaffected – if not so much in Americans' belief in God, or a higher spiritual power, at least in their relationship to mainstream religious institutions. But is this trend real and/or lasting? Was *Newsweek*'s cover story headline on April 13, 2009, accurate, when it announced: "The End of Christian America"?[12]

As alluded to earlier, what lies at the core of this anticipated secularization is the decline of America's mainline, Protestant churches, a decline that some have argued has gone on for a century or more, but most agree began in earnest in the mid-1970s. While the total Protestant population has now fallen below 50 percent of American adults (48 percent), the mainline churches (identified earlier), which once constituted the considerable majority of Americans, by the end of the twentieth century, accounted for no more than a quarter of Americans. The decline of these churches has been addressed by several different researchers, who, as of the mid-1990s, pointed out that, while those churches had accounted for every president of the United States except for Roman Catholic John Kennedy and Southern Baptists Jimmy Carter and Bill Clinton, they had produced the majority of US Supreme Court justices, and they were overrepresented by far in Congress, "these one-time pillars of the religious establishment are frequently ignored, their power to bestow social prestige has greatly dissipated, and their defining theological doctrines have been largely forgotten."[13]

Since then many critics, especially on the right, have argued that these liberal churches are at least in part responsible for the moral and spiritual decline that they believe has pervaded the nation down to the present. As Thomas Reeves put forth their questions: "Why are these churches failing to teach right from wrong? Why are young people abandoning them? Why are church leaders so quiet in the face of growing moral anarchy? And why do they spend much if not most of their time promoting counterproductive social and political causes?" Reeves continued: "In the story of America's mainline churches, especially since the sixties, we encounter the larger drama of a country and a civilization in intense turmoil over the nature of truth . . . [that, in the midst of] the deterioration of the religious bodies that once established our spiritual and moral standards."[14]

Over the course of the past two decades polls have shown that Americans believe that the many problems facing our country have been "primarily moral and social," even going so far as to suggest that the nation is suffering from moral decay. Social scientist Os Guinness has speculated that "Under the conditions of late twentieth-century modernity, the cultural authority of American belief, ideals, and traditions is dissolving." In 1994, classics professor Donald Kagan observed in the *Wall Street Journal*: "By now . . . the power of religion has faded, and for many the basis for a modern political and moral order has been demolished." All of this, and more, fairly or not, is often placed at the foot of the declining, liberal mainstream Protestant churches.[15]

Since the cultural turmoil of the 1960s and 1970s, the mainline churches have lost adherents in unprecedented numbers, losing between one-fifth and one-third of their membership by the end of the century. A major reason for this decline has been the failure to retain their own youth when they become young adults and make their own decisions. The result has been that, by the turn of the twenty-first century, fully half of all mainline members were over 50 years old and continuing to age, whereas conservative Protestants and Roman Catholics have aged more slowly because they have been more successful in keeping their young, the latter group being helped by an influx of comparatively young Catholic immigrants, as well.[16]

Colleges and universities founded by mainline churches have become either secular or so unintentional in their mission so as to lack any readily identifiable connection to their founding churches. Morale in the mainline ranks has declined. In 1995, one major study concluded that: "The liberal Protestant community is mired in a depression, one that is far more serious and deeper than it has suffered at any time in this century." A Gallup Poll showed that only 27 percent of Protestants gave their church an excellent rating. The Methodists, scoring the highest among the mainline bodies, reported 25 percent; the Presbyterians, 18 percent; and the Episcopalians, 9 percent. And missionary zeal has been almost lost, Gallup reported, "invitation and evangelism" going "virtually ignored by the mainline churches." In 1985, one-third of the nation's Methodist churches had performed no baptisms; almost two-thirds offered no membership training or confirmation classes; and nearly one-half lacked a list of potential new members. The Episcopal Church in 1996 sponsored just twenty-five overseas missionaries worldwide, down from fifty-nine in 1989.[17]

Reasons for the decline of mainline Protestant churches from the left have differed considerably from those offered from the right. One common explanation is that the churches have failed to keep pace with the times and become too conservative, suggesting that they would do better by abandoning their "old-fashioned" ways or moral positions. As Thomas Reeves has summarized this proposition; "To many liberals, in short, the mainline denominations are declining because they have been insufficiently attentive to the 'progressive' [social] forces of our time. Churches stuck in the past, they argue, must pay the price for their ignorance and insensitivity."[18]

Some observers, especially conservatives, have challenged this position. As one critic of the left has put it: "To politicize the church by focusing its attention and energies on pronouncements dealing with social issues about which Christians are bitterly divided is to lead the church away from its destiny and toward eventual paralysis." Moreover, most observers have seen this insistence on political neutrality as unrealistic. As history suggests, and as we have seen, in the vast majority of cases, a close relationship between religious belief and social action is inevitable. As Richard John Neuhaus has argued: "Christian truth, if it is truth, is public truth. It is accessible to public reason. It impinges upon public space. At some critical points of morality and ethics it speaks to public policy."[19]

Other observers see the mainline Protestant churches as the victims of modernism, or more specifically urbanism, industrialism, rising educational levels, prosperity, social mobility, the changing nature of the family, and the changing demands on the religion that have resulted. Dean M. Kelley, an official of the National Council of Churches, raised this prospect in 1972 in what was then a highly controversial book, *Why Conservative Churches Are Growing*. In the midst of the rebellious sixties and early seventies, widespread challenges to organized religion in America occurred, which in turn caused many mainstream Protestant churches to back off on their demands on their members. Kelley posed what then appeared to be the counterintuitive thesis that the successful churches, which he identified as the more conservative denominations, not only had taken positions that challenged the more socially liberal stances of the mainstream, but also made strict demands both of faith and practice on their members. He contended that the "business" of religion is "to explain the ultimate meaning of life" and that what makes "one system of ultimate meaning more convincing than another is not its content but its seriousness/strictness/costliness/bindingness." The mainline churches, he contended, had lost sight of this and not only failed to address the essential questions of life – its meaning and purpose – but had lost their distinctive identity and become too permissive.[20]

Kelley's thesis remained just that, some suggesting that what he found was a temporary response to the turmoil of the 1960s, but it was carefully studied for several years thereafter, gradually producing evidence that it was substantially correct. In 1987, Wade Clark Roof and William McKinney, two liberal scholars of religion, provided data in support of Kelley's thesis. They concluded: "Careful analysis of membership trends shows that the churches hardest hit were those highest in socioeconomic status, those stressing individualism and pluralism in belief, and those most affirming of American culture." That was followed in 1992 by similar findings by sociologists Roger Finke and Rodney Stark, who, looking at data from the very founding of the nation, found that "to the degree that denominations rejected traditional doctrines and ceased to make serious demands on their followers, they ceased to prosper. The churching of America was accomplished by aggressive churches committed to vivid otherworldliness."[21]

In the run-up to the new millennium, several studies offered similar conclusions as to the state of the mainstream Protestant churches. Sociologist Daniel V. A. Olson argued that conservative churches prosper because their members are united in basic, orthodox Christian beliefs and values that are distinctive from mainstream American culture. And looking ahead to what challenges to religion the twenty-first century would bring, sociologist of religion Robert Wuthnow argued that, opposed to those who chose more conservative denominations, a large number of more liberal Americans lacked firm commitments to mainstream Protestant denominations and that many switched denominations several times during their adult years, seeing little of substance that differentiated one from the other. He cited a national survey of Presbyterians, by way of example, wherein 73 percent of those polled agreed with the statement: "There are several other denominations where I could serve and be just as satisfied."[22]

By the end of the century, whether or not they agreed with Kelley's findings, it was widely accepted that, while established religions overall had suffered some loss of membership and conservative denominations' growth had begun to taper off, they were faring better than mainline denominations. Nevertheless, some have suggested that even the conservative churches are now feeling some of "the secularism and relativism plaguing their spiritual cousins in the mainline churches." One of the earliest to offer this perspective was theologian David Wells: "We now have less biblical fidelity, less interest in truth, less seriousness, less depth, and less capacity to speak the Word of God to our own generation in a way that offers an alternative to what it already thinks." Wells also suggested that evangelicals had "come to terms psychologically with our society's structural pluralism and its lack of interest in matters of truth," which might constitute their "death rattle."[23]

During the first decade and more of the twenty-first century, several prognosticators, mostly those bemoaning what they see as a loss in traditional spirituality, have weighed in on the subject of loss of church membership, most painting a less than optimistic picture of religion in the future. Most start from current trends documented in the numerous polls discussed earlier and from that base venture into less well-charted waters as to what the future will bring. A brief sampling of those representative of this genre would include Eric Jay Miller, whose book title says it all: *The Fading Light – The State of the Church in 21st Century America* (2012). In brief, Miller argues that, in light of the declining affiliation of Americans with not only mainstream, but any organized religious entities, the influence of Christianity is ceasing to be significant in America. Thomas Goehle stakes out a more dramatic position, describing what he calls a "post-Christian apocalypse," in which Christianity has lost its moral authority. Americans may say they believe in God, he suggests, but that is not reflected in the nation's laws, morals, or behavior. The result is a "secular modernism" that is "leaving God behind."[24]

Joseph Bottum begins from a similar position, that mainstream Protestantism has been losing its hold on the spiritual beliefs of Americans, on its "moral center," for a half-century or more. He found its origins in the Social Gospel of the early twentieth century and its greater emphasis placed on social justice over individual salvation. But he also argues that what has resulted, rather than a more secular society, is a more spiritual age marked by heightened anxiety at the loss of the traditional mooring and the answers religion has provided. Bottum points to the unsuccessful efforts of Roman Catholics and evangelicals to create a new moral code and religious institutional ballast to fill the void left in American society by the decline of the Protestant mainline churches but holds out some hope for a revitalized Protestant mainstream that better meets the spiritual needs of America.[25]

And as we have seen repeatedly, there are those who once again take the jeremiad approach, at once driving home the point that Christian America has lost its way and in the process its special covenantal relationship with God, or its exceptionalism. But not all is lost, they insist, as the United States stands at a critical juncture if it is to survive. Most of these authors issue a clarion call for a spiritual renewal that must begin with humility, repentance, and a return to the Christian faith of their fathers, an opportunity this particular group believes is still available to us.[26]

The "nones"

Perhaps the most discussed development in Americans' religious affiliations has been the continual rise as a percentage of American adults of those identified as "nones." In the 1950s, only 2 percent fit that definition. But in 2014, nearly 23 percent (22.8) of adults reported that they were religiously unaffiliated, describing themselves as atheists, agnostics, or "nothing in particular." As noted earlier, that represented some 56 million adults, which would make the "nones" more numerous than Roman Catholics and mainline Protestants, respectively, and second in size only to evangelical Protestants. More specifically, roughly 3 percent of those polled self-identified as atheists, 4 percent as agnostics, and nearly 16 percent as "nothing in particular." Fewer "nones" were looking for a religion, as religion was "not too" or "not at all" important in the lives of 39 percent of the unaffiliated, while 30 percent reported that religion was "very important" or "somewhat important" in their lives, down from 39 percent in 2007. Digging deeper, however, Pew found that, among the "nones," 68 percent said they believed in God, while 37 percent classified themselves as "spiritual" but not religious. This would suggest that, although some of the "nones" may well be losing, or have lost, their faith in God, it is likely that a considerably larger proportion of them have become disaffected from organized religion. This may simply be the result of a lessening of the social stigma attached to those without a religious affiliation, which was clearly present in the 1950s. Nevertheless, as there is a growing number of self-reported "nones," at least four theories have been posed and received sufficient attention to be noted here, two of which have already been alluded to.[27]

The first is secularization. An idea floated as early as the 1960s, but that failed to gain any traction until the 1990s, the rise of the unaffiliated in America has rekindled interest in the theory that basically linked economic development with loss of faith and predicted that religion in the United States would wither away by the twenty-first century as it has in Europe. By way of example, sociologist Peter Berger predicted that, by the twenty-first century, traditional religions would survive only in "small enclaves and pockets," a prediction he later called back. Studies since then have shown that, in much of the world, there is a correlation between a country's wealth and measures of its religiosity, more specifically that people in countries with a high per capita gross domestic product tend to be less religious, while those in countries with a low GDP tend to be more religious. But as Pew Global Attitudes reported in 2007, Americans have proven to be a major exception to that rule, combining both a high GDP per capita and high levels of religious commitment. As summarized in Chapter 4 of that study: "Americans are different when compared with the citizens of other wealthy nations. Americans are more religious. . . . On many issues, Americans share values with their traditional transatlantic allies in Europe, but on others – especially issues related to religion – Americans more closely resemble the publics of developing countries." Nonetheless, encouraged by the rise of the "nones," many theorists continue to look to the day when their prediction will come to pass. Among the factors they point to as delaying the process of secularization are economic inequality and insecurity that serve as a counterbalance to America's overall high GDP and the continued arrival of new immigrants who bring relatively strong religiosity with them.[28]

A second theory argues for backlash. This theory contends that young adults, in particular, have turned away from organized religion because they perceive it as deeply entangled with conservative politics and do not want to be associated with it. As sociologists Michael

Hout and Claude S. Fischer wrote in 2002, "part of the increase in 'nones' can be viewed as a symbolic statement against the Religious Right." Luis Lugo, of the Pew Research Center, has argued that "what we are seeing is not secularization but polarization," which is also reflected in the finding that "nones" now constitute the largest single religious group of Democrats, while religious conservatives are the largest constituency within the Republican Party. Political scientists Robert Putnam and David Campbell have pulled together polling data to support this thesis. From the 1970s through the 1990s, they have found, "religiosity and conservative politics became increasingly aligned, and abortion and gay rights became emblematic of the emergent culture wars," one result of which was that many young people came to view religion as "judgmental, homophobic, hypocritical, and too political."[29]

A Pew Research Center/Religion & Ethics News Weekly survey conducted in 2012 offers further support for the backlash theory. The survey found that the unaffiliated are concentrated among younger adults, political liberals, and people who take liberal positions on most issues. Two-thirds or more of the unaffiliated say the churches and other religious institutions are too concerned with money and power (70 percent) and too involved in politics (67 percent), both of which are significantly more common among the unaffiliated than they are in the general public. The survey shows that the unaffiliated are less likely than the affiliated to believe it is important to have a president with strong religious beliefs and that the unaffiliated are more likely than those with a religious affiliation to say that churches should stay out of political matters. And finally, although the percentage of religiously unaffiliated people has risen among Republican voters as well as among Democratic voters, the increase is greater among Democrats.[30]

A third theory on the rise of the unaffiliated is related to delays in marriage, the common assumption being that marrying and starting a family brings younger adults back to religion. This delay is consistent with the general population as well, but Pew surveys have consistently shown that the increase among the unaffiliated has taken place almost entirely among those who seldom or never attend religious services. Sociologist Robert Wuthnow, among others, has found not only an overall decline in church attendance since the 1970s, but also attributed it to broader social and demographic trends, including the postponement of marriage and parenthood by growing numbers of young adults. Pew research shows that, among adults under thirty, married people are more likely to have a religious affiliation than are unmarried people. On the other hand, although the frequency of prayer and the degree of importance people assign to religion in their lives do increase with age, Americans do not generally become more affiliated as they age. Rather, the percentage of people in each generation who are religiously affiliated has remained stable or decreased only slightly.[31]

Finally, there is the well-documented theory based on broad social disengagement, or what is often referred to as a decline in "social capital," as more Americans tend to live more separate lives and engage in fewer communal activities – "bowling alone," as Robert Putnam has put it. This theory suggests that the growth of the unaffiliated is just one manifestation of much broader social disengagement. Pew evidence includes data that show that the 40 percent of Americans who describe themselves as "active" in religious organizations – a higher bar than affiliation with a religious group – are more likely than other Americans to be involved in all types of volunteer and community groups. Further, the data show that religiously unaffiliated Americans are less inclined than Americans as a whole to feel that it is very important to belong to "a community of people who share your values and beliefs" (28 percent versus 49 percent).[32]

Atheism and agnosticism in twenty-first century America

Although more diverse than ever, and with some signs of reluctance to affiliate with established religions, as the United States enters the twenty-first century, America appears to be nearly as religious as ever. It is the case that for several years prior to 2001, beginning in the 1990s, proponents of unbelief entered into an aggressive state. Perhaps it was to be expected as a reaction to the equally ardent Christian evangelical movement marked by Biblical literalism, Christian conservatism, and distrust of, even hostility toward, modern science and rationalism. But following 9/11, there was a noticeable uptick in such activity. As reported in the previously discussed report, "America's Changing Religious Landscape," in 2014, 3.1 percent of those polled self-identified as atheists, up from 1.6 percent, while 4 percent considered themselves agnostic, an increase from 2.4 percent in 2007.[33]

In part, the growth in the number of atheists and agnostics may be the result of an increased willingness to self-identify. It may also be prompted by terrorists' religious pronouncements. Still others may have responded to highly public figures, the "New Atheists," like Sam Harris, author of *The End of Faith* (2004); Richard Dawkins, author of *The God Delusion* (2006); journalist Christopher Hitchens; and others, who launched a major campaign not merely attacking institutionalized religion but also denying the existence of God. As David Silverman, president of American Atheists, put it: "Atheists were driven to become more vocal because of 9/11 attacks and America's reaction to it," especially among the religious right with their invoking "God is on our side" rhetoric in their advocating for a "war on terror." Silverman added: "It really showed atheists why religion should not be in power. Religion is dangerous, even our own religion."[34]

Of the several New Atheist spokesmen, author Christopher Hitchens was among the best known, largely because of his impassioned – some would say polemical – attacks on religion, well represented by his *God Is Not Great: How Religion Poisons Everything* (2007). A close second to Hitchens would be Sam Harris's *The End of Faith*, aptly subtitled: *Religion, Terror, and the Future of Reason*, whose first chapter is titled "Reason in Exile" with a section headed: "The Myth of 'Moderation' in Religion." But Oxford University evolutionary biologist Richard Dawkins has been the most influential, some arguing that his *The God Delusion*, published in 2006, helped make atheism more mainstream. In that book, Dawkins argues against the existence of a supreme being. He does so in what likely will stand for the foreseeable future as the most comprehensive response to those who have defended religion and opposed atheism. For example, he takes on those who insist that atheism is as dogmatic as religious belief and that agnosticism is the more "reasonable position," by arguing that "the God hypothesis" is "a scientific hypothesis about the universe, which should be analysed as sceptically as any other," and not accepted as a matter of faith. He addresses the major arguments for God's existence finding them to be "spectacularly weak" and debunking each one. He follows that chapter with his own answer as to "why there almost certainly is no God." In the process, he takes on those who have based their belief in God on the argument of "irreducible complexity," concluding that "the illusion of design in the living world is explained with far greater economy and with devastating elegance by Darwinian natural selection." He takes on the commonly raised question: "Don't we need God, in order to be good?" In this chapter, Dawkins builds on his earlier book, *The Selfish Gene* (1976), in which he addresses the common understanding of being selfish as essential to the survival of the fittest. He argues that such an interpretation is a misreading of its theorists, that what might be seen as selfish actions among humans actually have altruistic ends, that our sense of right and wrong can be derived from our Darwinian past, and that it can be credited with the survival of species.[35]

Beyond making his case against the existence of God, Dawkins acknowledges that one of his goals in this and all of his writings on the subject is to provide a "consciousness raiser" for "atheist pride": "Being an atheist is nothing to be apologetic about. On the contrary, it is something to be proud of, standing tall to face the far horizon, for atheism nearly always indicates a healthy independence of mind and, indeed, a healthy mind." Addressing Americans in particular, acknowledging that "the religiosity of today's America is something truly remarkable," he insists that there are many more atheists than most people believe, but that they have chosen to keep it to themselves because "the very word 'atheist' has been assiduously built up as a terrible and frightening label." He insists that it is time for them to "come out," making reference to the gay movement and what followed their coming out. He explains that what many see as his hostility toward religion is his response to what he sees as the hostility of fundamentalist religion toward science, and he is critical of non-fundamentalists, who may not be so hostile toward science but that are "making the world safe for fundamentalism."[36]

This latest reoccurrence of unbelief appears to be waning as have similar episodes in the past, but as history suggests it will be back. As we have seen throughout this history of religion in America, although not widespread antichurch, anti-Christian, or antireligious movements in the United States have occurred on several occasions provoking widespread and often impassioned responses and then fading from the limelight. But whether or not they became a major factor in American life they have been an important part of our history.[37]

Bridging this section with the next, comparing Americans attitudes toward Muslims and atheists is revealing. Polling data over the last half-century suggests that, although overall American social tolerance toward suspect groups such as Catholics, Jews, African Americans, homosexuals, as well as Muslims (until 9/11) and atheists has increased, the gap of mistrust between all of these groups and atheists persists. In 2014, the Pew Research Center released its findings from a recently conducted poll that measured how "warmly" Americans felt toward various religious groups. The results showed that on its "feeling thermometer" evangelical Christians, Catholics, and Jews each received an average rating of 60 or higher on a scale from 0 to 100. Buddhists, Hindus, and Mormons received neutral ratings, ranging from 48 for Mormons to 53 for Buddhists, while atheists and Muslims scored only 41 and 40, respectively. Historically, atheists have been at the bottom of the "feeling thermometer" or its equivalent until after 9/11, when they were joined by Muslims, who previously scored closer to Buddhists, Hindus, and Mormons. Whereas fewer than 40 percent of Americans said that they would vote for an African American for president in 1958, that number rose to over 90 percent in 1999 (still pre-Obama days). American willingness to vote for homosexual candidates (not measured in 1958) increased from under 30 percent in 1978 to about 60 percent twenty years later. Atheists, in contrast, were seen as viable candidates by fewer than 20 percent of Americans in 1958 and that number rose to less than 50 percent some forty years later. Muslims were not included in this poll. But in 2003 – two years after 9/11 and in the still considerable heat of anti-Muslim rage in America – when Americans were asked if various groups agreed with their vision of American society, nearly 40 percent of those polled did not agree that atheists shared their vision, while only 26 percent doubted Muslims, and that number has decreased ever since despite continued anti-Muslim rhetoric. In sum, atheists have consistently been at the top of the list of groups that Americans find problematic in both public and private life, and the gap between acceptance of atheists and acceptance of other racial and religious minorities is large and persistent.[38]

As sociologist Will M. Gervais has commented: "Wherever there are religious majorities, atheists are among the least trusted people." As has been the case throughout American history, many Americans who are religious believe that those who are not religious – who do not believe in God – have no moral compass. Moreover, it has been a way of defining cultural membership in American life, based on belief about the role of religion in underpinning society's moral order as determined by whether society's standards of right and wrong should be based on God's laws. Put another way, the rejection of atheists is in large part correlated with Americans' rejection of the idea that a good society can have a secular basis. This was no doubt exacerbated over the past two decades by the New Atheist spokesmen, who, following in the footsteps of Madalyn Murray O'Hair, launched impassioned attacks on organized religion. Such attacks served to confirm the negative stereotype of atheists, despite the efforts of some atheists to counter it by making public statements as to the reasonableness of non-believers and insisting that they exemplify a positive moral and ethical lifestyle without belief in God based instead on a rational, secular understanding of the world. This has often involved their criticism of Dawkins and Hitchens, as well as making clear that they do not seek to destroy religion, but rather equality.[39]

Hispanics in America in the twenty-first century

Among the most significant changes in the American religious landscape of the twenty-first century has been the dramatic increase in the Hispanic population, a development that began before the turn of the century but remains strong. The impact of this migration on American Catholicism has been significant. Statistically, Hispanics now comprise 34 percent of Catholics, up from 29 percent as recently as 2007. And not surprisingly, given what we have seen among most immigrant groups, a significant amount of "hybrid religion spiritual belief and practices," or syncretism, has occurred among Hispanic migrants in their new land, making their particular "brand" of Catholicism distinctive. The incorporation of the mestiza, Spanish, and Indian figure of the Virgin of Guadalupe is among the best-known examples of this.[40]

Also telling has been the shift in religious affiliation among Hispanics since the 1960s. Although recent surveys indicate that 55 percent of Hispanics consider themselves Catholic, that number has steadily declined over the years, while the percentage of Protestants has increased to 22 percent – 16 percent Protestant evangelicals – and 18 percent unaffiliated. As recently as 2010, the percentage of Roman Catholics among Hispanics was 67 percent. Recent data show that the Pentecostal Assembly of God is now the most popular of all Protestant denominations among Hispanics. Although much smaller in number, significant increases have also occurred among the Mennonites, Mormons, Jehovah's Witnesses, and Seventh-Day Adventists. Historians point to the more welcoming environments these religious communities offered, where native Catholic were often leery of the newcomers, as well as the more emotionally satisfying aura they provided, more in keeping with their religious experience in their homeland. This has also been the case among Puerto Ricans and Cubans, who moved to the United States in large numbers at mid-century. Cuban Catholics, however, tended to reestablish themselves in communities in the Southeast, especially Florida, which replicated their religious life in Cuba. They were often accompanied by migrating Cuban Catholic priests, and they were more readily embraced by other Roman Catholics in large part the result of the political circumstances of their migration.[41]

Muslims in America in the twenty-first century

Among the most contentious changes in the American religious landscape has been the assimilation of Muslims. Muslims have been in America for centuries, if as a small minority and at times – among African slaves, for example – worshipping in the shadows. Further, at times forgetting their deep roots in America, attitudes toward Muslims have often been at least suspicious, and at times openly hostile, for nearly the same time period. Historians have argued that, rather than being a product of 9/11, anti-Muslim suspicion in America grew out of a socially constructed image in America far earlier, thereby providing an environment in which misunderstanding and hostility could thrive. We have already noted the hostility exhibited toward the African American Nation of Islam in the 1960s, seeing that group's demands for justice and its insistence on black superiority as threatening. But overall hostility toward non-black Muslims dominates. One of the earliest anti-Muslim statements branding Islam demonic and placing it into the context of end times eschatology came from the eighteenth-century theologian Jonathan Edwards. He identified Islam as one of "two great kingdoms [the other being Roman Catholicism] which the devil . . . erected in opposition to the kingdom of Christ," and that Christ would destroy at the battle of Armageddon."[42] By way of another historical example that resonates with attitudes expressed since 9/11, a letter to the editor of the *Cleveland Herald* in 1845 by "An Anti-Mohammedan" contrasts the peaceful character with references to the New Testament and the Koran. It reads, in part:

> The spirit of Mohammedanism says, 'War, then, is enjoined against you, the infidels. Kill the idolaters, wherever you shall find them – lay in wait for them in every convenient place – strike off their heads. Verily God hath purchased of the true believers their souls and their substance, promising them the enjoyments of Paradise on condition that they fight for the cause of God.'
>
> *Koran*

> The spirit of Christianity says, 'Love your enemies; do good to them that hate you; and pray for them that persecute and calumniate you.'
>
> *Matthew*

> The spirit of Mohammedanism says, 'The sword is the key of Heaven and Hell: a drop of blood shed in the cause of God, a night spent in arms, is of more avail than two months of fasting and prayer: whoever falls in battle, his sins are forgiven – and the loss of his limbs shall be supplied with the wings of Angels.'
>
> *Koran*

> The spirit of Christianity says, 'Put up again thy sword into its place. For all that take the sword shall perish by the sword.'
>
> *Matthew*

> Can men . . . utter more atrocious and blood-thirsty languages than that of the Koran? How peaceful is the word of Truth! May the spirit of Christianity teach us to shun the blood of Mohammedanism, is the prayer of him who is ever yours, AN ANTI-MOHAMMEDAN.

One final, and more recent, but still pre-9/11, example of outright violence rather than heated rhetoric, followed the false assumption that Muslims were responsible for the bombing of the Murrah Federal Building in Oklahoma City in 1995. That instigated a short-lived but vicious outbreak of over 200 cases of anti-Muslim harassment and acts of vandalism, including the burning of mosques.[43]

Nevertheless, between 1995 and 2000, the number of Muslim mosques and religious centers increased by 25 percent to over 1200, attended by about 2 million Muslims with another 2 to 3 million Muslim immigrants unaffiliated. And since 2000, Muslims have been the largest group of non-Christian immigrants to the United States. As a result, Islam has surpassed Judaism as the nation's second largest faith. But their numbers were not the source of the more sustained hostility that followed. That grew out of the association of Islam with the events of 9/11; the calls of al-Qaeda leader Osama bin Laden for attacks on "crusader infidels"; armed conflicts in Iraq, Iran, Afghanistan, and elsewhere; and most recently the rise of the self-styled Islamic State, all of which persuaded many Americans that Harvard professor and former National Security Council official Samuel P. Huntington was correct in his prediction during the 1990s of a "clash of civilizations." Islamic and other non-Western civilizations are fundamentally irreconcilable with Western civilization, he argued, and conflict in the post-Cold War era would occur along religious and cultural lines.[44]

On the one hand, many Americans have responded to 9/11 by seeking to better understand Islam and to engage in interfaith dialogue. Religious leaders of all faiths, including Islam, have made numerous attempts to make clear American Muslim patriotism and rejection of the hostile activities of radical Muslims, as well as to provide for a better understanding of Islam as a peaceful religion, which Americans need not fear. Immediately following 9/11, mosques across the country flew American flags and opened their doors to non-Muslims to provide for dialogue among various faiths about the course of events. Muslims along with Christians and Jews participated in interfaith services for the victims and their families followed by other interfaith efforts to achieve better understanding among the diverse religions in America, notable examples being the work of Muslim Eboo Patel and Omid Safi as well as organizations such as the Islamic Society of North America and the Council for American–Islamic Relations. The American Muslim Political Coordination Council, an umbrella body for several Muslim groups in the United States, issued a press release making clear that "American Muslims utterly condemn what are apparently vicious and cowardly acts of terrorism against innocent civilians. We join with all Americans in calling for the swift apprehension and punishment of the perpetrators. No political cause could ever be assisted by such immoral acts." And two weeks after 9/11, on September 17, 2001, President George W. Bush, at the Islamic Center of Washington, DC, spoke of Islam as a peaceful religion, explaining that the acts [of 9/11] "of violence against innocents violate the fundamental tenets of the Islamic faith" and that "those who feel like they can intimidate our fellow citizens to take out their anger don't represent the best of America. They represent the worst of humankind, and they should be ashamed of that kind of behavior." President Obama took the same position.[45]

On the other hand, despite these attempts to allay the anger of Americans in the immediate aftermath of the attack on the United States, there was a reemergence of Christo-Americanism, "a distorted form of Christianity that blends nationalism, conservative paranoia and Christian rhetoric" that, as we have seen, has emerged from time to time in American history. At an official level, American Muslim charities came under scrutiny and in some cases were shut down, charged with having ties to terrorist groups. Government officials identified Sharia (Muslim moral and religious law) as, in the case of former Speaker of the House of Representatives Newt Gingrich, "a moral threat to the survival of freedom in the United States. And US Congressman from Illinois Joe Walsh said that here were "radical" Muslims in American neighborhoods that "try to kill Americans every week." Over the course of the decade, instances of outright violence and hostility decreased, although suspicion and at times heated rhetoric persist.[46]

Some went beyond rhetoric seeking revenge, and there was a spike in anti-Muslim hate crimes immediately following 9/11 including assaults on Muslims and the burning of mosques. In the years leading up to 9/11, the FBI typically reported between 20 and 30 anti-Muslim hate crimes per year. In 2001, that number rose to nearly 500, but in the years since – to 2015 – annual hate crimes against Muslims has hovered in the 100 to 150 range. To provide some perspective, overall, anti-Muslim crimes now make up about 13 percent of religiously motivated hate crimes and 2 percent of all hate crimes. Anti-Semitic (anti-Jewish) crimes consistently rank number 1 (anti-Muslim crimes number 2), in 2014 accounting for about 60 percent of religious hate crimes. And, finally, religious hate crimes do not reach the level of racially motivated hate crimes, which outnumber religiously motivated hate crimes by about two to one.[47]

Thomas Kidd has pointed to a dramatic resurgence in anti-Muslim rhetoric among conservative evangelicals in the wake of 9/11. Among several different figures, he points to the popular conservative Christian writer and pastor John MacArthur and his book, published soon after 9/11, *Terrorism, Jihad, and the Bible: A Response to the Terrorist Attacks.* But MacArthur was not alone in using incendiary language to describe Islam in a highly negative light and in particular in characterizing Mohammed as a demon-possessed pedophile, based on the view that the prophet's revelations were conveyed by Satan and on a common belief in the youth of the woman Mohammed took as his wife. To the former point, MacArthur argued that Mohammed received his revelations while in a trance or while suffering seizures, which he was certain were induced by Satan, the result of which was a text that contradicted the Bible and therefore was not only wrong but Satan's ploy to topple Christianity.[48]

Kidd also points to at least two more theological explanations for the hostility toward Muslims among conservative evangelicals, which paradoxically have grown out of an increased knowledge of Islam. First, he explains an essential point concerning the belief that the origin of the Arab-Israel conflict can be traced to the biblical hostility between Isaac and Ishmael, and Arab Muslim hatred of Jews to whom God promised the land of Canaan. Second, Kidd has argued that "the most distinctive change in Christian eschatology since 2001 has been the rise of speculation in conservative evangelical circles that the Antichrist would come from Islam, and particularly that he would be (mis) identified by Muslims as the messianic Mahdi." He explains that some conservative evangelicals have discovered in Muslim anticipation of Mahdi's return "an eschatological narrative easily inverted and employed for Christian uses." Among the various expressions of this idea is professor Ralph Stice's *From 9/11 to 666*, which begins with a speculative account of how America might be taken over by Mahdi, the Antichrist, following the failure of the Iraq War and the resulting collapse of American power. The Muslim states of the world would unite under Mahdi, who would be supported by Isa. Isa would claim to be the resurrected Christ and would advise people to convert to Islam, whereupon they would receive the mark of Islam. True Christians would refuse the mark, whereupon they would be beheaded in the streets, interpreted as the biblical prophecy of the tribulation which would be followed by the rapture.[49]

It is important to understand, and Kidd agrees, that most conservative evangelicals have taken a more moderate stance, stressing the importance of gaining a better understanding of

Islam and assumed a less hostile posture toward Muslims, while not compromising on the essential differences between Islam and Christianity. But along with Paul Boyer and others, Kidd makes the case for the role of dispensational beliefs in American foreign policy in the Middle East among conservative evangelicals, although "subterranean and indirect." Kidd argues that this eschatology shapes their views of conflicts in the Middle East and has led to conservative evangelicals becoming Israel's most enthusiastic supporters. This, he adds, has led many evangelicals "to essentialize Muslims, terrorism, the Middle East and the Iraq War into an inevitable spiritual clash hurtling toward Judgment Day."[50]

It is difficult to predict at this point how all of this will play out. History suggests that what is often referred to as Islamophobia and belief among some in the inevitability of a "clash of civilizations," will pass in time, as it has for the acceptance of many new religions in America – perhaps when international events lessen external pressures on domestic Muslim-Christian relations. But again, it is too soon to tell, and the most recent observations by authorities in the field have been mixed. Within months of 9/11, Diana Eck, professor of comparative religions, held out hope that this would be the case. While acknowledging that 9/11 unleashed "an unprecedented rash of xenophobic incidents," she also pointed to the efforts of many religious and interfaith leaders and groups to calm the anger through a better understanding of Muslims, especially American Muslims, and their religious and cultural traditions. This response, rather than that of hostility, "revealed something more complex, and more heartening, about American society," she argued, namely that "the multireligious and multicultural fabric of the US was already too strong to rend by random violence." The "iconography of inclusion," as she put it, took a quantum leap in the weeks after September 11."[51]

By mid-decade commentators painted a largely dark portrait of America. In 2005, for example, Mark Lewis Taylor argued that many of the forces eroding our democracy existed before 2001, namely the dangerous and formidable combined alliance of neoconservatives, the Christian right, and the corporate elite, providing fertile ground for the rise of a "theocratic plutocracy." The events of 9/11, however, prompted the fear that allowed their policies to be implemented taking their toll on minorities in America, not just Muslims. Similarly in 2006, Richard W. Blumberg portrayed the nation as heading in the wrong direction since 9/11, arguing that politics in America, driven by religious extremists but manipulated by political operatives was being dominated by an atmosphere of hate, dividing and inflaming the electorate. Both Taylor and Blumberg held out hope, based on an enlightened electorate, but they were not terribly optimistic.[52]

In contrast, in 2007, Geneive Abdo presented a largely optimistic perspective for the future of the nation's 6 million Muslims. From her study of a representative sampling of the Muslim community, she found that Muslim Americans were seeking to be better understood and judged on their own merits and compatibility with other Americans rather than by Americans' perceptions based on Muslim extremists abroad. This was followed two years later by an ethnographic study published by Louis Cainkar, involving more than a hundred interviews and five in-depth oral histories of native born and immigrant Muslim Americans. He found that the vast majority of those interviewed were optimistic about the future of Arab and Muslim life in the United States, as evidenced by increased interest in Islam and the effective mediation of various organizations, religious and secular. All were helping to build bridges between the Muslim community and others, reinforcing stronger ties and greater inclusion in American social and political life. This was followed in 2012 by a similarly cautious but optimistic observation by Evelyn Alsultany, who studied how Muslims were represented in the media over the course of the last decade. Alsultany found that negative images of Muslims were commonplace immediately following 9/11, contributing to the atmosphere of anti-Muslim sentiment in America's "war on terror." She also found, however, that a fair number of sympathetic images appeared as well, and that gradually the latter grew in number over the years, thereby either leading or reflecting a change in Americans' attitude toward Muslims – at least Muslim Americans.[53]

Finally, on the tenth anniversary of 9/11, Stephen Prothero remained optimistic but more guarded. He admitted that, in the immediate aftermath of 9/11, he thought "things were going to get very ugly, very fast for American Muslims." And they did. Prothero dismissed them as "the isolated activities of individual bigots," but polls showed that Americans' unfavorable view of Islam rose from 33 percent in 2002 to 53 percent in 2010 in large part because of ongoing acts of terrorism on the part of Islamic extremists. The result, Prothero observed, has been not only widespread fear and mistrust of Muslims and Islam, but also a resurgence of explicitly Christian language resurgent in American politics, adding fuel to the fire. A decade after the fact, he concluded that things "are not looking good for Americans like myself who see religious liberty as one of the great achievements of the American experiment." Nevertheless, he continued, "Take heart":

> The United States has survived a series of culture wars in which Catholics, Mormons and members of other religious minorities were anathematized as un-American. In each case, Americans as a group have eventually decided to live not by fear but by first principles, not least the constitutional protection of liberty afforded in the First Amendment to Americans of all creeds. . . . It is always there in our cultural DNA.

Whether the "many frayed edges in the common fabric" as Eck described it, will be mended, as she predicted, remains to be seen. The heightened anti-Muslim rhetoric in the 2016 presidential election was not encouraging.[54]

Summary

Chapter 8 opens with the question: Whither religion in the twenty-first century? And that is appropriate as where evidence has surfaced that suggests changes in the American religious landscape, it is too soon to tell if they are lasting or merely passing aberrations. Historians are far better at examining the past than foretelling the future. As the data gathered over the past two decades suggest, the United States remains the most religious developed nation on earth. It continues to be the most Christian nation, as well as one of the most religiously diverse. Yet many of the traditional measures of its religiosity have gradually but steadily declined. For example, as noted, in 2013 the percentage of adults who described themselves as Christian stood at just over 70 percent, a comparatively large number, but that constituted a drop of 8 percentage points since 2007. As also reported in this chapter, a strong majority of Americans continue to believe in God, but from 2005 to 2013 that number has declined from 82 percent to 74 percent. At the same time, in the most noticeable change in polling data gathered over the past two decades, the percentage of adults who describe themselves as unaffiliated with any particular religious organization has steadily increased to nearly one in four. Moreover, although it is the case that the "nones," as they are called, have drawn heavily on the young, recent polling data indicates that the ranks of the "nones" among older population groups are growing. However, as also reported, only 3 percent self-identified as atheists and among the "nones" 68 percent continue to believe in God, which suggests that the "nones" disaffection may be more from organized religion than from religion itself. Whether this will continue, or what the reasons are for this development, remain speculative, as does what is asked at the close of Chapter 8, namely if the widespread and comparatively consistent level of distrust and outright hostility toward Muslims since 2001 will continue. As noted, history suggests it will not, but, one final time, it is too soon to tell.

Review questions

1   Just one question on which to end: Whither religion in twenty-first century America? What is your best guess based on the evidence?

Notes

1   Edwin S. Gaustad and Leigh E. Schmidt, *The Religious History of America: The Heart of the American Story from Colonial Times to Today*, rev. edn. (New York: HarperSanFrancisco, 2002), 412. For an international perspective on religion in the twenty-first century, see Lisbet Christoffersen, Hans Raun Iversen, Hanne Petersen, and Margit Warburg, eds., *Religion in the 21st Century: Challenges and Transformations* (Farnham, UK: Ashgate Publishers, 2010), and Pascal-Emmanuel Gobry, "Why Religion Will Dominate the 21st Century," theweek.com (May 18, 2015). http://theweek.com/articles/555371/why-religion-dominate-21st-century
2   Roger Finke and Rodney Stark, *The Churching of America, 1776–1990: Winners and Losers in Our Religious Economy* (New Brunswick, NJ: Rutgers University Press, 1992), 40–6; Roof is quoted in Gaustad and Schmidt, *The Religious History of America*, 426.
3   Those interested in looking at membership reported by denominations should see "U.S. Religion Census 1952 to 2010." www.rcms2010.org/
4   See "How America's Faith Has Changed since 9–11," Barna Group Update (November 26, 2001). www.barna.org/barna-update/5-barna-update/63-how-americas-faith-has-changed-since-9-11#.ViVdLyskpZI
5   "How America's Faith Has Changed since 9–11."
6   "Americans' Belief in God, Miracles and Heaven Declines," Harris Interactive, (December 16, 2013). www.theharrispoll.com/health-and-life/Americans__Belief_in_God__Miracles_and_Heaven_Declines.html
7   "America's Changing Religious Landscape," Pew Research Center (May 12, 2015). www.pewforum.org/2015/05/12/americas-changing-religious-landscape/. For comparison numbers on the size of Christian populations in other countries, see "The Future of World Religions: Population Growth Projections, 2010–2015," also done by the Pew Research Center. It offers two comparative observations that provide some perspective on what is happening in the US, namely that Muslims increasing their number faster than any other religion in the world and that the unaffiliated are shrinking as a share of the world's population: www.pewforum.org/2015/04/02/religious-projections-2010-2050/. For more on how the finding in this Pew Survey compare to other surveys, see www.pewforum.org/2015/05/12/appendix-c-putting-findings-from-the-religious-landscape-study-into-context/
8   On the longer-term decline of mainstream Protestants and for a brief discussion of the measuring of Catholic membership losses, see Finke and Stark, *The Churching of America*, 236–75, and Thomas C. Reeves, *The Empty Church: The Suicide of Liberal Christianity* (New York: The Free Press, 1996), 1–36, 62–4.
9   "'Nones' on the Rise," Pew Research Center: Religion and Public & Life (October 9, 2012). www.pewforum.org/2012/10/09/nones-on-the-rise/
10 As noted earlier, Finke and Stark provide an explanation for this historical phenomenon in terms of the free and competitive marketplace of religious groups in America: Finke and Starke, *The Churching of America*, 18–19. The drop among Roman Catholics might well be the result of the sex abuse scandal among the clergy. See, for example: "The Rise of Atheism in America," theweek.com (April 13, 2012). http://theweek.com/articles/476559/rise-atheism-america
11 "Gallup Historical Trends: Religion," (2015). www.gallup.com/poll/1690/religion.aspx
12 See Harvey Cox, *The Secular City: A Celebration of Its Liberties and an Invitation to Its Discipline* (New York: Macmillan Company, 1965); Thomas Luckmann, *The Invisible Religion: The*

Problem of Religion in Modern Society (New York: Macmillan Company, 1967); and Alan Wolfe, *The Transformation of American Religion: How We Actually Practice Our Faith* (Chicago: University of Chicago Press, 2003).

13 Barry A. Kosmin and Seymour P. Lachman, *One Nation under God: Religion in Contemporary American Society* (New York: Crown Publishing, 1993), 43, 253–63; William R. Hutchison, "Past Imperfect: History and the Prospect for Liberalism," in *Liberal Protestantism: Realities and Possibilities*, ed. Robert S. Michaelsen and Wade Clark Roof (New York: Pilgrim, 1986), 65–82; "'Nones' on the Rise."

14 Reeves, *The Empty Church*, 2–3.

15 Os Guinness, *The American Hour: A Time of Reckoning and the Once and Future Role of Faith* (New York: The Free Press, 1993), 29; Kagan is quoted in Reeves, *The Empty Church*, 3–4.

16 Over the same time period, the ranks of Mormons, Southern Baptists, and Roman Catholics held steady. For a summary of data on church membership, see Reeves, *The Empty Church*, 10–11. Dean R. Hogue, Benton Johnson, Donald A. Luidens, *Vanishing Boundaries: The Religion of Mainline Protestant Baby Boomers* (Louisville, KY: Presbyterian Publishing Corporation, 1994), 4–8; Wade Clark Roof and William McKinney, *American Mainline Religion: Its Changing Shape and Future* (New Brunswick, NJ: Rutgers University Press, 1987), 152–4.

17 Robert Wood Lunn, "The Survival of Recognizably Protestant Colleges: Reflections on Old-Line Protestantism, 1950–1990," in *The Secularization of the Academy*, ed. George M. Marsden and Bradley J. Longfield (New York: Oxford University Press, 1992), 171; George Gallup, Jr., and Jim Castelli, *The People's Religion: American Faith in the 90s* (New York: Macmillan Publishing Company, 1989), 141, 259, 263; Finke and Stark, *The Churching of America*, 167; Reeves, *The Empty Church*, 13.

18 Reeves, *The Empty Church*, 27–8.

19 Charles S. MacKenzie, "Deformation of the Church," in *Churches on the Wrong Road*, ed. Stanley Atkins and Theodore McConnell (Chicago, IL: University Press of America, 1986), 30; Richard John Neuhaus, *The Naked Public Square: Religion and Democracy in America*, 2nd edn. (Grand Rapids, MI: Eerdmans Publishing Company, 1986), 19, 110.

20 Dean M. Kelley, *Why Conservative Churches Are Growing: A Study in Sociology of Religion* (Macon, GA: Mercer University Press, 1986), xxii. See also Rodney Stark, "Why Religious Movements Succeed or Fail: A Revised General Model," *Journal of Contemporary Religion*, 11 (May 1996): 133, 261–2, 265.

21 Roof and McKinney, *American Mainline Religion*, 20; Finke and Stark, *The Churching of America*, 245–50; Stark, *Why Religious Movements Fail*, 133–46.

22 Daniel V. A. Olson, "Fellowship Ties and the Transmission of Religious Identity," in *Beyond Establishment: Protestant Identity in a Post-Protestant Age*, ed. Jackson Carroll and Wade Clark Roofe (Louisville, KY: Westminster/John Knox Press, 1993), 32–51; Robert Wuthnow, *Christianity in the 21st Century: Reflections on the Challenges Ahead* (New York: Oxford University Press, 1993), 39–40.

23 Reeves, *The Empty Church*, 33. David F. Wells, *No Place for Truth, or Whatever Happened to Evangelical Theology?* (Grand Rapids, MI: Eerdmans, 1993), 12, 131.

24 Eric Jay Miller, *The Fading Light – the State of the Church in 21st Century America*, Kindle edn. (Seattle, WA: Amazon Digital Services, 2012); Thomas R. Goehle, *America's Post-Christian Apocalypse: How Secular Modernism Marginalized Christianity and the Peril of Leaving God Behind at the End of the Age* (Leesburg, VA: Aletheia, 2015).

25 Joseph Bottum, *An Anxious Age: The Post-Protestant Ethic and the Spirit of America* (New York: Image Press, 2014).

26 See, for example: Christopher Robert Walling, *The Price of Christian Revival in 21st Century America* (London, UK: Pavilion Books, 2014), and Jerry Combee and Cline Hall, *America – Destined for Destiny: America's Compelling Opportunity for Spiritual and Political Renewal in the Twenty-First Century*, 3rd edn. (Newport Beach, CA: Publish Authority, 2015).

27 Jim Eckman, "21st Century America and Religion: The Secularization of America?," *Issues in Perspective* (April 20, 2013). https://graceuniversity.edu/iip/2013/04/13-04-20-1/; "America's Changing Religious Landscape: Christians Decline Sharply as Share of Population; Unaffiliated and Other Faiths Continue to Grow," Pew Research Center (May 12, 2015). www.pewforum.org/2015/05/12/americas-changing-religious-landscape/; "'Nones' on the Rise."; *American Piety in the 21st Century: New Insights to the Depth and Complexity of Religion in the United States* (Waco, TX: Baylor Institute for Studies of Religion, 2006), 12–14.

28 "World Publics Welcome Global Trade – but Not Immigration," Pew Research Center's Global Attitudes Project (October 4, 2007). www.pewglobal.org/2007/10/04/world-publics-welcome-global-trade-but-not-immigration/; see also www.pewglobal.org/2007/10/04/chapter-4-values-and-american-exceptionalism/. See, for example: Pippa Norris and Ronald Inglehart, *Sacred and Secular: Religion and Politics Worldwide* (New York: Cambridge University Press, 2004), 89–95, 107–8, 225–6.

29 "'Nones' on the Rise."; Michael Hout and Claude S. Fischer, "Why More Americans Have No Religious Preference: Politics and Generations," *American Sociological Review*, 67 (April 2002): 165–90; Eckman, "21st Century America and Religion: The Secularization of America?," (April 20, 2013). http://graceuniversity.edu/iip/2013/04/13-04-20-1/; Robert D. Putnam and David E. Campbell, *American Grace: How Religion Divides and Unites Us* (New York: Simon and Schuster, 2010), 120–1.

30 See "Little Voter Discomfort with Romney's Mormon Religion," Pew Research Center (July 16, 2012). www.pewforum.org/2012/07/26/2012-romney-mormonism-obamas-religion/; "More See 'Too Much' Religious Talk by Politicians," Pew Research Center (March 21, 2012). www.pewforum.org/2012/03/21/more-see-too-much-religious-talk-by-politicians/; "'Nones' on the Rise."

31 Robert Wuthnow, *After the Baby Boomers: How Twenty- and Thirty-Somethings Are Shaping the Future of American Religion* (Princeton, NJ: Princeton University Press, 2007), 51–70; "Religion Among the Millennials," Pew Religious Forum (February 17, 2010). www.pewforum.org/2010/02/17/religion-among-the-millennials/; "'Nones' on the Rise."

32 Robert D. Putnam, *Bowling Alone: The Collapse and Revival of American Community* (New York: Simon and Schuster, 2000), 127; "Little Voter Discomfort with Romney's Mormon Religion," Pew Research Center (July 16, 2012). www.pewforum.org/2012/07/26/2012-romney-mormonism-obamas-religion/; "'Nones' on the Rise."

33 "America's Changing Religious Landscape: Christians Decline Sharply as Share of Population; Unaffiliated and Other Faiths Continue to Grow"; "'Nones' on the Rise"; *American Piety in the 21st Century: New Insights to the Depth and Complexity of Religion in the United States.*

34 John Blake, "Four Ways 9/11 Changed America's Attitude toward Religion," CNN Online (September 3, 2011). http://religion.blogs.cnn.com/2011/09/03/four-ways-911-changed-americas-attitude-toward-religion/

35 Sam Harris, *The End of Faith: Religion, Terror, and the Future of Reason* (New York: W. W. Norton, 2004), ch. 1; Richard Dawkins, *The Selfish Gene* (Oxford, UK: Oxford University Press, 1976); Dawkins also makes reference to several other books he believes have supported his hypothesis. For example: Robert Hinde, *Why Good Is Good: The Sources of Morality* (New York: Routledge, 2002); Michael Shermer, *The Science of Good and Evil: Why People Cheat, Gossip, Care, Share, and Follow the Golden Rule* (New York: Holt, 2004); Robert Buckman, *Can We Be Good without God?* (Toronto: Viking, 2000); and Marc Hauser, *Moral Minds: How Nature Designed Our Universal Sense of Right and Wrong* (New Yok: Ecco, 2006); Richard Dawkins, *The God Delusion* (Boston: Houghton Mifflin Company, 2006), 2–5, 75–109, 111–59, 209–33.

36 Dawkins, *The God Delusion*, 2–5, 284–6. A survey of scientists who are members of the American Association for the Advancement of Science, conducted by the Pew Research Center for the People and the Press in May and June 2009, found that scientists are roughly half as likely as the general public to believe in God or a higher power – 51 percent versus 95 percent. "Religion and Science in the United States: Scientists and Belief," Pew Research Center for the People and the Press (November 5, 2009). www.pewforum.org/2009/11/05/scientists-and-belief/. Often quoted is Harvard biologist E. O. Wilson's more moderate statement in a 1998 issue of *The Atlantic Monthly*: "On Religion I lean toward deism, but consider its proof largely a problem in astrophysics. The existence of a God who created the universe is possible, and the question may eventually be settled, perhaps by forms of material evidence not yet imagined." Edward O. Wilson, "The Biological Basis of Morality," *The Atlantic Monthly* (April 1998): 54.

37 For an overview of what we have covered in this book as to the earlier history of unbelief, see Martin E. Marty, *Varieties of Unbelief* (New York: Doubleday, 1966).

38 "How Americans Feel about Religious Groups," Pew Research Center (July 16, 2014). www.pewforum.org/2014/07/16/new-pew-research-survey-explores-how-americans-feel-about-religious-groups/

39 A good example of the counteroffensive of atheists is the "Reason Rally" held on the National Mall in Washington, DC, on March 24, 2001. "The Rise of Atheism in America." See, for example: Phil

Zuckerman, *Living the Secular Life: New Answers to Old Questions* (New York: Penguin Press, 2014), and Lex Bayer, *Atheist Mind, Humanist Heart: Rewriting the Ten Commandments for the Twenty-First Century* (Lanham, MD: Rowman and Littlefield, 2014). Among the several existing organizations that include atheists, agnostics, humanists, non-theists, and skeptics – the dividing line between them often blurred – are: American Atheists, American Ethical Union, American Humanist Association, and Americans United for Separation of Church and State.

40 While realizing the multiplicity of cultural heritages among this population, for simplicity's sake, the term Hispanic – a term employed by the US government in 1970 – will be used here, while also recognizing the common usage of Latino. www.pewresearch.org/fact-tank/2015/09/14/a-closer-look-at-catholic-america/; David A. Brading, *Mexican Phoenix: Our Lady of Guadalupe Across Five Centuries* (New York: Cambridge University Press, 2001); and Jeanette Favrot Peterson, *Visualizing Guadalupe: From Black Madonna to Queen of the Americas* (Austin: University of Texas Press, 2015).

41 www.pewforum.org/2014/05/07/the-shifting-religious-identity-of-latinos-in-the-united-states/. See Edwin David Aponte, *Santo: Varieties of Latino/a Spirituality* (New York: Orbis, 2012), 43–5; and Gaston Espinoza, *Latino Pentecostals in America: Faith and Politics in Action* (Cambridge, MA: Harvard University Press, 2014); Jaime Vidal, *Puerto Rican and Cuban Catholics in the U.S., 1900–1965* (Notre Dame, IN: University of Notre Dame Press, 1994), 79; Ana Maria Diaz-Stevens, *Oxcart Catholicism on Fifth Avenue: The Impact of Puerto Rican Migration on the Archdiocese of New York* (Notre Dame, IN: University of Notre Dame Press, 1995).

42 Louis A. Cainkar, *Homeland Insecurity: The Arab American and Muslim American Experience after 9/11* (New York: Russell Sage Foundation, 2009). See also Karine V. Walther, *Sacred Interests: The United States and the Islamic World, 1821–1921* (Chapel Hill: University of North Carolina Press, 2015); John Corrigan and Lynn S. Neal, eds., *Religious Intolerance in America: A Documentary History* (Chapel Hill: University of North Carolina, 2010); Thomas S. Kidd, *American Christians and Islam: Evangelical Culture and Muslims from the Colonial Period to the Age of Terrorism* (Princeton, NJ: Princeton University Press, 2009), xi.

43 Gaustad and Schmidt, *The Religious History of America*, 417–18. For a brief discussion on how federal agencies and officials have viewed and worked both against and with Islamic groups at home and abroad, see Edward E. Curtis, IV, "For American Muslims, Everything Did Not Change after 9/11," *Religion and Politics* (July 5, 2012). http://religionandpolitics.org/2012/07/05/for-american-muslims-everything-did-not-change-after-911/. For a history of American anti-Muslim sentiment, focused especially on conservative evangelicals, see Thomas Kidd, *American Christians and Islam*.

44 Samuel P. Huntington, "The Clash of Civilization," *Foreign Affairs*, 72 (Summer 1993): 22–49; see also Samuel P. Huntington, *The Clash of Civilizations and the Remaking of World Order* (New York: Simon and Schuster, 1996); Curtis, "For American Muslims," 97–8; and Harvard's Pluralism Project. www.pluralism.org/religion/islam/issues/post-911

45 Curtis, "For American Muslims," 98–9, 113–14; Blake, "Four Ways 9/11 Changed America's Attitude Toward Religion." See Eboo Patel, *Acts of Faith: The Story of an American Muslim: The Struggle for the Soul of a Generation* (Boston: Beacon Press, 2007); Harvard's Pluralism Project; and Curtis, "For American Muslims, Everything Did Not Change after 9/11."

46 Curtis, "For American Muslims," 100; Harvard's Pluralism Project.

47 Blake, "Four Ways 9/11 Changed America's Attitude Toward Religion." For a list of anti-Arab and anti-Islamic attacks for the first year after 9/11, see Hussein Ibish, ed., *Report on Hate Crimes and Discrimination against Arab Americans: The Post-September 11th Backlash, September 11, 2001–October 11, 2002* (Washington, DC: American-Arab Anti-Discrimination Committee, 2003). See also Christopher Ingraham, "Anti-Muslim Hate Crimes Are Still Five Times More Common Today Than before 9/11," *The Washington Post* (February 11, 2015). www.washingtonpost.com/news/wonkblog/wp/2015/02/11/anti-muslim-hate-crimes-are-still-five-times-more-common-today-than-before-9/11; "How Americans Feel about Religious Groups"; "2013 Hate Crime Statistics," Federal Bureau of Investigation (see especially Table 1). www.fbi.gov/about-us/cjis/ucr/hate-crime/2013/tables/1tabledatadecpdf/table_1_incidents_offenses_victims_and_known_offenders_by_bias_motivation_2013.xls; Corrigan and Neal, *Religious Intolerance in America*, 9.

48 John MacArthur, *Terrorism, Jihad, and the Bible: A Response to the Terrorist Attacks* (Nashville, TN: Thomas Nelson, 2001); Kidd, *American Christians and Islam*, 150.

49 Kidd, *American Christians and Islam*, 150–9; Ralph Stice, *From 9/11 to 666* (Ozark, AL: ACW Press, 2005). For more on Mahdi in Islam, see Timothy R. Furnish, *Holiest Wars: Islamic Mahdis, Their Jihads, and Osama Bin Ladin* (Westport, CT: Praeger, 2005).
50 Kidd, *American Christians and Islam*, 163. See Paul Boyer, *When Time Shall Be No More: Prophecy Belief in Modern American Culture* (Cambridge, MA; Harvard University Press, 1992), 142–6. Also, as an example of a more moderate position taken by a conservative evangelical, see Timothy George, *Is the Father of Jesus the God of Muhammad: Understanding the Differences between Christianity and Islam* (Grand Rapids, MI: Zondervan, 2002).
51 See the excerpt from Diana Eck's, "Preface" to *A New Religious America: How a "Christian Country" Has become the World's Most Religiously Diverse Nation* (New York: HarperSanFrancisco, 2002) at PBS Frontline. www.pbs.org/wgbh/pages/frontline/shows/faith/neighbors/excerpt.html
52 Mark Lewis Taylor, *Religion, Politics, and the Christian Right: Post-9/11 Powers in American Empire* (Minneapolis, MN: Fortress Press, 2005); Richard W. Blumberg, *Politics and Religion in America – Post 9/11* (Bloomington, IN: AuthorHouse, 2006).
53 Geneive Abdo, *Mecca and Main Street: Muslim Life in America after 9/11* (New York: Oxford University Press, 2007); Cainkar, *Homeland Insecurity*; Evelyn Alsultany, *The Arabs and Muslim in the Media: Race and Representation after 9/11* (New York: New York University Press, 2012).
54 Stephen Prothero, "How 9/11 Changed Religion in America," *USA Today* (September 10, 2011). http://usatoday30.usatoday.com/news/opinion/forum/story/2011-09-10/911-religion-islam-christianity/50354708/1; Gaustad and Schmidt, *The Religious History of America*, 417; Catherina L. Albanese, *America: Religions and Religion*, 4th edn. (Belmont, CA: Thomson/Wadsworth, 2007), 210–1; Yvonne Yazback Haddad, *Not Quite American: The Shaping of Arab and Muslim Identity in the United States* (Waco, TX: Baylor University Press, 2004); and Yvonne Yazback Haddad, *Becoming American? The Forging of Arab and Muslim Identity in Pluralistic America* (Waco, TX: Baylor University Press, 2011); Harvard's Pluralism Project. See also Michael Wolfe, ed., *Taking Back Islam: American Muslims Reclaim Their Faith* (New York: Rodale, 2002).

Recommended for further reading

Abdo, Geneive. *Mecca and Main Street: Muslim Life in America after 9/11*. New York: Oxford University Press, 2007.

Alsultany, Evelyn. *The Arabs and Muslims in the Media: Race and Representation after 9/11*. New York: New York University Press, 2012.

American Piety in the 21st Century: New Insights to the Depth and Complexity of Religion in the United States. Waco, TX: Baylor Institute for Studies of Religion, 2006.

Dawkins, Richard. *The God Delusion*. Boston: Houghton Mifflin Company, 2006.

Eck, Diana. *A New Religious America: How a "Christian Country" Has Become the World's Most Religiously Diverse Nation*. New York: HarperSanFrancisco, 2002.

Kelley, Dean M. *Why Conservative Churches Are Growing: A Study in Sociology of Religion*. Macon, GA: Mercer University Press, 1986.

Kidd, Thomas S. *American Christians and Islam: Evangelical Culture and Muslims from the Colonial Period to the Age of Terrorism*. Princeton, NJ: Princeton University Press, 2009.

Reeves, Thomas C. *The Empty Church: The Suicide of Liberal Christianity*. New York: The Free Press, 1996.

Wuthnow, Robert. *After the Baby Boomers: How Twenty- and Thirty-Somethings Are Shaping the Future of American Religion*. Princeton, NJ: Princeton University Press, 2007.

Wuthnow, Robert. *Christianity in the 21st Century: Reflections on the Challenges Ahead*. New York: Oxford University Press, 1993.

Index

Note: Page numbers in *italics* denote references to Figures and Tables.

Jesus: imperative of love 37; as source of Christian ethics 36–7; as spiritual guardian 14; Zionist movement 43
Jesus Movement 174
Jews: abortion issue 164; environmental movement 167; immigration 4–5, 7; interfaith worship 43; on same-sex marriage 169; skeptical of Catholic presidency 154; Social Gospel and 41–3; women's ordination and 165. *See also* Conservative Jews; Orthodox Jews
Jodock, Darrell 2
John Paul II (pope) 167
Johnson, Lyndon 170
Johnson, Texas v. 192
John XXIII (pope) 155
Joiner, Thekla Ellen 17, 22, 23
Jones, Charles P. 79
Jones, Jim 112, 175–6
Jonestown massacre 176
Judeo-Christian tradition 139–40
Jungle, The (Sinclair) 44
just ware theory 121–2, 146

Kagan, Donald 223
Keepers of the Earth (Shomrei Adamah) 167
Kelley, Dean M. 203, 224
Kemp, Jack 191
Kennedy, John F. 153
Kerry, John 193
Kidd, Thomas 233–4
Kimball, Edward 15–16
kindergarten movement, Women's Christian Temperance Union 46
King, Martin Luther, Jr. 129, 143–6, 156–8, *157*
King's Business, The (Torrey) 94
Kitzmiller v. Dover Area School District 208
Knights of Columbus 134
Knights of Labor 40–1
Koresh, David 176
Kugelmass, Jack 7–8
Ku Klux Klan 37, 43, 143
Kurtz, Lester 4

Ladies' Council of the Chicago Evangelization Society 24
La Guardia, Fiorello 133
LaHaye, Beverly 187, 196, 199
LaHaye, Tim 196
Lakota Ghost Dance 10–12
Lamarck, Jean Baptiste 63
LaPorte, Roger 170
Larson, Edward 97
Larson, Orvin 69
Late, Great Planet Earth, The (Lindsey) 195
LaVey, Anton 175

law of competition 73
Leadership Conference of Women Religious 165
Leary, James 41
Leavelle, Tracy Neal 13
Lee, Ann 20, 91
Lee v. Weisman 206
Left Behind series 196–7
Leo XIII (pope) 3–4, 41, 130
"Letter from Birmingham Jail" 156
Lewinski, Monica 193
Lewis, John 155
Liberal Christians 43, 89, 188
Liberty Baptist College 185
Liebman, Joshua Loth 135–6
Lienesch, Michael 90
Life Amendment PAC 198
Life Is Worth Living (television show) 132
Life of Jesus (Strauss) 58–60
Lincoln, Abraham 16
Lindsey, Hal 195
lived religion, in ethnic communities 6–8
Living Wage: Its Ethical and Economic Aspects, A (Ryan) 39–40
Lord is My Shepherd and He Knows I'm Gay, The (Perry) 169
Los Angeles revival 126–7
Love, E. K. 8
Luce, Henry 124, 127
Luckmann, Thomas 222
Lucy (Black Elk's daughter) 13, 14
Lugo, Luis 227
Lutherans 165
Lyell, Charles 63

MacArthur, Douglas 134
Macartney, Charles 95–6
Machen, John Gresham 96
MacIntire, Carl 130
"Madonna of 115th Street Revisited, The" (McAlister) 7
Mahan, Asa 77–8
Mahdi 233
Malcolm X 158–9
Mann Act 109
March of the Flag, The (Beveridge) 49
Maritain, Jacques 131
Marshall, Thurgood 143, 172–3
Mary, Martin 71
Maryknoll fathers 51
Mason, Charles H. 79, 81
Massa, Mark 136
mass migration 7. *See also* immigration
Mathews, Shailer 36–7, 48
Mattachine Society 168
Matthews, John Brown 137
McAlister, Elizabeth 7